THE MANUSCRIPT JOURNAL

OF

THE REVEREND CHARLES WESLEY, M.A.

VOLUME I

D1598589

THE MANUSCRIPT JOURNAL OF THE REVEREND CHARLES WESLEY, M.A.

VOLUME I

EDITED BY

S T Kimbrough, Jr.
and
Kenneth G. C. Newport

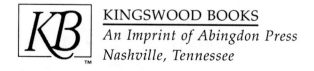

KINGSWOOD BOOKS
An Imprint of Abingdon Press
Nashville, Tennessee

THE MANUSCRIPT JOURNAL OF THE REVEREND CHARLES WESLEY, M.A.
VOLUME 1

Library of Congress Cataloging-in-Publication Data

Wesley, Charles, 1707–1788.
   The manuscript journal of the Rev. Charles Wesley, M.A. / edited by S T Kimbrough, Jr. and
Kenneth G. C. Newport.
     p. cm.
   ISBN-13: 978-0-687-64604-3 (pbk. : alk. paper)
   1. Wesley, Charles, 1707-1788—Diaries. 2. Wesley, Charles, 1707–1788—Manuscripts
3. England—Social life and customs—18th century. 4. Oxford (England)—Social life and customs.
5. Methodist Church—Clergy—Diaries. 6. Clergy—England—Diaries. I. Kimbrough, S T, 1936–
II. Newport, Kenneth G. C. III. Title.
   BX8495.W4A34 2007
   287.092—dc22
   [B]

                                                                                    2007028665

The Graeca (R) font used to print this work is available from Linguist's Software, Inc., PO Box 580,
Edmonds, WA 98020-0580 tel (206) 775-1130.

Image on page vii is reproduced by courtesy of the University Librarian and Director, The John
Rylands University Library, The University of Manchester. Used by permission. All rights reserved.

08 09 10 11 12 13 14 15 16 17—10 9 8 7 6 5 4 3 2 1
MANUFACTURED IN THE UNITED STATES OF AMERICA

This edition of Charles Wesley's manuscript journal is dedicated to the memory of the Rev. Dr. Oliver A. Beckerlegge, British Methodist minister, friend, and lifelong committed Charles Wesley scholar.

May. 1738.

firmly believed y.t his faith wou.d be avail-
-able for the healing of me.

The Day of Pentecost

Sunday May 21. 1738. I waked in hope
& expectation of his Coming. At 9 my Bro.r
& some friends came, & sang an hymn to the
Holy Ghost. My Comfort & Hope were hereby
increased. In about half an hour they went,
I betook myself to prayer, y.e substance as fol-
-lows; "O Jesus, Thou hast said, I will come un-
~~to you send the Comforter unto you~~ come un-
-to you: Thou hast said, I will send y.e Com-
-forter unto you. Thou hast said, My Father
& I will come unto you, & make our abode
with you. Thou art GOD who canst not lie.
I wholly rely upon thy most true promise,
accomplish it in thy time & manner." Ha-
-ving said this I was composing myself to
sleep, in quietness & peace, when I heard one
come in (Mrs Musgrave, I thought, by the
voice) & say "In the name of Jesus of Na-
-zareth, arise, & believe, & thou shalt be hea-
-led of all thy infirmities!" I wondered how
it shou.d enter into her head to speak in that
manner. The words struck me to the heart.
I sighed, & said within myself "O y.t Christ
wou.d but speak thus to me." I lay musing
& trembling: then thought, "But what if it
shou.d be Him?" I will send at least to see.
I rang, & Mrs Turner coming, desired her
to send up Mrs Musgrave. She went down, &
returning said, "M.rs Musgrave had not been
here." My heart sunk within me at the word,
& I hoped it might be Christ indeed. However
I sent her down again to inquire, & felt in
y.e mean time a strange palpitation of heart.
I said, yet hard to say, "I believe, I believe!"

She

CHARLES WESLEY SOCIETY SERIES

The Manuscript Journal of the
Reverend Charles Wesley, M.A., Volume I

The Manuscript Journal of the
Reverend Charles Wesley, M.A., Volume II

The Journal Letters of the
Reverend Charles Wesley, M.A.

The Letters of the
Reverend Charles Wesley, M.A.

CONTENTS

ACKNOWLEDGMENTS

This new edition of the manuscript journal of Charles Wesley began as a publication idea of The Charles Wesley Society over ten years ago. Persons who contributed to the early discussions include the late Drs. Frank Baker and Oliver A. Beckerlegge, Dr. Richard P. Heitzenrater, The Rev. Thomas Albin, Dr. S T Kimbrough, Jr., and other members of the Society. A parallel project was conceived about the same time of the publication of the "journal letters" of Charles Wesley, now being completed by Dr. Heitzenrater.

Special words of gratitude are expressed to the late Dr. Beckerlegge and to Dr. Heitzenrater for their counsel and assistance with the decipherment of some of the shorthand passages. Thanks are due to Dr. Gareth Lloyd of the John Rylands University Library of Manchester, who has assisted with this as he has with other Charles Wesley projects. His extensive knowledge of the Methodist Archive has again been generously shared with the editors. We also appreciate the time that Dr. Colin Podmore, an authority on the early development of Moravianism in Great Britain, provided in identifying many of the persons and settings mentioned by Wesley.

Practical support has been given to this project by Liverpool Hope University and by the Epworth Trust. In particular, at a time when what turned out to be a very long journey indeed had barely begun, Dr. Ian Markham, then Foundation Dean at the university, was a constant source of encouragement. Professor Suzanne Schwarz, also of Liverpool Hope, who has extensive experience in editing diaries and journals, has been a very welcome conversation partner as the project has progressed. Others at the university, including the present Vice-Chancellor and Rector, Professor Gerald

Pillay, have been more than generous in allowing time and space for a project of this size to be undertaken.

Finally, deep appreciation is expressed to Kingswood/Abingdon Press for its commitment to publish this new edition of the manuscript journal of Charles Wesley and particularly to Dr. Randy Maddox, General Editor for Kingswood Books, for his indefatigable editorial efforts to provide the work with consistency and transparency.

S T Kimbrough, Jr.
Kenneth G. C. Newport

ABBREVIATIONS

AV   *Holy Bible,* Authorized Version, 1611 ("King James Version").

BCP   Church of England. *Book of Common Prayer.* London, 1662.

CPH (1737)   John Wesley, ed. *A Collection of Psalms and Hymns.* Charleston: Lewis Timothy, 1737.

CPH (1738)   John Wesley, ed. *A Collection of Psalms and Hymns.* London: Bowyer for Hutton, 1738.

CPH (1741)   John Wesley, ed. *A Collection of Psalms and Hymns.* London: Strahan, 1741.

CPH (1743)   John and Charles Wesley. *A Collection of Psalms and Hymns* (2nd ed. of 1741). London: Strahan, 1743.

Funeral Hymns (1746)   [Charles Wesley.] *Funeral Hymns.* [London: Strahan, 1746.]

Funeral Hymns (1759)   [Charles Wesley.] *Funeral Hymns.* London: [Strahan,] 1759.

Hoole   Elijah Hoole. *Oglethorpe and the Wesleys in America.* London: R. Needham, 1863.

HSP (1739)   John and Charles Wesley. *Hymns and Sacred Poems.* London: Strahan, 1739.

HSP (1740)	John and Charles Wesley. *Hymns and Sacred Poems*. London: Strahan, 1740.
HSP (1749)	Charles Wesley. *Hymns and Sacred Poems*. 2 vols. Bristol: Farley, 1749.
Jackson	Thomas Jackson, ed. *The Journal of the Rev. Charles Wesley, M.A., . . . to which are Appended Selections from his Correspondence and Poetry*. 2 vols. London: Wesleyan Methodist Book-Room, 1849; reprinted Grand Rapids: Baker Book House, 1980.
MARC	The Methodist Archives Research Centre, John Rylands University Library of Manchester, England.
MS Journal	Charles Wesley's manuscript journal, bound in one volume, running from March 1736 through November 1756, residing in MARC (ref. DDCW 10/2).
MSP	John Wesley, ed. *A Collection of Moral and Sacred Poems from the Most Celebrated English Authors*. Bristol: Farley, 1744.
OED	*The Oxford English Dictionary*.
Poetical Works	*The Poetical Works of John and Charles Wesley*. Edited by George Osborn. 13 vols. London: Wesleyan-Methodist Conference, 1868–72.
PWHS	*Proceedings of the Wesley Historical Society*.
Redemption Hymns	[Charles Wesley.] *Hymns for those that seek, and those that have, Redemption in the Blood of Jesus Christ*. London: Strahan, 1747.

Sermons	*The Sermons of Charles Wesley: A Critical Edition with Introduction and Notes.* Edited by Kenneth G. C. Newport. Oxford: Oxford University Press, 2001.
Telford	John Telford, ed. *The Journal of the Rev. Charles Wesley, M.A., sometime student of Christ Church, Oxford.* Vol. 1: *The Early Journal, 1736–39.* London: Robert Cully, 1910; reprinted Taylors, SC: Methodist Reprint Society, 1977.
Works	*The Works of John Wesley;* begun as "The Oxford Edition of The Works of John Wesley" (Oxford: Clarendon Press, 1975–1983); continued as "The Bicentennial Edition of The Works of John Wesley" (Nashville: Abingdon, 1984–); 16 of 35 vols. published to date.

INTRODUCTION

As we observe the 300th anniversary of the birth of Charles Wesley, his importance is broadly recognized within Western religious and literary history. While remaining firmly committed to the Church of England, Charles shared in the founding of Methodism, a religious movement that has had far-reaching social and religious influence worldwide. His literary abilities and output were also extraordinary. Wesley wrote an estimated 9,000 poetical compositions, many of which are still in active use as hymns. The appeal of these hymns stretches across denominational boundaries, bearing witness to their author's theological insight and his ability to express in flowing poetic form some of humankind's most recurrent and heartfelt concerns.

One might assume that a figure of such acknowledged importance would have been thoroughly researched and analyzed by this point after his birth. But the most recent survey of relevant secondary literature makes clear that research into Charles Wesley's life and thought is still at a rudimentary stage.[1] The problem is not just the limited number (and uneven quality) of secondary studies. More fundamental is the need for reliable editions of all of Charles's primary works, to provide the basis for more adequate secondary study.

There has been some recent progress in this regard. For example, three volumes of Charles Wesley's manuscript poetry have been issued to supplement the earlier collection of his published poetry by George Osborn.[2] While the Osborn collection is not a critical edition, or fully reliable, there is now at least a complete set of the

---

1. See the opening chapter of Gareth Lloyd, *Charles Wesley and the Struggle for Methodist Identity* (Oxford: Oxford University Press, 2007).

2. S T Kimbrough, Jr., and Oliver A. Beckerlegge, eds., *The Unpublished Poetry of Charles Wesley*, 3 vols. (Nashville, TN: Kingswood Books, 1988–1992). Cf. George Osborn, ed., *The Poetical Works of John and Charles Wesley* (London: Wesleyan-Methodist Conference, 1868–1872).

poetic texts available. The situation with Charles Wesley's sermons is even better, with the recent publication of a complete—and annotated—edition.[3] But major work remains to be done, such as a complete edition of Charles Wesley's personal correspondence (a need that Frank Baker voiced over fifty years ago[4]).

The present volume is dedicated to one of the most pressing needs, as regards primary texts, for future study of Charles Wesley—to provide a *complete, accurate,* and *accessible* edition of his manuscript journal (MS Journal). The journal is a crucial resource for the study of Charles Wesley because it conveys a select glimpse into some of the most pivotal events in his life and highlights the major role he played in the emergence and early development of the Methodist movement. The journal also reveals Charles's perspective on many practices within early Methodism, including some pointed disagreements with his brother John.

THE NATURE OF THE MANUSCRIPT JOURNAL

Although written by Charles Wesley, the MS Journal is not an autobiography. It makes no attempt to cover the whole of his life. The account begins (without introduction) in March 1736, with the twenty-eight-year-old Wesley arriving in the Georgia colony as a missionary pastor and an aide to Governor Oglethorpe. It ends in November 1756, with the completion of Charles's last trip into northern England as an itinerant leader of the Wesleyan Methodist connexion. Moreover, the material included between these two boundaries is selective, often minimizing or ignoring developments in his personal life, while emphasizing details of his ministry and instances of persecution of the movement. But within these parameters the MS Journal provides important insights into Charles's life, ministry, and convictions that are available nowhere else.

The character of the MS Journal is a reflection of its original purpose. The journal form, common in eighteenth-century England, was adopted by several members of the Oxford Methodists in the

---

3. Kenneth G. C. Newport, ed., *The Sermons of Charles Wesley: A Critical Edition with an Introduction and Notes* (Oxford: Oxford University Press, 2001).

4. See Frank Baker, *Charles Wesley as Revealed by His Letters* (London: Epworth, 1948), 4.

1730s and was recommended by John Wesley to his preachers later in the century. This form involved regular recording of one's activities and encounters, supplemented with frequent devotional, pastoral, or other reflections on the events of the day. Such journaling is broadly valued for its contribution to nurturing spiritual self-awareness. When the Wesleys went to Georgia in 1736, they recognized that the accounts could also serve as a means of continuing their practice of encouraging one another in their daily lives and ministry. So they began to send selected transcripts of their journals to one another, and to the agencies supporting their ministry.[5]

As the manuscript journals came into circulation, the range of their uses broadened. Their devotional and hortatory value led naturally to a practice of reading selections from them to family members and other Christian friends.[6] The agencies supporting the ministry of the various writers also sensed the value the accounts had for publicizing the work and helping to raise funds. Such potential uses pushed for making the manuscript journals—or some edited extract from them—available more widely. Thus, in 1738, an extract of George Whitefield's earliest journal was rushed into print (without his explicit permission). While Charles Wesley eventually helped edit this extract for publication, he had advised against its release.[7] Charles likely feared that the frank negative comments that Methodist writers were prone to make to one another about nominal Christian practice would spawn criticism and concern. This consequence certainly proved to be the case. In response, both Whitefield and John Wesley soon published further extracts from their journals—extracts now selected with an eye toward clarifying and defending the doctrine and practices of the emerging Methodist movement.

These published *Journals* were often "extracts of extracts." That is, the manuscript journals from which they were drawn were themselves already a selective redaction of earlier materials.[8] Such is clearly the case with Charles Wesley's manuscript journal, which

---

5. Note Charles's comment immediately after his return to England from Georgia about the circulation of manuscript copies of the journals of Benjamin Ingham and John Wesley among their Oxford friends, the Georgia trustees, and others (in entries for December 5 and December 15, 1736, below).

6. Charles records reading from John's manuscript journal to a group in February 8, 1737.

7. See his comments in the entry for August 3, 1738.

8. Note the interrelationship of John Wesley's diary, his manuscript journal, and his published *Journal* in *Works*, volume 18.

he labels on the first page as an "extract of [my] journal." What is the larger "journal" from which this extract was drawn? It was likely never a bound volume in its own right. Rather, by the outset of his mission to Georgia, Charles had adopted the habit of recording accounts of his daily experience on loose sheets of paper and including transcripts of some of these accounts in letters to his friends. Some letters, particularly those sent to his brother John, detailed the struggles and opposition he was facing and sought advice. This practice continued as Charles became involved in the early Methodist movement upon his return to England. From the period of his active itinerant ministry (1739–1756), in addition to numerous personal letters to family and friends that contain some journal-like material, nearly three dozen "journal letters" have survived.[9] These letters (usually sent to his brother or his wife) are devoted entirely to accounts of Charles's activities. Compared to the MS Journal for the same period, the journal letters are frequently more extensive and are evidently a major source from which the journal itself is excerpted. Consider the example of the parallel entries for Sunday, July 7, 1751:

Manuscript Journal	Journal Letter
	Sunday, July 7. Went to church and heard a very harmless sermon. What was once their one subject, the poor Methodists are now rarely mentioned from their pulpits. At five, I preached
Sunday, July 7. Preached out to a numerous congregation, whom I could not look upon without tears. My text was Rev. 3:3: "Remember therefore how thou hast received and heard, and hold fast, and repent." Out of the	out in Wednesbury to a very numerous congregation whom I could not look upon without tears. My text was Revelation 3:3, "Remember therefore how thou hast received and heard, and hold

---

9. These "journal letters" are scheduled to be published soon, as a companion to the present volume.

abundance of my heart my mouth spake, and called them back to their first love and first works. It was a solemn season of sorrow. The Lord, I trust, knocked at many hearts, which will hear his voice, and open to him again. He stirred up the faithful remnant to pray for their backsliding brethren; and their prayers shall not return empty.
 	
    Another hour I employed in earnestly exhorting the Society to repentance.
	fast, and repent." Out of the abundance of my heart my mouth spake, and called them back to their first love and first works. It was a solemn season of sorrow. The Lord, I trust, knocked at many hearts which will hear his voice and open to him again. He stirred up the faithful remnant to pray for their backsliding brethren; and the prayer of faith shall not return empty.
	    Another hour I employed in strongly exhorting the society to repentance. And my faith revived: and many, I believe, saw the door of hope opening.
	    Lodged at Mr E——, who did run well; but the world, that gulf of souls, has now quite swallowed him up. Still he acknowledges the truth and loves the witnesses thereof. O that he might strengthen the things that remain and are ready to die. His wife, sister, and a few neighbours, who had been my hearers at the beginning, seemed a good deal affected, and stirred up again to set their hand to the plough.

As this example illustrates, the MS Journal does not include everything that Charles Wesley may have recorded about a particular day or event; it contains only that which he deemed worthy of retaining for the purposes of this document. The example also hints that immediate publication was not among these purposes. Like the sample, the style of the entire MS Journal is terse, often omitting the subject term in sentences, and constructing long run-on passages. Charles utilizes throughout a series of standard abbreviations for words like "Mrs," "brother," and "sister," as well as abbreviating names whenever possible. Moreover, at several places in the document dealing with sensitive issues Charles switches to writing in a type of shorthand developed by John Byrom. Charles and his brother John had resorted to the use of this shorthand (and writing in Greek) when dealing with sensitive matters in their letters after one of the letters had been intercepted and used against them.[10] Charles was clearly intending to protect these sections of the MS Journal from prying eyes as well.

But this very protective act suggests that Charles was preparing the MS Journal so that he could share at least parts of it in some settings. Indeed, he records in its pages several instances where he reads short selections of his journal to individuals or groups, both for their edification and to clarify specific events.[11] External evidence also suggests that Charles let some friends, like his brother and Lady Huntingdon, read his journal.[12] Finally, there are indications that he was preparing the MS Journal as a resource from which he could generate a printed version, if needed, in order to defend himself or the Wesleyan Methodist movement from unjust attack. This potential purpose would explain, for example, the extended accounts he includes showing that Methodists were vindicated from the charge that they were "Jacobites" or supporters of the rebel forces seeking to overthrow King George.[13] Charles specifically invokes such an apologetic potential in the entry for March 16, 1739, in the context of his role of helping adjudicate a charge that had been made against Thomas Broughton of a sexual indiscretion. When Broughton began to threaten (false) public insinuations about Charles's partiality to the accuser, Wesley specified his line of defense: "I shall simply print my journal."

---

10. See below the entry for April 16, 1736.

11. For a few examples, see January 7, 1737 (to Oglethorpe); September 11, 1737 (to Mrs Delamotte); June 24, 1740 (to the bands); and April 12, 1741 (to the bands). Since we do not know how soon Charles prepared his "extract" from his initial journaling papers, we cannot be sure that he was reading from the MS Journal in these cases.

12. Cf. Lady Huntingdon's letter to John Wesley (October 24, 1741), in *Works* 26:67.

13. See in particular the entries for March 10–15, 1744.

THE FORTUNES AND NATURE OF THE JOURNAL MANUSCRIPT

In fact, Charles never did publish his journal, though he apparently had much of the manuscript material bound into a single octavo volume. At his death (1788) this volume passed into the care of his wife, Sally. With her death in 1822, and the death of their daughter Sarah in 1828, Wesley's manuscript materials became the concern of his eldest son, Charles, Jr. The younger Charles (who had always relied upon his sister to manage his resources) was ill-equipped for this responsibility and in need of money. Recognizing both realities, Thomas Jackson approached Charles, Jr. with the proposal of purchasing his father's manuscript remains on behalf of the Wesleyan Methodist connexion. Jackson's account of the current state of the MS Journal has become almost legendary: "It was found among some loose straw on the floor of a public warehouse in London, where the furniture of the owner [Charles Wesley Jr.] was for a time deposited, several leaves in the volume being cut from the binding, and yet not removed."[14]

The sale of Charles Wesley's manuscript materials (and his personal library) to Jackson was finalized in 1831.[15] The next Wesleyan Methodist Conference received the manuscript materials from Jackson, gladly reimbursing his expense and allowing him full access to them.[16] Thereby, Charles's MS Journal became the property of the British Methodists. In the mid-1970s the Methodist Church of Great Britain decided to accept an offer from the John Rylands University Library of Manchester to house on permanent deposit much of their archives, and this is where the MS Journal currently resides.[17]

As it now exists, the MS Journal is made up of three documents that have been bound together. The first document begins at March 9, 1736, and runs through November 6, 1739, covering 286 pages. The numbering in the bound volume then starts over with page "1"

---

14. Thomas Jackson, ed., *The Journal of Charles Wesley*, 2 vols. (London: Wesleyan Methodist Book-Room, 1849), 1:v.

15. The deed of conveyance, dated August 4, 1831, is in MARC: ref. MAW Ra (Box 6).

16. See Thomas Jackson, *Recollections of My Own Life and Times* (London: Wesleyan Conference Office, 1874), 230.

17. The journal is classified in MARC as DDCW 10/2.

of a second document that is 446 pages in length, covering March 14, 1740, through August 26, 1751. This in turn is followed immediately by a third separately numbered (thirty-page) document that opens on September 17, 1756, and ends on November 5, 1756. Jackson makes clear that the volume was bound together in this fashion when it came into his possession. The leaves that he mentioned had become detached from the binding can be clearly identified. Pages 396–445 of document two (August 1749 to August 1751) and the entirety of document three are taped together and stitched back into the volume.

There are some significant gaps in this "extract" of Charles Wesley's broader journal letters and notes. In addition to the absence of the years 1752–55, the entirety of 1742 is also missing, and some of the other material is rather patchy. In none of these cases does it appear that material has been cut out of the bound volume; rather, it was never included.

PRIOR PUBLISHED EDITIONS OF THE MANUSCRIPT JOURNAL

While Charles Wesley never published the MS Journal, it was too important a resource to be left untapped by later Methodist writers, once they gained access to it. The first instance of such use came shortly after Charles's death. While Charles may have desired his wife to keep the volume in her exclusive possession,[18] it was made available to Dr. John Whitehead (a Methodist, and Wesley's physician) in the early 1790s. Whitehead was preparing a biography of John Wesley, which he planned to preface with brief accounts of the larger Wesley family. Given the wealth of material in the MS Journal, Whitehead's account of Charles Wesley grew to over 275 pages and included numerous direct extracts from the volume.[19]

When he purchased Charles Wesley's literary remains in 1831, Thomas Jackson became the second Methodist writer with access to the MS Journal. His first tapping of this resource, and of the many unpublished letters included in the remains, was for a two-

---

18. Jackson claims this was the case (*Journal*, 1:v), but cites no evidence for the claim.
19. Cf. John Whitehead, *The Life of the Rev. John Wesley . . . to which is prefixed . . . The Life of the Rev. Charles Wesley*, 2 vols. (London: Stephen Couchman, 1793–1796), 1:97–374.

volume biography of Charles Wesley, published in 1841.[20] With its greater length, Jackson's biography added a significant number of published excerpts from the MS Journal to those that had appeared in the earlier work by Whitehead.

Then, in 1849, Jackson published another two-volume work: *The Journal of the Rev. Charles Wesley, M. A., . . . to which are Appended Selections from his Correspondence and Poetry*. The title would suggest that Jackson was now publishing the MS Journal in its entirety. But this was not quite the case. To begin with, Jackson did not know how to read the shorthand that Charles used for several "sensitive" sections, so all of these are omitted (with almost no indication of the omission[21]). On top of this, Jackson omitted several longhand sections of the MS Journal that he considered indiscreet, unflattering to Charles, or open to misunderstanding by readers of his day.[22] As such, Jackson's published version is an *incomplete* presentation of the MS Journal.

Jackson's version also conveys an *inaccurate* sense of the MS Journal in two major ways. The first way concerns scope. Without indicating their different origin, Jackson added two sections to the published *Journal* that are not found in the bound volume. One of these sections runs from November 29, 1753, through December 6, 1753.[23] It was drawn from a separate small manuscript that was among Charles's remains and now resides in the Methodist Archives at the John Rylands University Library of Manchester.[24] The other section that Jackson added runs from July 8, 1754, to August 13, 1754.[25] There is a "journal letter" still extant that includes all the material for July 8–31, but Jackson's source for the

---

20. Thomas Jackson, *The Life of the Rev. Charles Wesley, M. A.*, 2 vols. (London: John Mason, 1841).

21. The one exception is the entry for April 16, 1736, where Jackson inserts a note after the first paragraph: "Several paragraphs following are written in a private character" (*Journal*, 1:19).

22. Even with these deletions, Jackson was criticized by some of his contemporaries for "betraying Methodism" by revealing Charles's disagreements with his brother; cf. Jackson, *Recollections*, 313.

23. Cf. Jackson, *Journal*, 2:95–100.

24. MARC, ref. DDCW 8/4. This is not a section of the MS Journal that fell out. The paper is a different size, the text has a different layout, and no running header of the date is used. It may be an instance of Charles's initial journal notes. The manuscript actually runs through December 11, 1753, and contains some shorthand sections that Jackson omits. Some of that shorthand can be found in John R. Tyson and Douglas Lister, "Charles Wesley, Pastor: A Glimpse Inside His Shorthand Journal," *Quarterly Review* 4.1 (1984): 9–21.

25. Cf. Jackson, *Journal*, 2:100–113.

material in August is not clear. The second way in which Jackson's edition conveys an inaccurate sense of the MS Journal concerns style. We observed earlier that Charles used a terse style in his extract, omitting the subject term in many instances, and creating complex run-on sentences. Jackson consistently supplies missing words (without noting that they are his insertions) and smooths Wesley's style, thereby creating the impression that the MS Journal was more of a final product than was the case.

The initial step in supplementing Jackson's published edition of Wesley's *Journal* came in 1863, when Elijah Hoole issued an essay on the relationship of James Oglethorpe and the Wesley brothers. Hoole included in his essay the first transcription of some of the shorthand sections in the original manuscript.[26] While helpful, Hoole's topic restricted his attention to a few of the shorthand passages in the period between March 22 and May 31, 1736. Moreover, his transcriptions of these passages were rather "free" in nature.

No further significant improvement upon Jackson's edition of the MS Journal was offered until the sixtieth anniversary of its appearance. In 1909 John Telford issued the first volume of his new edition of Charles Wesley's *Journal*.[27] A major advantage that Telford touted for his edition was that it included "some of the shorthand passages" that had been deciphered by Nehemiah Curnock.[28] Telford also expanded several of the abbreviated names, and included an index that gave brief identifications for some of the persons named in the journal accounts. Despite these advantages, Telford's edition still fell short of providing a *complete* and *accurate* edition of the MS Journal. To begin with, his first volume covered only through August 27, 1739, and he died before further volumes could be prepared. Moreover, Telford did not include *all* of the shorthand passages in the years covered by the first volume, apparently censoring some due to their sensitive nature. For example, instead of reproducing Charles's shorthand account on March 18, 1736, of Mrs Welch (falsely) accusing James Oglethorpe of making sexual advances, Telford simply inserted the note: "The record of her vile accusations is in shorthand." Add to this the fact that Telford relied heavily on Jackson's transcription of the longhand

---

26. See Elijah Hoole, *Oglethorpe and the Wesleys* (London: R. Needham, 1863), 8–9.

27. *The Journal of the Rev. Charles Wesley, M.A. sometime student of Christ Church, Oxford; The Early Journal, 1736–39* (London: Robert Cully, 1909).

28. Ibid., 6.

entries, meaning that he reproduced many of Jackson's omissions of "indiscrete" material here as well.[29] In the process, of course, he also replicated Jackson's smoothing of the terse style of the MS Journal.

While many have recognized the limitations of the published editions of Jackson and Telford, it has been nearly one hundred years since anyone has undertaken to provide a more complete and accurate edition of the MS Journal. The time is surely ripe!

CHARACTERISTICS OF THIS EDITION OF THE MANUSCRIPT JOURNAL

A *Complete* Edition. This edition of Charles Wesley's MS Journal is the first to include *all* of the material—shorthand and long-hand—in his manuscript. We have even included words that Charles struck out, in every instance where they may be significant. The following technical matters should be noted in this regard:

1) All transcribed shorthand passages are printed in <u>underlined</u> font.

2) Words that Charles underlined in the manuscript are *italicized*.

3) Other forms of emphasis or peculiarities in Charles's script are footnoted.

4) Words that Charles struck out are printed in ~~strikeout~~ font.

5) Any uncertainty of a reading or transcription is indicated in the footnotes.

For comparative purposes, we have identified in footnotes those sections of the longhand that were omitted by Jackson or Telford, and those sections of the shorthand omitted by Telford or Hoole (remember that Jackson omitted *all* of the shorthand). This will allow readers to gauge the sensibilities of these earlier editors of Wesley's manuscript.

An *Accurate* Edition. We have sought to reproduce the MS Journal accurately. As such, we have not included the sections which Jackson added to his published edition.[30] Likewise, we have

---

29. See the examples (concerning Peter Appee) that are footnoted in the entries for November 27 and December 29, 1736.

30. This additional material appears in the companion volume devoted to the "journal letters."

tried to preserve the terse style of Charles's writing in the MS Journal. When it has been necessary to add anything for clarity, we have been careful to mark the addition as an editorial insertion. Likewise, in those scattered instances where Charles enters a wrong date, we have identified our correction in the text. We have used square brackets [ ] to indicate all such editorial insertions.

An *Accessible* **Edition.** We have also devoted significant attention to making this edition of the MS Journal more accessible for general readers and for Wesley scholarship.

Part of this attention has been directed to the presentation of the text, where we have balanced our commitment to replication of Charles's style in the following ways:[31]

1) We have followed current rules of capitalization, rather than the eighteenth-century pattern of more frequent use of capital letters.

2) We have also followed current guidelines on punctuation, reducing Charles's typical eighteenth-century profligate use of commas, colons, and semi-colons.

3) We have retained Charles's practice, common in his time in Britain, of using double quotation marks as the primary form (with single quotation marks being used for quotations within quotations).

4) Charles routinely abbreviates the days of the week; such titles as "Mrs," "sister," or "brother"; and the names of persons or places. We have (silently) expanded all such abbreviations when there was certainty about the expansion. Uncertain cases are left in abbreviated form, though probable suggestions are sometimes given in footnotes.

5) Charles's spelling of the names of persons and places is often phonetic-based, and varies from the standard spelling. We have been able to identify the intended referent in nearly all cases for places (by context and use of contemporary gazettes), and in many cases for persons (by comparison to parallel accounts). Whenever there is an agreed spelling that differs from the one that Charles gives, we substitute the correct spelling in the text, but note Charles's variant spelling in a footnote (for the first occurrence) and the relevant index.

---

31. In most of these cases we are adopting the practices used in the current production of John Wesley's *Works*.

6) Charles's spelling of a few names changes through the course of the MS Journal. In these cases we have standardized all instances to their most correct form.

The other dimension of accessibility that drew our attention was identification of the events, people, places, and writings to which Charles refers. Our goal was not a highly annotated edition, with its own description for each person and place, but an edition that provided (when known) sufficient details to enable readers to consult standard reference sources for further information. The major principles we observed were as follows:

1) Charles typically refers to persons using only their last name. When the first name could be determined, either from elsewhere in the MS Journal or in parallel materials, we have inserted it [in brackets] on the first occurrence of the person in the MS Journal and wherever else it is necessary to make clear the individual in question. This is to aid the reader in locating the individual in the Index of Personal Names, where we often provide further distinguishing details like dates of birth and death. With these details the reader can consult other primary materials in eighteenth-century Methodism, as well as relevant reference sources.[32]

2) When Charles refers to persons by title—such as "the bishop of Oxford"—we have provided a note identifying the person holding the title or office.

3) We have provided footnotes for places that Charles names only when this is necessary (such as distinguishing between two places with the same name). Otherwise, the reader is directed to the Index of Places for further details. In particular, every town is identified in the Index by its *traditional* shire or county,[33] and with detailed location information when this is deemed helpful.

---

32. See, in particular, Samuel J. Rogal, *Biographical Dictionary of Eighteenth-Century Methodism*, 10 vols. (Lewiston, ME: Edwin Mellen, 1997–1999); John A. Vickers, editor, *Dictionary of Methodism in Britain and Ireland* (London: Epworth, 2000); Donald M. Lewis, editor, *The Blackwell Dictionary of Evangelical Biography, 1730–1860* (Oxford: Blackwell, 1995); and H. C. G. Matthew, editor, *Oxford Dictionary of National Biography* (Oxford University Press, 2004). A very helpful resource providing details on overlapping Moravian developments and persons is Colin Podmore, *The Moravian Church in England, 1728–60* (Oxford University Press, 1998).

33. We use the traditional shire or county because this identification remains the same, whatever the later merging, dividing, or renaming of governmental districts.

4) Charles frequently cites both classical and contemporary writers. We provide notes identifying the sources for these quotations, and translate all quotations that are not in English. Since Wesley often quoted his classical sources from memory, we also point out the occasional mistakes in his citation.

5) Wesley's most frequent source for quotations and allusions throughout the MS Journal is the Bible. We have ensured that references are supplied for all direct quotations and for clear biblical allusions. The quotations are typically identified in the text (using [brackets] when necessary). The allusions are identified in footnotes. In both cases the references should be understood as denoting the Authorized Version, unless it is a psalm. Wesley's daily source for reading psalms was the Psalter in the *Book of Common Prayer*, which can differ from the AV in both wording and numbering. When it is clear that Charles is quoting from the Psalter, this is specified in the reference; and the Psalter should be assumed as the more likely source for those instances where it parallels the AV.

6) One of the rich resources that the MS Journal provides for study of Charles Wesley is its record of numerous instances of his preaching. Our final contribution to the accessibility of this edition was to identify the scripture text for as many of these instances as possible.

CONCLUSION

Charles Wesley has with good reason been called the greatest hymnographer of the English language. But he should be remembered as more than just the "sweet singer of Methodism." With his brother John, he was one of the founders of the Methodist movement within the Church of England. The primary sources indicate that he was a powerful preacher-evangelist, a determined leader, and an individual who lived within, had imbibed, and expressed well the general spirit of the eighteenth-century evangelical revival. This first *complete* edition of the MS Journal allows us to catch a richer glimpse of Charles and his world, his triumphs and his sorrows, his pleasures and his pains (including his disagreements with brother John), than has been possible until now. The editors hope that the publication of the journal will inspire and enable further research into the life and work of Charles Wesley and into the cauldron of religious ferment that was the "real-life situation" out of which the document evolved.

The editors,
S T Kimbrough, Jr.
Kenneth G. C. Newport

EXTRACT OF JOURNAL

[MARCH] 1736[1]

Tuesday, March 9, 1736. About three in the afternoon, I first set foot on St Simons Island, and immediately my spirit revived. No sooner did I enter upon my ministry than God gave me, like Saul, another heart.[2] So true is that [remark] of Bishop Hall: "The calling of God never leaves a man unchanged. Neither did God ever employ any one in his service whom He did not enable to the work He set him, especially those whom he raises up to the supply of his place and the representation of Himself."[3] The people, with Mr [James] Oglethorpe, were all arrived the day before.

The first who saluted me on my landing was honest Mr [Benjamin] Ingham, and that with his usual heartiness. Never did I more rejoice at the sight of him, especially when he told me the treatment he has met with for vindicating the Lord's Day. Such as every minister of Christ must meet with. The people seemed overjoyed to see me. Mr Oglethorpe in particular received me very kindly.

I spent the afternoon in conference with my parishioners. (With what trembling ought I to call them mine!) At seven we had evening prayers, in the open air, at which Mr Oglethorpe was present. The lesson gave me the fullest direction and greatest encouragement:

1. Charles consistently switches the year at January 1, rather than March 25, even though this New Style dating did not become official until 1752.
2. Cf. 1 Sam. 10:9.
3. Joseph Hall (1574–1656), *Contemplations upon the Principal Passages of the Holy Story* (London: Henry Featherstone, 1618), 4:94.

Continue instant in prayer, and watch in the same with thanksgiving; withal praying also for us, that God would open unto us a
door of utterance, to speak the mystery of Christ, that I may make
it manifest, as I ought to speak. Walk in wisdom toward them that
are without, redeeming the time. Let your speech be alway [. . .]
seasoned with salt, that ye may know how ye ought to answer
every man. [. . .] Say to Archippus, take heed to the ministry which
thou hast received of the Lord, that thou fulfil it [Col. 4:2-17].

At nine I returned and lay in the boat.

Wednesday, March 10. Between five and six in the morning read
short prayers to a few at the fire, before Mr Oglethorpe's tent, in a
hard shower of rain. Mr Oglethorpe had set up a tent for the
women near his own. Toward noon I found an opportunity of talking at the tent-door with Mrs [Anne] Welch. I laboured to guard her
against the cares of the world, and to give herself to God in the
Christian sacrifice; but to no purpose. God was pleased not to add
weight to my words, therefore they could make no impression.

After dinner I began talking with Mrs Germain, about baptizing
her child by immersion. She was much averse to it, though she
owned it a strong, healthy child. I then spoke to her husband, who
was soon satisfied, and brought his wife to be so too.

In the evening I endeavoured to reconcile Mrs Welch to Mrs
[Beata] Hawkins, who, I assured her, bore her no ill-will. She
replied, "You must not tell me that. Mrs Hawkins is a very subtle
woman. I understand her perfectly. There is a great man in the case,
therefore I cannot speak—only, that she is exceedingly jealous of
me." Company stopped her saying more.

Thursday, March 11. At ten this morning I began the full service
to about a dozen women whom I had got together, intending to
continue it and only to read a few prayers to the men before they
went to work. I also expounded the second lesson with some boldness, as I had a few times before.

After prayers I met Mrs Hawkins's maid, in a great passion of
tears, at being struck by her mistress. She seemed resolved to make
away with herself, to escape her Egyptian bondage. With much difficulty I prevailed upon her to return, and carried her back to her
mistress. Upon my asking Mrs Hawkins to forgive her she refused
me with the utmost roughness, rage, and almost reviling.

Mr [Ambrose] Tackner, whom I talked with next, made me full amends. He was in an excellent temper, resolved to strive, not with his wife, but himself, in putting off the old man and putting on the new.[4]

In the evening I heard the first harsh word from Mr Oglethorpe, when I asked for something for a poor woman. The next day I was surprised by a rougher answer, in a matter that deserved still greater encouragement. I knew not how to account for his increasing coldness.

My encouragement was the same in speaking with Mrs Welch, whom I found all storm and tempest. The meek, the teachable Mrs Welch (that *was* in the ship) was now so wilful, so untractable, so fierce, that I could not bear to stay near her. I did not mend myself by stumbling again upon Mr Oglethorpe, who was with the men under arms, in expectation of an enemy. I stayed as long as I could, however,

> Unsafe within the wind
> Of such commotion.[5]

But at last the hurricane of his passion drove me away.

Sunday, March 14. We had prayers under a great tree. In the epistle I was plainly shown what I ought to be, and what to expect.

Giving no offence in anything, that the ministry be not blamed, but in all things approving ourselves as the ministers of God, in much patience, in afflictions, in necessities, in distresses, in stripes, in imprisonments, in tumults, in labours, in watchings, in fastings; by pureness, by knowledge, by longsuffering, by kindness, by the Holy Ghost, by love unfeigned, by the word of truth, by the power of God, by the armour of righteousness on the right hand and on the left, by honour and dishonour, by evil report and good report; as deceivers, and yet true; as unknown, and yet well known; as dying, and, behold, we live; as chastened, and not killed; as sorrowful, yet always rejoicing; as poor, yet making many rich; as having nothing, and yet possessing all things [2 Cor. 6:3-10].

---

4. Cf. Eph. 4:22-24.
5. Milton, *Paradise Lost*, vi.309–10.

I preached with boldness on singleness of intention,[6] to about twenty people among whom was Mr Oglethorpe. Soon after, as he was in Mrs Hawkins's hut, a bullet (through the carelessness of one of the people who were exercising today) flew through the wall, close by him.

Mrs Germain now retracted her consent for having her child baptized. However, Mrs Colwell's I did baptize by trine immersion, before a numerous congregation.

At night I found myself exceeding faint, but had no better bed to go to than the ground, on which I slept very comfortably, before a great fire, and waked the next morning perfectly well.

Tuesday, March 16, was wholly spent in writing letters for Mr Oglethorpe.[7] I would not spend 6 days more in the same manner for all of Georgia.

Wednesday, March 17. Found an opportunity to tell Mrs Welch the reason why I had not talked with her lately was my despair of doing her any good. She acknowledged herself entirely changed, "but could never tell me the cause." I immediately guessed it, and mentioned my conjecture. She confessed the truth of it. My soul was filled with pity, and I prayed God the sin of others might not ruin her.

Thursday, March 18. Today Mr Oglethorpe set out with the Indians, to hunt the buffalo upon the main, and to see the utmost limits of what they claimed. In the afternoon Mrs Welch discovered to me the whole mystery of iniquity. <u>What she said was as follows: Mr Oglethorpe is a wicked man and a perfect stranger to righteousness. He kept a mistress in England to my knowledge, and even there solicited me. He forebore while I was sick, pretending he had laid aside all such designs, but resumed them upon my recovery. He would persuade me righteousness is but a church teaching. Mrs Hawkins persuaded me he has the same designs, I fear with better hopes of success, his gratitude led to set him against your brother. In regard to this, she has told him, your brother was in love with her, has kissed her a thousand times and wept bitterly in the ship at the thought of parting from her. Mr Oglethorpe refused a long time to believe it. She is exceeding jealous</u>

---

6. Cf. Matt. 6:22-23. The text of this sermon, which Charles copied from his brother John, has survived. See *Sermons*, 306–13.

7. At least one such letter has survived. It is now held in MARC (ref. DDCW 1/5).

of me; fell upon me lately with "Must I have the character of Mr Oglethorpe's whore to secure on you?" She has also used him with the utmost insolence.

He is extremely jealous of you; having done all he could to persuade me you have the same design upon me which he has. He contrived your going in the other boat without answers to hinder your speaking to me.

She further owned that she loved him and was much grieved at the thought of losing his love. Besides she dreaded the consequence of its being changed into hatred as she would then be entirely exposed to the mercy of a wicked man with absolute power. I encouraged her to trust in God and only then pressed her to seek for strength in the means of grace.

From her.[8]

Went to my myrtle-walk, where, as I was repeating "I will thank Thee, for Thou hast heard me, and art become my salvation," [Ps. 118:21, BCP] a gun was fired from the other side of the bushes. Providence had that moment turned me from that end of the walk which the shot flew through, but I heard them pass by me![9]

Sunday, March 21. Mr Oglethorpe had ordered oftener than once that no man should shoot on a Sunday. [Michael] Germain had been committed to the guardroom for it in the morning, but was upon his submission released. In the midst of [the] sermon a gun was fired. [Samuel] Davison the constable ran out and found it was the doctor, told him it was contrary to orders and he was obliged to desire him to come to the officer. Upon this the doctor flew into a great passion, and said, "What, don't you know I am not to be looked upon as a common fellow?" Not knowing what to do the constable went and returned after consulting with [Captain] Hermsdorf, with two sentinels, and brought him to the guardroom. Hereupon Mrs Hawkins charged and fired a gun, and then ran thither, like a madwoman, crying she had shot, and would be confined too. The constable and Hermsdorf persuaded her to go away. She cursed and swore in the utmost transport of passion, threatening to kill the first man that should come near her. (Alas, my brother, what is become of thy hopeful convert!)

---

8. Not included in either Telford or Hoole.
9. The exclamation mark has more the form of a question mark in the MS, though an exclamation mark seems intended.

In the afternoon, while I was talking in the street with poor Catherine, her mistress came up to us, and fell upon me with the utmost bitterness and scurrility; said she would blow me up and my brother, whom she once thought honest, but was now undeceived; that I was the cause of her husband's confinement, but she would be revenged, and expose my damned hypocrisy, my prayers four times a day by beat of drum, my intrigue with her maid, and abundance more, which I cannot write, and thought no *woman*, though taken from Drury Lane,[10] could have spoken. I only said I pitied her, but defied all she or the devil could do, for she could not hurt me. I was strangely preserved from passion, and at parting told her I hoped she would soon come to a better mind.

In the evening hour of retirement I resigned myself to God, in my brother's prayer for conformity to a suffering Saviour.[11]

<u>I was interrupted by the following note.</u>

Mr Wesley,
Being by your priestly order confined, the care of the sick is no longer incumbent on me. As you have been busy in intermeddling with my affairs, I desire the following patients may have proper assistance, which ought to have been before this time, and no neglect laid to your injured friend John[12] Hawkins.

PS.—I dispute the authority of confining a surgeon, and especially for a thing I know nothing of.

<u>After a short prayer for meekness I went and visited all his patients, only saying, "I had no hand in your confinement. The gun was fired in sermon time, and before the constable came back I went directly in my surplice to the tent and gave the Sacrament. Immediately after this I took a walk in the woods, whence I did not return till dinner time, about an hour after your confinement, which I then first heard of. You misunderstood Hermsdorf, if you say he lays it to me. He wholly denies it."</u>

---

10. Drury Lane, in the Covent Garden area of London, was in Wesley's day (as it still is today) the site of the Theatre Royal.

11. Cf. the Prayer for Friday Morning in John Wesley's *Collection of Forms of Prayer for Every Day of the Week* (London: n.p., 1738 [original, 1733]), which includes the line: "O Jesus, hanging on the accursed tree, bowing the head, giving up the ghost, have mercy upon me, and conform my whole soul to thy holy, humble, suffering spirit" (p. 65).

12. The shorthand clearly reads "John," but his first name was actually Thomas.

"But when you did know it," he replied, "why did you not tell him he had no business or authority to confine me, no more than a captain to confine his lieutenant."[13]

"Because I did presume they understood their own business best, and your having charged the matter upon me made me resolve to have no concern in it."

Going from home I was informed of the compliments Mrs Hawkins' husband was very surely paying my brother and me. Hawkins, seeing me from the guardroom walking with his maid between the two rows of houses, had said, "There goes the parson with his whore. I myself saw her and him were under the bushes." Modest Mrs Hawkins added, "upon the ground."

Monday, March 22. While I was persuading Mr [John] Welch not to concern himself in this disturbance, I heard Mrs Hawkins cry out "Murder!" and walked away. Returning out of the woods, I was informed by Mr[14] Welch that poor blockhead Mrs Welch had joined with Mrs Hawkins and the devil in their slanders of me. I would not believe it till half the town told me the same, and exclaimed against her ingratitude. Soon after Haydon informed me that he had civilly told Mrs Hawkins his orders were not to suffer her to come within the camp, but he would carry those bottles for her. She replied she would come, and, upon his holding open his arms to hinder her, broke one of the bottles on his head. He caught her in his arms, she striking him continually and crying out "Murder!" Hawkins at the same time ran up and struck him. He closed and threw him down, set his foot upon him, and said if he resisted he would run his bayonet into him. Mr [Thomas] Hird, the other constable, was meantime engaged in keeping off Mrs Hawkins, who broke the other bottle on his head. Welch coming up to her assistance, Davison the constable desired him to keep off the camp. Nevertheless, he ran upon him, took the gun out of his hand, and struck him with all his strength on his sides and face; till Haydon interposed and parted them. Welch then ran and gave the doctor a bayonet, which was immediately taken from him. Mrs Hawkins cried out continually against the parsons, and swore revenge against my brother and me. But the bridle is in her mouth.

13. The shorthand here follows the British pronunciation of the word with an "f" at the end of the first syllable.
14. Original: "Mrs."

At three, I carried Mrs Perkins to Mrs Welch; but finding her as the troubled sea, thought this no time for expostulating her treatment of me. Asked whether I could do anything for her or her husband, now confined for his violence towards the officers. Her railing forced me to leave her.

Mr Hird soon after told me he had followed Mrs Hawkins to her house, and entreated her to return quietly to her husband and trouble the public peace no longer. Upon no greater provocation than this, she snatched up an iron pistol and offered to strike him. He laid hold of her husband's gun, and she as quickly caught up another. She presented it, but was seized before she could discharge it. The pistol, gun, and other arms were now taken from her, and she put in a guard of two sentinels.[15]

Faint and weary with the day's fatigue, I found my want of true holiness, and begged God to give me comfort from his word. I then read, in the evening lesson,

> But thou, O man of God, flee these things; and follow after righteousness, goodness, faith, love, patience, meekness. Fight the good fight of faith, lay hold on eternal life, whereunto thou art also called, and hast professed a good profession before many witnesses [1 Tim. 6:11, 12].

Before prayers I took a walk with Mr Ingham, who was surprized I should not think innocence a sufficient protection. I had not indeed acquainted him with what Mrs Welch had told me. At night I was forced to exchange my usual bed the ground for a chest, being almost speechless through a violent cold.

Tuesday, March 23. In reading Heb. 11, I felt my faith revive and I was confident God would either turn aside the trial, or strengthen me to bear it. In the afternoon Mr Davison informed me the doctor had sent his wife word to arm herself from the case of instruments, and forcibly make her escape to speak to Mr Oglethorpe first and even to stab any that should oppose her. Mrs Perkins told me she had heard Mrs Hawkins say "Mr Oglethorpe dares not punish me." I was encouraged by the lesson:

> God hath not given us the spirit of fear but of power. . . . Be not thou therefore ashamed of the testimony of our Lord, nor of me his

---

15. Telford includes this entire section of shorthand; Hoole (pp. 8–9) transcribes only the material for March 22.

prisoner. But be thou partaker of the afflictions of the gospel according to the power of God. [. . .] Whereunto I am appointed a preacher—for the which cause also I suffer these things. Nevertheless I am not ashamed, for I know whom I have believed, and am persuaded that He is able to keep that which I have committed to him against that day [2 Tim. 1:7-12].

Wednesday, March 24. Was enabled to pray earnestly for my enemies, particularly Mr Oglethorpe, whom I now looked upon as the chief of them. Then gave myself up entirely to God's disposal, desiring I might not now want power to pray, when I most of all needed it. Mr Ingham then came, and read the 37th Psalm, a glorious exhortation to patience and confidence in God, from the different estate of the good and wicked. After breakfast I again betook myself to intercession, particularly for Mrs Welch, that Satan, in the shape of that other bad woman, might not stand at her right hand. Doubting whether I should not interpose for the prisoners, I consulted the oracle, and met Jer. 44:16-17, "As for the word which thou hast spoken to us in the name of the Lord, we will not hearken unto it. But we will certainly do whatsoever thing goeth forth out of our own mouth." This determined me not to meddle with them at all.

At eleven met Mrs Perkins, who told me of the infamy Mrs Hawkins has brought on Mr Oglethorpe, and the utter discouragement it will be to the people if she is supported. Farther she informed me that Mrs Welch begins to repent of having engaged so far with her, confessing she has done it through cowardice, as thinking Mr Oglethorpe will bear her out against all the world.

Soon after I talked with Mrs Welch *sub deo*,[16] and with the last degree of astonishment heard her accuse herself with Mr——! Horror of horrors! Never did I feel such excess of pity. I gave myself up to prayer for her. Mr Ingham soon joined me. All the prayers expressed a full confidence in God. When notice was given us of Mr Oglethorpe's landing, Mrs Hawkins, Mr Ingham, and myself were sent for. We found him in his tent with the people round it, Mr and Mrs Hawkins within. After a short hearing, the officers were reprimanded, and the prisoners dismissed. At going out Mrs Hawkins modestly told me she had something more to say

---

16. "Under God."

9

against me, but would take another time. I only answered, "You know, madam, it is impossible for *me* to fear *you*." When they were gone, Mr Oglethorpe said he was convinced and glad I had had no hand in all this. I told him I had something to impart of the last importance, when he was at leisure. He took no notice, but read his letter; and I walked away with Mr Ingham, who was utterly astonished. The issue is just what I expected.

I was struck with those words in the evening lesson:

> Thou therefore, my son, be strong in the grace that is in Christ
> Jesus. . . . Endure hardness, as a good soldier of Jesus Christ. . . .
> Remember that Jesus Christ was raised from the dead, according to
> my gospel, wherein I suffer trouble, as an evil-doer, even unto
> bonds; but the word of God is not bound. Therefore I endure all
> things for the elect['s] sake. It is a faithful saying, for if we be dead
> with him, we shall also live with him; if we suffer, we shall also
> reign with him [2 Tim. 2:1-12].

After reading I could not forbear adding, "I need say nothing. God will shortly apply this."

Glory be to God for my confidence hitherto. O, what am I if left to myself! but I can do and suffer all things through Christ strengthening me.[17]

Thursday, March 25. At five I heard the second drum beat for prayers, which I had desired Mr Ingham to read, being much weakened by my fever. But considering I ought to appear at this time especially, I rose and heard those animating words.

> If any man serve me, let him follow me; and where I am, there
> shall my servant be: if any man serve me, him will my Father hon-
> our. Now is my soul troubled; and what shall I say? Father, save
> me from this hour? But for this cause came I unto this hour. Father
> glorify thy name [John 12:26-28].

At half-hour past seven Mr Oglethorpe called me out of my hut. I looked up to God and went. He charged me with mutiny and sedition, with stirring up the people to desert the colony. Accordingly he said, they had had a meeting last night, and sent a

---

17. Cf. Phil. 4:13.

message to him this morning, desiring leave to go. That their speaker had informed against them, and me the spring of all. That the men were such as constantly came to prayers, therefore I must have instigated them. That he should not scruple shooting half a dozen of them at once; but that he had out of kindness *first* spoke to me. My answer was: "I desire, sir, you would have no regard to my brothers, my friends, or the love you had for me, if anything of this is made out against me. I know nothing of their meeting or designs. Of those you have mentioned, not one comes constantly to prayers, or Sacrament. I never incited any one to leave the colony. I desire to answer my accuser face to face." He told me my accuser was Mr [Richard] Lawley, whom he would bring, if I would wait here. I added, "Mr Lawley is a man who has declared he knows no reason for keeping fair with any man, but a design to get all he can by him. But there was nothing to be got by the poor parsons." I asked whether he himself was not assured that there were enough men in Frederica to say or swear anything against any man that should be in disgrace; whether, if he himself was removed, or succeeded ill, the whole stream of the people would not be turned against him; and even this Lawley, who was of all others the most violent in condemning the prisoners and justifying the officers. I observed this was the old cry, "Away with the Christians to the lions"; mentioned Hawkins and his wife's scandalizing my brother and me, and vowing revenge against us both, threatening me yesterday even in his presence. I asked what redress or satisfaction was due to my character; what good I could do in my parish if cut off by their calumnies from ever seeing one half of it? Ended with assuring him I had and should still make it my business to promote peace among all. I felt no disturbance while speaking, but lifted up my heart to God, and found him present with me. While Mr Oglethorpe was fetching Lawley I thought of our Lord's words, "Ye shall be brought before rulers," etc. [Matt. 10:18; Mark 13:9], and applied to him for help, and words to make my defence.

Before Mr Oglethorpe returned I called in upon Mr Ingham, and desired him to pray for me; then walked, and, musing on the event, opened the book on Acts 15:31-33: "Which when they had read, they rejoiced for the consolation, and we exhorted the brethren with many words and confirmed them. And after they had tarried

11

there a space, they were let go in 'peace'."[18] Mr Ingham coming, I related all that had passed. On sight of Mr Oglethorpe and Lawley, he retired.

Mr Oglethorpe observed the place was too public. I offered to carry him to my usual walk in the woods. In our way God put it into my heart to say, "Show only the least disinclination to find me guilty, and you shall see what a turn it will give to the accusation." He took the hint and instead of calling upon Lawley to make good his charge, began with the quarrel in general, but did not show himself angry with me, or desirous to find me to blame. Lawley, who appeared full of guilt and fear, upon this dropped his accusation, or shrunk it into my "forcing the people to prayers." I replied, that the people themselves would acquit me of that; and as to the *officers'* quarrel, I appealed to the officers for the truth of my assertion, that I had had no hand at all in it; professed my desire and resolution of promoting peace and obedience; and as to the people, was persuaded their desire of leaving the colony arose from mistake, not malice. Here Mr Oglethorpe spoke of reconciling matters, bade Lawley tell the petitioners he would not so much as ask who they were, if they were "but quiet for the future." "I hope," added he, "they will be so, and Mr Wesley here hopes so too." "Yes sir," says Lawley, "I really believe it of Mr Wesley, and had always a very great respect for him." I turned, and said to Mr Oglethorpe, "Did not I tell you it would be so?" He replied to Lawley, "Yes, you had always a very great respect for Mr Wesley. You told me he was a stirrer-up of sedition, and at the bottom of all this disturbance." With this gentle reproof he dismissed him, and I thanked him for having first spoken to me of what I was accused of, begging he would always do so. This he promised, and then I walked with him to Mrs Hawkins's door. She came out aghast to see me with him. He there left me, and I was delivered out of the mouth of the lion.[19]

I went to my hut, where I found Mr Ingham. He told me this was but the beginning of sorrows. Not as I will but as thou wilt [Matt. 26:39]. About noon, in the midst of a violent storm of thunder and lightning, I read the 18th Psalm and found it gloriously suited to my circumstances. I never felt the Scriptures as now. Now I need them, I find them all written for my instruction and comfort. At the

18. Wesley adds the quotation marks around "peace."
19. Cf. 2 Tim. 4:17.

same time I feel great joy in the expectation of our Saviour thus coming to judgment, when the secrets of all hearts shall be revealed, and God shall make my innocency as clear as the light, and my just dealing as the noonday.

At three walked with Mr Ingham, and read him the history of this amazing day. We rejoiced together in the protection of God, and through comfort of the Scriptures.

The evening lesson was full of encouragement.

> This know also, that in the last days perilous times shall come. For men shall be . . . *false accusers*, incontinent, fierce, despisers of those that are good, traitors, heady, highminded, . . . *but they shall proceed no further*, for their folly shall be made manifest [un]to all men. But thou hast fully known my doctrine, manner of life, . . . what persecutions I endured; but out of them all the Lord delivered me. Yea, and all that will live godly in Christ Jesus shall suffer persecution. But evil men and seducers shall wax worse and worse, deceiving and being deceived. . . . All Scripture is given by inspiration of God, and is profitable for doctrine, for reproof, for correction, for instruction in righteousness [2 Tim. 3:1-16].

Blessed be God that I begin to find them so!

Meeting with Mr Hird, I persuaded him to use all his interest with the people to lay aside all thoughts of leaving the colony. He told me he had assured Mr Oglethorpe that this was always my language towards him and the rest, and that I had had no hand in the late disturbance, but was answered short with "You must not tell me that. I know better."

After spending an hour at the camp in singing such psalms as suited the occasion, I went to bed in the hut, which was thoroughly wet with today's rain.

Friday, March 26. "My soul is always in my hand. Therefore will I not forget Thy law" [Ps. 119:109, BCP]. This morning, early, Mr Oglethorpe called me out to tell me of Mrs [Anne] Lawley's miscarriage, by being denied access to the doctor for bleeding. He seemed very angry, and to charge me with it, saying he should be the tyrant if he passed by such intolerable injuries. I answered I knew nothing of the matter, and 'twas hard it should be imputed to me; that from the first Hermsdorf told the doctor he might visit whom of his patients he pleased, but the doctor would not. I denied my having the least hand in the whole business, as Hermsdorf himself had declared. He said, "Hermsdorf himself assured me what he did, he did by your advice." I answered, "You must mistake his imperfect English, for many have heard him say the contradictory of this. Yet I must be charged with all the mischief." "How else can it be," said he, "that there should be no love, no meekness, no true religion among the people; but instead of that, mere formal prayers?" "As to that, I can answer for them that they have no more of the form of godliness than the power.[20] I have seldom above six at the public service." "But what would an unbeliever say to your raising these disorders?" "Why, if I had raised them, he might say there was nothing in religion. But what would that signify to those who had experienced it? They would not say so."

He told me the people were full of dread and confusion; that it was easier to govern 1,000 than sixty men, for in so small a number every one's passion was considerable; that he durst not leave them before they were settled; etc. I asked him, "Would you have me forbear conferring at all with my parishioners?" To this I could get no answer, and went on, "The reason why I did not interpose for or against the doctor was his having, at the beginning, charged me with his confinement. I talked less with my parishioners these 5 days past, than I had done in any one afternoon before. I shunned appearing in public, least my advice should be asked, or least, if I heard others talking my very silence should be deciphered into advice. But one argument of my innocence I can give, which will even convince you of it. I know my life is in your hands, and you know that was you to frown upon me, and give the least intimation that it would be agreeable to you, the generality of this wretched people would say or swear anything." (To this he agreed, and owned the case was so with them all.) "You see that my safety depends on your single opinion of me. Must I not therefore be mad, if I would in such a situation provoke you by disturbing the public peace? Innocence, I know, is not the best protection, but my sure trust is in God." Here company interrupted us, and I left him.

I was no longer careful of the event after reading those words in the morning lesson: "Thou shalt not follow me now. But thou shalt follow me afterwards" [John 13:36]. Amen. When thou pleasest. Thy time is best.

---

20. Cf. 2 Tim. 3:5.

Mr Oglethorpe, meeting me in the evening asked when I had prayers? I said I waited his pleasure. While the people came slowly, "You see, sir," said I, "they do not lay too great a stress on forms." "The reason of that is because others idolize them." "I believe few stay away for that reason." "I don't know that." Mr Oglethorpe stood over against me, and joined audibly in the prayers. The chapter was designed for me, and I read with great boldness, as follows:

> I charge thee before God and the Lord Jesus Christ, who shall judge the quick and dead at his appearing and his kingdom: preach the word, be instant in season, out of season; reprove, rebuke, exhort with all long-suffering and authority. For the time will come when they will not endure sound doctrine. . . . But watch thou in all things, endure affliction, do the work of an evangelist, make full proof of thy ministry. . . . At my first appearing no man stood with me, but all men forsook me. . . . Notwithstanding the Lord stood with me . . . that by me the preaching might be fully known, and that all the Gentiles might hear, and I was delivered from the mouth of the lion. And the Lord shall deliver me from every evil work, and will preserve me unto his heavenly kingdom, to whom be glory for ever and ever. Amen [2 Tim. 4:1-18].

Saturday, March 27. This morning we began our Lord's last discourses to his disciples. Every word was providentially directed to my comfort, but particularly those: "Let not your hearts be troubled. Ye believe in God. Believe also in me. . . . I will not leave you comfortless. I will come unto you. . . . Peace I leave with you, my peace I give unto you. Let not your heart be troubled, neither let it be afraid" [John 14:1-27]. I was sensibly concerned this afternoon at hearing that Mrs Welch is growing more and more like Mrs Hawkins; declares she will be no longer priest-ridden, jests upon prayers, and talks in the loose, scandalous dialect of her friend. In the evening a thought came into my mind of sending Mr Ingham for my brother. He was much averse to leaving me in my trials, but was at last persuaded to go.

Sunday, March 28. Went to the storehouse (our tabernacle at present) to hearken what the Lord God would say concerning me. Both myself and the congregation was struck with the first lesson: Joseph and Potiphar's wife [Gen. 39]. The second was still more animating: "If the world hate you, ye know it hated me before it hated you. If ye were of the world . . ." [John 15:18-20]. After prayers poor Mr Davison stayed behind to take his leave of Mr Ingham. He burst into tears, and said, "One good man is leaving us already. I foresee nothing but desolation. Must my poor children be brought up like these savages?" We endeavoured to comfort him by showing him his calling. At ten Mr Ingham preached an alarming sermon on the day of judgment, and joined with me in offering up the Christian sacrifice.

In my walked at noon I was full of heaviness. Complained to God that I had no friend but Him, and even in Him could now find no comfort. Immediately I received power to pray, then opening my Bible read as follows: "Hearken unto me, ye that seek the Lord. Look unto the rock whence ye are hewn. . . . Fear ye not the reproach of men, neither be ye afraid of their reviling[s]. Awake, awake . . . flee away. Who art thou, that thou shouldst be afraid of a man that shall die . . . and hast feared continually every day because of the fury of the oppressor?" [Isa. 51:1-13] After reading this no wonder I found myself renewed in confidence.

While Mr Ingham waited for the boat, I took a turn with Mr [William] Horton. He fully convinced me of Mrs Hawkins's true character—ungrateful in the highest degree, a common prostitute, a complete hypocrite. He told me her husband and she had begged him upon their knees to intercede with Mr Oglethorpe not to turn them out of the ship, which would be their utter ruin. This he accordingly did, though Mr Oglethorpe at first assured him he had rather given 100£ than take them. The first person she fell upon after this, was Mr Horton himself, whom she abused as she has since done me. From him I hastened to the waterside, where I found Mr Ingham just put off. O happy, happy friend! *Abiit, erupit, evasit!*[21] But woe is me, that I am still constrained to dwell with Meshech![22] I languished to bear him company, followed him with my eyes till out of sight, and then sunk into deeper dejection than I had known before.

Monday, March 29. Was revived by those words of our Lord: "These things have I spoken unto you that ye should not be offended.

---

21. "He has gone, [he has departed], he has escaped, he has broken out." This is an echo of Cicero, *Against Catiline*, 2.1. However, Charles omits *excessit* and reverses the order of *evasit* and *erupit*.
22. Cf. Ezek. 38–39.

They shall put you out of the synagogues. Yea the time cometh that whosoever killeth you will think that he doth God service. And these things will they do to you, because they have not known my Father, nor me. . . . In the world ye shall have tribulation, but be of good," etc. [John 16:1-3, 33].

Knowing I was to live with Mr Oglethorpe, I had brought nothing with me from England except my clothes and books. But this morning, asking a servant for something I wanted (I think a teakettle), I was told Mr Oglethorpe had given orders that no one should use any of his things. I answered that order, I supposed, did not extend to me. His "Yes, sir," says he, "you was excepted by name." Thanks be to God that it is not yet made capital to give me a morsel of bread.

Tuesday, March 30. Having laid hitherto on the ground in a corner of Mr [Will] Reed's hut, and hearing some boards were to be disposed of, I attempted in vain to get some of them to lay upon. They were given to all besides. The minister only of Frederica must be ἀφρήτωρ, ἀθέμιστος, ἀνέστιος.[23] Yet are we not hereunto called, ἀστατεῖν, κακοπαθεῖν?[24] Even the Son of man had not where to lay his head![25]

I find the Scripture an inexhaustible fund of comfort:

> Is my hand shortened at all, that it cannot save? or have I no power to deliver? . . . I gave my back to the smiters, and my cheeks to them that plucked off the hair. I hid not my face from shame and spitting. For the Lord God will help me, therefore shall I not be confounded. Therefore have I set my face like a flint, and I know that I shall not be ashamed. He is near that justifieth me, who will contend with me? Let us stand together. Who is mine adversary? Let him come near to me. Behold, the Lord God will help me, who is he that shall condemn me? [Isa. 50:2, 6-9]

Wednesday, March 31. I begin now to be abused and slighted into an opinion of my own considerableness. I could not be more trampled upon was I a fallen minister of state. The people have found out that I am in disgrace, and all the cry is:

---

23. Homer, *Iliad*, ix.63, "without clan, without law, without home."

24. The words mean "to be restless, to be wretched." The infinitives suggest that Wesley is not quoting a specific source. He may be recalling, however, the New Testament occurrences of these words: ἀστατοῦμεν (1 Cor. 4:11), κακοπαθῶ (2 Tim. 2:9), and κακοπαθεῖ (James 5:13).

25. Cf. Matt. 8:20; Luke 9:58.

*Curramus praecipites, et
Dum jacit in ripa calcemus Caesaris hostem.*[26]

My few well-wishers are afraid to speak to me. Some have turned out of the way to avoid me. Others desired I would not take it ill if they seemed not to know me when we should meet. The servant that used to wash my linen sent it back unwashed. It was great cause of triumph my being forbid the use of Mr Oglethorpe's things, and in effect debarred of most of the conveniences, if not necessaries, of life. I sometimes pitied and sometimes diverted myself with the odd expressions of their contempt, but found the benefit of having undergone a much lower degree of obloquy at Oxford.

APRIL 1736

Thursday, April 1. In the midst of morning service a poor scout-boatman was brought in, who was almost killed by the burst of a cannon. I found him senseless and dying. All I could do was to pray for him and try by his example to wake his two companions. He languished till the next day, and died.

Hitherto I have been born up by a spirit not my own, but exhausted nature at last prevails. 'Tis amazing she held out so long. My outward hardships and inward conflicts, the bitterness of reproach from the only man I wish to please,

At last have worn my boasted courage down.[27]

Accordingly, this afternoon, I was forced by a friendly fever to take my bed. My sickness, I knew, could not be of long continuance. But, as I was in want of every help and convenience, must either shortly leave me or release me from farther suffering.

In the evening Mrs [Grace] Hird and Mrs Robinson called to see me, and offered me all the assistance in their power. I thanked them, but desired they would not prejudice themselves by taking this notice of me. At that instant we were alarmed with a cry of the Spaniards being come, heard many guns fired and saw the people

---

26. Juvenal, *Satires*, x.85–86; "Let us run headlong (swiftly) and while he lies on the bank, let us trample the enemy of Caesar." (*Jacit* should be *jacet*.)

27. Nicholas Rowe, *Tamerlane*, 2nd ed. (London: Tonson, 1703), Act IV, Scene 1 (p. 51).

fly in great consternation to the fort. I felt not the least disturbance or surprise. Bade the women not fear, for God was with us. Within a few minutes news was brought us that the alarm was only a contrivance of Mr Oglethorpe, to try the people. My charitable visitants then left me, and soon returned with some gruel, which threw me into a sweat. The next morning, *April 2*, they ventured to call again. At night, when my fever was somewhat abated, I was led out to bury the scout-boatman, and envied him his quiet grave.

Saturday, April 3. Nature, I found, endeavoured to throw off the disease by excessive sweats, and therefore drank whatever my women brought me.

Sunday, April 4. Many of the people had been ill of the bloody flux. I escaped hitherto by my vegetable diet, but now my fever brought it. Notwithstanding this, I was obliged to go abroad, and preach and administer the Sacrament. My sermon on "Keep innocency, and take heed to the thing that is right, for that shall bring a man peace at the last" [Ps. 37:37], was deciphered into a satire against Mrs Hawkins. At night I got an old bedstead to lay on, being that on which the scout-boatman had died.

Monday, April 5. At one this morning the sandflies forced me to rise, and smoke them out of the hut. The whole town was employed in the same manner. My congregation in the evening consisted of Presbyterians and a Papist. I went home in great pain, my distemper being much increased with the little duty I could discharge.

Tuesday, April 6. I found myself so faint and weak that it was with the utmost difficulty I got through the prayers. Mr Davison, my good Samaritan, would often call or send his wife to tend me, and to their care, under God, I owe my life.

Today Mr Oglethorpe gave away my bedstead from under me, and refused to spare one of the carpenters to mend me up another.

Friday, April 9. While talking to Mrs Hird, I turned my eyes towards the huts, and saw Mr Lascelles's[28] all in a blaze. I walked towards the fire, which before I could come up to it had consumed the hut and everything in it. It was a corner hut, and the wind providentially blew from the others or they would have been all destroyed.

---

28. Henry Lascelles, Jr., Charles spells "Lassel."

Saturday, April 10. Mr Reed waked me with news of Mr [Charles] Delamotte and my brother being on their way to Frederica. I found the encouragement I sought in the Scriptures for the day, Psalm 52: "Why boastest thou thyself, thou tyrant, that thou canst do mischief; whereas the goodness of God endureth yet daily. Thy tongue imagineth wickedness, and with lies thou cuttest like a sharp razor. Thou hast loved . . ." [Ps. 52:1-4, BCP].

At six Mr Delamotte and my brother landed, when my strength was so exhausted I could not have read prayers once more. He helped me into the woods, for there was no talking among a people of spies and ruffians; nor even in the woods, unless in an unknown tongue. He told me the Scripture he met with at landing was, "If God be for us, who can be against us?" [Rom. 8:31] and that Mr Oglethorpe received him with abundant kindness. I begun my account of all that has passed, and continued it till prayers. It were endless to mention all that the Scriptures which have been for so many days adapted to my circumstances, but I cannot pass by the evening's lesson, Heb. 11. I was ashamed of having well nigh sunk under mine, when I beheld the conflicts of those triumphant sufferers, "of whom the world was not worthy" [Heb. 11:38].

Sunday, April 11. What words could more support our confidence than the following, out of the psalms for the day?

Be merciful unto me, O God, for man goeth about to devour me. He is daily fighting, and troubling me. Mine enemies are daily in hand to swallow me up, for they be many that fight against me, O thou most highest. Nevertheless, though I am sometimes afraid, yet put I my trust in Thee. I will put my trust in God, and will not fear what man can do unto me. They daily mistake my words. All that they imagine is to do me evil . . . land of the living [Ps. 56:1-5, BCP].

The next psalm was equally animating:

Be merciful unto me, O God, for my soul trusteth in thee, and under the shadow of thy wings shall be my refuge, until this tyranny be overpast I will call upon the most high God; even the God that shall perform the cause which I have in hand. He shall send down from heaven, and save me from the reproof of him that would eat me up. God shall send forth his mercy and truth. My soul is among lions. And I lie even among the children of men, that are set on fire, whose teeth are spears and arrows, and their tongue a sharp sword. Set up thyself, O God, above the heavens and thy glory above all the earth [Ps. 57:1-7, BCP].

I had just recovered strength enough to consecrate at the Sacrament, the rest my brother discharged. We then got out of the reach of informers, and proceeded in my account, being fully persuaded of the truth of Mrs Welch's information against Mr Oglethorpe, Mrs Hawkins, and herself.

Next morning [*April 12*] Mr Oglethorpe met and carried us to breakfast at the modest Mrs Hawkins's. At noon my brother repeated to me his last conference with Mrs Welch, in confirmation of all she had ever told me.

At night I took leave of Mr Horton, Mr Hermsdorf, and Major Richards, who were going with 30 men to build a fort over against the Spanish lookout, 12 leagues from [St] Augustine.

Wednesday, April 14. By a relation which my brother gave me of a late conference he had with her, I was again, in spite of all I had seen and heard, half persuaded into a good opinion of Mrs Hawkins—for the lasting honour of our sagacity, be it written!

Friday, April 16. My brother brought me off a resolution, which honour and indignation had formed, of starving rather than ask for necessaries. Accordingly I went to Mr Oglethorpe, in his tent, to ask for some little things I wanted. He sent for me back again, and said,

[*Oglethorpe:*] "Pray, sir, sit down. I have something to say to you. I hear you have spread several reports about me and Mrs Hawkins, in that you are the author of them. There is a great difference in telling such things to another and to me. In you, who told it your brother, it is scandal; in him who repeated it to me, it is friendship. My righteousness does not, like the Pharisee's, consist in long prayers,[29] but in forgiving injuries, as I do this of yours. Not but the thing is in itself a trifle and hardly deserves a serious answer, though I gave one to your brother because he believed the report true. It is not such a thing as this will hurt my character. They would pass for gallantries and rather recommend me to the world."

---

29. Cf. Matt. 6:5ff.

Here he made slight of the matter, at the same time vindicating himself from the imputations by the like ungrounded reports in the ship, by the example of others, by the impossibility of having opportunities, etc., and went on:

[*Oglethorpe:*] "I know many suppose a thirst of fame the motive of all my actions, but they are quite mistaken. I have had more than my share of it, and my fortune is now, I believe, upon the turn."

"Many judge of others' barren hearts. At my landing, one told me you had confined Welch that you might have an opportunity with his wife, but I silenced [him], and told him that was just as he would have done himself. I believe you guilty of the meeting and disturbance, because of your consequent shyness. I forbade you the use of my things without first speaking to me, lest others should use your name to justify the abuse of my goods. You cannot deny the charge of scandalising me, for you wrote your brother an account of it. I thought you would have been an help and relief to me. I shall still continue my beneficence to Mrs Hawkins, for it is needless trying to ward off scandal. I refused on this account to take a poor woman into my ship and she was almost lost by going on Thomas's."[30]

After lifting up my heart to God I replied:

[*Wesley:*] "I acknowledge first, that as you suppose me guilty, it is the greatest kindness that you can forgive me. I shall only speak the truth and leave you to judge of it. I absolutely deny the whole charge. I have neither raised nor spread this report, but wherever I heard, checked it immediately. Some who themselves spoke it in my hearing have, I suppose, gone, and fettered their own words upon me. I had myself reported these stories to you, had I still continued in your favour. I did mention it to my brother, that he might tell it [to] you. Suppose I myself believed it, I should never have propagated [it], because I am not to speak evil of the ruler of my people.[31] The ground of the people's supposition was Mrs Hawkins's great assurance during her confinement. What they say of you they say of my brother and her. She said so herself, at first, but has since eaten her words. The letter she intercepted was wrote before this report was heard of. I own, to suffer thus as an evildoer, and from you, is the severest trial I have ever known. My shyness

---

30. I.e., Captain Thomas's ship.
31. Cf. Acts 23:5; Exod. 22:28.

was caused by yours. As I shall always think it my duty to please you to the utmost of my power, I hope you will look upon me as you used to do. I know your unforgiving temper, and that if you once entertain a suspicion of dislike, it is next to impossible to remove it."

He promised to be the same to me as before.

At night Mrs Welch sent for my brother. He being engaged with Mr Oglethorpe, I went, and found her half dead with fear. She began accusing me of betraying her.

[*Wesley:*] "Be not imposed upon; your betraying me shall never make me betray you."

[*Mrs Welch:*] "But he will get it out of your brother."

[*Wesley:*] "No, my brother is a Christian; I am so much of one to prefer any sufferings to breach of promise."

[*Mrs Welch:*] "He [Mr Oglethorpe] came to me just now, and in a transport of anger said, 'So, Madam, you have been so wise as to tell Charles Wesley of your affair. It is nothing to me, but you have exposed yourself for ever.' I answered, 'If Charles Wesley told you so, he is the greatest villain upon earth; and denied it to the last. I did tell him, indeed, that it was you [who] informed me of his affair with Mrs Hawkins.' He denied his having any regard for her, and said he preferred an hour of my company to a week of hers. I am almost distracted at the thought of his knowing I told you."

[*Wesley:*] "Be not troubled. You are entirely safe on this head."

[*Mrs Welch:*] "If you have really said anything, he is the greatest villain upon earth. I hear him now. He is falling upon your brother. He will get it out of him."

[*Wesley:*] "It is impossible. My brother put his life in his hand by speaking to him about Mrs Hawkins."

[*Mrs Welch:*] "Pray, send your brother to my master."

[*Wesley:*] "I will."[32]

At ten[, I] related this conversation to my brother. He then gave me a surprising account of Mr Oglethorpe. Oh that it were true! Who knows but he may still be innocent? God. God make and keep us all so! The Spaniards, he informed my brother, were expected every moment, and was himself in a calm expectation of death.

Saturday, April 17. I called on Mrs Welch, and asked what Mr Oglethorpe had said last night.

---

32. The last six short paragraphs are found in Hoole (p. 12), but not included in Telford.

[*Mrs Welch:*] "He again charged me with having told you, and thereby your brother; said I was in love with him, which I owned, but not as he thought. I told him he was all made up of art. He was exceeding sad when he left me."

[*Wesley:*] "Mrs Welch, you have deeply injured me. I never built upon Mr Oglethorpe's friendship, for I have no worldly expectations. But you have turned my best friend into an enemy for life. When in the openness of my heart I warned you against that evil woman, how could you go immediately and betray me to her? Why would you even invent falsehoods to hurt me, and say to her and Mr Oglethorpe that I raised the report about them? Did I deserve this at your hands? Was this gratitude?"

[*Mrs Welch:*] "No; very far from it. I know not what I meant; I was mad, I was out of my senses. But I beg you would not say anything to Mr Oglethorpe."

[*Wesley:*] "No; you are safe. I cannot return evil for evil.[33] But must in justice tell Mr Oglethorpe 'twas not I informed you, but you informed me of the scandalous reports. But what was your end in saying what you did of Mrs Hawkins?"

[*Mrs Welch:*] "Oh, do not ask me. I was mad, I was bewitched. I said I don't know what."

[*Wesley:*] "But was that false which you told us of yourself?"

[*Mrs Welch:*] "It was. I never saw Mr Oglethorpe till I came into the ship."

[*Wesley:*] "What end had you in fooling yourself?"

[*Mrs Welch:*] "Do not ask me; I cannot tell."

[*Wesley:*] "Then I will for you. Answer me sincerely. Are you not in love with Mr Oglethorpe? and did you not invent all these falsehoods to gain credit with my brother and thereby employ him to throw out Mrs Hawkins, and so make room for you?"

[*Mrs Welch:*] "You say the very thing; it is so."

An hour after, I was with her again, and informed her I intended to set Mr Oglethorpe right, as she in justice to me ought to do. She replied:

[*Mrs Welch:*] "I have been almost distracted at the thoughts of my treatment of you; that I should incense Mr Oglethorpe to such a devilish outrage; that I should be the devil's instrument in crushing you, in destroying the innocent. The devil surely was in me.

---

33. Cf. 1 Pet. 3:9.

I raised Mr Oglethorpe's suspicions of you. I complained of your being so troublesome to me. I accused you against my conscience of a base design, and have estranged him from you entirely."

[*Wesley:*] "How had I provoked you to it? Did you ever receive aught but good from me?"

[*Mrs Welch:*] "No; but Mrs Hawkins was continually inciting me to it, saying, 'We must supplant these parsons, and then we shall have Mr Oglethorpe to ourselves. Do you accuse Charles Wesley to him, and I will accuse the other.' I hear she said that of your brother which I said of you. I am not sure, but find she has laid all upon me, and would have me ruin you, that she may ruin me."

[*Wesley:*] "Then what you said of her history to my brother is true again?"

[*Mrs Welch:*] "Every word of it. Her design of drawing him in and then exposing him, with all the account I gave your brother, is true."

[*Wesley:*] Upon her again falling into self-condemnation, I said, "God forgive you as freely as I do. You owe me a public vindication, but my innocence shall surely meet with the fullest vindication from God."

[*Mrs Welch:*] "I will unsay all, the first opportunity I have with Mr Oglethorpe. I know how enraged he is against you. At his landing he accosted me with, 'I hear Charles Wesley has secured your husband and I suppose came to bed to you.' I denied it with horror. But what shocked me above all, was his saying, 'Could not you get him into the shadows, then run away screaming out that he had offered you violence? I know he will say it is a false accusation, but leave me to manage him then.' I so dreaded the consequence, that I have had no rest ever since."

[*Wesley:*] "But does not your concern arise not from any regard to my anger or danger, but from the fear of losing him?"

[*Mrs Welch:*] "No. For though I love him to distraction, it is as a brother. Even last night, I absolutely refused him when he offered to come to bed to me."

[*Wesley:*] "Do you believe a life after this? Do you believe a future judgment? And that the secrets of all hearts shall then be revealed? As you believe this, tell me, if all you now speak be true."

[*Mrs Welch:*] She answered with another solemn oath, 'It is.'"[34]

---

34. The section beginning with Mrs Welch's comment "I will unsay all" and concluding with her words "It is" is found in Hoole (p. 14), but not in Telford.

I related to my brother this conversation, and we were both utterly confounded.

Soon after, I got some time for meditating on death, and felt an hope of being accepted through Christ. When I had finished this relation, he seemed entirely changed.[35]

The next day [*April 18*] my brother and Mr Delamotte set out in an open boat for Savannah. I preached in the afternoon on "He that now goeth on his way weeping, and beareth forth good seed, shall doubtless come again with joy, and bring his sheaves with him" [Ps. 126:7, BCP].[36]

Easter Eve, April 24. At ten I was sent for by Mr Oglethorpe. He began,

[*Oglethorpe:*] "Mr Wesley, you know what has passed between us. I took some pains to satisfy your brother about the reports concerning me, but in vain. He here renews his suspicions in writing. I did desire to convince him, because I had an esteem for him, and he is just so considerable to me as my esteem makes him. I could clear up all, but it matters not. You will soon see the reason for my actions."

"I am now going to death. You will see me no more. Take this ring, and carry it from me to Mr [James] Vernon. If there is a friend to be depended upon, he is one. His interest is next to Sir Robert's.[37] Whatever you ask, within his power, he will do for you, your brother, and your family. I have expected death for some days. These letters show that the Spaniards have long been seducing our allies, and intend to cut us off at a blow. I fall by my friends— Gascoin, whom I have made; the Carolina people, whom I depended upon to send their promised succours. But death is to me nothing. T.[38] will pursue all my designs, and to him I recommend them and you."

He then gave me a diamond ring. I took it, and said:

[*Wesley:*] "If, as I believe,

postremum fato, quod te alloquor, hoc est.[39]

---

35. This sentence appears in both the shorthand and longhand in the MS Journal.
36. The text of this sermon has survived; see *Sermons*, 123–29.
37. Probably Sir Robert Walpole (1676–1745), first earl of Oxford.
38. Probably Thomas Tower; cf. entry for July 25, 1736.
39. "These are my last words to you." Cf. Virgil, *Aeneid*, vi.466: "*extremon fato quo te alloquor, hoc est.*"

Hear what you will quickly know to be true, as soon as you are entered upon the separate state. This ring I shall never make any use of for myself. I have no worldly hopes. I have renounced the world. Life is bitterness to me. I came hither to lay it down."

"You have been deceived, as well as I. I protest my innocence as to the crimes I am charged with, and take myself to be now at liberty to tell you what I thought never to have uttered. Mrs Welch had excited in me the first suspicion of you after we were come here. She afterwards told you her own words as if they had been mine. This she confessed both to my brother and me, as likewise that she had falsely accused me to you of making love to her. She was put upon it by Mrs Hawkins saying, 'Let us supplant those parsons and we shall have Mr Oglethorpe to ourselves.'"

When I had finished this relation, he seemed entirely changed, full of his old love and confidence in me.[40] After some expressions of kindness, I asked him, "Are you satisfied?" He replied, "Yes, entirely." "Why then, sir, I desire nothing more upon earth, and care not how soon I follow you." He added, he much desired the conversion of the heathen, and believed my brother intended for it. "But I believe," said I, "it will never be under your patronage, for then men would account for it without taking in God." He replied, "I believe so too," then embraced and kissed me with the most cordial affection. I attended him to the scoutboat, where he waited some minutes for his sword. They brought him first, and a second time, a mourning sword. At last they gave him his own, which had been his father's. "With this sword," says he, "I was never yet unsuccessful." "I hope, sir," (said I) "you carry with you a better, even the sword of the Lord, and of Gideon."[41] "I hope so too," he added.

When the boat put off, I ran before into the woods, to see my last of him. Seeing me and two others running after him, he stopped the boat and asked whether we wanted anything. Captain [John Mohr] Mackintosh, left commander, desired his last orders. I then said, "God is with you. Go forth, *Christo duce, et auspice Christo!*"[42] "You have," says he, "I think, some verses of mine. You there see my

---

40. The first sentence of this paragraph in longhand also appears in the shorthand.
41. Cf. Judg. 7:18, 20.
42. "Christ being your leader, and Christ your aid." Hoole (p. 16) includes the following footnote: "Oglethorpe's motto, given him by Charles Wesley, was, 'Nothing is to be despaired of with Christ for leader'—*Christo duce nil desperandum.*"

thoughts of success." His last word to the people was, "God bless you all." The boat then carried him out of sight. I interceded for him, that God would save him from death, would wash out all his sins,[43] and prepare before he took the sacrifice to himself.

Easter Day, April 25. The people were alarmed at night by the sight of two great fires on either side of the town, not knowing if they were made by friends or enemies. Next morning news was brought of a boat coming up. Every one seemed under a consternation, though no one but myself was fully apprized of our danger. At night the watch was doubled by Captain Mackintosh. The people being unwilling to comply with his orders, I was forced to tell Mr Hird the constable that there might be danger which Mackintosh alone knew of, and therefore they ought to obey. He promised it for himself and the rest. Though I expected every hour that the Spaniards would *bring* us the news of Mr Oglethorpe's death, yet I was insensible of fear, and careless of the consequence. But my indifference arose from stupidity rather than faith. There was nothing I cared for in life, and therefore the loss of it appeared a trifle.

Thursday, April 29. About half-hour past eight I went down to the bluff to see a boat coming up. At nine it arrived with Mr Oglethorpe. I blessed God for still holding his soul in life. In the evening we took a walk together and he informed me more particularly of our past danger. Three great ships, and four smaller, had been seen for three weeks together at the mouth of the river. But the wind continuing full against them, [they] were kept from making a descent, till they could stay no longer. I gave him back his ring and said, "I need not, sir, and indeed I cannot, tell you how joyfully and thankfully I return this." "When I gave it to you," said he, "I never expected to receive it again, but thought it would be of service to your brother and you. I had many omens of my death, particularly their bringing me my mourning sword. But God has been pleased to preserve a life which was never valuable to me; and yet in the continuance of it, I thank God, I can rejoice." "I am now glad of all that has happened here, since without it I could never have had such a proof of your affection as that you gave me, when you looked upon me as the most ungrateful of villains." While I was

---

43. Cf. Acts 22:16.

speaking this he appeared full of tenderness, and passed on to observe the strangeness of his deliverance, when betrayed on all sides, without human support and utterly defenceless. He condemned himself for his anger (God forgive those who made me the object of it), which he imputed to his want of time for consideration. "I longed, sir, to see you once more, that I might tell you some things before we finally parted. But then I considered, that if you died, you would know them all in a moment." "I know not whether separate spirits regard our little concerns. If they do, it is as men regard the follies of their childhood, or as I my late passionateness."

Friday, April 30. I had some farther talk with him in bed. He ordered me whatever he could think I wanted, promised to have me an house built immediately, and was just the same to me he had formerly been.

MAY 1736

Sunday, May 2. I went to him to ask if there was any truth in the report that Major Richards and Mr Horton were detained at [St] Augustine, and the men at St George's [Point] run away. He told me he hoped that the gentlemen were well received, but the people had been frightened away by two soldiers bringing a civil proffer of refreshment; that thereupon the men mutinied and obliged Captain Hermsdorf to quit the advanced post and turn homeward, which he had done pursuant to [William] Ferguson's advice; that he intended immediately to go in quest of them. In an hour's time he set out accordingly.

In the evening I endeavoured to convince Mr [Francis] Moore (as I had done some few besides) of Mr Oglethorpe's innocency. He then read me a list of the officers that were to be, and who should be appointed head-bailiff but my dear friend the doctor!

Monday, May 3. The people had observed that I was taken into favour again, which I found by their provoking civilities.

Wednesday, May 5. At night news was brought of a boat being seen off the point which would not come to, though the soldiers had fired at her several times. The people were greatly alarmed, being in no preparation for an enemy. I went to bed, but was soon awakened by the firing of a gun and, rising, found all the town flocking towards the fort in the utmost consternation. I walked leizurely after them without fear, yet without faith. Found the uproar was occasioned by a friendly Indian, and walked back again.

Saturday, May 8. I had some affecting talk with a poor man belonging to the scoutboat who had broke his arm. He owned himself greatly moved by the *Christian Monitor*[44] I had given him; convinced thereby of the truth of religion, unable to read for tears, and fully resolved to obey the motions of the Holy Spirit by leading a new life.

Between ten and eleven I was waked again by an alarm. I rose, as did all the women, and found a signal had been made from the man-of-war. I sent away the women, and being myself of equal service, soon followed their example and went to sleep again.

Sunday, May 9. Notice was given me that Mr [Edward] Dyson, chaplain to the Independent Company,[45] was landed and walking toward me. His moral character did not recommend him. I had just time to run away into the woods, and so escaped his visit. The next morning Mr Oglethorpe returned, from whom I had the following account of his expedition:

> On *Saturday, May 1.* Late at night, arrived the *Caroline* scout-boat with Captain [William] Ferguson, bringing advice that Major Richards and Mr Horton (who had carried answers to the Spanish governor's letters) had landed at their lookout, and he believed were made prisoners by the Spaniards, for they had heard no more of them except by a blind letter written with a pencil. That the boats, in which were the men under Captain Hermsdorf, were come about thirty miles on this side of St George's Point and there waited for orders. That the men were mutinous, and Hermsdorf believed he should be forced to retire to Fort St Andrew. That he was apprehensive they would either murder their officers and turn pirates, or be cut off by the Spaniards. Mr Oglethorpe, on Sunday, went on board the man-of-war, and proceeded from thence with the man-of-war's boat, commanded by the Lieutenant, and the Georgia scoutboat. They arrived that night at Fort St Andrew. On

---

44. John Rawlet, *The Christian Monitor; Containing an Earnest Exhortation to a Holy Life; with some Directions in Order Thereto* (London: Samuel Tidmarsh, 1686).

45. The Independent Company was a group of Scottish Highlander foot soldiers, recruited by Oglethorpe to help protect the Georgia Colony.

Monday they came up with the south point of Cumberland, where they met with the boats under the command of Captain Hermsdorf. Mr Oglethorpe immediately took them out to sea with him, round Amelia Island. He found upon examination that the men did not intend to mutiny, but that the suspicion was occasioned by the lies of one man, who was hereupon sentenced by Mr Oglethorpe to run the gauntlet.

He went to Point St George, within sight of the Spanish lookout, and resettled them on the same place where Mr Hermsdorf had before taken up his quarters. It had been agreed that the Spaniards should make a signal and from thence he would repair with his boats, to fetch Major Richards back, who was gone to [St] Augustine at the request of the governour, who promised to send horses to conduct him but did not. It likewise was agreed that the boats should patrol up and down the rivers to prevent the Indians, our allies, passing over to molest the Spaniards, as they should prevent their Indians passing over to molest us.

Mr Oglethorpe went that afternoon to the Spanish lookout, with a flag of truce. But not being able to perceive anyone, leaving the boat at her grapling, he leaped ashore himself to see if he could discover anybody there, and going along the beach, at distance from the sandy hillocks to prevent surprize, he surrounded the hillocks where he found two horses hobbled. He went forward to a palmetto hut but could find no man. After this he sent the flag of truce into a great savannah to see if that would draw down any people to a conference. Upon this, William Frazier, a Scotch lad, going into the neighbouring woods and finding a Spaniard, brought him to Mr Oglethorpe, to whom he delivered two letters, one from Major Richards, the other from Mr Horton directed to Mr Hermsdorf, acquainting him that he should be back with him in two days' time. Mr Oglethorpe gave the man a bottle of wine, victuals, and tobacco, and a *moidore*[46] for his trouble of bringing the letters, and inquired where Major Richards and Mr Horton were. The man said he knew nothing concerning them; that he was an horseman, and sent by the colonel of the cavalry from the headquarters, which were about twelve leagues off, with those letters, to wait there till he should see an English boat appear, and deliver it to them; that he had laid 4 days on the beach, and had not discovered a boat in that time. Mr Oglethorpe delivered to him letters for the

46. A *moidore* was a Portugese gold coin.

governour of [St] Augustine, and between ten and eleven on Thursday morning set out with the man-of-war's boat and Georgia scoutboat to meet the man again, according to appointment.

He discovered a guardecoast full of men that lay behind a sandbank, beyond the breakers, on the English side of the water, and soon after he discovered several men hid in the woods, next to some sandhills. Two horsemen showed themselves and beckoned to the boats, which had a flag of truce flying, to come down to a point beyond which the guardecoast lay concealed; on which Mr Oglethorpe rowed with the two boats toward the guardecoast, that he might not leave her behind to intercept us and our people at St George's Point. There seemed to be about seventy men on board her, and there were in our boats twenty-four. She lay still for some time, but when they found plainly that they were discovered, they rowed away with incredible swiftness, directly out to sea, toward [St] Augustine.

Mr Oglethorpe returned to the horsemen, who seemed very unwilling to approach the boats, but at last agreed to receive a letter if Mr Oglethorpe would send an unarmed man ashore. One of them, seemingly an officer, forbade the boats to land on the King of Spain's ground. Mr Oglethorpe answered that as it was the King of Spain's ground, the English would forbear landing on it, since the Spaniards requested it; but that the Spaniards should be very welcome to land on the King of England's ground, which was on the opposite side of the river, and should be welcome to a glass of wine with him there. He asked him for news of Mr Horton and Mr Richards, and whether he could not send anything to them. The man said he knew nothing of them; that he received his orders from the Colonel of horse, who was quartered at twelve leagues' distance; and that he could carry no news but to him. Upon this, Mr Moore, Lieutenant of the *Hawk* man-of-war, wrote a letter to the Colonel of horse acquainting him that he was come thither with boats to conduct back the gentlemen who were sent by Mr Oglethorpe to treat with the governour of [St] Augustine; and that, if at any time he would make three fires on the Spanish main, he would take it as a signal that the gentlemen were come and would come over with a boat and fetch them. The Spanish officer promised to deliver the letter by night to the colonel of horse. Mr Oglethorpe stayed till Saturday night, expecting an answer, and sent over to the Spanish side every day, but could find nobody to have conference with. By the lookout within land they have a vineyard, flocks of turkeys, cattle, and horses. But great care was taken that none of our people should touch any of them. On Saturday night Mr Oglethorpe set out, leaving Captain Hermsdorf with an armed *periagua*,[47] the Georgia scoutboat, and another boat.

Tuesday, May 11. I had now so far recovered my strength, that I could again expound the lesson. In the lesson next morning was Elisha incompassed with the host at Dothan.[48] It is our privilege, as Christians, to apply those words to ourselves: "There be more that be for us than those that be against us" [2 Kings 6:16]. God spoke to us yet plainer in the second lesson:

> Behold, I send you forth as sheep in the midst of wolves. Be ye therefore wise as serpents, and harmless as doves. But beware of men, for they will deliver you up . . . and ye shall be brought before governours and kings for my name's sake . . . and ye shall be hated of all men. But he that endureth to the end shall be saved. But when they persecute you in this city, flee ye into another. . . . The disciple is not above his master. . . . Fear ye not therefore, for there is nothing covered, that shall not be revealed, and hid that shall not be known [Matt. 10:16-26].

In explaining this, I dwelt on that blessed topic of consolation to the innocent, that however he suffers under a false accusation here, he will shortly be cleared at God's righteous bar, where the accuser and the accused shall meet face to face, and the guilty person acquit him whom he unjustly charged, and take back the wickedness to himself. Poor Mrs Welch, who was just over against me, could not stand it, but first turned her back, and then retired behind the congregation.

While I waited for Mr Oglethorpe setting out again for the southward, Mr [Peter] Appee accosted me, a young gentleman lately come from Savannah. He mentioned his desire of being baptized (having only received lay-baptism before). I thought he ought to have a longer trial of his own sincerity. He passed on to his intended marriage with Miss [Rebecca] Bovey, which I dissuaded him from, not thinking either sufficiently prepared for it. He owned he had made little progress in subduing his will, and ought to be more dead to the world before he threw himself into it. Near midnight I took leave of Mr Oglethorpe, who set out in the scout

---

47. Spanish name for a canoe formed out of the trunk of a tree.
48. Cf. 2 Kings 6:17.

boat, after the other boats, for St George's. The remainder of the night I passed upon the ground in the guardroom.

At four the next day set out for Savannah, whither the Indian traders were coming down to meet me and take out licences. I was overjoyed at my deliverance out of this furnace,[49] and not a little ashamed of myself for being so.

Sunday, May 16. We landed at Skidaway, and dined at Mrs [Lucy] Mouse's. I then went round and asked the few people there were upon the island to come to prayers, which accordingly I read and preached to about ten in the guard-room, and promised so to contrive, if possible, that they should be supplied once a month.

At four we returned to our boat, and by six reached Thunderbolt, whence I walked the five remaining miles to Savannah. Mr Ingham, Mr Delamotte, and my brother were surprized at my unexpected visit. But, it being late, we each retired to his respective corner of the room, where, without the help of a bed, we slept soundly till the morning.

Wednesday, May 19. According to our agreement, my brother set forward for Frederica, and I took charge of Savannah in his absence. The hardest duty imposed on me was the expounding the lesson morning and evening to one hundred hearers. I was surprised at my own confidence, and acknowledged it not my own. The day was usually divided between visiting my parishioners, considering the lesson, and conversing with Mr Ingham, Delamotte, and Appee.

Tuesday, May 25. I visited a girl of fifteen who lay a-dying of an incurable illness. She had been in that condition for many months, as her parents, some of the best people of the town, informed me. I started at the sight of a breathing corpse. Never was real corpse half so ghastly. Her groans and screams alone distinguished her from one. They had no intermission, yet was she perfectly sensible, as appeared by her feebly lifting up her eyes when I bad her trust in God, and read the prayers for the *energumens*.[50] We were all in tears. She made signs for me to come again.

---

49. Cf. Dan. 3.

50. That is, prayers for one possessed by an evil spirit. Wesley almost certainly was using the text in Thomas Deacon, *A Complete Collection of Devotions, both Public and Private: Taken from the Apostolical Constitutions, the Ancient Liturgies, and the Common Prayer Book of the Church of England* (London: for the author, 1734), 46–47.

Friday, May 28. Mr Oglethorpe returned from the frontiers. The following account of his expedition I extracted out of his letter to the trustees:

> After that flagrant breach of the law of nations, putting our messengers, sent with a flag of truce, under arrest, I could expect nothing but farther hostilities, and therefore prepared to repel force by force. We fortified, with the utmost speed that the smallness of our number would allow, St George's Point, within sight of the Spanish outguards, and were much facilitated by finding the ruins of a fort built by Sir Francis Drake; so that we had nothing to do but to repair and palisade the breaches made by time, and to clear the ditches, which were originally 30 foot deep.
>
> The Independent Company and man-of-war being posted below Frederica, I drew out from thence, and from the Scotch settlements, what men I possibly could, to increase the garrison on St George's Point. While we were getting down recruits and cannon, the governor of [St] Augustine, having before put our messengers under arrest, sent out Don Ignacio [Cob],[51] colonel of foot, with 30 of his picked men, some Yamasaw Indians, and a strong boat's crew, about sixty men, in a launch to reconnoitre our settlements; and, if he found us so weak as the advices from Carolina said we were, to dislodge us. Don Ignacio came out by sea, and attempted to get undiscovered into Jekyl's Sound;[52] was discovered by Ensign Delegall, who commanded a guard upon the sea-point. He haled them to give an account who they were; which they refusing, he fired some cannon with powder; and about the same time they discovered the man-of-war lying within the sound. They ran out to sea with great precipitation, and strove to get in at another inlet by the island of Cumberland, where the Scotch from St Andrews challenged them. They neither answered nor hung out colours, but rowed away in such haste that the same night they reached the Spanish outguards on St John's River, near sixty miles distant.
>
> Don Ignacio landed in the night, and had a conference with Don Pedro de Lamberto, the commander of the Spanish horse, who was come up by land to the lookout with one hundred sixty foot and fifty horse [soldiers]. They concluded by the two forts they had met with, and the man-of-war's being there, that all our strength lay at Frederica, and that we were weak at Fort St George. Therefore resolved to try to surprise some of our boats, and upon

---

51. Charles spells "Ignatio."
52. Jekyl's Island is just south of St Simons Island, and Jekyl's Sound is on its southern end.

their intelligence to leave their horses, carry over their men by water, and attack us the night following. This was on Wednesday. I, having discovered some fires on the Spanish main, concluded troops come down, and therefore, in order to make them delay attacking us till our succours should arrive on Thursday morning, I had two carriage-guns and two swivel-guns which we had brought with us carried into the woods, that the Spaniards might not distinguish where they were fired, and ordered the swivel-guns to be discharged so often as to make a salute of seven, and with the carriage-guns fired five shot in answer. The swivel-guns, by reason of the smallness of the report, seemed like a ship at a distance saluting, and the carriage-guns like batteries answering from the shore.

I set out with two boats and a flag of truce to meet the Spaniards. They concluded from the guns, as I have heard since, that there was a new strength arrived; in which they were confirmed by our boats rowing briskly toward them, on which their launch thought proper to make the best of her way toward [St] Augustine. There the soldiers and boatmen, fatigued with overlabour, spread such dismal accounts magnifying our strength and diligence, in order to save their own reputation, that they created a general uproar among the people.

That night I had several fires made in the woods, some at two, some at three miles' distance from Point St George. On Friday morning the foot and horse, under the command of Don Pedro, finding themselves abandoned by the launch, and therefore in no possibility of passing over into the island against us; and from the many fires in the woods collecting that the Creek Indians were come up; having left a small guard of horse to observe our motions, retired in good order to [St] Augustine. Their arrival doubled the confusion, they apprehending that if the Indians should cut off their communication by land, as the man-of-war might do by sea, they should perish by famine. The governour was obliged to call a council of war, in which the oldest officers, and indeed almost all, gave their opinion that the gentlemen sent by me should be immediately released and sent back in the most honourable manner, with an officer attending them, to treat with me and desire me to restrain the Indians from invading them; at the same time to ask me why we settled upon lands and territories belonging to the King of Spain.

Not knowing anything of these proceedings, except that the Spaniards were retired, I lay at Fort St George from Thursday to Sunday, in which time fresh troops arrived. And falling all of us to work, with the officers and men of the King's sloop, who distinguished themselves upon this occasion, we mounted some guns upon the batteries along the river and got the fortifications in good forwardness; and having left the fort under the command of Captain Hermsdorf, retired with the utmost diligence to Frederica.

There I found the King of the Uchees, with thirty men, who offered to assist me with hundred more against the Spaniards. King Tomochichi[53] was also there, with thirty men, and an account that several hundreds of the Creeks eagerly desired to fall upon the Spaniards. In three days I set out with a large *periagua* and fifty men, cannon, and provision for two months, two ten-oared boats, and the Indians in their own boats, to relieve St George, which I imagined by that time might be besieged. God was pleased to prosper us, so that about fifteen miles from St George's, being fortunately an hour ahead of the rest of the boats, I met a Spanish boat with a flag of truce flying and Mr [Charles] Dempsey and the gentlemen sent to [St] Augustine in her, together with Don Pedro de Lamberto, captain of their troop horse, and Don Manuel [Gonzalez], secretary to the governour and adjutant of the garrison. It was lucky the Indians were not foremost, for if they had been they would certainly have engaged the Spanish boat; which, as it was, I could hardly prevent by sending a ten-oared boat to guard them to Frederica. Then I ordered them to be received on board the man-of-war, where they dined with me. I received them with the greatest form I could, having a guard of the King's troops on the right hand, with their bayonets fixed, and on the left hand the Highlanders, with their targets and broad swords drawn.

After dinner we drank the King of Britain's and the King of Spain's health, under the discharge of the cannon from the ship, which was answered with fifteen pieces of cannon from Delegall's fort at the sea-point. That again was followed by the cannon from Fort St Andrew, and that by those of Frederica and the Darien,[54] as I had before ordered. The Spaniards seemed extremely surprized that there should be so many forts, and all within hearing of one another. Don Pedro smiled and said, "No wonder Don Ignacio made more haste home than out." After the healths were done, a great number of Indians came on board, naked, painted, and their heads dressed in feathers. They demanded of me justice against the Spaniards for having killed some of their men in time of full peace.

---

53. This is the most widely used spelling for this chief of the Yamacraw Indians, a branch of the Creek people. Charles spells "Tomo-chachi."

54. The fortified camp for the Independent Company, on the north bank of the Altamaha River, about fifteen miles north of Frederica (now Darien, Georgia).

They farther proved that after the woman was taken, she was abused by numbers of men, and when she had satisfied their lust for two days, they inhumanly burned her alive.

Don Pedro, having asked several questions, acknowledged himself fully satisfied of the fact, excusing it by saying he was then in Mexico, and that the governour, being newly come from Spain, and not knowing the customs of the country, had sent out Indians under the command of the Pohoia King of the Floridas, who had exceeded his orders, which were not to make war with the Creeks. But the Indians not being content with that answer, he undertook that, at his return to [St] Augustine, he would have the Pohoia King put to death, if he could be taken; and if he could not, that the Spaniards would supply his people with neither powder, arms, nor anything else, but leave them to the Creeks. The Indians answered that he spake well; and, if the Spaniards did what he said, all should be white between them; but if not, they would take revenge, from which, at my desire, they would abstain till a final answer came.

The Indian matters being thus settled, we had a conference with the Spanish commissioners. They thanked me first for my restraining the Indians who were in my power, and hoped I would extend that care to the upper Indians. They then, after having produced their credentials, presented a paper, the contents whereof were to know by what title I settled upon St Simons, being lands belonging to the King of Spain. I took the paper promising an answer the next day. The substance was that the lands belonged to the King of England by undoubted right; that I had proceeded with the utmost caution, having taken with me Indians, the natives and possessors of those lands; that I had examined every place to see if there were any Spanish possessions, and went forward till I found an outguard of theirs, over against which I settled the English, without committing any hostilities or dislodging any. Therefore I did not extend the King's dominions, but only settled with regular garrisons that part of them which was before a shelter for Indians, Pircks,[55] and such sort of disorderly men.

The rest of the evening we spent in conversation, which chiefly turned upon the convenience it would be, both to the Spaniards and English, to have regular garrisons in sight of each other. Don Pedro smiled, and said he readily agreed to that, and should like very well to have their Spanish guard upon the south

---

55. *OED* defines "pirck" as a person who behaves "proudly, impudently, or conceitedly."

side of H——[56] River (which is within five miles of Charleston[57] and where the Spaniards had a garrison in King Charles the First's time). I replied, I thought it was better as it was, for there were a great many people living between who could never be persuaded to come into his sentiments. At last Don Pedro acquainted me that he thought the Spaniards would refer the settling of the limits to the courts of Europe, for which purpose he would write to their court, and in the meantime desired no hostilities might be committed, and that I would send up a commissary to sign with the governour an agreement to this purpose. I thereupon appointed Mr Dempsey to be my commissary, and to return with them.

Don Pedro is the ruling man in [St] Augustine, and has more interest with the Council of War than the governour. As he passed by St George's Point, he sent a whole ox as a present to their garrison. He gave me some sweetmeats and chocolate. I gave him a gold watch, a gun, and fresh provisions. To Don Manuel I gave a silver watch, and sent back a boat to escort them. If the Spaniards had committed any hostilities, I could, by the help of the Indians, have destroyed [St] Augustine with great facility. But God be praised that by his blessing, the diligence of Dempsey, and the prudence of Don Pedro, all bloodshed was avoided.

Saturday, May 29. At ten this evening I first met my traders at Mr [Thomas] Causton's, the head bailiff, as I did some or other of them every day for some weeks.

Monday, May 31. About noon Mr Oglethorpe sent us word that he was going to court. We went and heard his speech to the people, in the close of which he said, "If any one here has been abused or oppressed by any man, in or out of employment, he has free and full liberty of complaining. Let him deliver in his complaints in writing at my house. I will read them all over by myself, and do every particular man justice."

At eight in the evening I waited upon him and found the 3 magistrates, who seemed much alarmed by his speech and hoped he would not discourage government. He dismissed them and told me he feared his following my brother's advice, in hearing all complaints, would ruin the people and he should never have any to

56. There is a blank space in the MS Journal at this point, suggesting Charles was unsure of the name. It is identified as the Edisto River in Oglethorpe's letters.
57. Charles spells "Charlestown."

serve him. I replied I thought the contrary, and that such liberty
was the happiest thing that could happen to the colony, and much
to be desired by all *good* men. He fell, I know not how, into talk of
Frederica and said:

[*Oglethorpe:*] "Your brother read me his diary, which astonished
me to the last degree, and fully convinced me of your innocence.
For if Mrs Welch could so blacken me, she could you. Accordingly,
she came crying to me upon my arrival, with complaints that you
had confined her husband, and come to bed with her. I asked her
whether she would suffer it. She said, out of fear, and to save her
husband's life. From that time I shuddered at the sight of you.
'Twas such a complication of villainy! To make a fool of poor
Hermsdorf; to half kill the miserable husband by keeping him
three days under a tree; to take this opportunity of ruining his life,
and all under the mask of religion! I could not bear you, or suppress my strong antipathy. She told me you was continually solic-
iting her to walk with you into the woods, and had persecuted her
throughout the beach, and had now actually ruined her. I asked
whether she would witness this publicly against you; she
answered, 'No, by no means'; she would not be brought in evidence against you; (observing, I suppose, that I did not appear forward enough for it). 'But why then,' said I, 'did you tell it me? You
must now be silent and keep it to yourself.' 'Would,' said she,
'would you have me continually priest-ridden?'[58] I had intended, if
she would have stood to her charge, to have sent for you and tried
you before all the people, pulled off the mask and punished you
with the utmost severity, especially when I heard from your
brother of your having defamed me with Mrs Hawkins. I thought
you a very devil, so to divert all inquiries into your own guilt by
throwing the charge upon me! I had entirely excommunicated
[you] from my little church within, and determined to make an
example of you. Everything concurred to convince me of your
guilt. All you did and said—your very silence and shyness; your
telling me you should be cut off from doing good to one half of
your parishioners, if I did not vindicate you from Mrs Hawkins's
aspersions; your pretended tenderness for Mrs Welch in the ship;
your seeing her since, especially when your brother was here, run-

---

58. The section beginning at "Accordingly she came" and ending here is found in Hoole
(pp. 16–17), but not in Telford.

ning thither continually and staying till midnight, for I had you dogged for several days. All men would have condemned you upon your trial, the circumstances were so strong. And tried and sentenced you would infallibly have been, but that I considered the effect it would have upon religion. That that should be wounded through your sides I could not bear. Your history would be made a play or novel of. The character you had in your former life, your coming here a missionary, would altogether have made as good a story as Madame Cellier's.[59] These thoughts first staggered me; but above all, your uncle![60] His triumph over you and religion turned the scale; and I verily believe God sent me that night to be insulted by him, to save you."

[Wesley:] "But what did you think of my former life, and my end in coming here?"

[Oglethorpe:] "I thought you was then sincere; but never meeting with any woman before, and being perhaps sometimes encouraged and sometimes checked by an artful woman, was drawn in unawares into such depths of wickedness, and was now wholly given up and abandoned to the power of the devil."

[Wesley:] "But my guilt would never have been believed by my friends in England."

[Oglethorpe:] "The good who did believe it would think you fell as Santon Barsisa."[61]

[Wesley:] I said among other things: "The reason of my shyness was the opinion I had entertained of you from Mrs Welch's account, which I am now at liberty to mention, since you know it all, in great measure from my brother. I thought you as very a devil as you thought me. The character she had given me of you was, if possible, worse than mine. She knew three of your mistresses in England.[62] She was herself seduced by you, as well as Mrs Hawkins. You believed no more of Christianity than Mahomet; was a truly wicked man, and intended to take away my life. I expected no other for many days, never hoping to come alive from Frederica.

---

59. Elizabeth Cellier was a midwife, and convert to Roman Catholicism, who gained notoriety in late seventeenth-century England when she published an account seeking to vindicate herself from the accusation of plotting to charge several leading Protestants, including the King's son, with treason.

60. Matthew Wesley (1667–1737), the London doctor.

61. Oglethorpe is referring to a popular Islamic legend about a saintly ascetic named Barsisa who succumbed to temptation and seduced a woman.

62. This sentence is not included in Telford.

41

What freed me at once from all anxiety was a word of Scripture: 'Thou canst not follow me now, but thou shalt follow me hereafter'" [John 13:36].

[*Oglethorpe:*] He then assured me of his firm belief of the Christian revelation, "which alone," said he, "has tied my hands, and hampered me from putting an end to a miserable life."

[[*Wesley:*] "But when," said I, "did you first begin to suspect that I might be innocent?"

[*Oglethorpe:*] He answered, "Not till I went to the southward, as I thought upon certain death. For upon your saying in my tent: 'If you can believe this you must think me a most complete villain.' Alas! thought I, you well know what a villain I ought to think you!"

[*Wesley:*] "What was it at last that convinced you too of the contrary?"

[*Oglethorpe:*] "A dream made the first impression upon me, while I was asleep in a boat towards the southward. The manner is not all exact; but I never knew a dream deceive me. I thought you came to me and said something which quite convinced me of your innocence. This, when I waked, put me upon reconsidering everything. What sprung the first doubt was what I had observed from the beginning, that Mrs Welch was an exceedingly subtle woman. Next, her telling me the story of you, and stopping short when she observed me, as she thought, not sufficiently forward to destroy you."

[*Wesley:*] "But you told me just as you went to the southward, that you was satisfied."

[*Oglethorpe:*] "I did so, and I was satisfied then, at least of your being penitent."

[*Wesley:*] "Did what I said conduce to it?"

[*Oglethorpe:*] "No. 'Twas your looks, so sad, so pale and mortified! that I could not but say unto myself, This man must either be innocent, or deeply penitent; whichever it is, it is the same to me. I am going to cast myself in death upon the mercy of God, and shall I refuse forgiveness to my fellow creature? No, I will not only forgive him, but so forgive him as I would God should forgive me; leave him entirely acquitted and satisfied. All this I tell you that you may give God the glory for your deliverance, and beware of men. But I did not tell it your brother. Pride, I own, hindered me, lest my relating what Mrs Welch had said of you immediately upon his telling me what she had said of me might look like retaliation. A second reason was my regard for him; for he would doubt my having entirely renounced my ill opinion of you; and as to what is past, though he forgive, he will never forget it. You, I am satisfied, will be tender of the poor unhappy woman, as I was, leaving her full of comfort, though I am determined never to mention any word of all this to her, and desire you would not.

[*Wesley:*] "That I can readily promise, for my intercourse with her is over. I am no longer obliged to look upon her as one of my charge, and shall never speak to her of this matter. Indeed, my caution in conversing with her did not spring from any fear of these consequences, but from an advice of S.[63] Spangenberg's, 'never to talk with a woman without a witness, or in the face of the sun.' I followed his directions; but did not see the providential reason of it until now."

JUNE 1736

Sunday, June 6. I passed good part of this as of every day in conversing with Mr Appee, who generally breakfasted and supped at our house. The subject of our discourse was my intention of resigning my place, which I resolved to do after my last conference with Mr Oglethorpe. The giving up my salary and certain hopes of preferment weighed nothing against my resolution. I made Mr Appee a proffer of them, which he did not accept, being obliged to return, to look after his fortune in Holland.

Tuesday, June 8. I was present at court, and heard the accusations against Mr Causton, who stood by while [Henry] Parker, the first tribune of the people, on whom the malcontents had built all their hopes, brought the heaviest charges, I suppose, that could be brought against him. But they were so incredible, trifling, and childish, that I thought them a full vindication of the magistrates, and admired Mr Oglethorpe's patience in hearing them.

Wednesday, June 16. This and many foregoing days have been mostly spent in drawing up bonds, affidavits, licences, and instructions

---

63. The shorthand certainly has "S. Spangenberg's," but his full name was August Gottlieb Spangenberg.

for the traders; the evenings in writing letters for Mr Oglethorpe. We seldom parted till midnight. Tonight, at half-hour past twelve, he set out in the scoutboat for Frederica. I went to bed at one and rose again at four, but found no effect this variety of fatigue had upon my body till some time after.

Sunday, June 20. Walking in the trustees' garden, I met the Miss Boveys, whom I had never been in company with. I found some inclination to join them, but it was a very short-lived curiosity.

Saturday, June 26. Mr Oglethorpe and my brother returned from Frederica.

JULY 1736

Thursday, July 1. I was at court while the Creek Indians had an audience of Mr Oglethorpe, which I took down (as several afterwards) in shorthand.

Wednesday, July 7. Between four and five this morning Mr Delamotte and I went into the Savannah. We chose this hour for bathing both for the coolness and because the alligators were not stirring so soon. We heard them indeed snoring all around us, and one very early riser swam by with a few yards of us. On Friday morning we had hardly left our usual place of swimming when we saw an alligator in possession of it. Once afterwards Mr Delamotte was in great danger, for an alligator rose just behind him and pursued him to the land, whither he narrowly escaped.

Saturday, July 10. I was waked by the news my brother brought us of Miss Bovey's sudden death.[64] It called up all my sorrow and envy. "Ah, poor Ophelia!" was continually in my mind, "I thought thou shouldest have been my Hamlet's wife."[65] Mr Appee was just set out for *Charleston*[66] [on his way to] Holland, intending to return when he had settled his affairs and marry her.

But death had quicker wings than love.[67]

---

64. Cf. John Wesley's *Journal* (3–8 July 1736), *Works* 18:164–65.
65. Shakespeare, *Hamlet*, Act V, Scene 1. Should be "I hoped" instead of "I thought."
66. Charles has underlined the name for some reason.
67. This is the last line of "Epigram, from the Greek," by Samuel Wesley, Jr., Charles's eldest brother. See his *Poems on Several Occasions* (London: E. Say, 1736), 81.

The following evening I saw her in her coffin, and soon after in her grave.

Wednesday, July 21. I heard by my brother that I was to set sail in a few days for England.

Thursday, July 22. Today I got their licenses signed by Mr Oglethorpe, countersigned them myself, and so entirely washed my hands of the traders.

Sunday, July 25. I resigned my secretary's place in a letter to Mr Oglethorpe. After prayers he took me aside and asked me whether all I had said was not summed up in the line he showed me on my letter:

Magis apta tuis tua dona relinquo.[68]

Sir, to yourself your slighted gifts I leave,
Less fit for me to take, than you to give.[69]

I answered, I desired not to lose his esteem, but could not preserve it with the loss of my soul. He answered he was satisfied of my regard for him, owned my argument drawn from the heart unanswerable, and yet, said he,

I would desire you not to let the trustees know your resolution of resigning. There are many hungry fellows ready to catch at the office, and in my absence I cannot put in one of my own choosing. The best I can hope for is an honest Presbyterian, as many of the trustees are such. Perhaps they may send me a bad man, and how far such an one may influence the traders and obstruct the reception of the gospel among the heathen, you know. I shall be in England before you leave it. Then you may either put in a deputy or resign.

You need not be detained in London above three days, and only speak to some of my particular friends (Vernon, Hutchinson, and Tower[70]), to the Board of Trustees, when called upon, and to the Board of Trade.

---

68. Cf. Horace, *Epistles*, I.vii.43: "*Atride, magis apta tibi tua dona relinguam.*"
69. This poetic translation may be Wesley's own. More literally Horace's text would translate:
    [Son of Atreus,] your gifts are better suited to yourself,
    I shall leave them for you to use.
70. Thomas Tower, a trustee of the Georgia Colony. Charles spells "Towers."

On many accounts I should recommend to you marriage, rather than celibacy. You are of a social temper, and would find in a marriage state the difficulties of working out your salvation exceedingly lessened, and your helps as much increased.

Monday, July 26. The words which concluded the lesson, and my stay in Georgia, were, "Arise, let us go hence" [John 14:31]. Accordingly at twelve, I took my final leave of Savannah. When the boat put off, I was surprised that I felt no more joy in leaving such a scene of sorrows.

Saturday, July 31. I arrived with my brother at Charleston. Lay that night at an inn. Next morning I was much rejoiced at hearing Mr Appee was still in town, waiting for my company to England. His ingenuous, open temper, and disengagement from the world, made me promise myself a very improving and agreeable voyage—especially as I doubted not but the sudden death of his mistress had taken off that appearance of lightness, which I attributed rather to his youth and education than any natural inconstancy. After breakfasting with Mr [Samuel] Eveleigh,[71] a merchant who had bespoke lodgings for us, I went in quest of my friend. We met with equal satisfaction on both sides, but I did not observe those deep traces of sorrow and seriousness, which I expected. I asked him whether his loss had had its due effect, in making his heart more tender and susceptible of divine impressions. By his answer I concluded his heart was right, and its uppermost desire to recover the divine image.

Something of this desire I felt myself at the holy Sacrament, and found myself encouraged, by an unusual hope of pardon, to strive against sin.

AUGUST 1736

Monday, August 2. I had observed much, and heard more, of the cruelty of masters towards their negroes. But now I received an authentic account of some horrid instances thereof. The giving a child a slave of its own age to tyrannize over, to beat and abuse out of sport, was, I myself saw, a common practice. Nor is it strange that

---

71. Charles spells "Eveley."

being thus trained up in cruelty, they should afterwards arrive at so great perfection in it; that Mr Star, a gentleman I often met at Mr Laserre's, should, as he himself informed Laserre, first nail up a negro by the ears, then order him to be whipped in the severest manner, and then to have scalding water thrown all over him, so that the poor creature could not stir for four months after. Another much applauded punishment is drawing their slaves' teeth. One Colonel Lynch is universally known to have cut off a poor negro's legs, and to kill several of them every year by his barbarities.

It were endless to recount all the shocking instances of diabolical cruelty which these men (as they call themselves) daily practice upon their fellow-creatures, and that on the most trivial occasions. I shall only mention one more, related to me by a Swiss gentleman, Mr [Sebastian] Zouberbuhler, an eyewitness of Mr Hill, a dancing-master in Charleston. He whipped a she-slave so long, that she fell down at his feet for dead. When by the help of a physician she was so far recovered as to show signs of life, he repeated the whipping with equal rigour, and concluded with dropping hot sealing wax upon her flesh. Her crime was overfilling a tea-cup.

These horrid cruelties are the less to be wondered at, because the government itself in effect countenances and allows them to kill their slaves by the ridiculous penalty appointed for it, of about 7 pounds sterling (half of which is usually saved by the criminal's informing against himself). This I can look upon as no other than a public act to indemnify murder.

Wednesday, August 11. Coming on board our ship, I found the honest captain had let my cabin to another. My flux and fever that has hung upon me forced me for some nights past to go into a bed. But now my only bed was a chest, on which I threw myself in my boots, and was not overmuch troubled with sleep till the morning. What was still worse, I then had no asylum to fly to from the captain, the most beastly man I ever saw, a lewd, drunken, quarrelsome fool; praying and yet swearing continually. The first sight I had of him was upon the cabin-floor, stark naked, and dead drunk.

Friday, August 13. The wind was still contrary, so that we were forced to lie off the bar about five miles from Charleston.

Monday, August 16. A faint breeze springing up, the pilot, weary of waiting a week to no purpose, said he would venture over the bar, though he feared there was not water enough. Accordingly we attempted it, and had got above half of the two miles between us and the sea, when a violent squall arose, and drove the ship before it with incredible swiftness. Before it began we were almost becalmed, so that it saved the ship, at least, from being aground, though with the immediate hazard both of that, and our lives. The sailors were in great consternation, expecting to be stranded every moment. The pilot cursed the ship most heartily, and the hour he set foot in her. Having scraped along the ground for some minutes before, the ship at last stuck. She got clear, and stuck fast a second time and immediately fell into seven-fathom water.

The mate afterwards told me it was thousand to one but she had been lost by the captain's folly and ignorance, in letting fly the mainsail while we stuck on the bar—which was the surest way to fix her there, as it must have done had we not been then on the very edge of it.

Tuesday, August 17. We were much surprised, the passengers I mean, at finding, as soon as over the bar, that two of our twelve sailors were obliged to pump every half-hour.

Monday, August 23. I rose in the night to appease a quarrel between the second mate and the captain, who was continually interrupting the officers in their duty, giving out, as they informed me, such orders as would, if followed, cost them the ship and their lives. His indignation at present was occasioned by their furling some of the sails in the greatest squall we have yet met with.

Thursday, August 25. We saw a brigantine standing to the windward of us, but quickly lost sight of her. Had she come near us, Mr Appee and I intended to have gone on board her, for we cannot yet believe we shall come to England in this ship.

Friday, August 26. We came to an allowance of water, the captain knowing nothing of what we had on board till the officers informed him. Indeed, at his rate of drinking we must quickly come to a shorter allowance, for while any of his half-hogshead of rum remains, here will be nothing but punch and drams, and drunkenness without end.

This morning Mr Appee laid aside his mask. He began by telling me all Mr Oglethorpe had ever said to him, particularly his inmost thoughts of my brother and me. That he ridiculed our pretended fasting in the ship. That he took all my abstentiousness for mere hypocrisy, and put on for fear of my brother, for he saw how very uneasy I was under the restraint. That he much blamed my carelessness, my closeness, my frightening the people, and stirring them up to mutiny, etc. That he found I apprehended being turned out of my office, and therefore pretended to be weary of it. That to save my reputation he had found me an errand to England, but never expected my return, any more than my brother's going to the Indians, which he well knew he never intended, but he would make his own use of him. That he greatly admired his *finesse* in offering to go to the Choctaws in all haste, but at the same time procuring the Germans to dissuade him. In a word, he believed him to have a little sincerity, but more vanity; me to have much vanity, but no sincerity at all.

I asked Appee whether his judgment was the same? He answered, "Yes." That my brother, he believed, was labouring to establish a character for sanctity, was exceedingly subtle, keeping me in the dark as well as all others, yet credulous, and easy to be imposed upon himself. That he pitied his ignorance in taking him (Appee) to be sincere, particularly in regard to his breaking off with Miss Bovey, which he intended, not in pursuance of his ghostly advice, but of Mr Oglethorpe's, who had told him she was below one of his aspiring genius. That after his fine talk with my brother, he never made the least alteration in his own behaviour, or thought any farther about it.

While he was giving this blessed account of himself I could not help reflecting on the profound sagacity and spiritual discernment of my brother and myself—particularly *his,* who was born for the benefit of knaves. *Si vult decipi decipiatur.*[72] For my own part, I will never imitate, I will ever beware of men, as he who best knows them advises. I will not think all men rogues till I find them otherwise (according to Appee's avowed principle), but I will insist upon a far different probation from what my brother requires before I take anyone into my confidence!

I next enquired what his thoughts were of me. He frankly replied he took me to be partly in earnest, but I had a much greater mind

---

72. This is likely Wesley's shortened version of a common Latin proverb: *Si populus vult decipi, decipiatur,* "If the crowd wants to be deceived, let them be deceived."

to please myself than to please God. That as for money, I did not much value it, but in my eagerness for pleasure and praise I was a man after his own heart. That as I could not hold it, he wished I would leave off my strictness, for I should then be much better company.

As for himself, he said his only principle was an insatiable thirst of glory. That Georgia was too narrow a sphere for him, and therefore he should never see it more. That he desired my friendship, because I had learning, was sincere, and of his temper, but he should like me much better if I were not a parson. I had before let him into my own affairs, and read him my letter of resignation to Mr Oglethorpe. His remark upon that was, "'Tis finely calculated for the end you propose, the engaging Mr Oglethorpe's opinion and interest, but he will understand you."

Saturday, August 28. After a restless, tempestuous night, I hardly rose at eight. Our happier captain, having got his dose, could sleep a day and a night upon the stretch, and defy either pumps or squall to wake him.

Monday, August 30. At noon we were alarmed by an outcry of the sailors at their having continued pumping several hours without being able to keep the water under. They desired the captain to put into some port before they were got out to sea too far for returning, but he was too drunk to regard them. At five the sailors came down in a body to the great cabin, waked, and told him it was much as their lives were worth to proceed on the voyage unless their leaks were stopped. That he remembered it was as much as ever they could do to keep the ship above water in their passage from Boston, being forced to pump without ceasing. That the turpentine fell down upon and choked up the pumps continually. Nor was it possible for them to get at it, or to hold out in such continual labour, which made them so thirsty they could not live on their allowance of water. That they must come to shorter still through his neglect to take in five more hogsheads of water, as his mate advised him. That one of them, Benjamin Arnold, had been forced to drink his own water. That he owned they had no candles for half of the voyage. On all which accounts they begged him to consider whether their common safety did not require them to put in at some land for more water and candles, and, above all, to stop their leaks. The captain, having now slept out his rum, replied, "To be sure, the men talked reason," and, without consulting any of his officers, immediately gave orders to stand away for Boston.

SEPTEMBER 1736

Saturday, September 4. Appee laid a train for the captain and betrayed him into talking lewdly, for which I reproved him too sharply and thereby increased his beastliness. He abused me plentifully, till I ceased to take any notice of him. In the evening he set upon me again, but I turned from him, and talked Latin to Zouberbuhler. This made him more outrageous. He blew out the candle by which I was writing. Zouberbuhler lit it, and he blew it out again. On which we all set upon him, I only talking Latin or Greek. He told me I was drunk, mad, an emissary, a Jesuit, a devil; but could not get one English word from me. The gentlemen, particularly Appee, baited him to his heart's content; and having laughed upon the stretch till near midnight, we then suffered the poor beast to return to his litter.

The next day we said neither good nor bad to him, but he was not so continent of speech. His indignation was mostly vented upon me, "the arch-rebel," as he called me, for "my audacious talk." In the evening he again put out Zouberbuhler's candle, upon which Appee pulled out the spicket of the rum and let it run about the cabin. This was the cruelest punishment [that] could have been devised and farther heightened by our mirth at his inimitable resentment. Zouberbuhler lighted up the candle in his own cabin every now and then, bringing it into the great cabin, and when the captain (whose motions were none of the nimblest) had come out of bed to put it out, Zouberbuhler carried it back again. He called down his men ten times, ordering them to bind us in our beds, to ours and their no small diversion. He offered to get the candle in Zouberbuhler's cabin, but the Swiss stood sentinel at his cabin door and then might as well have wrenched a bone from Cerberus.[73] The captain gave it over as impossible, drank a hearty dram, and dropped asleep.

---

73. In Greek mythology, Cerberus was the three-headed watchdog of the underworld.

Wednesday, September 15. This is the first time I have heard a sailor confess, "It was a storm." We lay under our mainsail, and let the ship drive, being by conjecture about sixty leagues from Boston, upon George's Bank, though, as we hoped, past the shoals in it. The captain never troubled himself about anything, but lay snoring even in such a night as the last, though frequently called, without ever stirring, either for squalls, or soundings, or shoals.

In the afternoon the mate came down having sounded and found forty, and soon after twenty fathom, told the captain he apprehended coming into shallower water still, and therefore it would be necessary to reef the foresail and mainsail in readiness, that in case we fell foul of the shallows (being upon George's Bank, and in a storm), the ship might have head-way, to get clear again. This the captain absolutely refused, and, though told it could do no possible harm, and might be the saving of the ship and us, persisted in his obstinacy, so that the mate left him to sleep, and the ship to take care of itself. But it pleased God to abate the storm and, on Thursday, about twelve, entirely to remove it.

Monday, September 20. At seven, Mr Graham, the first mate, came to ask for directions, as he constantly does, the captain as constantly shifting him off, and leaving the whole management of the ship to him, or chance, or anybody. The conversation being somewhat remarkable, I took it down in shorthand, as they were speaking.

Mate: "Captain Indivine, what would you have us do? What course would you have us to steer tonight?"
Capt.: "Even what course you will, we have a fair wind."
Mate: "Yes Sir, and it drives us full upon the land, which cannot be many leagues off."
Capt.: "Then I think you had best keep forward."
Mate: "Would you have us go on all night, and venture running upon the land?"
Capt.: "I don't know. Go on."
Mate: "But there are shallows and rocks before us."
Capt.: "Why, then, have a good lookout."
Mate: "But you cannot see twice the ship's length. What would you order me to do?"
Capt.: "These rebels and emissaries have excited you to come and ask for orders. I don't know what you mean."

Mate: "Sir, nobody has excited me. I come, as it is my duty, to my captain for directions."

Capt.: "Have you a mind to quarrel with me?"

Mate: "I have a mind to know what you will do."

Capt.: "Nay, what will you do, if it come to that?"

Mate: "Am I your captain? or you mine?"

Capt.: "I am your captain, and will make you know it, Mr Man. Do what I order you, for you must and shall."

Mate: "Why, Sir, you order me nothing."

Capt.: "You would not have me come upon deck myself, sure."

Mate: "If you did, I should not think it would be much amiss. Some captains would not have stirred off deck a moment in such a night as this. Here you lie, without so much as ever once looking out, to see how things are."

Capt.: "Yes, I have been upon deck this very day."

Mate: "But you have taken no account of anything, or given yourself the least trouble about the ship for many days past."

Capt.: "'Tis all one for that. I know where we are exactly."

Mate: "How far do you think we may be from land?"

Capt.: "Why just thirty-five leagues. I am sure of it."

Mate: "How is that possible? You have taken no observation this fortnight, nor have we got one these four days."

Capt.: "No matter for that. I know we are safe."

Mate: "The most skilful sailor alive cannot know it. Be pleased only to declare what you would have done. Shall we sail on? Shall we lay by? Shall we alter our course? Shall we stand in and off?"

He went on repeating such questions again and again. But as to giving an answer, the captain chose to be excused, till the mate, quite out of patience, having waited an hour to no purpose, left him. And the captain (concluded all with) "Jack, give me a dram!"

Tuesday, September 21. The sailors, who were upon deck all night, saw three large ships coming as they supposed, out of the bay, but in vain attempted to speak with them. At three I was waked by a cry of "Land." The mate said we were just upon it, for he saw the light of the watch-house, and if they did not tack about immediately they would be upon the rocks which lay just before them under the water. At the same time it blew a storm. The uproar was so great that it even waked the captain, who started up, ran to his rum, drank an hearty draught, and then looked upon deck, but not much liking things there, came down again immediately, cried, "Aye, aye; all will be well," and dropped asleep again.

Wednesday, September 22. Having sailed for some hours without discovering land, we began to think the light, which the mate had seen, was of some ship, and not the lighthouse. At two we made land, which the men soon found to be Cape Cod, about eighteen leagues from Boston. The wind blew from shore, yet we kept our course. At midnight the storm gave place to a calm. These have constantly succeeded each other since our leaving Charleston.

Thursday, September 23. The fineness of the weather invited even Mr Appee upon deck, who usually disposes of twenty-three of the twenty-four hours in bed. His vanity betrayed him into farther discoveries of himself. He laboured to show me the only difference between us lay in externals, through the difference of our education. I had the same views that he had, but was forced by the restraints of a narrower education to dissemble those inclinations which he had given a loose to. The case was the same with my brother—a much better hypocrite, he said, than me, and who would have made an excellent Jesuit. But Mr Oglethorpe understood him, though for his own convenience he would not seem to do so.

Upon my asking him how he accounted for the great pains my brother had taken with him, he readily answered, "That was all grimace. My brother could not but be mightily pleased with the reputation such a convert would gain to his sanctity, which had charms to win over so wild a young gentleman of his parts." But how could you bear him so long, if you had no esteem for him, or regard to his advice? "Why, it was so new a gratification to ~~him~~ me to be thought religious, that I found no difficulty in keeping on the mask, and I had got such a knack of going to prayers and Sacrament that I don't know but I should have been actually caught at last."

Friday, September 24. Being within sight of the lighthouse, at nine in the morning, the pilot came on board us. At two I gladly obeyed his hasty summons, and went into his boat with the other passengers, bidding an hearty farewell to our wretched ship, and more wretched captain, who for the last two days had, most happily for us, lain dead drunk on the floor, without sense or motion.

I was at leisure now to contemplate a prospect entirely new, and beautiful beyond all I had ever seen. We sailed smoothly on, in a vast basin, as it seemed, bounded on all sides with small innumerable islands. Some of these were entire rock in height and colour not unlike Dover Cliffs; others steep, and covered with woods. Here and there lay a round hill, entirely clothed with green, and all at such equal distances that the passages seemed artificially made to admit the narrow streams between.

Having passed one of these passages, we were presented with a new set of hills and rocks and woods, in endless variety, till we came to the castle,[74] three miles from Boston. From thence we had a full view of the town, stretched out a mile and a half upon the shore, in a semicircle. We landed at Long Wharf, which we walked straight up, having a row of houses on one side, and near 200 sail of ships on the other. Lodged in a public house. Went to bed at eleven. Appee followed me, drunk, between one and two in the morning.

Saturday, September 25. Called several times at Mr [Roger] Price, the commissary's, before I found him at home. At first he looked as not believing me to be a clergyman (my ship-clothes not being the best credentials). But when I returned in my habit (Dr [Timothy] Cutler having met him meantime, and informed him of me), he received me very cordially, and pressed me to live with him, while I stayed in Boston.

Sunday, September 26. Preached in the morning at Dr Cutler's church,[75] in the afternoon at Mr Price's,[76] on "The One Thing Needful" [Luke 10:42].[77]

---

74. Castle Island, in Boston harbor, the fortified defense for the city of Boston.

75. Cutler was rector of Christ Church, Boston (now known also as "Old North Church").

76. Price also served as rector of King's Chapel, Boston. The best source for the names and individuals cited by Wesley during his Boston visit is volume 1 of H. W. Foote, *Annals of King's Chapel from the Puritan Age of New England to the Present Day,* 2 vols. (Boston: Little, Brown, and Company, 1882).

77. This is one of John Wesley's sermons that Charles transcribed and preached often. See Richard P. Heitzenrater, "Early Sermons of John and Charles Wesley," in *Mirror and Memory* (Nashville: Kingswood Books, 1989), 150–61. While Charles varies a little in the several subsequent listings of preaching this sermon, all citations have been regularized as in this entry. Cf. *Sermons,* 79, 360–68.

In the evening I first fell into company with Mr John Checkley,[78] a right honest zealous advocate for the Church of England, who has on that account, been cruelly persecuted by the Presbyterians.

Thursday, September 30. In the morning I waited upon the governor.[79] At noon Mr Miller,[80] a good-natured clergyman, visited me. The rest of this and the following day I employed in writing to my friends at Charleston.

OCTOBER 1736

Friday, October 1. Wrote to my brother concerning my return to Georgia,[81] which I found myself inclined to refer wholly to God.

Saturday, October 2. I rode out with Mr Price in his chaise, to see the country, which is wonderfully delightful. The only passage out of town is a neck of land about 200 yards over, all the rest being encircled with the sea. The temperate air, the clear rivulets, and the beautiful hills and dales, which we everywhere met with, seemed to present the very reverse of Georgia.

Sunday, October 3. After near two months' want of it, I again enjoyed the benefit of the Sacrament, which I assisted Dr Cutler to administer. I preached on "There the wicked cease from troubling, [and] there the weary are at rest" [Job 3:17],[82] as I did again in the afternoon for Mr Price, though I found my strength sensibly abated.

Monday, October 4. I rode with Mr and Mrs Price, Dr Cutler (his son,[83] and Mr Bridge,[84] two Cambridge scholars), to see Mr Miller, at Braintree. At our return we found Mr Davenport,[85] who was come

---

78. John Checkley (1680–1754). Cf. *The Speech of Mr John Checkley, upon his trial at Boston in New England . . .* (London: J. Applebee, 1738). Charles spells "Chicheley."

79. Jonathan Belcher (1681/2–1757) was currently colonial governor of Massachusetts.

80. Rev. Ebenezer Miller (d. 1763) was rector of Christ Church in Braintree, and the brother-in-law of John Checkley. Charles spells "Millar."

81. This letter can be found in John Wesley, *Works* 25:476–79.

82. Charles was possibly preaching his brother John's sermon on this text; cf. "The Trouble and Rest of Good Men," *Works* 3:533–41.

83. John Cutler (1713–1771).

84. Christopher Bridge (b. 1712). Charles spells "Brig."

85. Rev. Addington Davenport (1701–1746), then minister at Scituate, Massachusetts; in 1737 became Price's assistant at King's Chapel, and rector of Trinity Church in 1740.

to see me, a worthy clergyman, as deserving of the name as any I see in New England.

Tuesday, October 5. I dined at Mr Plasted's, a London acquaintance of my brother's who from thence took occasion to find me out, and showed me all the friendship and civility he could, while I stayed in Boston. After dinner drove Mr Cutler to Cambridge. I had only time to observe the civility of the fellows, the regularity of the buildings, and pleasantness of the situation.

Saturday, October 9. Was dragged out to consult Dr Greaves[86] about my increasing flux. He prescribed a vomit, from which I received much benefit.

Sunday, October 10. Recovered a little strength in the Sacrament, but my body was extremely weakened by preaching twice.[87]

Tuesday, October 12. Supped with several of the clergy at Mr Checkley's, who entertained us very agreeably with his adventures. He seems to have excellent natural parts, much solid learning, and true primitive piety; is acquainted with the power, and therefore holds fast the form of godliness; obstinate as was my father in good, and not to be borne down by evil.

Thursday, October 14. Was taken up with the clergy, in drawing up recommendation of him to the Bishop of London for orders. The bishop had been formerly frightened from ordaining him, by the outcries of the Presbyterians. They were wise to keep a man out of the ministry who had in a private capacity approved himself such a champion for the Church.

Saturday, October 16. My illness increasing, notwithstanding all the doctors could do for me, I began seriously to consider my condition, and at my evening hour of retirement found benefit from Pascal's prayer in sickness.[88]

Sunday, October 17. While I was talking at Mr Checkley's on spiritual religion, his wife observed that I seemed to have much the

---

86. Dr. Thomas Greaves (1683–1747). Charles spells "Graves."
87. One of these was Charles's sermon on Ps. 126:7, BCP; cf. *Sermons*, 123.
88. Blaise Pascal, "A Prayer Composed in Sickness," in *Thoughts on Religion and Other Subjects*, translated by Basil Kennett (London: A. & J. Churchill, 1704), 369–92.

same way of thinking with Mr Law. Glad I was and surprised to hear that good man mentioned, and confessed all I knew of religion was through him. I found she was well acquainted with his *Serious Call*,[89] and has one of the two that are in New England. I borrowed it, and passed the evening in reading it to the family (Mr Williams's, where I have been some days). His daughter and he seemed satisfied and affected.

Monday, October 18. Many appointed days of embarkation had come and gone, without our embarking, but this was certainly to be the last. Accordingly Mr Miller came very early to attend me to the ship. I took occasion to mention the book I had borrowed of his sister, Mrs Checkley, and read him the characters of Cognatus and Uranius.[90] He liked them much and promised he would carefully read the whole. Breakfast and dinner past, but no summons to go on board.

Tuesday and *Wednesday* I grew worse and worse, and on *Thursday, October 21,* was forced to keep [to] my chamber through pain. Appee came, and laboured all he could to dissuade me from the voyage, promising himself to deliver my letters and papers, and excuse me to Mr Oglethorpe. Mr Price, Williams, etc., joined with him. But I put an end to their importunity by assuring them nothing less than death should hinder my embarking.

Friday, October 22. All things being at last in readiness, the wind providentially changed and afforded me three days more to try experiments. Within that time I vomited, purged, bled, sweated, and took laudanum,[91] which entirely drained me of the little strength I had left.

It may be of use hereafter to remember Appee's behaviour at Boston. He gave out that his design in coming to Georgia had been to take charge of the people there. But finding Mr Oglethorpe just a genius as himself, he thought his own stay there was not so necessary, but he might safely quit the interest of the colony, which, had it not been to such an hand, he could never have prevailed on himself to do. That at present he was unresolved where to bestow

89. William Law, *A Serious Call to a Devout and Holy Life* (London: William Innys, 1729).
90. In ibid., ch. 13.
91. An alcoholic extract of opium; a drug used fairly widely in the eighteenth century as a painkiller.

himself, only that it should be on that part of mankind which needed him the most. That he was going to England about matters of the last importance. Two or three letters of no moment, he said, I carried; but all secret dispatches to the Duke of Newcastle, and other ministers of state, he was charged with. From the court of Great Britain he was to be sent envoy to Spain. His money, a few 100s of pounds, he had (in some companies) sent before him to England; in others had turned it into silver, and freighted Indivine's ship.

Monday, October 25. I waked surprisingly better, though not yet able to walk. This morning Dr Greaves came over from Charlestown[92] to see me, gave me physic and advice, which he likewise left in writing, but would take no fee for either. The same civility I have received from Dr Gibbons, Dr Gardener, and others. A little after Mr Checkley came and brought me a summons to go aboard. Mr Price drove me to the wharf, having called by the way on some of my new friends, from whom I received all the instances of kindness in their power to show.

When we came to the wharf, the boat was not ready, so we were forced to wait half an hour in the open cold air. Mr Checkley helped me into the boat and covered me up. In about two hours we reached the ship,[93] and with Mr Zouberbuhler, Mr Appee, Mr [John] Cutler, and Mr [Christopher] Bridge went on board. I laid down in the stateroom, less fatigued with the passage than I expected.

Finding Appee wanted his stateroom again, I quitted it, and accepted Mr Cutler's offer of his cabin. I had a tolerable night, though stripped of the conveniences I so long enjoyed on shore.

Tuesday, October 26. Entered upon the doctor's regimen, and quickly found the benefit.

When five leagues onward on our voyage, the wind changing forced us back again. In the evening it came fair, and by the next day carried us clear of all land.

Wednesday, October 27. I began public prayers in the great cabin. We had seldom any present but the passengers. Had not yet

---

92. Charlestown, Massachusetts.
93. The ship on which Charles returned to London was named the *Hannah*.

strength to read the lesson; nor attention for any harder study than Clarendon's *History*.[94] In the night I was much disquieted by the cholic.

Thursday, October 28. The captain warned me of a storm approaching. In the evening, at eight, it came, and rose higher and higher, after I thought it must have come to its height. For I did not lose a moment of it, being obliged by the return of my flux to rise continually. At last the long-wished for morning came, and brought no abatement of the storm. There was so prodigious a sea, that it quickly washed away our sheep and half our hogs, and drowned most of our fowl. The ship had been new caulked at Boston; how carefully, it now appeared—for being deeply laden, the sea streamed in at the sides so plentifully, that it was as much as four men could do, by continually pumping, to keep her above water. I rose and lay down by turns, but could remain in no posture long; strove vehemently to pray, but in vain, persisted in striving yet still without effect. I prayed for power to pray, for faith in Jesus Christ, continually repeating his name, till I felt the virtue of it at last, and knew that I abode under the shadow of the Almighty.[95]

It was now about three in the afternoon and the storm at the height I endeavoured to encourage poor Mr Bridge and Cutler, who were in the utmost agony of fear. I prayed with them, and for them till four, at which time the ship made so much water that the captain, finding it otherwise impossible to save her from sinking, cut down the mizen-mast. In this dreadful moment, I bless God, I found the comfort of hope—and such joy in finding I could hope, as the world can neither give nor take away. I had that conviction of the power of God present with me, overruling my strongest passion, fear, and raising me above what I am by nature, as surpassed all rational evidence, and gave me a taste of the divine goodness.

At the same time I found myself constrained in spirit to bear witness to the truth, perhaps for the last time, before my poor friend Appee. I went to him, declared the difference between one that feareth God and one that feareth him not; avowed by hope, not

---

94. Edward Hyde, Earl of Clarendon, *The History of the Rebellion and Civil Wars in England* (Oxford: Sheldonian, 1705–1706).
95. Cf. Ps. 91:1.

because I had attained but because I had endeavoured it, and testified my expectation, if God should now require my soul of me, that he would receive it to his mercy.

My poor friend was convinced, but stupid; owned the happiness of the most imperfect Christian, an happiness he himself was a stranger to; and therefore, he said, all his refuge was, in time of danger, to persuade himself there was none. Mr Cutler frequently calling upon God to have mercy upon his soul, Appee confessed he greatly envied him, as he had no manner of concern for his own. I advised him to pray. He answered it was mocking God to begin praying in danger when he had never done it in safety. I only added I then hoped, if God spared him now, he would immediately set himself about the working out his salvation, which depended on the one condition of exchanging this world for the next. Mr Zouberbuhler was present at this conference, and behaved as a Christian ought to do.

I returned to Mr Bridge and Mr Cutler and endeavoured from their fear to show them the want of religion, which was intended for our support on such occasions; urged them to resolve, if God saved them from this distress, that they would instantly and entirely give themselves up to him.

The wind was still as high as ever but the motion rather less violent since the cutting of the mast, and we did not ship quite so much water. I laid me down, utterly exhausted, but my distemper was so increased it would not suffer me to rest. Toward morning the sea heard and obeyed the divine voice, "Peace, be still!"[96]

Sunday, October 31. My first business today (may it be the business of all my days!) was to offer up the sacrifice of praise and thanksgiving. Then we all joined in thanks for our deliverance. Most of the day I was on the bed, faint, and full of pain. At night I rose to prayers, but could not read them. I took a vomit, which gave me immediate ease, in which I passed the rest of the night.

NOVEMBER 1736

Monday, November 1. In the afternoon the wind rose, and promised a storm. I endeavoured to prepare myself and companions for

---

96. Cf. Mark 4:39.

it. It did not fail our expectation, but was not so violent as the last. The sea broke over us every ten minutes, and the ceaseless noise of the pumps either kept off sleep or continually interrupted it.

Tuesday, November 2. Still the poor sailors could have no respite; and as their strength abated, their murmurings increased. At night when almost exhausted, they were relieved by a calm.

Wednesday, November 3. In the evening the wind arose again, and with that the sea, which at ten broke in through one of the dark lights and filled the great cabin. It was in vain to look for rest in such a hurricane. I waited till two in the morning for its abatement but it continued all the following day in full majesty.

On *Friday, November 5*, we met a ship bound for Boston, which had been ten weeks on her passage from Bristol, and forced in the last storm to throw out most of their cargo overboard. Being short of provisions they desired a barrel of beef which our Captain very readily sent them (though at the expense of much time and pains), and a keg[97] of rum, to encourage their sailors to pump.

The wind came fair about midnight, but soon returned to the same quarter.

Monday, November 8. My flux returned with great violence.

Tuesday, November 9. The men came down and declared they could keep the water under no longer, it gaining upon them every moment. Therefore they desired the captain would be pleased to lighten the ship. He told them, he knew what he had to do, bade them return to their pumping, and ordered others to take in all the sails but the mainsail. He stayed some time (as he since told us, that he might not discourage *us*), and then went up, and as we lay by, stopped several leaks upon deck. This did considerable service, though it was still the constant business of four men to keep the ship from filling.

During this time I often threw myself upon my bed, seeking rest but finding none. I asked of God to spare me a little, that I might recover strength, then cast my eye upon the word: "For my name's sake I will defer my anger, and for my praise will I refrain from it, that I cut thee off" [Isa. 48:9]. My soul immediately returned to its rest, and I no longer felt the continuance of the storm.

---

97. Charles spells "cag."

Wednesday, November 10. Toward night it pleased God to abate the wind, so that I once more enjoyed the comfort of sleep.

Saturday, November 13. Never was a calm more reasonable than that which providence this day sent us. The men were so harassed they could work no longer, and the leaks increased so fast that no less than their uninterrupted labour could have kept the vessel from foundering. All hands were now employed in stopping the leaks. The captain himself told us he had been heartily frightened yesterday with danger he would now acquaint us with, since it was over—the total stoppage of one of the pumps. He further informed us that he had stopped several openings in the sides of the ship wide enough to lay his fingers in, so that he wondered the poor men had been able to keep her above water; and added that the utmost he hoped for was that they might hold out till they could reach some of the western islands. Just as the men had finished their work, the calm gave place to a fair wind.

Tuesday, November 23. I imparted to Mr Zouberbuhler my intention of discarding Appee as soon as we landed. He told me he wondered I had not done it before, for he was such a man, so unprofitable, so pernicious, that he himself would not be bound to go another voyage with him for all the world. That he was so excessively vain, he thought himself admired wherever he came; and I was so fond of him, that, for all my talk of parting, I could not live without him. He added, he was so notorious a liar that he had long since ceased to believe one word he said; and so utterly irreligious, that it was impossible to make a friend of him. He talked so well on this subject that I was convinced he is not the mere man of honour Appee had represented him, but has some better principle than the dream of a shadow to depend upon.

At midnight I was waked by a great uproar. So prodigious a sea broke upon the ship as filled it, and half-drowned the men upon deck, though by particular providence none were washed overboard. The swell lasted something longer than the rain and high wind, and in the morning we had our fair wind again, being the twelfth day since it was first commanded to attend us.

In the afternoon we had another short but fierce blast, which brought the wind still fairer for our running into the channel, whence all agreed we could not be far distant. At night I found Mr

Zouberbuhler alone, who, anticipating what I intended to say, addressed me very cordially, desiring my friendship and correspondence; complained of having been linked so long to Appee, that he was become dead like him, though he had had a fear of God, and some acquaintance with him, till this fatal voyage. He was full of care and thought about his countrymen, whether he should bring them to New England or Georgia. In the latter, he said, he saw little encouragement for true piety (which many of his poor Swiss were yet possessed of), and feared, if they were settled there, they would be corrupted, like the miserable Purisburgers.[98] He told me Appee had proffered, if his Spanish embassy failed to attend him to Switzerland, but he would never more trust such a man near him or his people—such an abominable liar, scoundrel, and thief; one who had been forced to fly his country and the pursuit of justice for robbing his father of 300 guineas.

A fair account of my friend Appee—and of the twenty-four pounds I had lent him! That a Dutchman should cheat me is nothing strange; but how did he evade the wary eye of Mr Oglethorpe? Happy Miss Bovey, to be delivered by death from such a man!

On Thursday night our wind failed us. When it was first sent, we had not, in three weeks' sailing, reached the banks of Newfoundland which is a third part of our way. But this fortnight has almost brought us home. The next day I was perfectly satisfied in the wind's turning against us.

Saturday, November 27. Towards the evening it came fair as we could wish.

Ecce iterum Crispinus![99] Mr Zouberbuhler came to me, full of abhorrence. "That Appee," said he, "is a very devil! Made up of falseness and lies! He is ever railing against you behind your back, to the captain and passengers, ridiculing the prayers, etc. He tells the captain (as he did everybody at Boston) that you are so ignorant Mr Oglethorpe was forced to send him to take care of you. At Charleston he declared in all companies, he was come with full powers to put an end to the dispute between them and Georgia. Last night I overheard him giving a blessed account of you to Mr Bridge. He was lately boasting of women he had had in Boston

---

98. Swiss Huguenot immigrants who settled in Purisburg (now "Purrysburg"), a South Carolina town on the Savannah River just before it goes into Georgia.

99. "Crispinus once again!" Juvenal, *Satires*, iv.1. Crispinus is a horrible, wretched person.

with such abominable circumstances I could not bear to hear him.[100] As soon as ever I come to land I shall cast him off, and advise you to do the same, for while you suffer him near you, he will not fail to do you all the mischief he can."

Monday, November 29. We were waked between six and seven by the captain crying out, "Land." It was the Lizard Point, about a league distant. What wind there was, was for us! I felt thankful for the divine mercies.

While I was walking upon deck, Appee stood up to me, *me tuens tale votum creptum a faucibus;*[101] began with many professions of friendship, hoped all little misunderstandings would be forgot; fell into familiar discourse as formerly; was sure I should never return to Georgia, where Mr Oglethorpe would allow none but his creatures, or such as were some way subservient to his glory, "which, take my word for it," says he, "is the principle of all his actions, as well as mine. Christianity he has about as much of as myself. I have given him some unanswerable reasons against it." He was undetermined where to spend the next year, but resolved to spend it all in quest of pleasure and glory—and confident I was just of his mind.

DECEMBER 1736

Wednesday, December 1. The first thing I heard at daybreak was the captain in an outrageous passion. For the ship, which, according to the course he had ordered, ought to have been near the coast of France, was, through the carelessness of the mate, just upon the land of Shoreham.[102] He told me that had not the day broke out as it did, the ship must have run aground, and then all the art of man could not have saved her, for we were land-locked on three sides, and had the wind right astern. So that it was with the utmost difficulty, and not till the afternoon, that we got clear. This lost us a day, for by the evening we should have reached the Downs.[103]

---

100. This sentence is omitted in Jackson and Telford.
101. "Fearing that such a promise/vow had been wrested from [his] throat." Note: The text should read *"me vens tale votum creptum a faucibus."*
102. I.e., Shoreham-by-Sea, Sussex.
103. A sheltered anchorage in the English Channel off the east coast of Kent.

Appee took me aside once more, to try his skill upon me, besought me not to alter my behaviour toward him when we should come to land; denied, as ever he hoped for salvation, that he had ever spoke or wrote disrespectfully of me; detested the thought of such treachery, with so many horrid imprecations as I believed even a Dutchman would have trembled at. The burden of all was, John Bull and Nicholas Frog were too dear friends ever to think of parting.[104] . . . But John Bull begged to be excused. Though I stood in admiration of his parts, I did not choose they should be any longer exercised on me. In vain did he resume our lodging together. I was deaf on that ear, and shifted the discourse, which he still brought back again, "Well, my dear friend, wherever you are," said he, "I will take a lodging next door."

Thursday, December 2. By four in the afternoon we came within sight of Beachy Head. But the wind freshening, by nine we found ourselves almost unawares over against Dover. We fired a gun for a pilot, but none would come to us. We fell down into the Downs, over against Deal, and fired two more. The captain gave us warning that he expected a pilot in an hour or two at the farthest. I returned thanks to God for bringing us to the haven where we would be, got my few things in readiness, and laid me down, without disquiet or impatience, for two or three hours.

Friday, December 3. At six the pilot came on board. It was with much difficulty we got down into his boat. The sea was so rough that nothing less than our late series of deliverances could have supported our confidence. In half an hour we reached the shore. I knelt down and blessed the hand that had conducted me through such inextricable mazes, and desired I might give up my country again to God, whenever he should require.

Zouberbuhler appeared full of gratitude to God and affection to me. We all adjourned to an inn. Zouberbuhler and I walked to bespeak a coach. Joined with the passengers in an hearty thanksgiving for our safe arrival.

---

104 "John Bull" is the typical Englishman (kindhearted and bullheaded) and "Nicholas Frog" the scheming Dutchman (like Appee) in the widely popular satirical play by John Arbuthnot (or Jonathan Swift), *Law Is a Bottomless Pit* (London: John Morphew, 1712); and in the further elaboration by Swift, "The History of John Bull," *Miscellanies in Prose and Verse*, 2nd ed. (Dublin: Samuel Fairbrother, 1728), 1:241–388.

Between ten and eleven set out in the coach, and by three reached Canterbury, and by ten Sittingbourne.[105] I had intended to lay with Zouberbuhler, but upon an intimation from him, went and lay with Appee, to hinder his having a different kind of bedfellow.

Saturday, December 4. Appee was so very grievous to us that not only I, but all the passengers, resolved this should be the last day of their acquaintance. At six in the evening we came safe to London. I immediately took coach for Charles Rivington's, leaving my friend Appee, who promised to come next day and pay me what he owed me.

My namesake was much rejoiced to see me and gave me great cause of rejoicing by his account of our Oxford friends.

Sunday, December 5. Received comfort with the Sacrament at St Paul's, and from thence went to Mr Tower's, who received me with great affection and heartily congratulated me on my arrival, which my friends had long despaired of. He told me the agreeable news of Mr Oglethorpe's being expected daily.

The next I waited upon was good old Sir John Philipps,[106] who received me as one alive from the dead. Here I heard a most blessed account of our friends at Oxford, their increase both in zeal and number. I then hastened to Mr Vernon to deliver my letters. He received me very affectionately, and pressed me to live with him during my stay in London.

While we were talking, young [James] Hutton called, having traced me hither, in order to carry me home with him. We took coach for my good old friend and host, his father.[107] I entered with fear and trembling. My reception was such as I expected from a family that entirely loved me but had given me over for dead and bewailed me as their own child. A captain had told them that fifty per cent assurance had been refused for Indivine's ship, and a report was spread abroad that she had been seen sink to the bottom.

The motion of the stage and hackney coaches occasioned the return of my flux, which prevents me preaching or talking to my admirers. Many such I have gained by Mr Ingham's magnificent

---

105. Charles spells "Sittenburn."
106. Sir John Philipps (c. 1666–1737), 4th baronet, of Picton. Charles spells "Philips."
107. Rev. John Hutton (1676–1750).

journal.[108] My brother's journal too (the last I hope will ever be sent hither) is in every one's hands.

libeat modo vivere, fient,
fient ista palam, cupient et in acta referri.[109]

Monday, December 6. I spent an hour at my uncle's, equally welcome and unexpected. They informed my brother Hall[110] was gone to a curacy, very melancholy, and impatient at the mention of Georgia. ~~What shocked me above measure was~~ That my sister Kezzy was gone to live with him.

Serpentes avibus geminentur tigribus agna[e]![111]

Waited upon Mr Hutchinson, who soon fell upon the controverted points. Here also I had an invitation to make his house my home.

Tuesday, December 7. Called in the morning on Charles Rivington, who gave me letters and a journal from my brother in Georgia. After leaving my secretary's book with Mr Tower, I waited upon the Bishop of London.[112] In the antechamber I began his journal, and read it through without either surprise or impatience. His dropping my fatal letter, I hope, will convince him of what I never could, his own great carelessness; and the sufferings that brought upon him of his inimitable blindness. His simplicity in telling what and who were meant by the two Greek words was "outdoing his own outdoings."[113] Surely all this will be sufficient to teach him a

---

108. This would be a manuscript copy of Benjamin Ingham's journal being circulated. Cf. Richard P. Heitzenrater, ed., *Diary of an Oxford Methodist; Benjamin Ingham, 1733–1734* (Durham, NC: Duke University Press, 1985).

109. "Yes, and if we only live long enough, we shall see these things done openly. People will wish to see them reported among the news of the day." Juvenal, *Satires*, ii.135–36. Note, in line 1 Juvenal has *"liceat,"* not *"libeat."*

110. This is Westley Hall, a student of John Wesley at Oxford, who had simultaneously courted two of Charles's sisters, Martha ("Patty") and Kezia ("Kezzy"). He ended up marrying Patty. After the death of Samuel Wesley, Sr., the couple invited Kezzy to live with them in Wootton-Rivers, where Hall was curate of a small parish. While the rest of the family scorned this arrangement, it was apparently innocent. In later years, however, Hall was repeatedly unfaithful to Patty, finally abandoning her.

111. "Serpents are joined with birds, lambs with tigers." Horace, *Art of Poetry*, 13. In Horace's original the last word is "agni."

112. Edmund Gibson (1669–1748) was Bishop of London, 1723–1748.

113. The manuscript journal of John that Charles was reading has been preserved. The relevant entry is August 20, 1736 (*Works* 18:411). John had apparently dropped a letter from

little wisdom of the serpent, of which he seems as utterly void, as his dear friend Mrs Hawkins is of the innocency of the dove.[114]

In the midst of these reflections I was called in to deliver my letters. His Lordship desired me to come next morning, having much to say to me. I drove to Colonel [Martin] Bladen, who was from home, then to Mrs Pendarves,[115] where we passed an agreeable hour in mutual accounts of our friends in England and America.

I returned to Mr Hutton's,[116] where Dr [Stephen] Hales, one of our trustees, came to see me. Much discourse we had of Georgia, particularly of Miss Bovey's death and my brother's persecutions among that stiff-necked people. He seems a truly pious, humble Christian, full of zeal for God and love to man.

Wednesday, December 8. Waited on Colonel Bladen, and then on the bishop, who asked abundance of curious questions, not worth remembering.

In the evening I obeyed a summons from my Lord Egmont[117] and gave him, as I did all I came to the speech of, a true account of the case between Georgia and Carolina.

Thursday, December 9. Called on Mr Tower, who desired me by all means to go home, and keep there whoever sent for me, promising, if he had any business, he would come to me. I took his advice and kept my chamber some days, which, with Dr Cockburn's electuary,[118] almost perfectly recovered me.

Saturday, December 11. Mr Bridge and Mr Cutler called, and informed me Captain Corney was heartily frightened by hearing on all sides Appee's real character. That he gave over for lost the money he had lent him, as well as that for passage and provisions.

Contrary to my doctor's advice, I ventured out *Sunday, December 12*, to the Sacrament in Duke Street. Mrs Rhodes challenged me after the service—with, "I am glad to see you. I hope you go back again to Georgia."

Charles and it was discovered by Mr. Hawkins. In this letter (which has not survived) Charles used two Greek terms to describe Mrs. Hawkins and Mrs. Welch in an unflattering way.

114. Cf. Matt. 10:16.

115. Mary Pendarves (née Granville) was living with her aunt, Lady Stanley, at Somerset House, London.

116. John Hutton lived on College Street (now 16 Great College Street) in Westminster.

117. Sir John Perceval (1683–1748), who became Earl of Egmont in 1733.

118. Dr. William Cockburn (1669–1739) made his fortune from a remedy for dysentery, which he developed for the British navy and the formula for which he kept secret.

In the evening a multitude came and went, most to inquire of their friends or relations in Georgia. I sent them away advocates for the colony.

Wednesday, December 15. About noon I waited upon the trustees at the office. It put me past all patience to hear they were reading Mr Ingham's and my brother's journals. I was called in, and delivered my letter for the trustees. Lord [George] Carpenter, being in the chair, desired me to speak that all gentlemen might hear me. Mr Tower interposed and told them I was so weakened by my illness that I could not speak aloud, and desired me to deliver my papers one by one to be read by Mr [Harman] Verelst.[119] At dinner they fell into discourse about the missioners, whom as yet they mightily commend, and wish for more of them; as that their journals might be forthwith printed, that the world might receive the benefit of their labours.

Thursday, December 16. I was extremely sick in the night, and by morning my flux returned.

Saturday, December 18. Began my twenty-seventh year[120] in a murmuring, discontented spirit, reading over and over the third of Job.

Tuesday, December 21. I dined at my uncle's, who bestowed abundance of wit on my brother and his apostolical project. He told me the French, if they had any remarkably dull fellows among them, sent them to convert the Indians. I checked this eloquence by those lines of my brother:

> To distant realms th' Apostle need not roam,
> Darkness alas, and heathens are at home.[121]

He made no reply, and I heard no more of my brother's apostleship.

---

119 Accountant for the Georgia Colony Trust. Charles spells the last name "Virelst."

120. Charles was actually now twenty-nine years old. The turmoil surrounding the burning of the Epworth rectory in his early childhood, and the accompanying destruction of records, led to vagueness about the year of his birth. Charles typically underestimated his age by two years (see the December 18, 1749, entry as well). Cf. Frank Baker, "The Birth of Charles Wesley," *PWHS* 31 (1957): 25–26.

121. It is not clear if Charles is attributing this to Samuel, Jr., or to John. In either case, it is not found among their published poetry.

Wednesday, December 22. Received a letter from Mr Whitefield, offering himself to go to Georgia.

Thursday, December 23. Had a long conference with Lord Fitzwalter[122] concerning Georgia. In the afternoon my old captain's owners came to desire me to testify the treatment I had received, for which reason I would not proceed [to England] with Indivine. This I promised with Zouberbuhler, if there should be occasion.

Sunday, December 26. I called upon my doctor, and was well chided for so doing. He told me that if I had not had a constitution of iron, I could not have held out so long; that he could do nothing for me, unless I would keep my chamber, through want of which I had undone all he had been doing, and had all to begin anew.

Wednesday, December 29. Called on Zouberbuhler, who gave me the poor Purisburgers' case to read, an eternal monument of Carolina's infamous breach of faith. Soon after Mr Lynn, his land-lord, came in and entertained us with some of Mr Appee's adventures; who, when he came from Surinam, where he had gamed away a plantation his father gave him, was reduced to the last extremity, and taken in naked and starving by one Mrs Legg, who was quickly forced to turn him out again for offering violence to a lady in her family,[123] that he had cheated a common whore of ten pounds at first, by giving her a bill upon his father for 100£.

Cedite Germani latrones, cedite Galli.[124]

He has not studied *Gil Blas*[125] for nothing (his inseparable companion throughout our voyage). As to his boasts, a specimen Mr Lynn helped me to may serve for all. "I wish that dear man, Mr Oglethorpe, would return. I am impatient to see him, but he is even with me. How would he throw open his arms to embrace me! We were always like two brothers. He could never be without me. We were constant bedfellows. Many an expedition have we made together, though in faith I had work enough of it as his secretary. What belonged to one, belonged to the other. He took a fancy to a

122. Benjamin Mildmay (1672–1756), Earl of Fitzwalter.
123. The remainder of this sentence is omitted in Jackson and Telford.
124. "Yield/make way German brigands, yield/make way Gauls."
125. This is the title of a novel, written in French in the early eighteenth century by Alain-René LeSage.

gold watch of mine. I gave it him that instant. It cost me indeed 20 guineas, but that is a trifle between friends."

Thursday, December 30. I waited upon the Bishop of London for some papers I had left with him concerning the state of the colony. Some effect they seemed to have had, for he appeared less reserved than I have ever seen him. I took the opportunity to recommend Mr Checkley for orders, and he said, "He should give his name to the Society,[126] in the list of missionaries."

JANUARY 1737

Monday, January 3, 1737. In the evening Mr Zouberbuhler brought Captain Corney to see me, from whom I received the following narration:

    I was walking with an officer last night, when in the Strand I met Mr Appee, the gentleman I had been two days in quest of. I let him pass to try if he would take any notice of me, but finding he would not, I called after him. He turned, ran to me, and embraced me with—

    Appee: "Dear Captain Corney, I am overjoyed to see you. 'Tis my great misfortune that I could not do it sooner. But I have been so extremely ill, and have such a multitude of business upon my hands, and of such consequence, as made it impossible."

    Captain: "I did hope indeed to have seen you in these three weeks."

    Appee: "But, dear Sir, you cannot conceive the load I have had upon me! What endless business of this Georgia! And all at this end of the town."

    Captain: "Well, since I have had the good fortune to meet you at last, we must take a glass of wine together."

    Appee: "That would be to me the greatest pleasure in life, but I am going home in all haste to dress, being forced abroad by business of the last importance."

    Captain: "Nay, but you shall bestow one half-hour upon me and my friend, since we have had the happiness of meeting you."

    With much ado he got him into the next tavern and, after some indifferent questions, mentioned his promise to freight the ship, which is now clear, said he, and all ready for the Georgia passengers.

---

126. That is, the Society for the Propagation of the Gospel.

Appee: "That is the very thing I wanted to talk with you about. I look for Mr Oglethorpe every hour, and as soon as ever he arrives the business shall be done. You may depend upon it, for I can do anything with him."

Captain: "Sir, I am infinitely obliged to you. But in the meanwhile I must pay off my men and refit my ship, which, you know, has suffered much in the passage. This will stand me in a good deal of money, and therefore I should be glad to settle that small account betwixt us."

Appee: "It was the very thing I was just going to mention, though it grieves me too. Surely I am the most unfortunate man breathing. Such disappointments and losses on all hands since my arrival—My father's failing! My mother's death! My dear friend Mr Oglethorpe's delay!—that really I am afraid it will be some days before I pay you."

The captain tried some time if he could not recover his money but finding nothing was to be got by fair means, at last told the officer that was the man, and bade him do his duty. Appee started up and cried, "I hope, Captain, you are not in earnest, he is not really an officer!" "Hands spake for Caska,"[1] and the catchpole told him he was his prisoner, offering to read his writ. Appee declined it, telling him he understood those things, and immediately fell to his entreaties: told the captain what an esteem he had for him, how he had everywhere extolled his honour, his good nature, and generosity; conjured him by their past friendship to release him directly; otherwise says he, Mr Wesley will hear of it, and bring his action for *his* money "which with your debt is all I owe in the world."

The captain replied, he had no intention to hurt him, but only to get his own money (a mere trifle for Mr Oglethorpe's secretary to pay) or to be sure his father would lay it down for him, the moment he heard of his confinement.

Appee: "I assure you, captain, if one shilling would set me free, I have not a relation in the world [who] would advance it for me."

Captain: "Why then I find you have behaved yourself as scurvily toward them as you have toward me. In the ship you was an agent, a secretary, a statesman; but on shore I perceive you are a bite, and a scoundrel; and as such I will use you."

---

1. Reference to Shakespeare's *The Tragedy of Julius Caesar*, in which Casca is the traitor who is the quickest to action, and says, "Speak, hands, for me!" as he stabs Caesar (Act. III, Sc. 1). The meaning in this case is that the catchpole's actions spoke his response, putting Appee under arrest.

Appee: "For God's sake, dear Captain, have pity upon me. I will give you all I have: 5 pounds in money; in clothes, watch, buckles, sword, snuffbox, and hat."

Captain: "Sir, I scorn to take a gentleman's clothes for such you passed upon me. And had you sent me a single line, with 'Here are three or four guineas for you, Corney, and I will pay the rest when I am able,' I would never have given you or myself any farther trouble about. But your design from the beginning was to cheat me, and I shall therefore make an example of you. In Boston when I would have had you lay in less wine, you told me, what signified 40£ New England money? Truly not much to you, who intended me to pay it. But how could you be so base, when I laid in your provisions, and lent you money?"

His answer to the last indictment was plainly,

Appee: "Necessity has no law."[2]

Captain: "None but an experienced rogue could have made such an answer. You thought me a soft, silly fellow, and was therefore resolved to skin me. But now you shall answer for all."

Appee: "Have patience with me till Mr Oglethorpe comes. You shall then have your freight passengers and money both. You may be sure of it, for I can have of him what money I please."

Captain: "I don't believe a word of it. Did Mr Oglethorpe see you in a gaol [jail], he would leave you there to consign punishment."

Appee: "O, how can you think so, when I have so often told you how intimate we are, and on what important affairs he sent me to England? It is not my liberty I value, for that he will restore me to the moment he hears of my confinement. But I fear I shall lose his good opinion."

Captain: "I don't believe you ever had it, or that he sent you hither for any other reason but to get rid of a vagrant that would else corrupt his colony. If you can pay me my money, do; or I must leave you to justice."

Appee: "Take my clothes in part of payment. I will give you my note for the remainder of the debt."

Captain: "Would you give me your note for the whole twenty-two pounds, I would sell it the first man that would give me sixpence for it."

The captain continuing inexorable, Appee cried like a child. Upon which he asked him how he could behave so abjectly, who had scorned on board to own himself in any danger (as soon as it was past), "when I myself," said he, "had little hope of escaping."

---

2. A proverb going back at least to St Augustine's *Soliloguium Animae.*

Appee: "O Sir, imprisonment, or death itself is nothing to me, but the loss of so dear a friend as Mr Oglethorpe—this is what sits so heavy at my heart. But I hope you will not be so cruel as to rob me of him."

Captain: "I shall be so just to myself, and the world, as to expose a common cheat, who lives upon the public, and lays all honest men that do not know him under contribution."

[*Saturday, January 8*][3] following the captain was prevailed upon by a friend of Appee (now in Newgate)[4] to go hear if he had anything farther to propose.

He began very oratorically: could not blame the captain for what he had done, but forgave him from his heart, and had still the utmost esteem and affection for him; always said, Captain Corney was a good-natured man and a gentleman; was sure therefore he would not ruin a poor young fellow, who was rising in the world, and on the very point of making his fortune. He then began casting up the worth of his snuffbox, etc.—his sword he valued at 7£, his bureau at four.

Captain: "That bureau, Mr Wesley told me, was a lady's in London."

Appee: "Why, that is very true. I had really forgot it. However a guinea I may ask her for the freight."

Captain: "Sir, you talk like what you are. I expected, when you sent for me, your father had supplied you with money to pay me."

Appee: "I assure you once more was I now going to be hanged, my father would not give a single shilling to save me from the gallows."

Captain: "You give a fine account of yourself, and perfectly consistent with that you gave at Boston. It is fit that such an one as you should be suffered any longer to impose upon honest people? 'Tis well you are at the end of your rogueries."

Appee: "I had a suspicion that you had laid a trap for me at Zouberbuhler's, but I was too wise to be caught there."

Captain: "'Tis full as well that I have caught you here. You have been so ungrateful a scoundrel to me that I was resolved to spend a little more money upon you."

---

3. Charles places this entry here, to keep material together, and then returns to January 7 in his next entry.
4. The notorious prison in London.

Appee: "I deserve it for a blockhead as I am, for not putting myself, as I intended, under the court of the green cloth."

Captain: "Why, what a precious rogue you describe yourself! Can you after this expect any favour from me?"

Appee: "I hope you will not take it ill, if I take the benefit of the act, through which I can come out next term."

Captain: "O, not at all, Sir. Take the benefit of the act by all means. I would do so myself, was I in your place. But when you are ready to come out, I will give you your keeping there for one half-year longer."

Here Appee's friend, Mr Joy, told him: "You have used the captain so villainously that I am ashamed to have had any dealings with you. I cannot say one word against his resolution, and desire you would never send or write to me again, or to any of your friends, for we wash our hands of you, and from this hour shall think of you no more."

With this speech he left him and, walking with the captain, observed what a poor unhappy young fellow he was. That ship-wreck of his, in particular, was as unfortunate an accident as one shall hear of. "What shipwreck," says the Captain? "Why, in his passage from Carolina: have you not heard of it?" "No," replied he, "nor I believe anybody else." "He told me," says Joy, "that the ship ran upon the rocks and all the men were lost, but the boatswain, a boy, and himself. That as he hung upon the rock, a sea came and washed him off, dashing him upon another rock with such violence that it broke his skull and tooth and three of his ribs. So that it cost him no less than ten guineas to the surgeon."

This account I made the captain repeat two or three times, and took it down from him in shorthand. I asked, what gave him the first suspicion of Appee's knavery? He answered that when the searchers had opened his bureau he saw several letters Appee had broke open and a memorandum of 900£ currency he had taken up at Charleston, upon (as he suspected) a forged bill of exchange.

Friday, January 7. The news was brought of Mr Oglethorpe's arrival. The next day I waited on him, and received a relation of his wonderful deliverance in the Bristol Channel. The people of Carolina, he told me, were quite mad, had hired men to murder the Indians—the Spaniards—had burnt Augusta, etc. He then inquired about Appee. I gave him some little account of his misbehaviour together with an extract from my journal. He seemed sorry he had ever employed him, talked admirably of resignation, and the impossibility of dying, when it is not best.

Sunday, January 9. I saw him again with Mr Tower's. He told me he had read my journal, which was writ with a great deal of spirit. I replied, all I could answer for was that it was writ with a great deal of truth.

Thursday, January 13. I met Mr Gershom at Mr Oglethorpe's. He told me of Appee's cheating D— a poor drunken P— of his gold watch. Mr Oglethorpe acquainted me that he had been sent to again by Appee in Newgate. Upon my expressing pity for him, he added, "I can do nothing. He has tied my hands. If I released him it would confirm all his lies. We are such dear friends that I must even leave him where he is."

Wednesday, January 19. Count [Nikolaus Ludwig von] Zinzendorf, just arrived from Germany, sent for me. When I came, he saluted me with all possible affection and made me promise to call every day. From him I went to the Bishop of Oxford,[5] where I met with an equally kind reception. He desired me to come as often as I could without ceremony, or farther invitation.

We had much talk of the state of religion, Count Zinzendorf's intended visit. Their bishops he acknowledged to have the true succession.

Thursday, January 20. I wrote and delivered my own state in a letter to the Count. He sent me to Mr Oglethorpe who talked much of the mischief of private journals, all which ought to be published, or never sent. A letter from my brother he read and argued. I could not but think the writer much too free, too bold, too credulous.

Saturday, January 22. I called upon Mrs Pendarves, while she was reading a letter of my being dead. Happy for me had the news been true. What a world of misery would it save me.

In the afternoon was overjoyed to meet at Mrs Essen's my old friend Miss [Anne] Granville.

---

5. John Potter (c. 1674–1747) was still Bishop of Oxford at this point. William Wake, the Archbishop of Canterbury, died on January 24 of this year, and Potter was elevated shortly after to Canterbury (see the August 26, 1737, entry below).

Sunday, January 23. Met Bishop Nitschmann[6] at the Count's, and was introduced to the Countess[7]—a woman of great seriousness and sweetness. I was present at their public service and thought myself in a quire of angels.

Tuesday, January 25. Paid a visit to Dr Hales in the country.

Wednesday, January 26. We took a walk to see Mr [Alexander] Pope's house and gardens,[8] justly called a burlesque upon human greatness. I was sensibly affected with the plain Latin sentence on the obelisk, in memory of his mother—"*Ah, Editha! matrium optima, mulierum amantissima, vale!*"[9] How far superior to the most laboured elegy that he, or [Matthew] Prior himself could have composed!

Sunday, January 30. At St Martin's[10] I heard an excellent sermon by Dr [Joseph] Trapp, on "In your patience possess ye (or be ye master of) your souls" [Luke 21:19], proving the miserable slavery of the passions.[11]

FEBRUARY 1737

Tuesday, February 1. I was again with the Bishop of Oxford and told him the Bishop of London had declined having anything to do with Georgia and said it belonged to the Archbishop only to unite the Moravians with us. He replied it was the Bishop of London's proper office, but bade me assure the Count we should acknowledge the Moravians as our brethren, and one church with ours.

Wednesday, February 2. Mr Oglethorpe told me Appee released from prison, desired to meet me at his house. The next morning I waited there some hours to confront him, but no Appee appeared.

At nine I was with the Count, who seemed resolved to carry his people from Georgia, if they might not be permitted to preach to the Indians. He much pressed me to go with him to Germany, which I am very willing to do if I can get clear of the trustees.

---

6. David Nitschmann (1696–1672), was consecrated in 1735 as the first bishop of the renewed "Moravian" church.

7. Erdmuth Dorothea von Zinzendorf (1700–1756).

8. In Twickenham, Middlesex.

9. "Ah, Edith! Best of mothers, most loving of women, farewell!"

10. St Martin-in-the-Fields Church, London.

11. This sermon was published in Joseph Trapp, *Sermons on Moral and Practical Subjects* (Reading: C. Mickelwright, 1752), 1:143–73.

Saturday, February 6. Had much conversation with the Count. Some of his words were "The Christian cannot yield to sin; cannot long fight against it; but must conquer it, if he will." Speaking of his own case, he said he and a lady were in love with each other, till finding something of nature, he resolved to renounce her— which he did, and persuaded her to accept of his friend. "From that moment," said he, "I was freed from all self-seeking. So that for ten years past I have not done my own will in anything great or small. My own will is hell to me. I can just now renounce my dearest friend without the least reluctance, if God require it." He kissed and blessed me at parting.

Monday, February 7. Before I set out for Oxford, called upon the Count and desired his prayers. He commended himself to our friends there and promised, if any of them would write to him, or the brethren, they would answer them.

Tuesday, February 8. I came to Oxford and took up my lodgings with Mr [John] Sarney. In the evening I met and encouraged our friends by the Count's and Moravians' example. Mr Kinchin[12] I found changed into a courageous soldier of Christ. Read them my brother's journal.

Wednesday, February 9. Met, and accompanied my friend Horne[13] to the convocation, where we carried the election (I came down about) for Mr [William] Bromley[14] our old member: 329 against 125.

Visited my old friends at the Castle,[15] and found honest Thomas Waite still a prisoner there. Mrs Topping was gone where "The prisoners rest together and hear not the voice of the oppressor."[16] Returning, I called at the Blue Posts and found my old pupil Robert Kirkham. Spent the evening as before, in mutual exhortation.

Thursday, February 10. Talked with some of my old proselytes in college. Paid my respects to the Dean,[17] and met with a sharp

---

12. Charles Kinchin (1711–1742), earlier member of the Oxford Methodists and now rector of Dummer, Hampshire.

13. Thomas Horne (b. 1708), a classmate of Charles at Christ Church, and now vicar of Spelsbury.

14. Bromley died very shortly after this election as bursar for the university.

15. "The Castle" here and in following occurrences is a reference to Oxford prison.

16. Cf. Job 3:18.

17. John Conybeare (1692–1755), Dean of Christ Church (1733–1755).

expostulation for voting against him (as he called it). In an hour we came to a right understanding and parted friends.

I dined with Mr Woods of Abingdon, the same kind friendly man he ever was. In the evening I saw Mr Carter[18] and Banny Kirkham and laboured to awaken one and confirm the other. At Mr Sarney's found good Mr [John] Gambold and Kinchin.

Friday, February 11. Exhorted poor languid Smith,[19] and then Carter, to resume all their rules of holy living! In the afternoon was the rector of Lincoln,[20] who received me very affectionately.

Saturday, February 12. By nine at night got back to the Count in London; and consulted him about my journey to Germany.

Tuesday, February 15. Told Mr Oglethorpe my desire of returning with him to Georgia, if I could be of any use there as a clergyman. But as to my secretary's place, I begged him to tell me where, when, and how I should resign it. He bade me think what I did, and when I had well considered the matter, he would talk with me farther.

Friday, February 18. In walking to St Martin's met my dearest friend[21] Appee, who accosted me with inimitable assurance and asked where he might meet me. I appointed Mr Oglethorpe's the next morning.

Saturday, February 19. Waited on Mr Oglethorpe with no great expectation of Appee. He was too wary to keep his appointment.

Sunday, February 20. Being to set out the next day to Tiverton, went to take my leave of the Count, who invited me again to Germany, bade not despair, and dismissed me with his blessing. My last words were *"Sit pax vobiscum;"* to which he replied *"Et cum spirito tuo."*[22]

Monday, February 21. Came in the coach to Reading, and the next evening to Marlborough where I found horses my brother Hall

---

18. Richard Carter (c. 1713–1737?), of Christ Church (1730–1734) and New College (M.A. 1737). He was ordained in 1737 and may have died the same year (see October 1, 1737, entry).

19. Most likely Richard Smith, who matriculated Christ Church in 1732 (age eighteen) and earned his B.A. in 1736 (and M.A. in 1739).

20. Euseby Isham (d. 1755), Rector of Lincoln College, 1731–1755.

21. Charles is speaking sarcastically.

22. "Peace be with you." "And with your spirit."

had sent to bring me to Wootton.[23] With him and my sisters Patty and Kezzy. I stayed till—

Monday, February 28, and then took horse for Bath. The next day got to Wellington, and

MARCH 1737

Wednesday, March 2, nine in the morning reached Tiverton. Ran up stairs to my sister who received me with tears of joy. I saw Phill next, and last my brother,[24] who seemed at least as well as when he left me at London, three years before. Went to comfort my mother, indisposed in her chamber.

Tuesday, March 8. I took horse and on Thursday afternoon got back again to Wootton.

Tuesday, March 15. Set out for London in the Marlborough coach, which had been robbed morning and evening for four days before. This fifth morning we passed unmolested. Scarce was I got to town, when they fell to robbing again.

Thursday, March 17. At Mrs Pendarves found Miss Granville and her brother,[25] who pressed me to bear him company to Mickleton.

Tuesday, March 22. Set out at three in the Oxford coach with Mr Granville, and his sister, and Mr D'Ewes.[26]

Wednesday, March 23. Was much moved at hearing Mr Gambold's history of my brother.

Thursday, March 24. Our company set out again for Mickleton, which we reached by night. We passed the time agreeably enough in walking, conversing, and reading.

---

23. I.e., Wootton Rivers, Wiltshire.
24. Samuel Wesley, Jr., was Headmaster of Blundell's Grammar School in Tiverton. Charles is greeting Samuel's wife, Ursula, and their daughter Phill, before reaching his brother. He then goes to his mother, Susanna, who is now living with Samuel, Jr.
25. Bernard Granville (1700–1776), Duke of Albemarle.
26. John D'Ewes, of Wellesbourne, who married Ann Granville in 1740. Charles spells "Dews."

Wednesday, March 30. Rode over to Stanton[27] where they were all overjoyed to see me, especially my first of friends, Varanese.[28]

[APRIL 1737]

Wednesday, April 6. I had some conversation with Miss Granville about the fewness of those that are saved. How little is she advanced in the school of Christ, who is not convinced of this truth!

Saturday, April 9. In the evening I had the satisfaction of seeing Mr Granville much affected to a chapter he had been reading of Mr Law.[29] He desired his sister might hear it. I read it a second time, and took that opportunity of pressing upon him a daily retirement.

Thursday, April 28. Took horse with Mr Granville and [Mr] D'Ewes. The former left us at Compton,[30] and we rode on towards Spelsbury.[31]

Saturday, April 30. Got back to Mr Sarney's weary and faint, and in a fever through want of sleep.

MAY 1737

Monday, May 2. Between one and two in the morning I betook myself to my usual bed, the floor. Charles Graves breakfasted with me, and owned with tears he had never felt any true joy but in religion. I earnestly recommended Law to him.

At noon visited Mr Gambold, right glad to see me. Found him much cheerfuller than usual. His sister [Martha] just the same. In the afternoon I talked with the prisoners, very attentive; with the Dean, very kind and friendly.

Tuesday, May 3. At two Mr Sarney rose to pray for me. I rose too, and set out for London, which I reached in a few hours.

---

27. Stanton, Gloucestershire, where Robert Kirkham was rector.
28. The Wesley brothers' nickname for Sarah ("Sally") Kirkham, who in 1725 married John Chapone. Charles spells "Varanes."
29. Most likely, again, Law's *Serious Call* (see October 17, 1736, entry above).
30. I.e., Long Compton, Warwickshire.
31. Charles spells "Spilsbury."

Thursday, May 5. I met Verelst and council at Mr Oglethorpe's about the hearing they are shortly to have before the Board of Trade. When they were gone, Mr Oglethorpe said if the government had dropped Georgia, he would not let the poor people perish, but sell his estate, which he could do for £45,000, and support them upon the interest.

Friday, May 20. At her desire, I waited upon Lady Betty Hastings. Her inquiries about Georgia were interrupted by the Bishop of Gloucester's coming.[32]

Saturday, May 21. Rode out of town to meet my brother and sister from Tiverton, and attended them to Mr Powel's.

Monday, May 30. Carried my brother to the good Archbishop,[33] who received us very kindly.

JUNE 1737

Wednesday, June 1. Accepted an invitation from Mrs Benson, and rode down to Cheshunt Nunnery.[34] Miss Kitty and Mrs Johnson were there before me. I was much delighted both with the place and the company. After dinner I missed my letter-book, and rode back to town, seeking it in vain. By seven next morning I was at the Nunnery again, and returned to London in the afternoon.

Friday, June 3. Between six and seven this evening I took horse for Cheshunt, eighteen miles from London; got there by nine; and the next morning rode eighteen miles farther, to Hatfield,[35] to see my sister Nancy.[36] In the afternoon I returned to the Nunnery.

Trinity Sunday, June 5. We all went in an hired coach to Wormley, where I preached "Few saved,"[37] and was pleased to see the family stay the unexpected Sacrament. In the evening rode back to town.

---

32. Martin Benson (1689–1752) was Bishop of Gloucester, 1734–1752.
33. John Potter (c. 1674–1747) had just been elevated to Archbishop of Canterbury.
34. The site of a medieval nunnery, this was now an estate near Cheshunt, Hertfordshire.
35. The descriptions here and in the August 17, 1737, entry rule out Hatfield, Herefordshire. It is most likely Hatfield Heath or Hatfield Broad Oak, Essex.
36. The nickname for his sister Anne, now married to John Lambert.
37. Cf. Luke 13:23.

Monday, June 6. At ten we were again before the Board of Trade. Till twelve Carolina side was heard. Then our council (confused enough) was heard for Georgia.

Wednesday, June 8. I made affidavit in Chancery Lane as to what I knew relating to Georgia. At one I called upon my uncle, and found him exceeding ill.

Thursday, June 9. At the Board, part of our Charter and Acts were read, etc. I declared upon oath that all the traders licensed were supposed to be within Georgia. After my affidavit was read, [William] Murray made our defence, but so little to Mr Oglethorpe's satisfaction that he started up and ran out.

I dined with my brother at Lord Oxford's.[38] Lady Oxford,[39] Lord Duplin,[40] and the famed Lady Mary[41] were of the company.

Saturday, June 11. Found my uncle dying. He pressed my hand, showed much natural affection, and bade me give his love to his sister. Spent the evening at Cheshunt, in reading Mr Law to the family—my usual employment there.

Sunday evening, [June 12]. I heard that my uncle died a little after I left him.

Monday, June [13]. Waited on my brother and sister a little way on their road to Tiverton.

On Wednesday I breakfasted at the nunnery.

On Thursday night attended my uncle to his grave.

Friday, June 17. I heard the last of my friend Appee's adventures here from one Mr Laba, a cutler; from whom he had just stole a watch, and run away with it to Paris.

Saturday, June 18. Before the Board of Trade for the last time, to hear Carolina's reply to Georgia. Spent the rest of the month between Cheshunt and Hatfield.

JULY 1737

Saturday, July 2. I was at the Nunnery, and the next day preached at Hatfield. Slept at Cheshunt.

---

38. Edward Harley, 2nd Earl of Oxford and Mortimer (1689–1741).
39. Henrietta Cavendish Harley (1693–1755).
40. Thomas Hay (1710–1797), Viscount Dupplin, and later 9th Earl of Kinnoull.
41. Lady Mary Wortley Montagu (1689–1762).

Monday, July 4. In the evening set out for Oxford. Came thither the next day, where James Hutton had got before me. In the evening young Graves came to me at Sarney's, in an excellent temper. I encouraged him to go on in the narrow way,[42] and strongly recommended stated hours of retirement.

Thursday, July 7. I pressed the same upon poor Smith in our walk to Mr Gambold's, where I found my sister Kezzy.[43] I got back to dinner with Lady Cox[44] and her sisters.

In the evening Graves told me that on this day he first felt the beginnings of the change, and was convinced of the reality of what he only believed before upon my brother's and my testimony. He appeared full of joy and love.

Saturday, July 9. Set out with James for Wootton. Quite spent, I laid me down and slept for a quarter of an hour upon the ground. By two we reached Marlborough, and by four, Wootton. My mother was lately come thither from Tiverton.

Monday, July 11. Meeting Charles Graves at Bath, we could get no farther. He carried us to see the quarries, where I narrowly missed being dashed to pieces.

On *Wednesday, July 13,* we came safe to Tiverton.

Saturday, July 23, and Sunday, 24. At Wootton. Days never to be forgot!

Monday, July 25. I heard at Oxford that Charles Graves had been carried away by his friends as stark mad.

Thursday, July 28. Spied Robinson[45] and Battely[46] in the Longwalk and crossed over to speak with them. They fell upon me unawares, desiring me to take some of the Cowley saints[47] to Georgia;

---

42. Cf. Matt. 7:14.

43. John Gambold was vicar of Stanton Harcourt, Oxfordshire. He had recently agreed to host Charles's sister Kezzy, so that she did not have to live with Westley Hall (cf. the December 6, 1736, entry above).

44. Lady Mary Cox (*née* Bethel), second wife of Sir Robert Cox (1659–1726), 2nd baronet, of Dumbleton. The last name is more properly "Cocks."

45. Matthew Robinson (c. 1713–1745), a student of John Wesley at Lincoln College and now a fellow at Brasenose.

46. Oliver Battely (b. 1697?), of Oxford (B.A. Christ Church, 1720; M.A. 1723/24; B.D. 1734). Charles spells "Bateley."

47. Battely had served for several years as curate at Cowley (Oxfordshire), and was likely using the term "saints" ironically in reference to some of his parishioners.

charged the Methodists with intrusion, schism, and bringing neglect upon the ministry. We differed *toto coelo*.[48] I left them with, "Remember, you will be of my mind when you come to die."

Friday, July 29. We set out for London with Mr Morgan[49] and Mr Kinchin, and on

Saturday, July [30],[50] finished our travels at College Street,[51] where I had the satisfaction of finding my old hearty friend, Benjamin Ingham.

AUGUST 1737

Monday, August 1. I read Mr Oglethorpe my brother's letter to the Trustees, charging Horton with raising a scandalous report about me. He would not advise one way or the other, which I interpreted as a dissuasive and therefore took no farther notice of the matter.

Wednesday, August 17. After spending some time at Hatfield, I set out with my brother Lambert[52] for London. At Epping he went back, full of good resolutions.

Thursday, August 18. Hearing that Mrs Delamotte[53] was now in town, I went to see her. We fell into discourse upon resignation, and she seemed resolved to acquiesce in the will of God, detaining her Isaac from her.

Sunday, August 21. Took horse again for Hatfield. Read prayers and preached at Wormley, called on Dr Nichols, and rode on.

My brother I left on [*Wednesday*] the twenty-fourth, in excellent temper. Called and dined at Dr Newton's.

Thursday, August 25. After giving the Sacrament to a sick woman, I breakfasted with Mr Chadwick. We had some close talk

---

48. A Latin phrase signifying the concurrence of "all the heavens"; i.e., entirely.
49. Richard Morgan (1714–1785), young brother of William Morgan, whose death in 1732 had been attributed to the rigorous discipline of the Oxford Methodists.
50. MS has "July 31," which is in error.
51. I.e., the home of John Hutton.
52. This is Charles's brother-in-law, John Lambert, married to Anne ("Nancy").
53. Elizabeth Delamotte (1685–1771), mother of Charles Delamotte.

about the new birth, with which he was greatly moved. I took opportunity of recommending regular retirement, and religious acquaintance. I preached at Ludgate,[54] dined with Mrs Musgrave, and called in the afternoon at Mrs Delamotte's. The Cambridge youth[55] was there; but we had no very useful conversation.

Friday, August 26. I waited upon His Majesty at Hampton Court, with the Oxford address,[56] by the advice of Mr Potter. The Archbishop told me he was glad to see me there. We kissed their Majesty's hands, and were invited to dinner. I left that, and the company, and hasted back to town. The next day [*August 27*] we waited upon his Royal Highness,[57] and dined all together at St James's [palace].

Wednesday, August 31. I talked at large upon my state with Mr [William] Law at Putney. The sum of his advice was, "Renounce yourself; and be not impatient."

SEPTEMBER 1737

Friday, September 9. Consulted Mr Law a second time, and asked him several questions:
[*Wesley:*] "With what comment shall I read the Scriptures?"
[*Law:*] "None."
[*Wesley:*] "What do you think of one who dies unrenewed, while endeavouring after it?"
[*Law:*] "It concerns neither you to ask, nor me to answer."
[*Wesley:*] "Shall I write once more to such a person?"
[*Law:*] "No."
[*Wesley:*] "But I am persuaded it will do him good."
[*Law:*] "Sir, I have told you my opinion."
[*Wesley:*] "Shall I write to you?"
[*Law:*] "Nothing I can either speak or write will do you any good."

---

54. A debtor's prison at one of the main gates in London Wall. George Whitefield had preached there regularly in 1736.
55. I.e., William ("Jack/Jacky") Delamotte (1718–1743), brother of Charles Delamotte, and a student at Cambridge.
56. The Vice-Chancellor and several heads of house of Oxford University came to the royal palace in Hampton, Middlesex, this day to present an address congratulating King George II and his wife, Caroline, on the birth of a new princess (granddaughter). As a fellow of Christ Church, Charles joined the party and met the royal couple.
57. Frederick, Prince of Wales, son of George II.

Saturday, September 10. Calling at Mr Delamotte's.[58] I found Miss Hetty[59] there, and gave her her brother's letter. We soon fell into talk about the new birth. She lamented her not being acquainted with me sooner, and that she could not be in the country now I was going thither. I walked back to Charles Rivington's and fetched her Mr Law,[60] and then took coach for Eltham and Blendon.[61] My friend Benjamin [Ingham] had been there before me, and met with such a reception as encouraged me to follow. He had preached to them with power, and still more powerfully by his life and conversation. The eldest sister,[62] and Cambridge scholar [William], were struck to the heart. The first evening passed in discourse of my namesake in America.

Sunday, September 11. I preached "The One Thing Needful" [Luke 10:42]. Had some serious talk with Miss Betsy, and read to Mrs Delamotte part of my journal relating to their intended visitant [Peter] Appee.

Monday, September 12. Returned to town and spent an hour with Hetty in discoursing on the inward change and reading Law. She received all his sayings with the utmost readiness.

Tuesday, September 13. I went again to my simple Hetty, to learn some of her humility. Her convictions were much deepened by my reading of the *Life of God in the Soul of Man*.[63] I took my leave and set out for Oxford, by way of Windsor and Mr Thorold's.[64]

Thursday, September 15. Rose (at Sarney's) with earnest desires of resigning myself up entirely to God. Had the satisfaction of seeing an excellent letter from young Graves in the country.

Friday, September 16. Walked over with Mr Gambold to Stanton Harcourt. After much talk of their states, we agreed that I should not speak at all to my sister [Kezzy] on religion, but fully to his.

---

58. Peter Delamotte (d. 1749), husband of Elizabeth. (Note: He is sometimes wrongly identified as a "Thomas" Delamotte.)

59. Esther ("Hetty") Delamotte (1712–1779), sister of Charles Delamotte.

60. That is, he fetched a copy of Law's book from Charles Rivington's bookstore.

61. Blendon Hall, home of the Delamotte family, near Bexley, Kent, about 12 miles southeast of London.

62. Elizabeth ("Betty/Betsy") Delamotte (1710–1780).

63. Henry Scougal (1650–1678), *The Life of God in the Soul of Man* (London: Charles Smith & William Jacob, 1677).

64. John Thorold (1703–1775), who had preceded John Wesley in a fellowship at Lincoln College, Oxford, and would later become Sir John Thorold, 8th baronet.

Calling accidentally in the evening at my sister's room, she fell upon my neck, and in a flood of tears begged me to pray for her. Seeing her so softened, I did not know but this might be her time, and sat down. She anticipated me by saying she had felt here what she never felt before, and believed now there was such a thing as the new creature. She was full of earnest wishes for divine love; owned there was a depth in religion she had never fathomed; that she was not, but longed to be, converted; would give up all to obtain the love of God; renewed her request with great vehemence that I would pray for her; often repeating, "I am weak, I am exceeding weak." I prayed over her, and blessed God from my heart. Then used Pascal's prayer for conversion,[65] with which she was much affected, and begged me to write it out for her.

After supper (at which I could not eat for joy), I read Mr Law's account of redemption.[66] She was greatly moved, full of tears, and sighs, and eagerness for more. Poor Mrs Gambold[67] was quite unaffected, her time being not yet come.

Saturday, September 17. I prayed with Kezzy, still in the same temper, convinced all her misery had proceeded from her not loving God.

This morning Mr [Christopher] Wells of Jesus College came in. I took occasion to mention Mr Law on the redemption, read part of it, and rejoiced in his so cordially joining us.

Sunday, September 18. I preached at the Castle, and gave the Sacrament to threescore communicants. In the afternoon at Stanton Harcourt. Was continually called upon by Kezzy to pray with her. We supped at Mr Bonnel's.

Wednesday, September 21. Rejoiced to hear at Oxford that Graves was returned from his friends unshaken. At night he came in (to Sarney's), fell upon my neck, and burst into tears. 'Tis hard to say whether his friends' hatred, or his love, of me exceeds.

Thursday, September 22. Breakfasted with Mr Rock at Newnham,[68] and dined at Mapledurham with Mr [John] Burton. Next

---

65. I.e., Pascal's "Prayer composed in Sickness," which is focused on conversion.
66. Likely Law, *Serious Call*, 472ff.
67. Elizabeth Gambold (d. 1744), mother of John.
68. Newnham Hill, Oxfordshire.

morning got to Mr Thorold's at Windsor, and in two hours to London. But my hard riding had nearly occasioned my being apprehended for an highwayman.

Saturday, September 24. At twelve set out for Blendon. Passing Mr Delamotte's I was reminded to call, though they were all out of town. Contrary to my expectation, I found Hetty left behind. We passed two hours in conference and prayer.

Two hours afterwards I was with her again, and read Scougal on "Few Saved." She was quite melted down, and after a prayer for love, said, "God knows my heart. I do desire nothing but him."

Sunday, September 25. I met her at the Sacrament in Crooked Lane,[69] and endeavoured to prepare her for persecution, which all must suffer who will live godly in Christ Jesus.

Tuesday, September 27. Rode to Windsor, and next day to Mapledurham by noon. An hour after I took horse, and quickly lost myself in a wood, but by breaking fences, and leaping ditches, got at last to Dorchester. I lost myself again between that and Nuneham,[70] but soon recovered it and by night came to honest Mr Sarney's.

Thursday, September 29. Found Graves and Kezzy still pressing forward.

In the afternoon met Mr Wells alone, and had some close talk with him upon the new birth, self-renunciation, etc. He confessed reputation was his idol; rejected his own righteousness; convinced, but fearful; longing to break loose. I went with him to the chapel, and afterwards resumed the subject. He seemed on the brink of the new birth.

OCTOBER 1737

Saturday, October 1. I prayed by Mr Carter, who lay a-dying; and by Mrs Sarney, in the same condition.

Sunday, October 2. Carried Graves to Stanton Harcourt, where I gave the Sacrament, and then preached at South Leigh. In the evening we returned to Oxford.

---

69. St Michael's Church, Crooked Lane, London.
70. Nuneham Courtenay, Oxfordshire.

Monday, October 3. At six took horse for Berkswell. A little on this side [of] Banbury my horse threw me, with great violence, over his head, and tumbled after, but not upon me. I rose first, unhurt, except that I sprained my leg. With much wandering through excessive bad roads by night, I got to Mr Boyce's, quite exhausted.

Tuesday, October 4. Waked much refreshed. The family showed me all possible civility, especially dear Susan, for whose sake I had come.

Wednesday, October 5. Parted as friends should part. I returned before night to Oxford.

Friday, October 7. Received a letter from James Hutton, summoning me on board in fourteen days.

Saturday, October 8. Endeavoured to fix Kinchin, Sarney, [Henry] Washington, and Hutchings[71] in meeting as my brother, etc., used formerly. Rode to Spelsbury to see my old friend Horne, and returned by night to read at Queen's.

Sunday, October 9. Gave the Sacrament and preached at South Leigh. In the evening at dear Charles [Grave]'s, still growing in humility and love.

Monday, October 10. Being determined not to leave England till I had come to a full explanation with Dicky Graves,[72] this morning I went to his rooms, talked the whole matter over, and were both entirely satisfied.

Then I spoke of my making his brother Charles mad; hoped he himself would be one of those whose life fools count madness; explained the nature of true religion: "no other than what you once laboured after, till the gentleman swallowed up the Christian." He was greatly moved, complained he could not pray. I appealed to him whether he had not formerly felt more solid pleasure in religion than in all the caresses of the world. He confessed it, and resolved to return. I earnestly recommended Law, and daily retirement, as my last legacy. "My heart's desire to God for you is, that you may be saved. In a little time, all I can do will be to pray for

---

71. John Hutchings (b. 1716), of Pembroke College, Oxford. Charles spells "Hutchins."
72. Richard Graves (1715–1804), older brother of Charles and later author of *The Spiritual Quixote* (London: Dodsley, 1773).

you. And I hope you will now pray for me, as for a friend, not an enemy."[73] He answered, "That I shall do heartily. I am satisfied you are my sincere friend." We then kissed, and parted—till that day.

Tuesday, October 11. Set out for London. In a mile's riding my horse fell lame. I sung the 91st Psalm, and put myself under the divine protection. I had scarce ended, and turned the hut, on Shotover Hill, when a man came up to me and demanded my money, showing, but not presenting, a pistol. I gave him my purse. He asked how much there was. "About thirty shillings." "Have you no more?" "I will see." Put my hand in my pocket, and gave him some halfpence. He repeated the question, "Have you no more?" I had thirty pounds in a private pocket. Bade him search himself, which he did not choose. He ordered me to dismount, which I did, but begged hard for my horse again, promising not to pursue him. He took my word, and restored him. I rode gently on, praising God. My bags, and watch, and gold, the robber was *forced* to leave me. By the evening I reached Westminster.

Friday, October 14. I was informed at the office that I was to go in three weeks with the Lieutenant Colonel by way of Gibraltar.

Sunday, October 16. Rode to Blendon, and read S. S.[74] to the two sisters, and prayed with them for conversion. Employed again in like manner after the opposers were gone to bed.

Tuesday, October 18. Jacky Delamotte and I took horse. Mine fell into a hole, but I kept my seat. His followed, and flung him over his head. Neither hurt.

Friday, October 28. Found Miss Betty[75] at Fresh Wharf, and spent an hour or two with her and Jacky. Next morning I was with her alone, and spoke largely of the danger of lukewarmness, and resting in negative goodness. I never saw her so moved before.

Sunday, October 30. Waked them at five, and attended them to Forster Lane,[76] where we heard Mr Whitefield and communicated

73. Cf. Rom. 10:11.
74. Almost certainly a reference to Samuel Shaw (1635–1696), *Immanuel: or, A Discourse of True Religion, as it imports a Living Principle in the Minds of Men* (London: s.n., 1667). John Wesley records reading this book together with Charles in his Oxford diary (3–6 Feb. 1735); and there is a copy in MARC (ref. MAW CW9) with Wesley's name (but not date) inscribed.
75. Charles uses both "Betsy" and "Betty" to refer to the eldest Delamotte sister.
76. This would be St Vedast's Church, on Forster Lane (now Foster Lane), London.

together. I preached at St Helen's[77] "The One Thing Needful" [Luke 10:42]. In the afternoon I carried her and her brother to Mr Chadwick's (my usual lodgings), and thence to Ironmonger's Lane.[78] After preaching the same sermon here, we drank tea at Mr Chadwick's, and then took coach for College Street.[79] They were much delighted with the singing there, and edified, I hope, by George Whitefield's example. 'Twas near eleven before I left them at their own house.

NOVEMBER 1737

Wednesday, November 2. I was at the office and returned the Trustees thanks for the £50 they had lately ordered me, as a missionary. Dined with them, and they desired me to draw up a scheme for an orphan-house. The evening I passed at Fresh Wharf. Good old Mr Delamotte was there, and pleased me much by his seeming so heartily to relish our reading Bishop Hall.

Friday, November 4. Heard an excellent sermon at St Antholin's[80] on holiness, or likeness to God; and passed the evening with brother Delamotte, who then told me the reason why I was not sent for to Blendon was Mrs Delamotte's fear of my making Hetty run mad. And when I gave them notice of my coming, she sent her up to town, that I might not see her—which Providence made the means of my having so many hours with her alone.

Saturday, November 5. I met and turned back with Betty, to hear Mr Whitefield preach, not with the persuasive words of man's wisdom, but with the demonstration of the Spirit and with power.[81] The churches will not contain the multitudes that throng to hear him.

Monday, November 7. I read over *Pietas Hallensis*[82] and desired our orphan-house might be begun in the power of faith.

---

77. St Helen's Church, Bishopsgate, London.
78. That is, at the Church of St Olave Jewry, which stood on the corner of St Olave's Court and Old Jewry (only the tower remains).
79. I.e., the home of Rev. John Hutton.
80. St Antholin's Church, Budge Row, London. The church is now gone, but there is a marker of its location at the intersection of Watling Street and Queen Victoria Street.
81. Cf. 1 Cor. 2:4.
82. August Hermann Franke, *Pietas Hallensis; or, A Public Demonstration of the Foot-steps of a Divine Being yet in the World. In an Historical Narration of the Orphan-House and other Charitable Institutions, at Glaucha, near Hall, in Saxony* (Edinburgh: J. Davidson, 1727).

Thursday, November 10. In obedience to a summons from Miss Betsy this morning, I took coach for Greenwich, and walked the rest of the way to Blendon. We had some animating discourse before Mrs Delamotte came in. Then we fell into talk of the new birth, which she did not at all relish, but continued still cold, averse, and prejudiced against the truth.

Sunday, November 13. Preached at Bexley on the love of God.[83] Mrs Delamotte thanked me for my sermon with tears, owned she had loved Charles too well, and was quite altered in her behaviour towards me. We had farther conversation on the love of God. Mr Delamotte confessed there could be no happiness in anything else.

Monday, November 14. Little Molly[84] burst into tears upon my telling her God loved her. The whole family now appear not far from the kingdom of God.

Sunday, November 20. At St Helen's I preached the circumcision of heart.[85] The next day my flux returned.

Tuesday, November 22. Mr Oglethorpe advised me to go to Tiverton. Went to take my leave of our friends at Blendon. Mrs Delamotte was quite open, and not afraid that her son should be called a Methodist.

Friday, November 25. At Mr Hutton's this evening, my brothers Lambert and Wright[86] visited me. The latter has corrupted the former, after all the pains I have taken with him, and brought him back to drinking. I was full, yet could not speak. Prayed for meekness, and then set before him the things he had done in the devil's name, toward reconverting a soul to him. He left us abruptly. I encouraged poor John Lambert to turn again unto God.

Monday, November 28. Took coach for Tiverton. The next day called on my mother in Salisbury.[87] She vehemently protested against our returning to Georgia.

---

83. Charles was preaching John Wesley's sermon on Mark 10:23; cf. *Sermons*, 348–59.
84. Miss Mary ("Molly") Delamotte (b. 1729), youngest sister of Charles Delamotte.
85. Charles was likely preaching a transcript of John Wesley's sermon by this title, on Rom. 2:29. Cf. John Wesley, *Works* 1:401–14.
86. This would be William Wright, married to Charles's sister Mehetabel ("Hetty").
87. Westley Hall had just moved to a small parish in Salisbury and Susannah was here visiting her daughter Patty (cf. the December 29 entry).

Wednesday, November 30. Had much serious conversation with a gentlewoman in the coach concerning the new birth. I read part of Mr Law. She was deeply struck, melted, conquered.

DECEMBER 1737

Thursday, December 1. We lodged at Dorchester, when my distemper fully returned.

Friday, December 2. Met horses at Honiton, and by four came to Tiverton, where I found my brother much better.

Sunday, December 4. Was much melted at the Sacrament. In the evening I reproved my sister[88] (which I am often forced to do) for evil speaking.

Thursday, December 22. Quite wearied out by her incessant slanders, today I had a downright quarrel with her about it. My brother on these occasions is either silent or on my side.

Tuesday, December 27. I was not sorry to set out for London. I rode as far as Taunton.

Wednesday, December 28. In the coach employed myself mostly in reading Cyrus's *Travels*,[89] and Leslie's *Short Method with the Deists*.[90]

Thursday, December 29. Narrowly escaped overturning, through the loss of a wheel. Supped in Salisbury, at my brother Hall's.

Saturday, December 31. Set out at two in the morning, and with the night came to James Hutton's.

JANUARY 1738

Thursday, January 5. Made frequent visits this month to Blendon, and rejoiced over Mrs Delamotte, now entirely cordial and

---

88. That is, his sister-in-law Ursula.

89. Andrew Michael Ramsay (1686–1743), *The Travels of Cyrus*, 2 vols. (London: Woodward & Peele, 1727). The title on the binding for this set was "Cyrus's Travels." Charles later purchased a copy of the 1728 French edition, which is in MARC (ref. MAW CW52), with his signature and the date Feb. 22, 1762, inscribed.

90. Charles Leslie (1650–1722), *A Short and Easy Method with the Deists* (London: Brome, 1699). There is a 1723 edition of this work in MARC (ref. MAW CW50), with Charles's signature and the date 1747 inscribed.

friendly. We were joined by Mr [Henry] Piers, the minister of Bexley, who delighted in every opportunity of conversing, singing, praying with us.

FEBRUARY 1738

Friday, February 3. In the afternoon news was brought me at James Hutton's that my brother was come from America. I could not believe, till at night I saw him. He comes, not driven away, but to tell the true state of the colony, which according to his account is truly deplorable.

Saturday, February 4. Informed Mr Oglethorpe of his arrival. He was very inquisitive into the cause of his coming; said he ought not to have returned without the Trustees' leave.

At ten, before the Council, heard the fresh pleadings for Carolina.

Monday, February 6. Waited on the good Archbishop, who received me with his usual kindness.

Wednesday, February 8. With the Trustees, who were surprised by my brother's account of Georgia, the fewness of the people, etc.

Friday, February 10. We dined at Mr Vernon's, who accosted me, "Well, sir, I hope you intend returning to Georgia." I answered, "That is my desire and design." Heard more of the great discouragements the poor people labour under.

Saturday, February 11. Heard clerk plead for Georgia before the Council, and Mr Oglethorpe's speech.

Thursday, February 16. Mr Oglethorpe told me, "Your brother must have a care. There is a very strong spirit raising against him. People say he is come over to do mischief to the colony. He will be called upon for his reasons why he left the people." I answered, "Sir, he has been twice before the Board for that purpose, but was not asked that question, and therefore had no opportunity to answer it. He will attend them again on Wednesday morning."

Waited on his Lordship of London, and informed him of my brother's return. He spoke honourably of him, expressed a great desire to see him, asked many questions about Georgia and the Trustees, forgot his usual reserve, and dismissed me very kindly.

Friday, February 17. Came in the Oxford coach to my old lodgings at Mr Sarney's.

Saturday, February 18. Rode over to Stanton Harcourt to see John Gambold and my sister [Kezzy]. My brother met us. We prayed and sang together. In the evening I prayed at Mr Sarney's with some scholars and a Moravian [Peter Böhler].

Sunday, February 19. Received the Sacrament once more at Christ Church.

Monday, February 20. Began teaching Peter Böhler English.

Tuesday, February 21. In the afternoon I lay down, half distracted with the toothache.

Wednesday, February 22. Waked much better. At five had some close conversation with Peter Böhler, who pressed upon our scholars the necessity of combining, and instanced in many awakened, but fallen asleep again, for want of it. He talked much of the necessity of prayer and faith.

Friday, February 24. At six in the evening, an hour after I had taken my electuary, the toothache returned more violently than ever. I smoked tobacco, which set me to avomiting, and took away my sense and pain together. At eleven I waked in extreme pain, which I thought would quickly separate soul and body. Soon after Peter Böhler came to my bedside. I asked him to pray for me. He seemed unwilling at first, but beginning very faintly he raised his voice by degrees, and prayed for my recovery with strange confidence. Then he took me by the hand and calmly said, "You will not die now." I thought within myself, "I cannot hold out in this pain till morning. If it abates before, I believe I may recover." He asked me, "Do you hope to be saved?" "Yes." "For what reason do you hope it?" "Because I have used my best endeavours to serve God?" He shook his head, and said no more. I thought him very uncharitable, saying in my heart, "What, are not my endeavours a sufficient ground of hope? Would he rob me of my endeavours? I have nothing else to trust to."

By morning my pain was moderated. Ted Bentham[1] calling then persuaded me to be blooded. I continued in great pain. In the evening he brought Dr [Pierce] Manaton. On Saturday morning I was blooded again; and at night a third time.

Sunday, February 26. Mr Wells brought my sister Kezzy. Dr Frewin[2] came. I dictated a letter to Dr Cockburn and James Hutton.

Monday, February 27. The scale seemed to turn for life. I had prayed that my pains might not outlast this day; and was answered.

Tuesday, February 28. My dear James Hutton came post from London, and brought me Dr Cockburn's letter and directions!

As soon as I was able, sent my brother at Tiverton the following account.

> Dear Brother, I borrow another's hand, as I cannot use my own. You remember Dr South's saying, "I have been within the jaws of death, but he was not suffered to shut his mouth upon me."[3] I ought never to forget it. Dr Manaton told me he expected to have found me dead at his second visit. This several remarkable accidents concurred to hinder. I had kept in a week before the pleurisy came, and taken physic twice. At midnight it seized me so violently, that I never expected to see the morning. In the preceding afternoon I had taken Dr Cockburn's electuary, and an hour after was visited by so outrageous a toothache, that it forced me to the abominable remedy of a pipe. This quickly made me discharge my astringent, and in all probability saved my life, binding medicines being poison in a pleuritic fever. I took my illness for the flux, and so never thought of sending for a physician. Ted Bentham fetched him against my will, and was probably the instrument of saving my life a second time. Dr Manaton called in Dr Frewin. They bled me three times, and poured down draughts, oils, and apozems without end. For four days the balance was even. Then, as Spencer says, "I over-wrestled my strong enemy."[4] Ever since I have been slowly gathering strength, and yesterday took my first journey to my sister's room, who has been with me from the beginning, and no small comfort to me.

---

1. Edward Bentham (1707–1776), earlier Oxford Methodist, tutor at Oriel College.
2. Richard Frewin, M.D. (c. 1681–1761), of Christ Church; physician and Professor of Ancient History. Charles spells "Fruin."
3. Cf. Robert South (1634–1716), *Twelve Sermons upon Several Subjects*, Vol. 3 (London: Thomas Bennett, 1698), 478. Charles's signed copy of this volume is in MARC (ref. MAW CW26).
4. Edmund Spenser (1552?–1599), *The Faerie Queen*, Bk. I, canto 7, st. 24.

One consequence of my sickness you will not be sorry for—its stopping my sudden return to Georgia. For the doctor tells me to undertake a voyage now would be certain death. Some reasons for *his* not going immediately my brother will mention to you in person.

Before I was taken ill, my brother set out for Tiverton, but came back instead of proceeding on his journey, stayed a week with me, and then went with Mr Kinchin to Manchester.

For some days that I continued mending, I was greatly tormented with the toothache. One day I prayed that the pain might be suspended, and it was for all that day.

Had Dr Frewin to my sister, taken ill. We communicated almost every day.

MARCH 1738

Tuesday, March 28. Was greatly moved in reading the *Life of Mr Halyburton*.[5]

APRIL 1738

Monday, April 3. By my brother's advice I resolved to give up my secretary's place, and today wrote my letter of resignation.

Saturday, April 8. Got abroad to the evening prayers at Christ Church, and received comfort from the lessons and anthem.

Wednesday, April 12. Received Mr Oglethorpe's answer to my letter of resignation, wherein he offered, if I would keep my place, to get it supplied in my absence by a deputy.

Saturday, April 15. Drs Frewin and Manaton called and forbade my voyage. Both as physicians and friends they advised me not to go, but stay at college, since I might, as Senior Master, expect *offices and preferment*.

Wednesday, April 19. I came up to town to take my leave of Mr Oglethorpe, who received me with his accustomed kindness. The next day I had the satisfaction of once more meeting that man of God, Peter Böhler.

---

5. Thomas Halyburton (1674–1712), *Memoirs of the Life of the Reverend Mr Thomas Halyburton* (Edinburgh: Andrew Anderson, 1714).

Monday, April 24. I took a ride to Blendon. In the afternoon we made Mr Piers a visit, and returning, found Mr [Thomas] Broughton and my brother at Blendon.

Tuesday, April 25. Soon after five, as we were met in the little chapel, Mrs Delamotte came to us. Sang, fell into a dispute whether conversion was gradual or instantaneous. My brother was very positive for the latter, and very shocking—mentioned some later instances of gross sinners believing in a moment. I was much offended at his worse than unedifying discourse. Mrs Delamotte left us abruptly. I stayed, and insisted a man need not know when first he had faith. His obstinacy in favouring the contrary drove me at last out of the room. Mr Broughton was only not so much scandalized as myself. After dinner, he and my brother returned to town. I stayed behind, and read them the *Life of Mr Halyburton*— one instance, but only one, of instantaneous conversion.

Wednesday, April 26. Passed the day at Mr Piers's in singing and reading and mutual encouragement. In the evening we finished *Halyburton*. The meltingness it occasioned in me (like those before) soon passed away as a morning cloud. Next morning I returned to London.

Friday, April 28. No sooner was I got to James Hutton's, having removed my things thither from his father's, than the pain in my side returned, and with that my fever. Having disappointed God in his last visitation, he has now again brought me to the bed of sickness. Towards midnight I received some relief by bleeding. In the morning Dr Cockburn came to see me; and a better physician, Peter Böhler, whom God had detained in England for my good. He stood by my bedside, and prayed over me, that now at least I might see the divine intention in this and my late illness. I immediately thought it might be that I should again consider Böhler's doctrine of faith; examine myself whether I was in *the faith*; and if I was not, never cease seeking and longing after it till I attained it.

MAY 1738

Monday, May 1. Mr Piers called to see me. I exhorted him to labour after that faith which he thinks I have, and I know I have not. After receiving the Sacrament, I felt a small anticipation of peace and said, "Now I have demonstrated against the Moravian doctrine that a man cannot have peace without assurance of his pardon. I now have peace, yet cannot say of a surety that my sins are forgiven." The next and several times after that I received the Sacrament, I had not so much as bare attention, God no longer trusting me with comfort, which I should immediately turn against himself.

For some days following I felt a faint longing for faith, and could pray for nothing else. My desires were quickened by a letter of Mr [John] Edmonds,[6] seeking Christ as in an agony.

Saturday, May 6. God still kept up the little spark of desire, which he himself had enkindled in me, and I seemed determined to speak of, and wish for, nothing but faith in Christ. Yet could not this preserve me from sin, which I this day ran into with my eyes open. So that after ten years' vain struggling, I own and feel it absolutely unconquerable.

By bearing witness to the truth before Miss Delamotte, Mr Baldwyn, and others, I found my desires of apprehending Christ increased.

Thursday, May 11. I was just going to remove to old Mr Hutton's when God sent Mr [John] Bray to me, a poor ignorant mechanic, who knows nothing but Christ—yet by knowing him, knows and discerns all things. Some time ago I had taken leave of Peter Böhler, confessed my unbelief and want of forgiveness, but declared my firm persuasion that I should receive the atonement before I died. His answer was, "Be it unto thee according to thy faith."

Mr Bray is now to supply Böhler's place. We prayed together for faith. I was quite overpowered and melted into tears, and hereby induced to think it was God's will that I should go to his house, and not to Mr Hutton's. He was of the same judgment. Accordingly I was carried thither in a chair.[7]

His sister I found in earnest pursuit of Christ; his wife well inclined to conversion. I had not been here long when Mr Broughton called. I hoped to find him altered like myself, but alas, his time is not yet come! As to Mrs Turner, he gave her up. "But for

---

6. Charles spells "Edmunds."
7. *OED* notes that "chair" was often used in the eighteenth century for a "chaise" or light vehicle pulled by a single horse.

you, Mrs Bray," said he, "I hope you are still in your senses, and not run mad after a faith which must be felt." He went on contradicting and blaspheming. I thought it my duty to withstand him, and to confess my want of faith. "God help you, poor man," he replied: "if I could think you have not faith, I am sure it would drive me to despair." I put all my hopes of ever attaining it, or eternal salvation, upon the truth of this assertion, "*I have not now the faith of the gospel.*"

As soon as he left us, Mr Bray read me many comfortable Scriptures, which greatly strengthened my desire. So that I was persuaded I should not leave his house before I believed with my heart unto righteousness.[8]

Friday, May 12. I waked in the same blessed temper, hungry and thirsty after God. I began Isaiah, and seemed to see that to me were the promises made, and would be fulfilled, for that Christ loved me. Found myself more desirous, more assured I should believe. This day (and indeed my whole time) I spent discoursing on faith, either with those that had it or those that sought it, in reading the Scripture, and in prayer.

I was much moved at the sight of Mr Ainsworth,[9] a man of great learning above seventy who, like old Simeon, was waiting to see the Lord's salvation, that he might depart in peace.[10] His tears, and vehemence, and childlike simplicity, showed him upon the entrance of the kingdom of heaven.[11]

In the afternoon I read Isaiah with Mr Edmonds, saw him full of promises, and that they belonged to me. In the midst of our reading Miss Claggetts[12] came and asked that they might hear us. We were all much encouraged to pursue the glorious prize held out to us by the evangelical prophet.

When the company was gone, I joined with Mr Bray in prayer and the Scripture, and was so greatly affected that I almost thought Christ was coming that moment. I concluded the night with private, vehement prayer.

---

8. Cf. Rom. 10:10.

9. This is Robert Ainsworth (1660–1743), author of a widely used Latin dictionary. He was actually sixty-eight at the time.

10. Cf. Luke 2:22-32.

11. Cf. Mark 12:34.

12. Two Claggett daughters are mentioned repeatedly in the MS Journal—Elizabeth ("Betsy," b. 1715) and Susanna ("Sukey," b. 1723). There appears to be a third (unnamed) sister as well. Charles uses this plural form of the last name when referring to them corporately.

Saturday, May 13. Waked without Christ, yet still desirous of finding him. Soon after, William Delamotte came and read me the 68th Psalm, strangely full of comfortable promises. Toward noon I was enabled to pray with desire and hope, and to lay claim to the promises in general.

The afternoon I spent with my friends in mutual exhortation to wait patiently for the Lord in prayer and reading. At night my brother came, exceeding heavy. I forced him (as he had often forced me) to sing an hymn to Christ, and almost thought he would come while we were singing, assured he would come quickly. *At night* received much light and comfort from the Scriptures.

Sunday, May 14. The beginning of the day I was very heavy, weary, and unable to pray. But the desire soon returned, and I found much comfort both in prayer and in the word, my eyes being opened more and more to discern and lay hold on the promises. I longed to find Christ, that I might show him to all mankind; that I might praise, that I might love him.

Several persons called today, and were convinced of unbelief. Some of them afterwards went to Mr Broughton, and were soon made as easy as Satan and their own hearts could wish.

Monday, May 15. I finished Halyburton's *Life* with Miss Claggetts, etc. Found comfort in the 102nd Psalm.

Tuesday, May 16. Waked weary, faith, and heartless. My brother Hall coming to see me, I urged him to examine himself whether he was in the faith. Two questions decided the matter. "Are you sure that is light?" "Yes." "Are you as sure of the things unseen, of Christ being in you of a truth?" "Yes, infinitely sure."

In the afternoon I seemed deeply sensible of my misery in being without Christ.

Wednesday, May 17. I experienced the power of Christ rescuing me in temptation.

Today I first saw Luther on the Galatians,[13] which Mr [William] Holland had accidentally lit upon. We began, and found him nobly full of faith. My friend, in hearing him, was so affected as to breathe out sighs and groans unutterable. I marveled that we were so soon,

---

13. Martin Luther, *A Commentary of M. Doctor Martin Luther upon the Epistle of St. Paul to the Galatians* (London: Thomas Vautrollier, 1575; or later reprint of this English translation).

and so entirely, removed from him that called us into the grace of Christ unto another gospel.[14] Who would believe our Church had been founded on this important article of justification by faith alone! I am astonished I should ever think this a new doctrine, especially while our Articles and Homilies stand unrepealed, and the key of knowledge is not yet taken away.

From this time I endeavoured to ground as many of our friends as came in this fundamental truth, salvation by faith alone, not an idle, dead faith, but a faith which works by love, and is necessarily productive of all good works and all holiness.

I spent some hours this evening in private with Martin Luther, who was greatly blessed to me, especially his conclusion of the second chapter. I laboured, waited, and prayed to see "who loved *me*, and gave himself for *me*" [Gal. 1:6-7]. When nature near exhausted forced me to bed, I opened the book upon "For he will finish the work, and cut it short in righteousness, because a short work will the Lord make upon earth" [Rom. 9:28]. After this comfortable assurance that he would come, and would not tarry, I slept in peace.

Thursday, May 18. In the approach of a temptation, I looked up to Christ, and confessed my helplessness. The temptation was immediately beat down, and continually kept off by a power not my own. About midnight I was waked by the return of my pleurisy. Felt great pain and straightness at my heart, but found immediate relief by bleeding. Had some discourse with Mr Bray. Thought myself willing to die the next moment, if I might but believe this. But was sure I could not die till I did believe. I earnestly desired it.

Friday, May 19. At five this morning the pain and difficulty in breathing returned. The surgeon was sent for, but I fell asleep before he could bleed me a second time. Easier all day, after taking Dr Cockburn's medicines. Not much desire. Received the Sacrament, but not Christ. At seven Mrs Turner came, and told me I should not rise from that bed till I believed. I believed her saying, and asked,

[*Wesley:*] "Has God then bestowed faith upon you?"

[*Mrs Turner:*] "Yes, he has."

[*Wesley:*] "Why, have you peace with God?"

[*Mrs Turner:*] "Yes, perfect peace."

---

14. Cf. Gal. 1:6-7.

[*Wesley:*] "And do you love Christ above all things?"
[*Mrs Turner:*] "I do, above all things incomparably."
[*Wesley:*] "Then you are willing to die?"
[*Mrs Turner:*] "I am, and would be glad to die this moment. For I know all my sins are blotted out. The handwriting that was against me is taken out of the way and nailed to his cross. He has saved me by his death. He has washed me with his blood. He has hid me in his wounds. I have peace in him, and rejoice with joy unspeakable, and full of glory."

Her answers were so full to these and the most searching questions I could ask, that I had no doubt of her having received the atonement, and waited for it myself with a more assured hope. Feeling an anticipation of joy upon her account, and thanking Christ as I could, I looked for him all night with prayers and sighs and unceasing desires.

Saturday, May 20. I waked much disappointed, and continued all day in great dejection, which the Sacrament did not in the least abate. Nevertheless God would not suffer me to doubt the truth of his promises. Mr Bray too seemed troubled at my not yet believing, and complained of his uneasiness and want of patience. "But so it is with me," says he. "When my faith begins to fail, God gives me some sign to support it." He then opened a Testament, and read the first words that presented, Matthew 9:1[-8]:

And he entered into a ship and passed over, and came into his own city. And, behold, they brought to him a man sick of the palsy, lying on a bed. And Jesus, seeing their faith, said unto the sick of the palsy, "Son, be of good cheer, thy sins be forgiven thee." And behold certain of the scribes and Pharisees said within themselves, "This man blasphemeth." And Jesus, knowing their thoughts said, "Wherefore think ye evil in your hearts? For whether is it easier to say, thy sins be forgiven thee, or to say, Arise and walk? But that ye may know that the Son of Man hath power on earth to forgive sins." (Then saith he to the sick of the palsy), "Arise, take up thy bed, and go unto thine own house." And he arose, and departed to his house. And when the multitude saw it, they marvelled, and glorified God, which had given such power unto man.

It was a long while before he could read this through, for tears of joy. And I saw herein, and firmly believed, that his faith would be available for the healing of me.

THE DAY OF PENTECOST

Sunday, May 21, 1738. I waked in hope and expectation of his coming. At nine my brother and some friends came and sang an hymn to the Holy Ghost.[15] My comfort and hope were hereby increased. In about half an hour they went. I betook myself to prayer; the substance as follows: "O Jesus, thou hast said, I will come unto you. Thou hast said, I will ~~come unto you send the Comforter unto you~~ send the Comforter to you. My father and I will come unto you, and make our abode with you. Thou art God who canst not lie. I wholly rely upon thy most true promise. Accomplish it in thy time and manner."[16] Having said this, I was composing myself to sleep, in quietness and peace, when I heard one come in (Mrs Musgrave, I thought, by the voice) and say, "In the name of Jesus of Nazareth, arise, and believe, and thou shalt be healed of all thy infirmities!"[17] I wondered how it should enter into her head to speak in that manner. The words struck me to the heart. I sighed and said within myself, "O that Christ would but speak thus to me!" Lay musing and trembling. Then thought, "But what if it should be him!" I will send at least to see. I sang, and Mrs Turner coming, desired her to send up Mrs Musgrave. She went down and returning said, "Mrs Musgrave had not been here." My heart sank within me at the word and I hoped it might be Christ indeed. However, I sent her down again to inquire, and felt in the mean time a strange palpitation of heart, I said, yet feared to say, "I believe, I believe!"

She came up again and said, "It was I, a weak sinful creature spoke, but the words were Christ's. He commanded me to say them and so constrained me that I could not forbear."

I sent for Mr Bray, and asked him whether I believed. He answered, I ought not to doubt of it—it was Christ spoke to me. He knew it, and willed us to pray together. But first, said he, I will read what I have casually opened upon: "Blessed is the man, whose unrighteousness is forgiven, and whose sin is covered. Blessed is

---

15. This was likely the "Hymn to the Holy Ghost" that John Wesley included in *CPH* (1737), 22–23 [and *CPH* (1738), 26–27]; taken from George Hickes, *Devotions in the Ancient Way of Offices* (London: Jones, 1700), 377–78.

16. Cf. John 14:23, 26.

17. Cf. Acts 3:1-11.

the man to whom the Lord imputeth no sin and in whose spirit is no guile" [Ps. 32:2, BCP]. Still I felt a violent opposition and reluctance to believe. Yet still the Spirit of God strove with my own and the evil spirit, till by degrees he chased away the darkness of my unbelief. I found myself convinced—I knew not how, nor when—and immediately fell to intercession.

Mr Bray then told me his sister had been ordered by Christ to come and say those words to me. This she afterwards confirmed and stated to me more at large the manner of her believing. At night, and nearly the moment I was taken ill, she dreamed she heard one knock at the door. She went down and opened it; saw a person in white; caught hold of and asked him who he was; was answered, "I am Jesus Christ"; and cried out with great vehemence, "Come in, come in!"[18]

She waked in a fright. It was immediately suggested to her, you must not mind this, 'tis all a dream and illusion. She continued wavering and uneasy all Friday till evening prayers. No sooner were they begun than she found herself full of the power of faith, so that she could scarce contain herself and almost doubted whether she was sober. At the same time she was enlarged in love and prayer for all mankind, and commanded to go and assure me from Christ of my recovery, soul and body. She returned home repeating with all joy and triumph, "I believe, I believe." Yet her heart failed her, and she durst not say the words to me that night.

On Sunday morning she took Mr Bray aside, burst into tears and informed him of the matter, objecting she was a poor, weak, sinful creature and should she go to a minister! She could not do it, nor rest till she did. He asked whether she had ever found herself so before? "No, never." Why then, said he, "Go. Remember Jonah. You declare promises not threatenings. Go in the name of the Lord. Fear not your own weakness. Speak you the words, He will do the work. 'Out of the mouths of babes and sucklings hath he ordained strength' [Ps. 8:2]."[19]

They prayed together and she then went up, but durst not come in till she had prayed again by herself. About six minutes after she had left him, he found and felt, while she was speaking the words, that Christ was with her. I never heard words uttered with

---

18. Cf. Rev. 3:20.
19. Charles has changed "hast thou" to "hath he."

like solemnity. The sound of her voice was entirely changed into that of Mrs Musgrave (if I can be sure of anything sensible). I rose and looked into the Scripture. The words that first presented were "And now, Lord, what is my hope? Truly my hope is even in thee" [Ps. 39:8, BCP]. I then cast down my eye and met, "He hath put a new song in my mouth, even a thanksgiving unto our God. Many shall see it and fear, and shall put their trust in the Lord" [Ps. 40:3-4, BCP]. Afterwards I opened upon Isaiah 40:1, "Comfort ye, comfort ye, my people, saith our God. Speak ye comfortably to Jerusalem, and cry unto her that her warfare is accomplished; that her iniquity is pardoned for she had received the Lord's hand double of all her sin."

I now found myself at peace with God and rejoiced in the hope of loving Christ. My temper for the rest of the day was mistrust of my own great, but before unknown, weakness. I saw that by faith I stood; by the continual support of faith, which kept me from falling, though of myself I am ever sinking into sin. I went to bed still sensible of my own weakness (I humbly hope to be more and more so), yet confident of Christ's protection.

Monday, May 22. Under his protection I waked next morning and rejoiced in reading the 107 Psalm, so nobly describing what God had done for my soul. I fell asleep again and waked out of a dream that I was fighting with two devils—had one under my feet; the other faced me some time, but faded, and sunk, and vanished away, upon my telling him I belonged to Christ.

Today I saw him chiefly as my King and found him in his power, but saw little of the love of Christ crucified, or of my sin's past— though more I humbly hope of my own weakness and his strength. I had many evil thoughts darted into my mind, but I rejected them immediately (yet not I[20]). At noon I rose continually fainting, nevertheless upheld. Was greatly strengthened by Isaiah 43, which God directed me to. "But now thus saith the Lord that created thee, Jacob, and he that formed thee. O Israel, fear not for I have redeemed thee. I have called thee by thy name, thou art mine. When thou passest through the waters I will be with thee, and through the rivers they shall not overflow thee. When thou walkest through the fire, thou shalt not be burned neither shall the flame kindle upon thee. For I am the Lord thy God, the holy one of Israel, thy Saviour" [Isa. 43:1-3].

---

20. Cf. Gal. 2:20.

My brother coming, we joined in intercession for him. In the midst of prayers I almost believed the Holy Ghost was coming upon him. In the evening we sang and prayed again. Found myself very weak in body, but thought I ought to pray for my friends, being the only priest among them. I kneeled down and was immediately strengthened both mind and body. The enemy did not lose such an opportunity of tempting me to pride. But God be praised, my strength did I ascribe unto him. I was often since assisted to pray readily and earnestly, without a form. Not unto me, O Lord, not unto me but to thy name be the glory![21]

An old friend called to see me under great apprehensions that I was running mad. His fears were not a little increased by my telling him the prayer of faith had healed me, when sick at Oxford. "He looked to see the rays of light about my head," he said, and more to that purpose. I begged him for his own sake not to pass sentence till he had his full evidence concerning me. This he could not promise, but faintly prayed me to flee from London and in despair of me took his leave.

It was morning before I could get to sleep. Many motions of pride arose and were continually broken down by Christ my King. The devil also tempted me to impatience through pain, but God turned it into an occasion of resignation.

Tuesday, May 23. I waked under the protection of Christ and gave myself up, soul and body, to him. At nine began an hymn upon my conversion, but was persuaded to break off for fear of pride. Mr Bray coming encouraged me to proceed in spite of Satan. I prayed Christ to stand by me and finished the hymn.[22]

Upon my afterwards showing it to Mr Bray, the devil threw in a fiery dart suggesting that it was wrong and I had displeased God. My heart sunk within me. When casting my eye upon a Prayerbook, I met with an answer for him, "Why boastest thou thyself, thou tyrant that thou canst do mischief?" [Ps. 52:1, BCP]. Upon this I clearly discovered it was a device of the enemy to keep back glory from God. And 'tis most usual with him to preach humility when speaking will endanger his kingdom or do honour to Christ. Least of all would he have us tell what things God has done for our

---

21. Cf. Ps. 115:1.
22. Most scholars believe that this first hymn on his conversion was "Christ, the Friend of Sinners," which can be found in *HSP* (1739), 101–3 (*Poetical Works*, 1:91–93).

souls, so tenderly does he guard us from pride. But God has showed me he can defend me from it, while speaking for him. In his name therefore, and through his strength, I will perform my vows unto the Lord. "Of not hiding his righteousness within my heart" [Ps. 40:10, BCP] if it should ever please him to plant it there.

Throughout this day he has kept up in me a constant sense of my own weakness. At night I was tempted to think the reason of my believing before others was my sincerity. I rejected the thought with honor, and remained more than conqueror through him that loved me.[23]

Wednesday, May 24. Being to receive the Sacrament today, I was assaulted by the fear of my old accustomed deadness, but soon recovered my confidence in Christ that he would give me so much sense of his love now as he saw good for me. I received without any sensible devotion, much as I used to be, only that I was afterwards perfectly active and satisfied, without doubt, or fear, or scruple.

Among our communicants was Mrs Pratt, who had been with me the night before, and related her receiving Christ in a dream, when under great trouble. His words to her were "Be of good cheer, thy prayer is heard."[24] From that time to this, being six years, she has enjoyed perfect peace. Most of Saturday night she had spent in intercession for me, as on Sunday morning I experienced.

Was much pleased today at the sight of Mr Ainsworth, a little child, full of grief and fears and love. At our repeating the line of the hymn, "Now descend, and shake the earth,"[25] he fell down, as in an agony. I found a general delight in their singing, but little attention, yet was not disquieted.

We passed the afternoon in prayer, singing and conference. For one half hour I was with Miss Delamotte, now unconvinced and full of dispute. I bore my testimony with plainness and confidence, declaring what God had done for my soul. Not hurt, but strengthened hereby.

From here I went to Miss Claggetts, young women of a better and more childlike spirit, who calmly and confidently looked for the promises. I was farther comforted by an excellent letter from

23. Cf. Rom. 8:37.
24. Cf. Luke 1:13.
25. "Hymn for Whitsunday," st. 8, *HSP* (1739), 213 (*Poetical Works*, 1:189).

my namesake in Georgia[26]—persecuted for Christ's sake; on the highest step, I trust, of the legal state.

At eight I prayed by myself for love with some feeling and assurances of feeling more. Towards ten my brother was brought in triumph by a troop of our friends and declared, "I believe." We sang the hymn with great joy and parted with prayer. At midnight I gave myself up to Christ, assured I was safe sleeping or waking. Had continual experience of his power to overrule all temptation, and confessed with joy and surprise that he was able to do exceeding abundantly for me, above what I can ask or think [Eph. 3:20].

Thursday, May 25. Commended myself to Christ my Prophet, Priest, and King. Miss Delamotte came in a better mind. Before communicating, I left it to Christ whether or in what measure he would please to manifest himself to me in this breaking of bread. I had no particular attention to the prayers, but in the prayer of consecration I saw, by the eye of faith, or rather had a glimpse of Christ's broken, mangled body, as taking down from the cross. Still I could not observe the prayer, but only repeat with tears, "O Love, Love!" At the same time I felt great peace and joy; assurance of feeling more when it is best.

Soon after I was a little cast down by feeling some temptation and foreseeing more but God lifted me up by his word— "Fear not, for I have redeemed thee. I have called thee by thy name, thou art mine. When thou passest through the waters, I will be with thee; and through the rivers, they shall not overflow thee. When thou walkest through the fire thou shalt not be burned, neither shall the flame kindle upon thee" (Isa. 43[:1-2]).

This promise was fulfilled in me when, under frequent motions of sin, I looked up to Christ, and found them broken down continually.

Friday, May 26. We joined this morning in supplication for the poor malefactors, while passing to execution, and in the Sacrament commended their souls to Christ. The great comfort we found those in made us confidently hope some of them were received as the penitent thief at the last hour.

I was much refreshed soon after by Miss Delamotte, who by the mercy of Christ is brought back again and more a thirst after him than ever.

---

26. Charles Delamotte.

I dined with great liberty of spirit, being amazed to find my old enemy intemperance so suddenly subdued that I have almost forgot I was ever in bondage to him. In the evening I broke through my own great unwillingness, and at last preached faith in Christ to an accidental visitant.

Saturday, May 27. I felt a motion of anger from a trifling disappointment, but it was no sooner felt than conquered. Received the Sacrament; still no sensible love, but comfort.

A gentle woman who has been long under the law, calling to see me, I thought, as she lived in the midst of opposers, no good could be done by speaking. Yet was I overruled to preach the gospel. She seemed convinced and comforted. After she was gone, I was much assisted to intercede for her, and for poor Mr Broughton, who continues the very life of all those that oppose the faith.

Two or three others calling were reproved of sin by the Holy Spirit of God. Miss Claggetts seemed on the very borders of Canaan, being fully convinced of righteousness also, of Christ's imputed righteousness, and looking to receive it every moment as by promise theirs.

Trinity Sunday, May 28. I rose in great heaviness, which neither private nor joint prayer could remove. At last I betook myself to intercession for my relations, which was greatly helped and enlarged herein, particularly in prayer for a most profligate sinner. I spent the morning with James Hutton in prayer and singing and rejoicing. In the afternoon my brother came, and after a short prayer for success upon our ministry, set out for Tiverton. I then began writing my first sermon in the name of Christ my prophet.[27]

Today Mrs Bray related to me the manner of her receiving faith in public prayer and the great conflicts she has since had with the enemy. For some days he so darkened the work of God that though her eye of faith had been opened to see herself encompassed with the blood of Christ, yet still he suggested to her that she did not believe, because she had not the joy which others had. She was just overpowered by his devices, when in great nearness she opened upon "Lord, I believe, help thou my unbelief" [Mark 9:24]. This stayed

---

27. This was his sermon on 1 John 3:14 (*Sermons*, 133–51). Note his second paragraph at the opening: "I trust there is no one here, who will not seriously attend, while in the name of our great prophet and teacher, now present among and with us, I endeavour. . . ."

her for a time but the tempter still pursued and in the very good words he had used to shake my brother's faith. She went to public prayers and was fervent throughout the whole. Toward the conclusion she saw, as it were, Satan under her feet and came home in all the triumph of faith.

After dinner Miss Claggetts and other friends came. I thought some would be now gathered into the fold, and was much assisted to pray. I rose and saw the younger Miss Claggett under the work of God. Asked, urged, believed that she believed. She thought so too but was afraid to confess it. While she stood trembling and in fears, I consulted the oracle for her and met with Isaiah 30:18[-19], "And therefore will the Lord wait, that he may be gracious unto you, and therefore will be exalted that he may have mercy upon you. For the Lord is a God of judgment. Blessed are all they that wait for him. For the people shall dwell in Sion at Jerusalem. Thou shalt weep no more. He will be very gracious to thee, at the voice of thy cry. When he shall hear it, he will answer thee."

She then opened the book on 2 Cor. 5:17, "Old things are passed away, behold all things are become new." She read so far and gave me the book to read on "And all things are of God, who hath reconciled us to himself by Jesus Christ, and hath given to us the ministry of reconciliation. To wit, that God was in Christ, reconciling the world unto himself, not imputing their trespasses unto them (and hath committed to us the word of reconciliation). Now then we are ambassadors for Christ, as though God did beseech you by us. We pray you in Christ['s] stead, be ye reconciled to God. For he hath made him to be sin for us, who knew no sin that we might be made the righteousness of God in him" [2 Cor. 5:18-21].

Mr Holland then read "Stand fast in the liberty wherewith Christ hath made us free and be not entangled again in the yoke of bondage" [Gal. 5:1]. She now openly professed her faith and increased her confidence every moment. We joined in hearty thanks to God for his unspeakable gift. Just before parting she opened the book upon Luke 8:37, "Return to thine own house and show how great things God hath done unto thee."

This success was followed with inward trials, but at the same time I experienced the superior power of Christ.

Wednesday, May 30. Today God enabled me in spite of the devil and my own heart to send Mr Wells a plain, simple account of what God hath done for my soul.

JUNE 1738

Thursday, June 1. Was troubled today that I could not pray; utterly dead at the Sacrament.

Friday, June 2. Still unable to pray; still dead in communicating; full of a cowardly desire of death.

Saturday, June 3. My deadness continued and the next day increased. I rose exceeding heavy and averse to prayer, so that I almost resolved not to go to church, which I had not been able to do till within these two or three days past. When I did go, the prayers and Sacrament were exceeding grievous to me, and could not help asking myself, "Where is the difference between what I am now and what I was before believing?" I immediately answered, that if darkness was not like the former darkness, because I was satisfied. There was no guilt in it, because I was assured it would be dispersed; and because, though I could not find I loved God, or feel that he loved me, yet I did and would believe he loved me notwithstanding.

I returned home and lay down with the same load upon me. This Mr Ingham's coming could not alleviate. They sung, but I had no heart to join; much less in public prayers. In the evening Mr Brown,[28] Holland, and others called. I was very averse to coming among them, but forced myself to it, and spent two or three hours in singing, reading, and prayers. This exercise a little revived me, and I found myself much assisted to pray.

We asked particularly that if it was the will of God, someone might now receive the atonement. While I was yet speaking of words, Mr Brown found power to believe. He rose and told me my prayer was heard, and answered in him. At the same time Mr Burton opened the Bible upon Col. 1:26[-27], "Even the mystery which has been hid from ages and from generations, but now is made manifest to his saints, to whom God would make known what

---

28. John Brown, a woollen draper in St Martin's-le-Grand parish.

is the riches of the glory of this mystery among the gentiles, which is Christ in you the hope of glory."

We were all full of joy and thanksgiving. Before we parted, I prayed with Mr Brown and praised God to the great confirmation of my faith. The weight was quite taken off. I found power to pray with great earnestness and rejoiced in my trial's having continued so long, to show me that it is then the best time to labor for our neighbour when we are most cast down and most unable to help ourselves.

Monday, June 5. I waked thankful with power to pray and praise. Had peace at the Sacrament, and some attention in public prayer. In the afternoon I met Mrs Syms[29] with Mr and Mrs Barton at Islington. He told me God had given him faith, while I was praying last night, but he thought it would do hurt to declare it then. Upon finding his heart burn within him, he desired God would show him some token of his faith and immediately opened on "Let there be light and there was light" [Gen. 1:3]. We rejoiced together in prayer and singing, and left the rest of the company much stirred up to wait for the same unspeakable gift.

Tuesday, June 6. In the evening I read Luther, as usual, to a large company of our friends. Mr Burton was greatly affected. My inward temptations are in a manner uninterrupted. I never knew the energy of sin till now that I experience the superior strength of Christ.

Wednesday, June 7. Found myself this morning under my Father's protection, and reading Matt. 7[:1], "Ask and ye shall receive." I asked some sense of his love in the Sacrament. It was there given me to believe assuredly that God loved me, even when I could have no sense of it. Some imperfect perception of his love I had, and was strengthened to hope against hope after communicating.

Went to Mrs Syms and passed the afternoon singing and reading the promises. Miss Claggetts, Mr Chapman,[30] [Joseph] Verding, and others dropped in, as by accident. We all went to public prayers; whence we again returned, contrary to my intention, to Mr Syms.[31] We joined in pleading the promises and asking some token

---

29. This may have been the aunt of John and Peter Syms. Their mother died in 1724, and Peter notes that he apprenticed under an uncle in London. Charles and John Wesley spell "Sims"; we have adopted the spelling used by the family.

30. George Chapman, a butcher, of Lime Street, near Leadenhall Market.

31. There are several possibilities for the various references to "Mr Syms" in the MS Journal. Two are brothers: John Syms (1714–1757) and Peter Syms (1716–1790), both currently bachelors

for good. I rose in confidence of our prayer being heard and at the same time Mr Verding declared with great simplicity and astonishment that he had seen as it were a whole army rushing by him and bearing the broken body of Christ. He found himself quite overpowered at the sight; was all in a cold sweat. While he spoke, my heart bore witness to the work of God in his and I felt myself affected as on Whitsunday. Was assured it was Christ. Said the written word would bear witness with the personal, and opened it for a sign upon Isaiah. "Surely shall one say in the Lord, have I righteousness and strength. Even to him shall men come and all that are incensed against him shall be ashamed. In the Lord shall all the seed of Israel be justified and shall glory" [Isa. 45:24]. Then said, "Look unto me and be ye saved all the ends of the earth, for I am God, and there is none else. I have sworn by myself, the word is gone out of my mouth in righteousness, ~~that~~ and shall not return, that unto me every knee shall bow, every tongue shall swear" [Isa. 45:22-23]. And then 1 Pet. 1:3[-5], "Blessed be the God and Father of our Lord Jesus Christ, who according to his abundant mercy hath begotten us again unto a lively hope by the resurrection of Jesus Christ from the dead to an inheritance incorruptible, undefiled, and that fadeth not away reserved in heaven for you which are kept by the power of God through faith unto salvation." After this he grew visibly in the faith and we rejoiced and gave God thanks for the consolation.

He appeared a very child, owned he had feared nothing so much as offending his Father; was ready to die that moment. In the beginning of prayer he could hardly persuade himself to kneel down, not thinking he could find any benefit, so poor, so sinful a creature. What should he pray for?

Returning home in triumph I found Dr [John] Byrom and, in defiance of the tempter, simply told him the great things Jesus had done for me and many others. This drew on a full explanation of the doctrine of faith, which he received with wonderful readiness. Toward midnight I slept in peace.

---

and in business together as butchers, in or near Leadenhall Street. Both brothers had contact with the Wesleys in religious societies in London, and meetings were often held in their house. A third possibility is their uncle, to whom Peter had been apprenticed. In 1743 the London Moravian congregation members included (in addition to Peter Syms) Robert Syms (married), William Syms (single), and Joseph Syms (single), while the (less committed) society members included Thomas Syms and Mrs Syms. Charles provides no clues as to which Syms he is naming. Again, Charles spells "Sims."

Thursday, June 8. I had the satisfaction of hearing Mr Sparks[32] confess himself convinced now that he is under the law, not under grace. In public prayer it pleased the Lord to melt me into humility and love.

At three I took coach for Blendon with Mr Bray. Had much talk with a lady about the fall and faith in Christ. She openly maintained the merit of good works. I would all who oppose the righteousness of faith were so ingenious, then would they no longer seek it as it were by the works of the law.

Before seven we came to Eltham. In riding thence to Blendon I was full of delight and seemed in a new heaven and a new earth. We prayed and sang and shouted all the way. We found Miss Betsy and Hetty at home and prayed that this day salvation might come to this house. In the lesson were those words, "This is the accepted time, this is the day of salvation" [2 Cor. 6:2].

Friday, June 9. Prayed with fervor for the family. The second lesson was Blind Bartimeus [Mark 10:46-52]. In riding to Bexley with Mr Piers, I spake of my experiences in simplicity and confidence and found him very ready to receive the faith. ~~The~~ We spent the day in the same manner, Mr Bray relating the inward workings of God upon his soul and I the great things he had lately done for me and our friends at London. He listened eagerly to all that was said, not making the least of objection, but confessing it was what he had never experienced. We walked and sang and prayed in the garden. He was greatly moved and testified his full conviction and desire of finding Christ. "But I must first," said he, "prepare myself by long exercise of prayer and good works."

At night we were joined in prayer for Hetty. Never did I pray with greater earnestness, expecting an immediate answer and being much disappointed at not finding it. I consulted then the Scripture and met with Jehu's words to his men, "Let none escape out of your hands!" [2 Kings 9:15]; then, "I trust . . . that I shall come shortly" [Phil. 2:24]; till I was in great heaviness for her and could not sleep till morning.

Waking full of desire for her conversion, those words were brought to my remembrance. "The Spirit and the bride say come, and

---

32. Mr. Sparks (or, possibly, Sparkes) was apparently an ordained Anglican (at least a deacon), but without a regular pastoral post; cf. the entries for July 11 and 17, 1738, below.

let him that heareth say come, and let him that is athirst come, and whosoever will let him take of the water of life freely" [Rev. 22:17]. At this instant came a flash of lightning, then thunder, then violent rain. I accepted it as a sign that the skies would soon pour down righteousness.

Yesterday (the devil of secrecy being expelled) Miss Betsy plainly informed me that after her last receiving the Sacrament, she had heard a voice, "Go thy way, thy sins are forgiven thee,"[33] and was filled thereby with joy unspeakable. She said within herself, "Now I do indeed feed upon Christ in my heart by faith," and continued all day in the spirit of humility and exultation. All her life she thought would be too little to thank God for that day. Yet, even after this it was that the enemy got so great advantage over her, in making her oppose the truth with such fierceness. For many days she did not know that she had in herself demonstration of that she denied. But after we had prayed that God would clear up his own work, the darkness of faith dispersed and those fears that her conversion was not real by little and little were all done away.

Saturday, June 10. In the morning lesson was that glorious description of the power of faith. "Jesus answering said unto them, have faith in God. For verily I say unto you that whosoever shall say unto this mountain, be thou removed, and be thou cast into the sea, and shall not doubt in his heart, but shall believe that those things which he said shall come to pass, he shall have whatsoever he saith. Therefore I say unto you, what things soever ye desire when ye pray believe that ye receive them and ye shall have them" [Mark 11:23-24]. We pleaded the promise in behalf of our seeking friends particularly Hetty and Mr Piers. He came with his wife. The day before our coming had been led to read the Homily on Justification, which convinced him that in him dwelt no good thing. Now he likewise saw that the thoughts of his heart were only evil continually for as much as whatsoever is not of faith is sin.

He asked God to give him some comfort and found it in Luke 5:23, etc., "Whether it is easier to say thy sins be forgiven thee, or to say rise up and walk? But that ye may know that the Son of Man hath power upon earth to forgive sins (he saith unto the sick of the palsy), I say unto thee, Arise, and take up thy bed and go unto

---

33. Cf. Luke 5:20.

thine own house. And immediately he rose up before them and took up that whereon he lay and departed to his own house glorifying God. And they were all amazed, and they glorified God, and were filled with fear, saying, we have seen strange things today" [Luke 5:23-26].

This was the very miracle I told him from which God had shown his intention to heal me, and it was a sign of the like to be done by him. Mr Bray moved for retiring to prayer. We prayed *after God*, again and again and asked him whether he believed Christ could just not manifest himself to his soul. He answered, yes. We read him the promise made to the prayer of faith. Mr Bray bid me speak some promise to him authoritatively, and he should find Christ make it good. I had not faith to do it. He made me pray again and then read Psalm 65. I felt every word of it for my friend, particularly "Thou that hearest the prayer unto thee shall all flesh come. Blessed is the man whom thou choosest and receivest unto thee. He shall dwell in thy court and shall be satisfied with the plenteousness of thy house, even of thy holy temple. Thou shalt show us wonderful things in thy righteousness. O God of our salvation, thou that art the hope of all the ends of the earth," etc. [Ps. 65:3-5].

Seeing the great confidence of Mr Bray, and the deep humility of Mr Piers, I began to think the promise would be fulfilled before we left the room. My fellow-worker with God seemed full of faith and the Holy Ghost and told him, if you can but touch the hem of his garment, you shall be made whole.[34]

We prayed for him a third time, the Spirit greatly helping our infirmities,[35] and then asked if he believed. He answered, "Yes." The Spirit witnessing with our spirits that his heart was as our heart, Bray said, "I now know of a truth that Christ is in you." We were all filled with joy, returned thanks, and prayed for a blessing on his ministry, and then brought him down in triumph. Miss Betsy was greatly strengthened hereby and bold to confess she believed. All her speech now was, "I only hope that I shall never lose this comfort."

The day was spent in prayer and confidence. Mrs Piers was with all ease convinced of unbelief. After supper I discoursed on faith from the lesson. The poor servants received the word gladly.

---

34. Cf. Matt. 14:36.
35. Cf. Rom. 8:26.

Sunday, June 11. While Mr Piers was preaching upon death, I found great joy in feeling myself willing, or rather desirous, to die. After prayers we joined in intercession for Mr and Mrs Delamotte, then for poor Hetty. Received much comfort in reading Luther.

We took coach for church. In singing I observed Hetty join with a mixture of fear and joy. I earnestly prayed and expected she should meet with something to confirm her in the service. Both the psalms and lessons were full of consolation.

We adjourned to Mr Piers and joined in prayer for a poor woman in despair, one Mrs Searle,[36] whom Satan had bound these many years. I saw her pass by in the morning and was touched with a sense of her misery. After pleading his promise of being with us to the end of the world, we went down to her in the name of Jesus. I asked her whether she thought God was love and not anger, as Satan would persuade her. Then I preached the gospel which she received with all imaginable eagerness. When we had for some time continued together in prayer, she rose up another creature, strongly and explicitly declaring her faith in the blood of Christ and full persuasion that she was accepted in the Beloved. Hetty then disclosed that she could not but believe ~~she could not be left out of the universal pardon, therefore~~ Christ died for her, even for her. We gave thanks for both with much exultation and triumph.

After family prayer I expounded the lesson, and going up to my chamber asked the maid (Mary) how she found herself. She answered, "O Sir, what you said was very comfortable, how that Christ was made sin for me, that I might be made the righteousness of God in him,[37] that is, he was put in my place, and I in his." "Do you then believe this, that Christ died for you?" "Yes, I do believe it and I found myself as I never did before, when you spoke the word." "But do you find within yourself that your sins are forgiven?" "Yes, I do." These and the like answers, which she made with great simplicity, convinced me that faith had come to her by hearing.[38] We joined in giving glory to God, for we perceived and confessed it was his doing. It pleased him likewise to bless me with a deep and hitherto unknown dread of ascribing anything to myself.

---

36. Charles spells "Searl."
37. Cf. 2 Cor. 5:21.
38. Cf. Gal. 3:2-5.

Monday, June 12. This morning Mrs Piers told she had always doubted her having true faith, but now declared with tears she was convinced her sins were forgiven and she did believe indeed. We all went to Mrs Searle in strong temptation, nothing doubting but we should see the power of Christ triumphing over that of Satan. The enemy had got no advantage over her, though he had laboured all night to trouble and confound her. As often as she named the name of Jesus, he was repelled and her soul at peace. We were much edified by her deep humility and preached the gospel to her and her husband, who received it readily. After prayer she rose with "How shall I be thankful enough to my Saviour?" We parted in a triumphant hymn.

Tuesday, June 13. Mr Piers was sent to a dying woman. She was in despair, having done so much evil and so little good. He declared to her the glad tidings of salvation, that as all her good, were it ten thousand times more, could never save her, so all her evil could never hurt her—if she could repent and believe, if she could lay hold on Christ by a living faith, and look for salvation by grace only. This was comfort indeed. She gladly quitted her own merits for Christ's. The Holy Ghost wrought faith in her heart, which expressed in a calm cheerful, triumphant expectation of death. Her fears and agonies were at an end. Being inspired by faith, she had peace with God, and only entered farther into her rest, by dying a few hours after. The spectators were melted into tears. She calmly passed into the heavenly Canaan, and has there brought up a good report of her faithful pastor, who, under Christ, hath saved her soul from death.

These were the first fruits of his ministry, and I find him strengthened hereby and more assured that the gospel is the power of God unto salvation to everyone that believeth [Rom. 1:16].

In the evening Mr Delamotte returned.

Wednesday, June 14. After morning prayer in the little chapel, I kept Hannah[39] from going, that we might first pray for her, but we quickly found there was greater cause of thanksgiving. She told me she was reading a collect last night, which gave her vast pleasure: "Almighty God, whom truly to know is eternal life, grant us perfectly to know thy Son Jesus Christ to be the way, the truth, and the

---

39. A maid in the Delamotte home.

life." "To be sure, sir," she said, "I found myself so easy immediately, that I cannot tell you." A few questions fully satisfied us that she was a true believer. Poor Hetty was tempted to imagine she did not believe, because she had not been affected exactly in the same manner with others. We used a prayer for her and parted.

On the road I overtook Frank and asked what he thought of these things. He answered, "I was greatly delighted with one thing you said, how that Christ was made sin for us that we might be made the righteousness of God in him."[40] Upon farther examination I found him manifestly in the faith. We talked and rejoiced together till we came to Eltham. He there left me, resolved to publish everywhere what things Jesus had done for him.

The coach was filled with young ladies. I was forced to leave off reading that I might interrupt their scandal. At London I was informed that my brother was gone with Mr Ingham and [Johann] Töltschig[41] to Herrnhuth.[42] The news surprised, but did not disquiet me.

Thursday, June 15. I was sent to baptize a child. It gave me occasion to speak upon faith. One of the company was full of self-righteousness. The rest were more patient of the truth, being only gross sinners.

Friday, June 16. After dinner Jack Delamotte came for me. We took coach, and by the way he told me that when we were last together at Blendon singing, "Who for me, for me hast died,"[43] he found the words sink into his soul; could have sung forever, being full of delightful joy; since then has thought himself led as it were in every thing; feared nothing so much as offending God; could pray with life, and in a word found that he did indeed believe in the Lord Jesus.

In the coach with Miss Delamotte. While it stopped I got out to reprove a man for swearing. He thanked me most heartily. We took up Hetty at Blendon and went on to Bexley.

Saturday, June 17. The next day we sang and prayed with Mrs Searle to our mutual encouragement. Mr Searle heard us gladly. The afternoon we passed with our friends at Blendon. Here I was

---

40. Cf. 2 Cor. 5:21.
41. Charles spells this name "Tilcheg" in this instance, and "Telchig" later.
42. Herrnhut, Saxony, the Moravian settlement established by Count Zinzendorf.
43. Line 6 of stanzas 1 and 9 of the hymn "O Filial Deity," *HSP* (1739), 108, 110 (*Poetical Works* 1:97, 99).

stopped by the return of my pain and forced to bed. Desires of death continually rose in me, which I laboured to check, not daring to form any wish concerning it.

Sunday, June 18. The pain abated and the next day left me, being carried off by a violent looseness.

Wednesday, June 21. Concerned at having been here several days and done nothing. Preached forgiveness to Mr Piers's man,[44] who seemed well disposed for receiving it by a true simplicity. We prayed together and went to public prayers. In the second lesson was the paralytic healed.[45] Came home with the Miss Delamotte, Mrs Searle, and the man, who declared before us all that God had given him faith by hearing "the sick of the palsy healed." We returned hearty thanks.

The Lord gave us more matter for thanksgiving at Blendon, where I read my brother's sermon on faith.[46] When it was over, the gardener declared, faith had come to him by hearing it, and he had no doubt of his sins being forgiven. "Nay, was I to die just now," he added, "I know I should be accepted by Christ Jesus."

Thursday, June 22. Comforted Hetty under a strong temptation, because she was not in all points affected like other believers, especially the poor, who have generally a much larger degree of confidence than the rich and learned. I had a proof of this today after Mrs Searle's, where meeting a poor woman, and convincing her of unbelief, I used a prayer for her that God who hath chosen the poor of this world to be rich in faith,[47] would now impart to her his unspeakable gift. In the midst of the prayer she received it, avowed it openly, and increased visibly therein.

In the evening we had a meeting at Mr Piers! And read my brother's sermon. God set his seal to the truth of it, by sending his Spirit upon Mr Searle and a maidservant, purifying their hearts by faith. This occasioned our triumphing in the name of Jesus our God.

Friday, June 23. Attended Mr Piers to a poor old woman whom he could never prevail upon to go to church. Expected we should be called to preach the law, but found her ready for the gospel, and

---

44. A gardener named "Frank" (cf. June 14 and July 4 entries).
45. Cf. Matt. 9:1-8.
46. John Wesley, "Salvation by Faith," *Works* 1:117–130. John preached this sermon at St Mary's Church, Oxford, on June 11, 1738, and published it soon after (London: Hutton, 1738).
47. Cf. James 2:5.

glad to exchange her merits for Christ's. The evening we prayed among our little flock and parted full of comfort and peace and joy.

Saturday, June 24. Riding to Blendon in the morning, I met William Delamotte just come from Cambridge. He had left town, well disposed to the obedience of faith, but now I observed his countenance altered. He had been strongly prejudiced by the good folk at London. At Blendon I found Mr Delamotte not over-cordial, yet civil. Met letters from my mother heavily complaining of my brother's forsaking her and requiring me to accept of the first preferment that offered, on pain of disobedience. This a little while disquieted me. Was not much comforted by William Delamotte, but I was extremely moved for him. Could not restrain from tears. His sister joined us. I began preaching faith and free grace. His objection was that it is unjust in God to make sinners equal with us, who had laboured perhaps many years. We proposed singing an hymn. We[48] saw the title, "Faith in Christ,"[49] and owned he could not bear it.

In our way to church I again proclaimed to him the glad tidings of salvation. He was exceeding heavy and by his own confession miserable. Yet could he not receive this saying, "We are justified freely by faith alone" [Rom. 3:28]. The lesson comforted me concerning him. "Behold, I will send my messenger, and he shall prepare the way before me. And the Lord, whom ye seek, shall suddenly come to his temple, even the messenger of the covenant, whom ye delight in. Behold, he shall come, saith the Lord" [Mal. 3:1]. To all such who think it is hard to lose the merit of their good works the Scripture spake as follows: "Your words have been stout against me, saith the Lord. Yet ye say, What have we spoken so much against thee! Ye have said, 'tis vain to serve God, and what profit is it, that we have kept his ordinances and that we have walked mournfully before the Lord of hosts?" [Mal. 3:13-14].

Sunday, June 25. Stayed to preach faith to Mrs Delamotte, whom providence brought home yesterday, I trust for that very purpose. I was so faint and full of passion that I had not power to speak. But I had no sooner begun my sermon than all my weakness vanished. God gave me strength and boldness, and after an hour's speaking I

---

48. "We" is struck through and "He" written above it. It is uncertain whether this is by Charles's hand.

49. Isaac Watts, "Faith in Christ," included by John Wesley in *CPH* (1737), 52. Original found in Watts, *Hymns and Spiritual Songs* (London: Humfreys, 1707), Bk. 2, no. 90.

found myself perfectly well. Went and accosted Mrs Delamotte in her pew. Just as shy as I expected. Let it work. God look to the event!

After evening prayer, she just spake to me. Betsy wondered she could bring herself to it. My sermon (I heard) occasioned much disturbance to more than her. Mrs Searle at night was full of triumph.

Monday, June 26. Waited upon Mrs Delamotte, expecting what happened. She fell abruptly upon my sermon for the false doctrine therein. I answered, "I staked my all upon the truth of it." She went on, "'Tis hard people must have their children seduced in their absence. If every one must have your faith, what will become of all the world? Have you this assurance, Mr Piers?" "Yes, Madam, in some degree. I thank God for it." "I am sorry to hear it." One of the company cried, "I am glad to hear it, and bless God for him, and wish all mankind had it too."

She moved for reading a sermon of Archbishop Sharp's.[50] Piers read. We excepted continually to his unscriptural doctrine. Much dispute ensued. She accused my brother with preaching an instantaneous faith. "As to that," I replied, "'we cannot but speak the things which we have seen and heard' [Acts 4:20]. I received it in that manner; as have above thirty others in my presence." She started up, said she could not bear it, and ran out of the house. William protested against her behaviour. In the beginning, I had found the old man rise. But I grew calmer and calmer the longer we talked. Glory be to God through Christ! I offered to go, but they would not let me. Betsy went, and at last prevailed upon her to come in. Nothing more was said. At six took my leave.

Poor Hannah and Mary came to the door, and caught hold of my hand. Hannah cried, "Don't be discouraged, sir. I hope we shall continue steadfast." I could not refrain from tears. Hetty came in. I exhorted her to persevere. Took horse. William seemed much better disposed than his mother, promised to come and see me the next day. I joined with Mr Piers in singing,

> Shall I, for fear of feeble man,
> Thy Spirit's course in me restrain?[51]

and in hearty prayer for Mrs Delamotte.

---

50. Cf. John Sharp (1645–1714), *Fifteen Sermons Preached on Several Occasions* (London: Walter Kettilby, 1700). Sharp was Archbishop of York, 1691–1714.

51. "From the German," st. 1, *CPH* (1738), 65. John Wesley's translation of Johann Joseph Winckler's hymn "Sollt ich, aus Furcht für Menschenkinder."

Tuesday, June 27. Calling upon poor Goody Dickenson, I asked if she had now forgiveness. "Yes," said she, "I received it in the midst of your sermon." "Do you then believe Christ died for you in particular?" "Yes, to be sure. I must believe it, if I would not deny the Scripture." She expressed strong confidence in God; appeared full of love to two beggars that called; believed she should be saved, if she died just now; would come to church, if all in rags. In short, she left me no reason to doubt but that she was taken in at the eleventh hour, being now near fourscore.

Coming back to Mr Piers's, I found William Delamotte. Full of hope for him. He told me he had wrote two sheets against the truth. But in seeking after more texts, had met one that quite spoiled all. "Not by works of righteousness which we have done, but according to his mercy he saved us" [Titus 3:5]. This convinced him, and immediately he burned all he had wrote. I asked what it was he still stuck at. "Nothing," said he, "but God's giving faith instantaneously." I replied, that alone hindered his receiving it just now, no more preparation being absolutely necessary thereto than what God is pleased to give.

We were directed to many apposite Scriptures, particularly Luke 7:47: "Wherefore I say unto thee, her sins, which were many, are forgiven." John 20:27-28, "Then said he to Thomas, 'Reach hither thy finger, and behold my hands; and reach hither thy hand, and thrust it into my side; and be not faithless, but believing.' And Thomas answered and said unto him, 'My Lord and my God.'"

We went to prayers, pleaded the promises for him with great earnestness and tears, then read 2 Thess. 1:11-12: "Wherefore also we pray always for you, that our God would count you worthy of this calling, and fulfill all the good pleasure of his goodness, and the work of faith with power; that the name of our Lord Jesus Christ may be glorified in you, and ye in him, according to the grace of our God and the Lord Jesus Christ." I observed the workings of God strong upon him, and prayed again. Then read the Scriptures that first offered: Titus 3:5, "Not by works of righteousness which we have done," etc. (The very text that stopped him in the morning.) Amos 4:12, "Because I will do this to thee, prepare to meet thy God." Psalm 88:6, "God setteth the solitary in families, he bringeth out those which are bound with chains." And lastly, Psalm 66:20, "Blessed be God, which hath not turned away my prayer, nor his mercy from me."

While we were praying, and singing, and reading, alternately, a poor man, one Mr Heather, came to talk with me. He had heard and liked the sermon upon faith. I asked him whether he had faith. "No." Whether forgiveness of sins. "No." Whether there was or could be any good in him, till he believed? "No." "But do you think Christ cannot give you faith and forgiveness in this hour?" "Yes, to be sure he can." "And do you believe his promise, that when two of his disciples shall agree upon earth, as touching anything they shall ask of him, he will give it them?" "I do." "Why, then, here is your minister, and I agree to ask faith for you." "Then I believe I shall receive it before I go out of this room."

We went to prayer directly, pleaded the promise, and rising, asked him whether he believed. His answer was, "Yes, I do believe with all my heart. I believe Christ died for my sins. I know they are all forgiven. I desire only to love him. I would suffer anything for him; could lay down my life for him this moment." I turned to my scholar and said, "Do you now believe that God can give faith instantaneously?" He was too full to speak, but told me afterwards he envied the unopposing ignorance and simplicity of the poor, and wished himself that illiterate carpenter.

[*Wednesday, June 28.*] Next day I returned to town, rejoicing that God had added to his living church seven more souls through my ministry. Not unto me, O Lord, not unto me, but to thy name be the praise, for thy loving-mercy, and for thy truth's sake.[52] I had hopes of seeing greater things than these, from a Scripture he this day directed me to: Luke 5:9, "For he was astonished, and all that were with him, at the draught of fishes which they had taken."

I went to Mr Syms's, in expectation of Christ. Several of our friends were providentially brought thither. We joined in singing and prayer. The last time we prayed I could not leave off, but was still forced to go on. Rose at last, and saw Mr Chapman still kneeling. Opened the book, and read aloud: "And, behold, a woman which was diseased with an issue of blood twelve years, came behind him, and touched the hem of his garment, for she said within herself, If I may but touch his garment, I shall be whole. And Jesus turned him about, and when he saw her, he said, Daughter, be of good comfort; thy faith hath made thee whole. And

---

52. Cf. Ps. 115:1, "Not unto us, O Lord, not to us, but to your name give glory. . . ."

the woman was made whole from that hour" [Matt. 9:20-22]. My heart burned within me while I was reading. At the same time I heard him cry out, with great struggling, "I do believe." We lifted him up, for he had not power to rise of himself, being quite helpless, exhausted, and in a profuse sweat. An old believer among us owned himself affected with wonderful sympathy. We had the satisfaction of *seeing* Mr Chapman increase in faith, and returned most hearty thanks to the God of his and our salvation.

Thursday, June 29. Miss Suky Claggett called, and to my no small comfort informed me of her sister's lately receiving faith. She likewise brought me an invitation from her mother. Mrs Turner would have sent for her (Miss Betsy Claggett), but I would not suffer it, that I might have no hand at all in the matter. I sat down to write, when Miss Betsy came for me. We joined in thanksgiving for her, and intercession for her mother, and then took coach. Mrs Turner made the fourth.

Sought to the oracle for direction, and was much strengthened by the answer from Acts 10:29, "Therefore came I unto you without gainsaying, as soon as I was sent for. I ask therefore for what intent ye have sent for me?" What makes it more remarkable is that it is St Peter's Day.[53] We all conceived great hopes of Mrs [Martha] Claggett. I found her very courteous, well-disposed, emptied of herself. We sang and at her desire prayed together. She freely confessed how greatly she had been prejudiced against the truth, but was thoroughly satisfied by my reading the sermon.[54] I prayed after it without much affection, again with more, and the third time strongly moved. *Knew* that she believed. Believed for her. The Scripture gave the strongest testimony of it. At first she said she must not presume to say she believed. But grew more and more confirmed. I left her in confidence God would soon clear up his own work in her soul, beyond all doubt or contradiction. Soon after, to keep me from being lifted up, the messenger of Satan was suffered to buffet me.[55]

Friday, June 30. Thanks be to God, the first thing I felt today was a fear of pride, and desire of love. Betsy Delamotte called, and gave me the following letter:

53. The day in the Christian calendar commemorating the Apostle Peter, who denied Christ three times but was restored and became an example of faith.
54. Again, his brother's sermon "Salvation by Faith."
55. Cf. 2 Cor. 12:7.

Dear Sir,

God hath heard your prayers. Yesterday, about twelve, he put his *fiat* to the desires of his distressed servant; and, glory be to him, I have enjoyed the fruits of his Holy Spirit ever since. The only uneasiness I feel is want of thankfulness and love for so unspeakable a gift. But I am confident of this also, that the same gracious hand which hath communicated will communicate even unto the end.

I am your sincere friend in Christ, William Delamotte.

O my friend, I am free indeed! I agonized some time betwixt darkness and light. But God was greater than my heart, and burst the cloud, and broke down the partition-wall, and opened to me the door of faith.

In reading this, I felt true thankfulness, and was quite melted down with God's goodness to my friend.

I followed his guidance in the afternoon to Mr Syms's. We spent the time as usual. Mrs Chapman called, said she could not stay, yet stayed [for] prayers. I was much assisted, rose, and asked her whether she believed. "I do not know but I do. For I never found myself so in my life. So strangely warmed! ~~Such strong beating of my heart~~. I seem to have a fire within me. Thought, while kneeling down, how could I expect to receive faith, when so many better than me were here? It then came into my mind that I had left my money upon the stall. But God, thought I, could take care of it, or give me a better thing."

We concluded the day with prayer at Mr Bray's.

JULY 1738

Saturday, July 1. Again at Mrs Claggett's. The younger daughter told me her mother many years ago had been cured of an incurable disease through faith. The eldest daughter and Mrs Claggett joined us. I related the cure of the lame girl at Bath. She rejoiced to hear a person might have faith, and have it long obscured by worldly cares, yet not lost; said the maid's case was hers; professed her now believing; and owned the darkness she had long lain under a just punishment for her not giving God the glory. We sang and rejoiced together, and went to the house of God as friends. In the lesson he related his past kindness to her. "And he was teaching in one of the synagogues on the sabbath day. And, behold, there was a woman which had a spirit of infirmity eighteen years, and was bowed together, and could in no wise lift up herself. And when Jesus saw her, he called her to him, and said unto her, Woman, thou art loosed from thine infirmity. And he laid his hands on her: and immediately she was made straight, and glorified God" [Luke 13:10-13]. Mrs Claggett was deeply affected, and told me afterwards that her not following the woman's example of glorifying God had occasioned all the troubles of her life. But she was now resolved, as far as in her lay, to repair her past unfaithfulness.

At Mr Syms's, extremely averse to prayer, would fain have stole away without it. But Mr Bray stopped me, saying my deadness could not hinder God, and forced me to pray. I had scarce begun when I was quite melted down, and prayed more fervently than ever before. A poor man, who came in at the beginning of the prayer, now confessed his faith before us all, being full of joy and triumph. He never found himself so before, knew his sins were forgiven, could gladly die that moment.

Sunday, July 2. Being to preach this morning for the first time, received strength for the work of the ministry in prayer and singing. The whole service at Basingshaw[56] was wonderfully animating, especially the gospel concerning the miraculous draught of fishes.[57] I preached "Salvation by Faith" to a deeply attentive audience. Gave the cup. Observing a woman full of reverence, I asked her if she had forgiveness of sins. She answered, with great sweetness and humility, "Yes, I know it now that I have forgiveness."

I preached again at London Wall,[58] without fear or weariness. As I was going into the church, a woman caught hold of my hand, and blessed me most heartily, telling me she had received forgiveness of sins while I was preaching in the morning.

In the evening we met, a troop of us, at Mr Syms's. There was one Mrs Harper there, who had this day in like manner received the Spirit by the hearing of faith, but feared to confess it. We sung

56. This would be St Michael's Church, Bassishaw, which used to stand on Basinghall Street in London.
57. Cf. Luke 5:9.
58. Either All Hallows' Church, London Wall, or St Alphage Church, London Wall.

the hymn to Christ. At the words, "Who for me, for me hath died,"[59] she burst out into tears and outcries, "I believe, I believe!" and sunk down. She continued, and increased in the assurance of faith; full of peace, and joy, and love.

We sang and prayed again. I observed one of the maids run out, and following, found her full of tears, and joy, and love. I asked what ailed her. She answered, as soon as joy would let her, that "Christ died for her!" She appeared quite overpowered with his love.

When the company were gone, she gave the following relation. That during the prayer she was encompassed with thick darkness, when a light broke in at a vast distance shining more and more as we proceeded in the prayer. At last the darkness seemed quite dispersed, and she saw our Saviour in a bright cloud, and laboured to run to him. The more she laboured, the nearer he seemed to come. She struggled as in an agony and dreaded the prayer being over before she should apprehend him. When she rose, she ran out, not knowing whither (for her face was covered) till she came close to him. He looked smiling upon her with outstretched arms, and with his crown of thorns on. She was confident, this was only the beginning of joy.[60]

Monday, July 3. Had some discourse with my friendly namesake, Charles Rivington. I begged him to suspend his judgment till he heard me preach.

Tuesday, July 4. Received a letter from my brother at Tiverton, full of heavy charges. At Mr Sparks's found Jephthah Harris. Convinced him so far that he owned he had been prejudiced against the truth, and had not faith. I carried him to Mr Bray's, prayed over him, and pleaded the promises. All were much affected.

Corrected a sermon of Mr Sparks on justification. Took coach for Bexley. In the way I was enabled to pray for my brother. I heard a good account of Mrs Delamotte, that she was almost beat out of her own righteousness.

---

59. "Hymn to the Son," st. 1, *HSP* (1739), 109 (*Poetical Works*, 1:97). Published version uses "hast died." This citation demonstrates that Charles introduced some of his hymns at gatherings of Methodists prior to their formal publication.

60. The preceding paragraph is crossed through with a diagonal line in the MS Journal. The passage is omitted in Jackson and Telford. It is doubtful that Wesley himself deleted the paragraph, since the diagonal line is Jackson's pencil marking.

Honest Frank made one of our congregation this evening, and gave a comfortable account of the little flock at Blendon. I received a fuller [account] from Hetty, informing me that her mother was convinced of unbelief, and much ashamed of her behaviour towards me.

Wednesday, July 5. William Delamotte came, and rejoiced with me for all God had done. We brought a woman home from church, and laboured hard to convince her she deserved hell. Another confessed her having received forgiveness of sins in sickness.

Friday, July 7. Mrs Delamotte followed me from church, sent for me down, hoped she did not interrupt me. Her third sentence was, "Well, Mr Wesley, are you still angry with me?" "No, Madam," I answered, "nor ever was. Before I gave myself time to consider, I was myself so violent against the truth, that I know to make allowance for others." Here we came to a full explanation. Produced the Scriptures which proved our justification by faith only, the witness of the Spirit, etc. By these and an excellent sermon of Bishop Beveridge's on the subject,[61] she seemed thoroughly convinced. All she stuck at was the instantaneousness of faith, or, in other words, the possibility of any one's perceiving when the life of faith first began.

She carried me in her coach to Blendon, where the poor servants were overjoyed to see me once more. While we were praying for her, she sent for me up to her closet. I found her quite melted into an humble, contrite, longing frame of spirit. She showed me several prayers attesting the true faith, especially that of Bishop Taylor:

> I know, O blessed Jesus, that thou didst take upon thee my nature, that thou mightest suffer for my sins; that thou didst suffer to deliver me from them, and from thy Father's wrath. And I was delivered from his wrath, that I might serve thee, in holiness and righteousness all my days. Lord, I am as sure thou didst the great work of redemption for me, and for all mankind, as that I am alive. This is my hope, the strength of my spirit, my joy, and my confi-

---

61. Most likely Sermon 74 in William Beveridge (1637–1708), *The Works of . . . William Beveridge . . . containing all the sermons*, 2nd ed. (London: Arthur Bettesworth & William Innys, 1729), 1:613–23. This sermon details justification by faith and insists it does not undercut good works. Beveridge was Bishop of St. Asaph, 1704–1708.

dence. And do thou never let the spirit of unbelief enter into me, and take me from this rock. Here I will dwell, for I have a delight therein. Here I will live, and here I desire to die.[62]

She asked me what she could do more, being convinced of her want of faith, and not able to give it herself. I preached the freeness of the grace, and betook myself to prayer for her, labouring, sighing, looking for the witness of the Spirit, the fullness of the promises, in her behalf. I conjured her to expect continually the accomplishment of the promise, and not think her confessed unworthiness any bar. Next morning I returned to town.

Sunday, July 9. Preached my brother's sermon upon faith at ____ and a second time in St Sepulchre's vestry. In walking home with Mrs Burton, I said, "Surely there must be something which you are not willing to give up, or God would have given you comfort before now." She answered only by her tears. After praying for her at Mr Bray's, I lay down, rose, stopped her going home, and carried her with James [Hutton] and Mrs Turner from the company to pray. After prayer, in which I was much assisted, I found her under a great concern, trembling, and cold; longing, yet dreading, to say "she believed." We prayed again. She then said, with much struggling, "Lord, I believe. Help thou my unbelief" [Mark 9:24]. She repeated it several times, and gained strength by each repetition.

Monday, July [10].[63] At Mr Sparks's request, I went with him, Mr Bray, and Mr Burnham to Newgate, and preached to the ten malefactors under sentence of death; but with a heavy heart. My old prejudices against the possibility of a death-bed repentance still hung upon me, and I could hardly hope there was mercy for those whose time was so short. But in the midst of my languid discourse a sudden spirit of faith came upon me, and I promised them all pardon, in the name of Jesus Christ, if they would then, as at the last hour, repent, and believe the gospel. Nay, I did believe they would accept of the proffered mercy, and could not help telling them I had no doubt but God would give me every soul of them.

---

62. This prayer is found in Sec. 10 of the concluding set of prayers in Jeremy Taylor (1613–1667), *The Rule and Exercises of Holy Living . . . Together with Prayers* (London: Francis Ash, 1650). Taylor was Bishop of Down and Connor, 1661–1667.
63. MS has "July 20," which is in error.

In going to Mr Chapman's I met Margaret Beutiman, and bade her follow, for we were several of us to join in prayer there. James Hutton, Mr Holland, Mr and Mrs Syms got thither soon after us. We sang, and pleaded the promises. In the midst of prayer, Margaret received the atonement, and professed her faith without wavering, her love to Christ, and willingness to die that moment. We returned thanks for her, and I then offered to go. They pressed me to stay a little longer. I did so, and heard Mrs Storer, a sister of Mr Bray's, complain of the hardness of her heart. She owned she had been under the utmost uneasiness since our last meeting at her brother's, unable to pray, or find any rest to her soul. While we were singing the Hymn to the Father,[64] she did find the rest she sighed after; was quite pierced, as she said; her heart ready to burst, and her whole nature overpowered. We went to prayers, and then opened the Scripture, "I thank thee, O Father, Lord of heaven and earth, that thou hast hid these things from the wise and prudent, and hast revealed them unto babes" [Matt. 11:25]. She then was strengthened to profess her faith, and increased in peace and joy. As we walked, she said she could not have conceived how these things could be, what the change was which we spoke of. Her faith was farther confirmed by public prayer, and she continued all the evening full of comfort, and peace that passeth all understanding.

Tuesday, July 11. Preached with earnestness to the prisoners from the second lesson. One or two of them were deeply affected. At Bray's I found a letter from William Delamotte, and read, with joy and thankfulness, as follows:

> I cannot keep peace. The mercies of God come in so abundantly on our unworthy family, that I am not able to declare them. Yet as they are his blessings through your ministry, I must inform you of them, as they will strengthen your hands, and prove helpers of your joy.
>
> Great, then, I believe was the struggle between nature and grace in the soul of my mother. But God, who knoweth the very heart and reins, hath searched her out. Her spirit, like Naaman's flesh,[65] is returned as that of a little child. She is converted, and

---

64. Almost certainly a reference to Wesley's "Hymn of Thanksgiving to the Father," which would soon be published in *HSP* (1739), 107–8 (*Poetical Works*, 1:96–97).
65. Cf. 2 Kings 5:1-27.

Christ hath spoken peace to her soul. This work was begun in her the morning you left us, though she concealed it from you.

When she waked, the following Scripture was strongly suggested to her, "Either what woman, having ten pieces of silver, if she lose one, doth not light a candle and sweep the house, and seek diligently till she find it" [Luke 15:8]. She rose immediately, took up Bishop Taylor, and opened upon a place which so strongly asserted this living faith, that she was fully convinced. But the enemy preached humility to her, that she could not deserve so great a gift. However, God still pursued, and she could not long forbear communicating the emotion of her soul to me. We prayed, read, and conversed for an hour. The Lord made use of a mean instrument to convince her of her ignorance in the word. Throughout that day her mind was more and more enlightened, till at length she broke out, "Where have I been? I know nothing. I see nothing. My mind is all darkness. How have I opposed the Scripture!" The tempter, thus enraged, excited all his powers to persuade her she was labouring after something that was not to be attained. But Christ suffered her not to fall. She flew to him in prayer and singing, and though Satan damped her much, yet could he not conquer her, because that which was conceived in her was of the Holy Ghost.

She continued agonizing all the evening. But how can I utter the sequel? The first object of her thoughts the next morning was Christ. She saw him approaching; and seeing, loved, believed, adored. Her prayers drew him still nearer, and everything she saw concurred to hasten the embrace of her Beloved. Thus she continued in the Spirit till four, when, reading in her closet, she received the kiss of reconciliation. Her own soul could not contain the joys attending it. She could not forbear imparting to her friends and neighbours that she had found the piece which she had lost. Satan in vain attempted to shake her, for she felt in herself,

Faith's assurance, hope's increase,
All the confidence of love.[66]

Mr Sparks this morning asked me whether I would preach for him at St Helen's. I agreed to supply Mr Broughton's place, who is now at Oxford, arming our friends against the faith. The pain in my side was very violent, but I looked up to Christ, and owned his healing power. At the same time, that came into my mind, "Out of

---

66. "Hymn to the Holy Ghost," st. 8, *HSP* (1739), 111 (*Poetical Works*, 1:101). Again they are using a hymn that had not yet been published.

weakness were made strong" [Heb. 11:34]. No sooner did I enter the coach than the pain left me, and I preached faith in Christ to a vast congregation with great boldness, adding much extempore.

After sermon, Mrs Hind, with whom Mr Broughton lodges, sent for me, owned her agreement to the doctrine, and pressed me to come and talk with Mr Broughton, who, she could not but believe, must himself agree to it.

From her I went to Mr Syms, and found that God had set his seal to my ministry, Mr Dandy and Miss Branford declaring faith had come to them by hearing me. We rejoiced, and gave thanks from the ground of the heart.

Wednesday, July 12. Preached at Newgate to the condemned felons. Visited one of them in his cell, sick of a fever—a poor black that had robbed his master. I told him of One who came down from heaven to save lost sinners, and him in particular. Described the sufferings of the Son of God, his sorrows, agony, and death. He listened with all the signs of eager astonishment. The tears trickled down his cheeks while he cried, "What! Was it for me? Did God suffer all this for so poor a creature as me!" I left him waiting for the salvation of God.

In the evening Mr Washington of Queen's came to dispute with me. I simply testified my want of faith three months ago, and my having it now. Asked whether he could lay down his life for the truth of his being in the faith, whether he allowed Christ to be as *really* present in the believing soul as in the third heavens. Told him he was yet in his sins, and knew nothing, and begged him to pray for direction.

Thursday, July 13. Read prayers and preached at Newgate, and administered the Sacrament to our friends, with five of the felons. Was much affected and assisted in prayer for them, and exhorted them with great comfort and confidence.

Friday, July 14. Received the Sacrament from the Ordinary.[67] Spake strongly to the poor malefactors, and to the sick negro in the condemned hole, moved by *his* sorrow and earnest desire of Christ Jesus.

---

67. The Anglican priest who served as the prison chaplain at Newgate.

Saturday, July 15. Preached there again with an enlarged heart and rejoiced with my poor happy black, who now *believes* the Son of God loved him, and gave himself for him.[68]

Sunday, July 16. [Charles] Metcalf and Savage came. The latter received faith on Friday night, in prayer, and is now filled with comfort, peace, and joy. Took coach with Metcalf. Preached the Threefold State[69] with boldness, gave the Sacrament. Went thence to Mrs Claggett's, sang, rejoiced, and gave thanks, in behalf of both the maids, now added to the church by true divine faith. Mr [Wyseman] Claggett coming in by mistake, we laid hold on and carried him with us to Blackfriars.[70] Very weak and faint, yet was I strengthened to preach for above an hour. Carried to bed full of pain, expecting my fever; yet believing it could not return, unless it were best.

Monday, July 17. Rose free from pain. At Newgate preached on death (which they must suffer the day after tomorrow). Mr Sparks assisted in giving the Sacrament. Another clergyman was there. Newington asked me to go in the coach with him. At one with the black in his cell, James Hutton assisting. Two more of the malefactors came. I had great help and power in prayer. One rose, and said he felt his heart all on fire, so as he never found himself before; was all in a sweat; believed Christ died for him. I found myself overwhelmed with the love of Christ to sinners. The black was quite happy. The other criminal was in an excellent temper; believing, or on the point of it.

Talked with another concerning faith in Christ. He was greatly moved. The Lord, I trust, will help *his* unbelief also.

Joined at Bray's with Hutton, Holland, Burton, in fervent prayer and thanksgiving. At six carried Bray and [William] Fish to Newgate again, and talked chiefly with Hudson and Newington. Newington declared he had felt, some time ago in prayer, inexpressible joy and love, but was much troubled at its being so soon withdrawn. The Lord gave power to pray. They were deeply affected. We have great hopes of both.

---

68. Cf. Titus 2:14.

69. This is Charles's sermon on 1 John 3:14. The surviving MS for the sermon carries Charles's note that he preached the sermon "July 16, 1738 at St George the Martyr's church, Queen's Square, [and later at] Blackfriars." See *Sermons*, 130–51.

70. This would be a society meeting in the Blackfriars region of London.

Tuesday, July 18. The Ordinary read prayers and preached. I administered the Sacrament to the black, and eight more, having first instructed them in the nature of it. Spake comfortably to them afterwards.

In the cells, one told me that whenever he offered to pray, or had a serious thought, something came and hindered him; was with him almost continually; and once appeared. After we had prayed for him in *faith*, he rose amazingly comforted, full of joy and love, so that we could not doubt his having received the atonement.

At night I was locked in with Bray in one of the cells. We wrestled in mighty prayer. All the criminals were present, and all delightfully cheerful. The soldier, in particular, found his comfort and joy increase every moment. Another, from the time he communicated, has been in perfect peace. Joy was visible in all their faces. We sang:

> Behold the Saviour of mankind,
>   Nail'd to the shameful Tree!
> How vast the Love that Him inclined
>   To bleed and die for Thee! etc.[71]

It was one of the most triumphant hours I have ever known. Yet on

Wednesday, July 19, I rose very heavy and backward to visit them for the last time. At six prayed and sang with them all together. The Ordinary would read prayers, and preach[ed] most miserably. Mr Sparks and Mr Broughton present, I felt my heart full of tender love to the latter. He administered. All the ten received. Then he prayed and I after him.

At half-hour past nine their irons were knocked off, and their hands tied. I went in a coach with Sparks, Washington, and a friend of Newington's (Newington himself not being permitted). By half-hour past ten we came to Tyburn.[72] Waited till eleven, then were brought the children appointed to die. I got upon the cart with Sparks and Broughton. The Ordinary endeavoured to follow, when the poor prisoners begged he might not come, and the mob kept him down.

---

71. "On the Crucifixion," st. 1, *CPH* (1737), 46. This poem by Samuel Wesley Sr was salvaged after the fire at the Epworth rectory in February 1709, and was first published in this *Collection*.

72. Tyburn, Middlesex, was the site for hangings in London, near present-day Tyburn Convent on the northern edge of Hyde Park.

I prayed first, then Sparks and Broughton. We had prayed before that our Lord would show there was a power superior to the fear of death. Newington had quite forgot his pain. They were all cheerful; full of comfort, peace, and triumph; assuredly persuaded Christ had died for them and waited to receive them into paradise. Greenaway was impatient to be with Christ.

The black had spied me coming out of the coach, and saluted me with his looks. As often as his eyes met mine, he smiled with the most composed, delightful countenance I ever saw. Read caught hold of my hand in a transport of joy. Newington seemed perfectly pleased. Hudson declared he was never better, or more at ease, in mind and body. None showed any natural terror of death—no fear, or crying, or tears. All expressed their desire of our following them to paradise. I never saw such calm triumph, such incredible indifference to dying. We sang several hymns, particularly,

> Behold the Saviour of mankind,
> Nail'd to the shameful Tree . . .

And the hymn entitled "Faith in Christ," which concludes,

> A guilty, weak, and helpless worm,
> Into thy hands I fall.
> Be thou my Life, my Righteousness,
> My Jesus, and my all.[73]

We prayed Him, in earnest faith, to receive their spirits. I could do nothing but rejoice. Kissed Newington and Hudson. Took leave of each in particular. Mr Broughton bade them not be surprised when the cart should draw away. They cheerfully replied they should not, expressed some concern how we should get back to the coach. We left them going to meet their Lord, ready for the Bridegroom. When the cart drew off, not one stirred, or struggled for life, but meekly gave up their spirits. Exactly at twelve they were turned off. I spoke a few suitable words to the crowd, and returned, full of peace and confidence in our friends' happiness.

That hour under the gallows was the most blessed hour of my life.

---

73. "Faith in Christ," st. 6, *CPH* (1737), 52; cf. the note for June 24, 1738, above.

At Mr Bray's we renewed our triumph. I found my brother and sister Lambert[74] there, and preached to them the gospel of forgiveness, which they received without opposition.

Thursday, July 20. At morning prayers in Islington. Had some serious conversation with Mr [George] Stonehouse, the vicar. Brought him home with me from evening prayers.

Friday, July 21. Mr [John] Robson[75] came. Received the strange doctrine of faith with surprising readiness. At night many joined us in prayer and praise. Brother[76] Edmonds bore his testimony. So did two others who had received the blessing of pardon in hearing my sermon upon "The voice of one crying in the wilderness, prepare ye the way of the Lord" [Matt. 3:3; Mark 1:3; Luke 3:3]. Another stood up (lately a notorious sinner) and declared the same. We continued until eleven, praying, and praising God.

Saturday, July 22. Mr Robson confessed he did believe there was such a faith, but it was impossible for him to obtain it, and it must necessarily bring on a persecution. We continued pleading the promises for him. He was greatly moved, and grew stronger and stronger in hope. I was full of expectation, as well as Mr Bray. In singing the Hymn to the Father,[77] our poor friend was quite overpowered, and even compelled to believe, till at last he was filled with strength and confidence.

At five Mr Chapman came from Mr Broughton, and appeared entirely estranged. He insisted that there is no need of our being persecuted now. I told him I was of a different judgment, and believed every doctrine of God must have these two marks: 1) meeting all the opposition of men and devils, 2) triumphing over all. I expressed my readiness to part with him, and all my friends and relations, for the truth's sake. Avowed my liberty and happiness since Whitsunday. Made a bridge for a flying enemy, and parted tolerable friends.

Monday, July 24. Preached faith at Mr Stonehouse's. Still he stuck upon fitness. We prayed most earnestly. Miss Claggetts dined

---

74. That is, Charles's sister Anne and her husband, John Lambert.

75. John Robson (b. 1715), had been a student of John Wesley at Lincoln College, 1732–1735, and member of the Oxford Methodists.

76. From this point Charles increasingly adopts the practice of referring to the members of the revival movement as "brother" and "sister."

77. Cf. the note for July 10 above.

with us. Prayed again with great comfort and hope for him. He continued insensible. We bade him open the Bible. He did, on these apposite words: 1 Thess. 1:5, "For our gospel came not unto you in word only, but also in power, and in the Holy Ghost, and in much assurance." Stayed with him after evening prayer, to keep him from Mr Chapman. Agreed to take charge of his parish, under him, as his curate.

At night Mrs Turner told me at Mrs Claggett's that she had been greatly strengthened to pray in faith for Mr Stonehouse.

Tuesday, July 25. William Delamotte came, and carried me to Bexley.

Wednesday, July 26. At Blendon. Mrs Delamotte called upon me to rejoice with her in the experience of the divine goodness. In the evening met several sincere seekers at Mr Piers's, with some who knew in whom they have believed, particularly one poor man whose ~~faith has cured him of an ague~~.[78] We had great power in prayer and joy in thanksgiving. William Delamotte often shouted for joy. Before nine we got back to Blendon. Mrs Delamotte then confessed that all her desire had been to affront, or make me angry; that she had long watched every word I said; had persecuted the truth, and all who professed it; etc.

Thursday, July 27. In the coach to London I preached faith in Christ. A lady was extremely offended, avowed her own merits in plain terms, asked if I was not a Methodist, threatened to beat me. I declared I deserved nothing but hell; so did she, and must confess it before she could have a title to heaven. This was most intolerable to her. The others were less offended, began to listen, asked where I preached. A maidservant devoured every word.

Friday, July 28. Mr [William] Exall received faith in immediate answer to our prayers. At Mr Stonehouse's met Charles Rivington and his wife, but could come to no agreement—I insisting on a particular manifestation of Christ in every soul, and he denying it.

Sunday, July 30. At six received the Sacrament. Preached faith at ten, and again in the afternoon at All Hallows' [church], Thames

---

78. The phrase "particularly one poor man whose faith has cured him of an ague" was not printed in Jackson or Telford.

Street. My strength increased with my labour. At Mr Syms's began expounding the Epistle to the Romans.

Monday, July 31. Began writing a sermon upon Gal. 3:22, "But the Scripture hath concluded all under sin, that the promise by faith of Jesus Christ might be given to them that believe."[79]

Met Mr Lynn, who had often asked me to his house. I went and found him again convinced of unbelief, and more uneasy than ever.

AUGUST 1738

Tuesday, August 1. Read prayers at Islington (as I do most days), and slept at Mr Stonehouse's.

Thursday, August 3. Met Lord Egmont and declared my intention of returning to Georgia if my health permitted, with which he was much pleased. I corrected Mr Whitefield's *Journal* for the press, my advice to suppress it being overruled.[80]

Sunday, August 6. Preached at Islington, and gave the cup. In the afternoon I read prayers in a church in London, and preached again. Faint, full of pain when I began, but my work quite cured me.

Thursday, August 10. Walked to Mrs Hind's. Mr Broughton and Washington were there. They denied explicitly that we are saved by Christ's imputed righteousness and affirmed that works do justify, have a share in making righteous before God. I appealed to the Homilies, which they had never read, for justification by faith only. When they were gone, I had much lively conversation with Mrs Hind and her son, well disposed to receive faith, if they have it not already.

Saturday, August 12. We were warmed by reading George Whitefield's *Journal*. I walked with Metcalf, etc., in great joy, wishing for a place to sing in, when a blacksmith stopped us. We turned into his house, sang an hymn, and went on our way rejoicing.[81]

---

79. This sermon has apparently not survived.
80. This volume was published, without George Whitefield's approval, as *A Journal of a Voyage from London to Savannah in Georgia* (London: James Hutton, 1738).
81. Cf. Acts 8:39.

Sunday, August 13. Preached at Islington.[82] Gave the Sacrament to a sick woman, who was therein assured of her reconciliation to God, through Christ Jesus.

Tuesday, August 15. Communicated again with the sick woman. Mrs Claggett and her daughters made the greater part of the congregation. We were all comforted. Seldom fail seeing them and Islington once a day.

Wednesday, August 16. Dragged out by Mr Bray to Jephthah Harris's religious society; where, after much disputing, I confuted, rather than convinced, them, by reading the Homily on Justification.

Thursday, August 17. Preached faith to a dying woman and administered the Sacrament. She was satisfied God had sent us, told me I was the instrument of saving her soul. I asked, "Had you then no faith before we came?" She answered, "No, how should I? It is the gift of God, and he never gave it me till now." Do you now think you shall be saved? "Yes," she replied smiling. "I have no doubt of it." "You need not then fear the devil's hating you." "I know that he is chained. I have nothing to do with him, or he with me." She promised to bring up a good report of us to those she was going to.

Read prayers at Islington. Met Mrs Brockmer,[83] one who in despair had been directed to Christ, and in a fortnight found peace to her soul, steadfastly believing her sin had been imputed to Christ and his righteousness to her. She asked me to go and see the sick woman again. Preached faith to a large company I found there. The woman bore a noble testimony. I asked her before them all: "Have you received forgiveness?" Her answer was, "Yes, I am assured of it by Christ himself." To them she said, they must not *think* they believe, but *feel* it, and have a full confidence thereof. They all thanked me much.

Friday, August 18. Prayed and rejoiced with her again, yet more ascertained of her salvation. Mrs Brockmer, the Claggetts, etc., were of the company. We got upon the leads[84] and sang; full of zeal, and life, and comfort. Read prayers, and with Mr Brockmer[85] and

---

82. Charles preached his sermon on 1 John 3:14; cf. *Sermons*, 132.
83. Charles spells "Brockmar."
84. This is a flat part of the roof of a house, often covered with lead.
85. John Paul Brockmer, a German gold-watch engraver of Salisbury Court, Fleet Street. Again, Charles spells "Brockmar."

others, returned to singing at Mr Stonehouse's. He read us an Homily. At seven we all walked out, were driven by the hard rain to a shed, where we sang and preached to those about us. I came wet through to Mr Bray's. I joined our friends there in singing, reading, and prayer. A young man received faith in that hour.

Saturday, August 19. At Mr Stonehouse's. Read prayers with some life. Gave the Sacrament to the women. Asked, "Do you still believe you shall be saved?" "Yes. I am humbly confident of it and care not how soon I depart. I desire to be dissolved, and to be with Christ." We sang on the leads as before.

At three found my friend Stonehouse exceeding heavy and sorely distressed through fear of marrying. I prayed earnestly that neither he nor I might ever be left to follow our own heart's desires. After reading prayers I buried a corpse, and went back to Bray's weighed down with my poor George's burden.

Sunday, August 20. Preached at Islington in the morning, at Clerkenwell[86] in the afternoon on "The Scripture hath concluded all under sin," etc. [Gal. 3:22]. God gave me great boldness; and the word, I trust, did not return empty.[87]

Monday, August 21. Mr Stonehouse's maid, Thomasin, told me she had found great peace, and comfort, and joy, in prayer last Saturday, so that her very inside (as she expressed it) was changed. Visited Mrs Hall, a-dying. (She made signs of her confident faith.) Then Mrs Hankinson, who told me she had been very uneasy ever since I said a person must be sure of their forgiveness. I preached faith, as the only instrument of justification. She was quite melted down. We prayed. She rose, and said her heart was set at liberty, her burden taken away, and her spirit joyful in Christ her Saviour.

Thursday, August 24. At Mrs Musgrave's met one Mrs Nichols, who readily owned she was not free, had not faith, but believed Christ could just then give it to her. We prayed for her in faith. She received immediate answer. Expressed her confidence, delight, and love of Jesus; and, at the same time, her utter defiance of Satan, sin, and death.

---

86. Likely at St John's Church, where John Wesley preached the following month; cf. *Journal* (September 23, 1738), *Works* 19:13.
87. Cf. Isa. 55:11.

Saturday, August 26. With Mr Stonehouse—possessed with a strange fancy that a man must be wholly sanctified before he can know that he is justified.

Sunday, August 27. Preached at St John's[88] the Three-fold State [1 John 3:14], and helped to administer the Sacrament to a very large congregation.

Monday, August 28. Came in the coach to Oxford. Rejoiced at Mr Fox's, with Mr Kinchin, Hutchings, and other Christian friends.

Tuesday, August 29. Preached to the poor prisoners in the Castle.[89] Many, with Mr [Robert] Watson, were present at the Society.[90] All of one mind, earnestly seeking Christ, I read the Homilies, and continued instant in prayer. A woman cried, "Where have I been so long? I have been in darkness. I shall never be delivered out of it"—and burst into tears. Mrs Cleminger too appeared in the pangs of the new birth.

Wednesday, August 30. Left Mr Watson convinced of unbelief, and rode to Stanton Harcourt. Spoke with great reluctance, yet fully and plainly, to my sister [Kezzy]; and then to Mr Gambold and Kinchin, who surprised me by receiving my hard saying that they had not faith. I was ashamed to see the great thankfulness, and childlike, loving spirit of Mr Kinchin, even before justification.

Thursday, August 31. Waited upon the Dean, but we could not quite agree in our notions of faith. He wondered we had not hit upon the Homilies sooner, treated me with great candour and friendliness.

At the Society read my sermon, "The Scripture hath concluded all under sin" [Gal. 3:22] and urged upon each my usual question, "Do you deserve to be damned?" Mrs Platt with the utmost vehemence cried out, "Yes. I do, I do!" Prayed that if God saw there any contrite soul, he would fulfill his promise of coming and making his abode with it. "If thou hast sent thy Spirit to reprove any sinner of sin, in the name of Jesus Christ, I claim salvation for that sinner!" Again she broke out into strong cries; but of joy, not sorrow, being

---

88. Charles's annotations on his sermon identify this as St John Zachary Church, which used to stand next to St Anne's and St Agnes's Church on Gresham Street, London.

89. Charles preached his sermon on 1 John 3:14; cf. *Sermons*, 132.

90. "Society" is capitalized throughout when it refers to the religious gatherings characteristic of the Moravian and Methodist movements.

quite overpowered with the love of Christ. I asked her if she believed in Jesus. She answered in full assurance of faith. We sang and rejoiced over her (she still continued kneeling), joined in thanksgiving; but her voice was heard above ours.

Mr Kinchin asked, "Have you forgiveness of sins?" "I am perfectly assured I have." "Have you the earnest of the Spirit in your heart?" "I have. I know I have. I feel it now within." Her answers to these and the like questions were expressive of the strongest confidence, to the great encouragement of all present.

Related this at Hutchings's before Mr Wells, who seems fully convinced of the truth.

SEPTEMBER 1738

Friday, September 1. Took coach for London. Between five and six reached Mrs Claggett's. They heartily joined me in praise and prayer. Mr Claggett was very friendly. James Hutton supped with us. Found several at Bray's. After prayer he told me God plainly forbids my return to America by my success here.

Sunday, September 3. Preached Salvation by Faith[91] at Westminster Abbey; gave the cup. In the afternoon preached at St Botolph's.[92] Expounded Rom. 2 at Syms's, to above two hundred people.

Monday, September 4. Charles Kinchin, now my inseparable companion, accompanied me to Bexley and Blendon. Prayed, and was comforted with the poor people.

Tuesday, September 5. Mr Piers agreed to board my sister Kezzy. Read my sermon, prayed, and rejoiced with Mrs Delamotte, and the rest at Blendon. Charles was all thankfulness and love. Returned to town very ill of a sore throat.

Sunday, September 10. Preached faith in the morning at Sir George Wheler's chapel,[93] and assisted at the Sacrament. In the afternoon

---

91. It is possible he was preaching his brother's sermon; cf. June 21, 1738, above.

92. Charles preached the first part of his sermon on 1 John 3:14; cf. *Sermons*, 132. The annotation makes clear it was St Botolph's Church on Aldersgate Street (at the intersection with Little Britain).

93. Charles spells "Wheeler's."

at St Botolph's.[94] In the evening at Syms's was much strengthened to pray and expound to above three hundred attentive souls. Another lost sheep was now brought home.

Friday, September 15. Meeting Charles Metcalf's mother, I laboured to convince her of unbelief (our first point with all). She yielded at last, and we joined in earnest prayer for her.

Saturday, September 16. James Hutton [came], and carried me perforce to Newgate, where we preached Christ to four condemned prisoners. At night my brother returned from Hernnhuth. We took sweet counsel together, comparing our experiences.

Sunday, September 17. At the early Sacrament my brother read prayers. I preached "All under Sin" in Grace-church-street,[95] the morning; at Queen's-Street chapel[96] in the afternoon. In the evening I preached faith, from Rom. 3, at the Savoy Society. My brother entertained us at night with the Moravian experiences.[97]

Friday, September 22. At Bray's expounded Eph. 1. A dispute arising about absolute predestination, I entered my protest against that doctrine.

Sunday, September 24. Comforted Mrs Claggett, much threatened by her husband; and then Mrs Hankinson, who has lost several boarders, yet is in nothing terrified by her adversaries. Read prayers in Islington church, and preached with great boldness.[98] There was a vast audience, better than usual. None went out as they had threatened, and frequently done heretofore; especially the well-dressed hearers, "where'er I mentioned hell to ears polite,"[99] and urged that rude question, "Do you deserve to be damned?"

---

94. Charles preached the second part of his sermon on 1 John 3:14; see *Sermons*, 132.

95. St Benet's Church, Gracechurch Street, London.

96. A chapel built by William Ragueley at the end of Great Queen Street. It operated at this time as an Anglican chapel, but later became a Methodist chapel.

97. John Wesley brought back from Germany a manuscript collection of accounts by the Moravians at Herrnhut of their spiritual experience. This manuscript does not seem to have survived. Cf. John Wesley, Letter to James Hutton (April 9, 1739), *Works* 25:629, n. 6.

98. There is some evidence he was preaching his brother's sermon on Exod. 20:8; cf. *Sermons*, 335.

99. A contrasting echo of Alexander Pope's sarcastic description of a "soft" Anglican cleric "who never mentions hell to ears polite," in *Epistle to the Right Honourable Richard Earl of Burlington* (London: L. Gilliver, 1731), 12.

Sang, rejoiced, and gave thanks at Mr Stonehouse's, and again at Mrs Hankinson's. Talked with one of her misses, to whom faith had come by hearing.

Wednesday, September 27. In our way to Oxford, I talked closely with my fellow traveller, Mr Coombs.[100] He expressed his desire of faith. Moved to sing "Salvation by Faith," then "Faith in Christ."[101] I told him, if the Spirit had convinced him of unbelief, he could of righteousness also, even before we reached Oxford. I stopped and prayed that he might believe. Immediately, he told me, he was in such a blessed temper as he never before experienced. We halted, and went to prayers. He testified that great delight he felt, saying, It was heaven, if it would but continue. While we were discoursing, the fire within him, he said, diffused itself through every part. He was brim-full of joy (yet not knowing he believed), and eager to praise God. He called upon me to join. "Was I now in heaven, I could not think of my sins. I should only think of praising God." We sang and shouted all the way to Oxford.

Met our friends with Mr Hutchings at Fox's. Mrs Platt was full of life and love. Read the experiences of the Moravians.

Thursday, September 28. Called on my friend that was, John Sarney, now entirely estranged by the offence of the cross. Rode to my *constant* friend, John Gambold. Mr Combes communicated with us. His warmth, he told me, had returned through his *professing* his faith. Left Mrs Gambold in confident hope of soon receiving it. Preached boldly at Oxford; prayed after God with Mr Wells.

Saturday, September 30. Returned to town having in some measure confirmed our friends at Oxford. My brother informed [me] of one who was yesterday an open sinner, and today received into Christ's church, or the company of faithful people. Mrs Claggett [said] that this morning, in utter despair, she had heard a distinct whisper, "I am the Lord thy God, mighty to save."[102]

---

100. Thomas Coombs, who matriculated at Corpus Christi in 1733, at the age of seventeen. Charles spells "Combes."

101. Charles is likely referring to the hymns "Faith in Christ" and "Salvation by Grace" found in *CPH* (1737), 52, 54–55. Both were by Isaac Watts.

102. Cf. Isa. 63:1.

OCTOBER 1738

Sunday, October 1. Read prayers and gave the Sacrament at the guest-room. In the afternoon I read prayers and preached at St Margaret's, Westminster.[103]

Monday, October 2. Dined at Mr Brockmer's, and we admonished one another in psalms and hymns and spiritual songs. Went with the three Miss Claggetts to our poor sick woman. My brother and James followed, then Mrs Metcalf and three of the Delamottes. We found her full of triumph, and vehement desires to be dissolved and to be with Christ. Did this in remembrance of Him.[104]

Thursday, October 5. Went with Sparks to Newgate; shamefully unwilling, yet preached on repentance with earnest zeal.

Sunday, October 8. Preached at Bexley "All under Sin." Finished my sermon in the afternoon. The people very outrageous. Mrs Delamotte carried me home. Exhorted my friends in the kitchen. A sermon read in the parlour, preached faith in Christ. Mr Delamotte made no objection, but seemed much pleased.

Monday, October 9. Walked with William Delamotte to Bexley, where my sermon has occasioned a great uproar.

Wednesday, October 11. Got back to my friends in London. Spoke plainly to Mr Claggett, who has been very violent toward his wife since I left them.

Thursday, October 12. At West's[105] with Bray and Sparks. Prayed, pleading the promises in much bodily pain. Asked in faith that it might leave me. It did, while I was walking to James's.

Friday, October 13. At seven read prayers and preached at St Antholin's.

Sunday, October 15. Heard Hutchings at St Lawrence's.[106] Much comfort and meltings in prayer after the Sacrament. Preached "The One Thing Needful" [Luke 10:42] at Islington, and added much extempore. Sang at Mr Stonehouse's. Syms's was excessively crowded

---

103. Charles preached his sermon on 1 John 3:14; cf. *Sermons*, 132.
104. Cf. Luke 22:19.
105. John West, black silk dyer of Thames Street, London.
106. St Lawrence Jewry Church, London.

in the evening, spake with much boldness and warmth. At Bray's found the bands meeting. Mr Stonehouse was there, in a most child-like spirit. Moved to pray for him earnestly, and according to God. Asked particularly that some one might *then* receive the atonement. While they were going, E—— came; complained of the pain and bur-den of sin that bruised him. I took him aside with Hutchings. He received faith in immediate answer to our prayer; professed it; full of peace, and joy, and love. Expressed a strong desire to pray for Mr Stonehouse. I prayed again with vehemence and tears. Bray greatly affected; so James and all the rest—yet no answer. Mr Stonehouse said the blessing was withheld from him to increase our importunity.

Friday, October 20. Seeing so few present at St Antholin's, I thought of preaching extempore. Afraid, yet ventured on the prom-ise, "Lo, I am with you always" [Matt. 28:20], and spake on justifi-cation from Rom. 3 for three-quarters of an hour without hesitation. Glory be to God, who keepeth his promise for ever.

Friday, October 20.[107] Waited with my brother on the Bishop of London, to answer the complaints he had heard against us, that we preached an absolute assurance of salvation. Some of his words were, "If by 'assurance' you mean an inward persuasion, whereby a man is conscious in himself, after examining his life by the law of God, and weighing his own sincerity, that he is in a state of salva-tion, and acceptable to God, I don't see how any good Christian can be without such an assurance." "This," we answered, "is what we contend for. But we have been charged as antinomians, for preach-ing justification by faith only." "Can anyone preach otherwise, who agrees to our Church and the Scriptures?" "Indeed, by preaching it strongly, and not inculcating good works, many have been made antinomians in theory, though not in practice: especially in King Charles's time." "But there is a heavy charge against us bishops, by your bringing the Archbishop's authority for rebaptizing an adult." My brother answered that he had expressly declared the contrary. "Yet," added he, "if a person dissatisfied with lay-baptism should desire episcopal, I should think it my duty to administer it, after having acquainted the bishop according to the canon." "Well, I am against it myself, where anyone has had the Dissenters' baptism."

---

107. Charles repeated the date because he was starting a new page. John's *Journal* confirms it was Friday, October 20 (see *Works* 19:359).

Next my brother enquired whether his reading in a religious society made it a conventicle. His Lordship warily referred us to the laws. But upon our urging the question, "Are the religious societies conventicles?" he answered, "No, I think not. However, you can read the acts and laws as well as I. I determine nothing." We hoped his Lordship would not henceforward receive an accusation against a presbyter, but at the mouth of two or three witnesses.[108] He said, "No, by no means. And you may have free access to me at all times." We thanked him, and took our leave.

Sunday, October 22. Preached "One Thing Needful" [Luke 10:42] at St Clement's,[109] to a very large audience (many of whom stayed the communion), and again at Sir George Wheler's chapel.

Tuesday, October 24. Told Mr Claggett, in one of his persecuting fits, that I should be glad to see him when on a sick-bed; that I had the satisfaction of having him my friend when he was most so to himself, and to God. He went out to fetch Bishop Taylor to confute me, but opened upon a place strongly asserting this living, justifying faith. He owned himself fully convinced; admired the hand of Providence; confessed he had loathed the sight of me, and hated me from his heart; but now loved me entirely, and all mankind; could hug me in his bosom; never knew such comfort in his life as at this moment; could not be beat out of it by all the world. Alas! that this morning-cloud should ever pass away!

Thursday, October 26. At Mrs Hind's charged by Mr Capell with particularly pleading the promises. Confessed, and justified it. James came to second me. We were both zealous, not angry.

Friday, October 27. Mr Sparks's, fully persuaded his sins are forgiven.

Sunday, October 29. Preached with strength at St George's,[110] then at Ironmongers' Almshouses,[111] and at night expounded Rom. 5 to a large audience in the Minories.[112]

---

108. Cf. 1 Tim. 5:19.

109. Almost certainly St Clement Danes Church, on the Strand, where John Wesley preached shortly after; cf *Journal* (November 5, 1738), *Works* 19:20.

110. St George's Church, Bloomsbury, London. Charles preached the first half of his sermon on 1 John 3:14; cf. *Sermons*, 132. (He preached the second half there on November 19.)

111. Charles again preached his sermon on 1 John 3:14; cf. *Sermons*, 132.

112. The Minories is a street that runs north from the Tower to Aldgate.

NOVEMBER 1738

Thursday, November 2. Much affected in praying for Mr Stonehouse.

Friday, November 3. Sang with him, envied his exquisite tenderness of conscience. Walked with Metcalf and Betsy Claggett to visit a woman dying in the faith, thence to Miss Reeves, who is now assured of her acceptance with God.

Saturday, November 4. Preached at St Antholin's, reconciling those who never differed—St Paul and St James.[113]

Sunday, November 5. Preached the Three-fold State [1 John 3:14] at St Alban's [church], Woodstreet, then expounded at Syms's.

Tuesday, November 7. At Newgate. Melted down under the word I spake.

Wednesday, November 8. At Bexley. Mr Piers, through fear of the world's threatenings, had left off the meeting on Wednesday night.
My sister [Kezzy] would not give up her pretensions to faith. Told me, half angry, "Well, you will know in the next world whether I have faith or no." I asked her, "Will you then discharge me, in the sight of God, from speaking to you again? If you will, I promise never more to open my mouth till we meet in eternity." She burst into tears, fell on my neck, and melted me into fervent prayer for her.

Saturday, November 11. Charles Graves came, and rejoiced my heart with the account of his having received the atonement.

Sunday, November 12. Mr Piers refused me his pulpit, through fear of man, pretending tenderness to his flock. I plainly told him, if he so rejected my testimony, I would come to see him no more. Walked back to town in the strength of the Lord, and expounded at Syms's. All dissolved in tears.

Monday, November 13. Charles brought Mr William Seward—a zealous soul, knowing only the baptism of John.[114]

---

113. Charles is referring to the apparent tension between James 2:20-26 and the Pauline teaching on justification by faith (alone). He was likely preaching his sermon on Titus 3:8, "On Good Works."
114. Cf. Acts 18:24-25.

Tuesday, November 14. Had another conference with his Lordship of London.

[*Wesley:*] "I have used your Lordship's permission to wait upon you. A woman desires me to baptize her, not being satisfied with her baptism by a Dissenter. She says sure and unsure is not the same."

He immediately took fire, and interrupted me: "I wholly disapprove of it. It is irregular."

[*Wesley:*] "My Lord, I did not expect your approbation. I only came, in obedience, to give you notice of my intention."

[*Bishop:*] "It is irregular. I never receive any such information but from the minister."

[*Wesley:*] "My Lord, the rubric does not so much as require the minister to give you notice, but any discreet person. I have the minister's leave."

[*Bishop:*] "Who gave you authority to baptize?"

[*Wesley:*] "Your Lordship—and I shall exercise it in any part of the known world."

[*Bishop:*] "Are you a licensed curate?"

[*Wesley:*] "I have the leave of the proper minister."

[*Bishop:*] "But don't you know, no man can exercise parochial duty in London without my leave? It is only *sub silentio.*"[115]

[*Wesley:*] "But you know many do take that permission for authority, and you yourself allow it."

[*Bishop:*] "It is one thing to connive, and another to approve. I have power to inhibit you."

[*Wesley:*] "Does your Lordship exert that power? Do you now inhibit me?"

[*Bishop:*] "O, why will you push things to an extreme? I do not inhibit you."

[*Wesley:*] "Why then, my Lord, according to your own concession, you permit or authorize me."

[*Bishop:*] "I have a power to punish, and to forbear punishing."

[*Wesley:*] "That seems to imply that I have done something worthy of punishment. I should be glad to know, that I may answer. Does your Lordship charge me with any crime?"

[*Bishop:*] "No, no; I charge you with no crime."

[*Wesley:*] "Do you then dispense with my giving you notice of any baptisms for the future?"

---

115. "Under silence."

153

[*Bishop:*] "I neither dispense, nor not dispense."

He railed at Lawrence on lay-baptism.[116] Blamed my brother's sermon, as inclining to antinomianism. I charged Archbishop Tillotson with denying the faith.[117] He allowed it, and owned they ran into one extreme to avoid another. He concluded the conference with, "Well, sir, you knew my judgment before, and you know it now. Good morrow to you."

Read prayers at Islington and baptized an adult, Mr Stonehouse, Mrs Syms, and Mrs Burton being the witnesses.

Wednesday, November 15. Dined at old Mr [John] Hutton's. They could scarcely be civil. Surely for Christ's sake have we lost this friendly family.

Thursday, November 16. After morning prayers, baptized Mrs [Richard] Bell with hypothetical baptism.[118] Sang and prayed with assistance at Mr Stonehouse's. Then Mrs Wren confessed she had been in bondage ten years, but received the atonement on Tuesday night, while we were praying—was now perfectly free, full of peace and joy in believing. Another professed her faith lately received. Dined at my friend Stonehouse's, who very kindly offers to keep my brother and me.

Mrs Hankinson carried me to a poor woman, broken, bruised, and bound by sin. After prayer she arose, loosed from her bond, and glorified God.

Saturday, November 18. Had a joyful meeting with my dear Charles Delamotte, just returned from Georgia. Found, in conversation, that he had received forgiveness five months ago, and continued in peace and liberty.

Sunday, November 19. At Dr Crowe's desire, preached in his church at Bishopsgate.[119] Dined at Mr Brockmer's, where Mr Seward testified faith.

---

116. See Henry Lawrence, *Of Baptism* (London: J. Macock, 1646). This was an early Baptist publication, and the last chapter insisted that it was the whole church, not just clergy, that could be called by God to baptize.

117. John Tillotson (1630–1694), Archbishop of Canterbury, 1691–1694. Wesley's signed copy of Tillotson's *Of Sincerity and Constancy in the Faith and Profession of the True Religion* (London: Richard Chiswell, 1695) is present in MARC (ref. MAW CW25).

118. "Hypothetical baptism" is baptism administered to persons in respect to whom it is unclear whether or not they have been baptized before.

119. Rev. Dr. William Crowe (c. 1691–1743), rector of St Botolph's Church, Bishopsgate (just north of London Wall). Charles preached his sermon on 1 John 3:14; cf. *Sermons*, 132.

Visited a poor woman of eighty-four, who told me she was reserved for some work of God; was soon beat out of her own words, and in the midst of prayer set at liberty. She rose, caught hold of me, declared her enlargement; that she was now at ease, ready to go into eternity this moment. She prayed for and blessed me with great earnestness.

Monday, November 20. Had a most comfortable Sacrament at Bray's; Mr Sparks, the three Claggetts, etc., partaking. Passed the evening at Blendon, in prayer and thanksgiving.

Tuesday, November 21. Communicated again at Bray's. Triumphed with some who are persecuted for righteousness' sake.

Wednesday, November 22. Set out in the coach for Oxford.

Friday, November 24. Met Charles Kinchin there. Received the blessed Sacrament at Mrs Townsend's, with much comfort.

Saturday, November 25. Felt a pining desire to die, foreseeing the infinite dangers and troubles of life. At Mr Wells's preached *the* faith of the gospel to him and Mr [Joseph] Hoare. Charles carried me to the Castle. Read prayers, and was afterwards constrained to speak freely and fully. Much cheered by it myself. Rode with Mr Wells and Kinchin to Cogges, where we spent the evening in prayer and the Scriptures.

Sunday, November 26. Preached the Three-fold State [1 John 3:14] at Cogges, then rode on to my brother Gambold's.

Tuesday, November 28. Dined in Christ-Church hall, as one not belonging to them.

Wednesday, November 29. After morning prayers, called on Mr Whitefield, who pressed me to accept of a college living. Read prayers, and preached at the Castle.

Thursday, November 30. Paid Mr Gambold another visit, and parted with the Sacrament.

DECEMBER 1738

Tuesday, December 5. At convocation, where honest John Checkley was presented with his degree, having before got orders, for which he came to England.

Thursday, December 7. Read prayers again to the poor prisoners in Bocardo.[120]

Saturday, December 9. With the Dean, who complained of my brother's obscurity in his sermon on salvation, and expressly denied the assurance of faith, and earnest of the Spirit.

Sunday, December 10. Preached at the Castle, "All under Sin," and helped to administer the Sacrament. Read prayers, and preached there again in the afternoon.

Monday, December 11. Came in the coach to Wycombe.[121] Lodged at Mr [Isaac] Hollis's, who entertained me with his French Prophets[122]—equal, in his account, if not superior, to the Old Testament ones. While we were undressing, he fell into violent agitations, and gobbled like a turkey-cock. I was frightened and began exorcising him with "Thou deaf and dumb devil," etc.[123] He soon recovered out of his fit of inspiration. I prayed, and went to bed, not half liking my bedfellow. Did not sleep very sound with Satan so near me. Got to London by one the next day. George Whitefield came to John Bray's soon after me. I was full of vehement desire in prayer. Heard him preach to a vast throng at St Helen's.

Thursday, December 14. Heard a glorious account of the success of the gospel at Islington. Some of the fiercest opposers were converted. James Hutton informed me what I could scarce believe, that a memorial is entered in the Trustee's book of my confining [James] Welch, that I might have an opportunity with his wife.

Friday, December 15. At Mr Stonehouse's I met Mrs Vaughan, full of joy in the Holy Ghost, but not without a mixture of nature.

Saturday, December 16. Hester Hopson[124] and her sister [Betty] called, being sick of love to Christ crucified. My soul, in and after prayer with them, was all desire and expectation.

---

120. A room over the north gate of the city of Oxford, used as a debtor's prison.
121. I.e., High Wycombe, Buckinghamshire.
122. See further Kenneth G. C. Newport, "The French Prophets and Early Methodism: Some New Evidence," *PWHS* 50 (1996): 127–40.
123. Cf. Mark 9:25.
124. Esther ("Hester") Sutton Hopson (1714–1794). Charles fluctuates between "Hobson" and the correct spelling, "Hopson."

Sunday, December 17. Met Mr Broughton at Mrs Hind's. The last time we had parted good friends, and he thanked me for my friendly offices with Miss Reeves. He now desired me to get from her a discharge.

Monday, December 18. She told me she fully released him from his promises, but durst not give him a written discharge, lest her brother should cast her off.

Tuesday, December 19. Asked my friend Stonehouse, "Dost thou believe in the Son of God?" And he could confidently answer, "Yes, I do, and now know that I believe." We sang (Mrs Hankinson joining us) in the spirit of faith, and triumphed in the name of the Lord our God.

Thursday, December 21. At St Antholin's the clerk asked me my name, and said, "Dr Venn[125] has forbidden any Methodist to preach. Do you call your self a Methodist?" "I do not. The world may call me what they please." "Well, sir," said he, "it is pity the people should go away without preaching. You may preach." I did so, on good works.[126]

Saturday, [December] 23. Deeply affected in singing at Blendon. Retired, and poured out my soul in prayer for love.

Christmas Day. I preached at Islington in the morning, and gave the cup. George Stonehouse in the afternoon.

Tuesday, December 26. George Whitefield preached. Had the Sacrament this and the four following days. On Thursday my brother preached; on Friday, George Whitefield; and on Saturday, Mr Robson. The whole week was a festival indeed; a joyful season, holy unto the Lord.

JANUARY 1739

Tuesday, January 2. At Mr Stonehouse's, with Mrs Vaughan and others. I urged him to throw away his mystics; but he adhered to them with the greater obstinacy. Saw myself in him.

---

125. Rev. Richard Venn, rector of St Antholin's, who would die two months later.
126. This was Charles's sermon on Titus 3:8; cf. *Sermons*, 152–66.

Wednesday, January 3. Today our sister Butcher died (the first that has) triumphant in the faith. At five she said, "I trust only to the blood of Christ. I cast myself at his feet; and if I perish, I perish." Soon after, "Now I am sure of heaven." Her last breath was spent in exhorting her husband and the rest to confide in Jesus Christ.

Friday, January 5. My brother, Mr Seward, Hall, Whitefield, Ingham, Kinchin, Hutchings, all set upon me. But I could not agree to settle at Oxford without farther direction from God.

Saturday, January 6. Mr Sparks and I at Mr Howard's, who denied any real communion we can have with God.

Sunday, January 7. Offended much at some orders which Bray, etc., were imposing on the Society.

Wednesday, January 10. I met Mr Broughton, who laboured hard to persuade me to make affidavit of what Miss Reeves had said. I positively refused it, as treachery to her, both in him and me.

Mr Thorold expounded at the Society. We had some discourse about agitations; no sign of grace, in my humble opinion.

Thursday, January 11. Met a Moravian and his wife.[1] She related her genuine conversion—had received forgiveness *before* the abiding witness of the Spirit.

Saturday, January 13. Pierced with the prayers of Hester Hopson, I expected a fresh manifestation of Christ continually, which I found the next day at the Sacrament.

Monday, January 15. At Mr Stonehouse's when Mr Silvester came. Mr Stonehouse insisted upon choosing a lecturer himself. I attended him to Mr Lloyd, the reader. Close talk of faith. Both he and his wife convinced.

Tuesday, January 16. Prayed in faith for her. Immediately she was filled with comfort. I called on Mr Wild, who tells me he lately received forgiveness under my sermon.

Wednesday, January 17. George Whitefield gave us so promising account of Oxford that I found myself strongly inclined to go.

---

1. Georg Piesch (1700–1753) and Rosina (*née* Münster) Piesch (1703–1779), who had arrived in London from Germany in early October 1738.

Sunday, January 21. I was much affected under Mr Stonehouse's sermon. Preached myself in the afternoon, to a crowded church, on Justification by Faith [Rom. 3:23-24].[2]

Monday, January 22. Lady Crispe[3] sent for me. Went and found Mr Stonehouse there. She behaved with great courtesy. I transcribed an hymn for Miss.[4] After supper, her Ladyship spoke largely in praise of marriage. I saw, and pitied, my poor friend, sorely beset. Sang. It was late before we parted.

Tuesday, January 23. Mrs Vaughan seemed deeply humbled, under a sense of her late vain, confident delusions.

Wednesday, January 24. Expounded (for the benefit of two clergymen present) on "Know ye not, that your bodies are the temples of the Holy Ghost?" [1 Cor. 6:19] and proved the promise of the Spirit to all, both from Scripture and our own Church.

Thursday, January 25. Expounded at Brockmer's. The Lord was present. A woman stopped me departing, confessed herself under the full power of the devil, fell at my feet. We prayed in confidence. On my mentioning in prayer the absolved adulteress,[5] she cried out, "I have received the comfort!" Rose full of love, and joy, and triumph—whereof we were all partakers.
Sent for to Bray. The three Miss Newtons were there. Expounded again with power.

Friday, January 26. At Dr Newton's. Sang and prayed with them—much affected now, well pleased last night.

Saturday, January 27. Carried Bray to Mrs Whitcomb's. The Claggetts, Metcalf and his mother, and Hester Hopson were there. Communicated, prayed, and sang with great life and comfort. Slept at Blendon.

Sunday, January 28. Preached on "The Three States" [1 John 3:14] at Bexley. Some went out of church. And more in the afternoon, while

---

2. This sermon survives, and annotations confirm its use on this occasion; cf. *Sermons,* 167–82.

3. Elizabeth Crispe (*née* Sayer, d. 1741), wife of Sir John Crispe (c. 1676–1728). Charles spells "Crisp."

4. Mary Crispe (1722–1751), daughter of Sir John and Lady Crispe, and future wife of George Stonehouse.

5. Cf. John 8:1-11.

I expounded, "Woe is unto me, if I preach not the gospel" [1 Cor. 9:16]. Quite spent, yet renewed my strength for the poor people at night.

Wednesday, January 31. Told Mr Delamotte he was not converted, had not the Spirit, or faith, and begged him to pray God to show him wherein he was wanting. He could not receive my saying, yet was not angry. Mrs Delamotte was quite transported with joy and love.

In the stagecoach with my sister Kezzy, I found three women, and very loathe to speak. Yet broke through, and laboured to convince them of sin and of righteousness. They all assented to the truth, and were, I hope, in some measure awakened to pursue "the one thing needful."[6] I left Kezzy at my aunt's[7] in Islington. I assisted to expound at the Society, slept at John Bray's in peace.

FEBRUARY 1739

Friday, February 2. With Charles Metcalf visited that worthy man, Zouberbouler, in the Marshalsea[8] for debt. Much moved at his afflictions.

Sunday, February 4. At night walked over the fields from Islington, several of us, with the voice of joy and thanksgiving.

Thursday, February 8. Carried Zouberbouler the news of his goods being redeemed by Mr Seward. Visited him again on Saturday, and was drawn in compassion towards him, and faith for him. At Islington rejoiced over a dying believer.

Saturday, February 10. I expounded to many hundreds at a Society in Beech Lane.

Sunday, February 11. We prayed for utterance this day. My brother preached. I was comforted in the Sacrament. Prayed again at Mr Stonehouse's for a blessing upon my ministry. (Lady Crisp with my brother.) I read prayers, and preached without notes on Blind Bartimeus [Mark 10:46-52],[9] the Lord being greatly my helper.

---

6. Cf. Luke 10:42.
7. Anne Annesley, sister of Susannah (Annesley) Wesley.
8. The Marshalsea was a debtor's prison in London.
9. There are several references to Charles preaching this sermon over the next few years.

Let him have all the glory. Returned to pray at Mr Stonehouse's. Miss Crisp asked to be admitted. We had close searching talk, before I expounded to the Society.

Monday, February 12. Mrs [Anne] Wheeler tells me she received Christ last Saturday, being weighed down with the fear of death, and delivered in a moment, melted into love, [and] able to apply Christ and all the promises to herself.

Mr Stonehouse informed me of a woman who had rejected him last week, but now sent for him, received the Sacrament, was reconciled to God and him, and died in peace.

Tuesday, February 13. Read a letter from Sarah Hurst, pressing me to Oxford, and Cowley (which is now vacant). Quite resigned, I offered myself. Opened the book upon those words, "With stammering lips, and with another tongue will he speak to this people" [Isa. 28:11]. Thought it a prohibition, yet continued without a will. With Captain Flatman at the Marshalsea. Read prayers and preached from Luke 7:36[-50], the woman washing Christ's feet. The word was with power; all attentive and thankful. Visited Zouberbouler, [who is] removed to the Fleet.[10]

Wednesday, February 14. Read prayers at Newgate, and preached the law first, and then the gospel. Sang "Invitation to Sinners."[11] All were affected.

Thursday, February 15. Preached again at the Marshalsea. Sent for by an harlot (supposed to be dying), and preached Christ, the friend of sinners, I trust to her heart.

Read prayers at Islington. Miss Crisp asked me home. My Lady was there. Pertinent discourse. The younger went with me to Mrs Hankinson's; extremely desirous of faith. Prayed for her with great earnestness. At the Society expounded the Woman of Samaria [John 4]. When I had done, she ran to me, and cried, "I do, I do believe! Those words which you spoke came with power, 'Him that

---

If he ever committed it to paper, it has not survived. But see possible related sermon in *Sermons*, 259–67.

10. The Fleet was another London prison, a little north of Ludgate Hill.

11. There was no hymn with this exact title in early Methodist collections. Charles may be referring to "Christ, the Friend of Sinners," which includes in its seventh stanza: "Come, O my guilty brethren, come. . . . He calls you now, invites you home!" Cf. *HSP* (1739), 101–3 (*Poetical Works*, 1:91–93). Or he may mean the hymn titled "The Invitation," taken from George Herbert's *The Temple*, that was included in *HSP* (1739), 125–26 (*Poetical Works*, 1:111–13).

cometh unto me, I will in no wise cast out' [John 6:37]. An unknown peace flowed with them into my soul." We sang, rejoiced, and gave thanks to the pardoning God in her behalf.

Sunday, February 18. Preached at Islington, on the woman that *was* a sinner [Luke 7:36-50]; at the Marshalsea, from Rom. 3. Prayed by the sick woman: expounded at Syms's to two several companies.

Monday, February 19. Prayed in the prison with Anne Dodd, well disposed, weary of sin, longing to break loose. Preached powerfully on the last day. Prayed after God for the poor harlots. Our sisters carried away one in triumph. I followed to Mrs [Mary] Hanson's, who took charge of the returning prodigal. Our hearts overflowed with pity for her. She seemed confounded, silent, testifying her joy and love by her tears only. We sang and prayed over her in great confidence.

At three met Miss Crisp at Mrs Claggett's, who helped me to rejoice for the lost sheep which I have found. In the evening I expounded at Mr Hind's. A lady was deeply wounded.

Tuesday, February 20. Waked full of concern for the poor harlot, began an hymn for her.[12] At five I called on Miss Crisp, then on Mr Stonehouse, where I expounded the Woman taken in adultery [John 8:1-11].

Wednesday, February 21. Heard that Cowley living was disposed of, and rejoiced. With my brother, I awaited on the Archbishop. He showed us great affection, spoke mildly of Mr Whitefield. Cautioned us to give no more umbrage than was necessary for our own defence, to forbear exceptionable phrases, to keep to the doctrines of the Church.

We told him we expected persecution, would abide by the Church till her Articles and Homilies were repealed. He assured us he knew of no design in the governors of the Church to innovate, and neither should there be any innovation while he lived. Avowed justification by faith only, and his joy to see us as often as we pleased.

From him we went to the Bishop of London, who denied his having condemned or even heard much of us. George Whitefield's *Journal*, he said, was tainted with enthusiasm, though he was him-

12. Published as "On the Conversion of a Common Harlot," HSP (1739), 103–4 (*Poetical Works*, 1:93–94).

self a pious, well-meaning youth.[13] He warned us against antinomianism, and dismissed us kindly.

Went in quest of a lost sheep, and found her coming with Bray from public prayers. She had been in deep distress; pierced with every word at the two last expoundings; almost fainted away this morning, weary and heavy-laden. She told Bray God could not forgive her, her sins were so great. She could not bear our triumph. We wrestled in prayer for her, and she declared her burden taken off and her soul at peace. The more we prayed, the clearer still she was, till at last she testified that she did believe in Jesus with her whole heart. We continued in mighty prayer for all gross sinners, and I offered myself willingly to be employed peculiarly in their service.

Sunday, February 25. Preached Justification by Faith at Bexley [Rom. 3:23-24]. In the beginning of my discourse about twenty went out of church. They were better pleased with (or at least more patient of) me in the afternoon, while I preached on the Woman at our Saviour's Feet [Luke 7:36-50].

Faint and spent at Blendon, I revived by exhorting above two hundred of the poor.

Monday, February 26. In our chapel I read Beveridge's sermon on the ministry.[14] Too much wanted[15] by Betsy, and others, who are running into wild notions. The people came at night, and we were all comforted together by the word.

Wednesday, February 28. Met the bands at John Bray's, and cautioned them against schism. I was violently opposed by one who should have seconded me. They urged me to go to Oxford, but I understood them, and begged to be excused.

MARCH 1739

Saturday, March 3. Expounded to upward of three hundred hearers at Beech Lane.

---

13. See August 3, 1738, entry above on the initial installment of Whitefield's *Journal*. The Bishop of London (Edmund Gibson) included an extensive critique of the first three installments in his *Pastoral Letter to the People of His Diocese ... By Way of Caution against Lukewarmness on One Hand, and Enthusiasm on the Other* (London: S. Buckley, 1739). Wesley comments on Whitefield's response to Gibson in the August 15, 1739, entry below.

14. See Sermon II, "The Institution of Ministers," in Beveridge, *Works*, 1:13–22.

15. "Wanted" is used here in the sense of "lacking."

Sunday, March 4. Read prayers, and preached,[16] and administered the Sacrament at St Katherine's;[17] at Islington from John 3; then expounded with much life at Mr Syms's; and lastly at Mr Bell's.[18] I concluded the labour of the day with prayer among the bands.

Thursday, March 8. In the midst of earnest prayer at John Bray's a woman received power to become a child of God. Felt pity for poor Mr Broughton (accused by H. T.) but not pity *enough*.[19]

Saturday, March 10. Went to Newgate with my usual reluctance. Preached with freedom, and in prayer had great power, as all present seemed to confess.

I expounded at Beech Lane. In prayer I asked some token if our gospel really is a ministration of the Spirit. Inquired if any had received an answer. One, and another, and another testified their sense of the Divine Presence. We rejoiced as men that divide the spoil.[20]

Sunday, March 11. I preached justification at St Katherine's.[21] Baptized two women at Islington (five adults I baptized some time before), and preached with great liberty from the Woman of Samaria [John 4].

My friend Stonehouse was very peevish with me (for a trifle), and very warm. I kept my temper, but was hindered in my expounding by his disputes. Encouraged Miss Crisp, now persecuted by her relations. Envied the dead at Mrs Vaughan's. Serious talk with Stonehouse, in defence of Miss Crisp. Both humbled.

Monday, March 12. Mr Broughton talked to me about H. T.'s charge. Called upon God to strike him dead, if it were true. I declared my belief of his innocency, and the woman's rashness. Proposed bringing her to be confronted by him.

Expounded in the Minories, where I met and asked her about it, before Mrs Claggett. She still persisted in her accusation.

---

16. Charles preached his sermon on Titus 3:8; cf. *Sermons*, 154.

17. It is unclear in this and subsequent cases whether Charles is at St Katherine Coleman Church, or St Katherine Cree Church; John Wesley preached at both during this same general period. Charles spells "St Catherine."

18. Richard Bell, a watchcase maker in Vine Court, Bishopsgate.

19. The concluding sentence for March 8 is not included in Jackson or Telford.

20. Cf. Isa. 9:3.

21. This was Charles's sermon on Rom. 3:23-24; cf. *Sermons*, 169.

Tuesday, March 13. Called on Mr Broughton at his lodgings. Burton present. Still I believe him innocent. James Hutton fetched H. T. She strongly insisted, as in the presence of God. He as strongly denied. I hoped both were innocent. Urged her to caution; would fain have her believe herself mistaken, but in vain. Broughton said he would prosecute her, still appearing innocent, acquitted me of the subornation.

I talked with her afterwards at J. Hagson's, to convince her of her fatal mistake. She said she was confirmed in the truth by seeing and hearing him. Called again in the afternoon, set before her the consequences, and urged her to retract. Went from her to Broughton.

[*Broughton:*] "Well, what says she now?"

[*Wesley:*] "She insists upon her not being mistaken."

[*Broughton:*] "I believe her suborned not by you, but by some [of] your followers."

[*Wesley:*] "That is very uncharitable. You have no ground for such belief."

[*Broughton:*] "I think you ought to withdraw your countenance from her."

[*Wesley:*] "And what shall I answer, if she perish through my neglecting her? I cannot consent to that."

[*Broughton:*] "Then you will not forsake her? It will fall upon yourself."

[*Wesley:*] "God do so to me, and more also,[22] if I choose to stand with the guilty rather than fall with the innocent."

[*Broughton:*] "Then you think me guilty."

[*Wesley:*] "No. I judge nothing before the time."

[*Broughton:*] "I declare what way I shall take. I shall first go to the Bishop of London, tell him I preached such a sermon, and immediately this followed."

[*Wesley:*] "Your conscience knows it is false. The account was given and written by me March 1, before that sermon was preached."

[*Broughton:*] "Well, it was for my other sermons then. The world will lay it to you."

[*Wesley:*] "I defy the world and the devil. They cannot hurt me. Neither can you, though you was to swear that I suborned her."

[*Broughton:*] "Would I have believed such a story of you?"

---

22. Cf. 2 Kings 6:31.

[*Wesley:*] "Who tells you I believe it?"

[*Broughton:*] "Last night you thought me innocent."

(Burton here came in)

[*Wesley:*] "I did so, but am now quite confounded, and can form no judgment at all concerning you."

[*Broughton:*] "But you think I have no faith, and she has; therefore you believe her, and not me."

[*Wesley:*] "Who told you so? I suspend my judgment. God knows the heart."

[*Broughton:*] "Suppose I prove myself absent at the time, what would you say?"

[*Wesley:*] "I should rejoice in your innocence, and believe her mistaken."

[*Broughton:*] "But you would not discard her."

[*Wesley:*] "If I do, and she should be lost by that means, would you answer for me at the day of judgment?"

[*Broughton:*] "But you own she has been a vile sinner."

[*Wesley:*] "Yes, and God sent me to seek this lost sheep, and shall I now cast her off? No, but I would again leave the ninety-nine sheep to seek the one,[23] and though I lost my life in so doing, I should find it again."

[*Broughton:*] "I suppose she will run away shortly."

[*Wesley:*] "I cannot say for that, but this I can say, that if she is a child of God (she *was* a child of the devil, as *we* were), then you cannot hurt her. God will be her support."

[*Broughton:*] "A fine story this! She shall stand in the pillory."

[*Wesley:*] "Well, may God direct you, and make this turn to your salvation. I wish you as well as I do myself."[24]

At Newgate with Bray. Prayed, sang, exhorted with great life and vehemence. Talked in the cells to two Papists, who renounced all merit but that of Jesus Christ. Expounded at Bray's on the day of judgment. The power of the Lord was present to wound. A woman cried out as in an agony. Another sank down overpowered. All moved and melted, as wax before the fire. At eight I expounded at Dowgate Hill.[25] Two were then taken into the fold.

---

23. Cf. Luke 15:4.

24. The section beginning with March 12 and ending here for March 13 is omitted from both Jackson and Telford. It is struck through in the MS Journal. The word "omit" is written in the upper left-hand corner of p. 20, but it is not in Charles Wesley's handwriting.

25. A society met at the home of Mr. Crouch in this neighborhood (cf. March 27, 1739, entry).

Wednesday, March 14. Found one of the Papists full of peace and joy in believing, immediately after we prayed.

Friday, March 16. Hearing Mr Broughton had been seeking me, I waited upon him at his lodgings. He said he had called to carry me to Sir John Ganson.[26] Read me his account of our conversation. I excepted to his saying I first asked to have the woman confront him, whereas his words were, "I will be confronted by this woman." He was very abusive; *hoped* my brother and I were not guilty of the subordination, yet applied Naboth and the lying spirit in the prophets to us;[27] charged me with bringing her out of prison for this purpose; threatened what mysteries of our iniquity he would discover; accused me with calling her sister. God kept me from speaking. Only at parting I said, "I lay under a much viler interpretation than you. I shall not be in haste to vindicate myself. When the time is, I shall simply print my journal."

Saturday, March 17. Sir John Ganson[28] sent me a message desiring to speak with me. I went, and met Mr Broughton. Talk of the woman; her sincerity doubtful; the reproach to Mr Broughton, who charged me with crediting and supporting her.

"Sir John, I appeal to you. As for crediting her—I believe her mistaken, Mr Broughton innocent. I charged her at first to mention it to none, which she observed. Mr Stonehouse told it [to] me. I discourage it among my friends. Did not take her out of prison, but prevailed upon a pious woman to take her in, else she was under a necessity of continuing in sin. How should such a poor creature ever reform, if all virtuous people spurn them away?"

To this he agreed. Mr Broughton mentioned my character's suffering.

"My character is in the hands of God. They cannot say more than all manner of evil against me falsely;[29] and that I expect. I beg your advice, Sir John, what can I do more?"

Mr Broughton said, "You should discourage, not encourage her."

I answered, "I shall encourage her to repent, till she is *proved* an hypocrite. But I declare to all, my belief in your innocence."

26. On this first occasion Charles writes "Garstone," but certainly means the same person who contacts him the next day. Sir John Ganson was a Middlesex magistrate sympathetic to the Methodists.
27. Cf. 2 Kings 9:25-26.
28. Charles here and hereafter spells "Gunson."
29. Cf. 1 Pet. 3:16.

Sir John said it was all I could do, except making affidavit of this, and giving it under my hand. This Broughton insisted upon.

"I will, upon this condition, that you in like manner vindicate me from a much blacker charge; and my friends also. Consider of it, as I will, and give you my answer tomorrow."

"People will believe it notwithstanding," said Sir John. He treated me with great civility and invited me to visit him again.

Satan by all this would frighten me from preaching the gospel to publicans and harlots, but I am not ignorant of his device.

Tuesday, March 20. Heard the poor H. T. persists in the truth of her report, notwithstanding the writ which is taken out against her. Mr Stonehouse voluntarily said to Bernard, "Go to the harlot from me, and tell her I believe her innocent, and will therefore bear all the expense of the suit." A double power and blessing accompanied my word at Fetter Lane.[30]

Thursday, March 22. At Marshalsea with Mr Okely.[31] Prayed with the sick, read prayers, and expounded the lesson.

Saturday, March 24. With the Bishop of London. Said,

[*Wesley:*] "Mr Broughton has been with your Lordship. I wait upon you to know how far you think me blameable with respect to him."

[*Bishop:*] "Did you hear that I blamed you?"

[*Wesley:*] "Yes, I heard that you was angry, and said, 'Will he to save a sheep, destroy a shepherd?'"

[*Bishop:*] "I never blamed you, nor said those words."

Here I declared my belief of Mr Broughton's innocence, and asked advice whether I should vindicate myself against the charge of subornation.

[*Bishop:*] "Has anyone accused you in particular? I dare say nobody believes it. I advise you to take no notice. It will soon die."

[*Wesley:*] "But your Lordship advised Mr Broughton to prosecute, for a much lighter accusation."

[*Bishop:*] "No, I did not. But what I say is mentioned again, which forces me to be upon my guard, though my nature is to be quite open."

---

30. Jackson and Telford omit the entries for March 16–17, and include only the last sentence of the March 20 entry, which Charles Wesley incorrectly dates "March 30."

31. Charles interacted with both Francis Okely (1719–1794) and his brother John Okely

I assured him I never mentioned anything of what he was pleased to say, thanked him for his advice, and promised to follow it.[32]

Sunday, March 25. Betty Hopson came, and prayed that today we might have a feast of fat things.[33] Mr Stonehouse was full of love, preached an excellent sermon on faith. After Sacrament, we continued our triumph. I preached with power, "Lazarus raised" [John 11]. Then sang and prayed at the room. Great was our rejoicing in the Lord.

Buried a corpse and exhorted the congregation. Expounded at Mr Stonehouse's with great enlargement. An opposer was troublesome, till we prayed him down. I visited Mr Lloyd and then Mrs Vaughan, both as full of love and joy as they could contain. By midnight I rested with Okely at John Bray's.

Tuesday, March 27. At Mr Crouch's I expounded on persecution. A man cried out, "That's a lie." We betook ourselves to prayer and singing. The shout of a king was in the midst of us.[34] The man came up quite affable. After another asked what that comfort and joy meant, I calmly invited him to experience it.

Wednesday, March 28. We dissuaded my brother from going to Bristol, from an unaccountable fear that it would prove fatal to him. A great power was among us. He offered himself willingly to whatsoever the Lord should appoint. The next day he set out, commended by us to the grace of God. He left a blessing behind. I desired to die with him.

APRIL 1739

Sunday, April 1. Preached at St Katherine's,[35] where I met my old friend Mrs Paine, of East Grinstead.[36] I administered the Sacrament. Dined at Chryssy Anderson's. Went in a coach with her and Esther to Islington, comforted in the way while singing. I expounded the

---

(1721–1792). Most of his references in the MS Journal do not make clear which of the brothers is intended. Charles spells "Oakley."
32. Jackson and Telford omit the March 24 entry.
33. Cf. Isa. 25:6.
34. Cf. Num. 23:21.
35. Charles preached his sermon on 1 John 3:14; cf. *Sermons*, 133.
36. East Grinstead, Sussex, eight miles east of Crawley.

Good Samaritan [Luke 10:29-37], with divine assistance. Prayed at Fetter Lane that the Lord might be in the midst of us. Received a remarkable answer: Brother [Edward] Nowers, in strong pangs, groaned, screamed, roared out. I was not offended by it—nor edified. We sang and praised God with all our might. I could not get home till eleven.

Wednesday, April 4. At Mr West's I rejoiced over an happy soul who received faith under my last expounding.

Friday, April 6. I convinced a woman of sin; found another convinced of righteousness. A man who had rejected me was now overpowered. Mrs Daniel and Winstone were apprehended by Christ.

Sunday, April 15. At Islington, in the vestry, the churchwardens demanded my license. I wrote down my name. Preached with increase of power, on the Woman taken in Adultery [John 8:1-11]. None went out. I gave the cup.

At night I waited upon Count Zinzendorf with Bray and Hutton. He received us very cordially. Told us of six hundred Moors converted, two hundred Greenlanders, three hundred Hottentots. *"Saluta meo nomine fratres et sorores. Christi Spiritum illis apprecor."*[37]

Found his prayers answered at the Society. Two received forgiveness. Many were filled with unutterable groanings. All received some spiritual gift. Could not part, but continued our triumph till the morning.

Monday, April 16. The Count visited us in Fetter Lane, and answered the several questions we proposed to him.

Today I first saw Miss Raymond[38] and Mr Rogers, at the expounding.

Tuesday, April 17. Tried in vain to check Mr [John] Shaw in his wild rambling talk against the Christian priesthood. At last I told him I would oppose him to the utmost, and either he or I must quit the Society.

Assisted Mr Stonehouse again (as every day this great and holy week) in administering the Sacrament. The presence of the Lord was much with us; and again at night, in the word expounded.

---

37. "Salute the brothers and sisters in my name. I pray Christ's Spirit will be with them."
38. Dinah Raymond, future wife of the Moravian Henry Conrad de Larisch.

Wednesday, April 18. Met Shaw at James's. He insisted that there is no priesthood, but he himself could baptize and administer the other Sacrament as well as any man.

At Mrs Claggett's met Mr Rogers and Miss Raymond, and prayed earnestly for her.

In my expounding warned them strongly against schism, into which Shaw's notions must necessarily lead. The Society were all for my brother's immediate return.

Thursday, April 19. Found Mr Stonehouse exactly right. Warned Mrs Vaughan (Hunter, half-perverted) and Brockmers against Shaw's pestilent errors, and spoke strongly at the Savoy Society in behalf of the Church of England.

Good Friday, April 20. Mrs Acourt was justified, in answer to our prayer. I felt life under Mr Stonehouse's sermon. From church I went to the house to pray. John Bray gave me the gospel for the day to expound. I besought them, in strong words, not to rend the seamless coat by their divisions. John Bray himself, that pillar of our church, begins to shake. At night I preached to the Society in Wapping.[39]

Saturday, April 21. With James [Hutton] at the Count's, who spoke much against the intended separation of our brethren.

Met Metcalf, wholly perverted, a rank Quaker!

Easter Day, April 22. Talked with the Count about motions, visions, dreams; and was confirmed in my dislike to them.

Wednesday, April 25. Began Potter on *Church Government*,[40] a seasonable antidote against the growing spirit of delusion. I heard George Whitefield, very powerful, at Fetter Lane. I was with him and Howell Harris,[41] a man after my own heart. George related the dismal effects of Shaw's doctrine at Oxford. Both Howell and he insisted on Shaw's expulsion from the Society. Poor Metcalf had little to say for his friend and master.

Friday, April 27. Heard George Whitefield in Islington churchyard. The numerous congregation could not have been more affected

---

39. There was a religious society meeting here, possibly in connection with St John's Church.

40. John Potter, *A Discourse of Church Government* (London: T. Childe, 1707). Cf. June 19, 1739, entry below.

41. Charles spells "Howel."

within the walls. I exhorted them at Fetter Lane to continue steadfast in the means of grace.

Saturday, April 28. Mr Stonehouse was much concerned that we should so misunderstand, as if he had forbid George Whitefield's preaching in his church. Today he preached out again. After him, [Thomas] Bowers got up to speak. I conjured him not, but he beat me down and *followed his impulse.* I carried many away with me. In the evening I expounded at Exall's. A woman received the atonement.

Sunday, April 29. At Islington vestry the churchwardens forbade my preaching, demanded my local license. I said nothing but that I heard them. Scions was very abusive, bidding me shake off the dust of my feet, etc.;[42] and said, "You have all the spirit of the devil," mentioning Mr Whitefield, Stonehouse, and me by name.

After prayers Mr Stonehouse made way for me to the pulpit. I offered to go up, when one [Mr] Cotteril and a beadle forcibly kept me back. I thought of, "The servant of the Lord must not strive" [2 Tim. 2:24], and yielded. Mr Streat preached. I assisted at the Sacrament.

Preached afterwards at our house, and prayed fervently for the opposers. Waited on Justice Elliot. He had gone with Sir John Ganson into the vestry, and severely chided the churchwardens, who had made the clerk read the canon, call a vestry, etc. Mr Streat advised to ask Mr Stonehouse to discharge me from ever preaching again.

In the afternoon Scions abused Streat himself at the vestry; abused us; owned he said, "the devil was in us all."

I read the prayers; Mr Scott preached. At night I was greatly strengthened to expound and pray for our persecutors. All were mild and peaceable among the bands. Heard that George had had above ten thousand hearers.

Monday, April 30. I preached at the Marshalsea. Mr Stonehouse told us he had been with the bishop, but left him close, shut up, sour, refusing to answer but to the written case.

At James's rejoiced to find Charles Metcalf coming back.

---

42. Cf. Luke 9:5.

MAY 1739

Tuesday, May 1. During the time of prayers the churchwardens still kept guard on the pulpit stairs. I was not inclined to fight my way through them. Mr Stonehouse preached a thundering sermon (unless their consciences are seared). I took notes of it.

I took water with James for Hastings. A poor harlot was struck down by the word. She, and all, were melted into tears, and prayers, and strong cries for her. I have a good hope this brand will also be plucked out of the fire.[43]

Wednesday, May 2. She was at Fetter Lane, where I expounded the Prodigal [Luke 15:11-32].

Thursday, [May] 10.[44] Expounded at Blendon, many fine folk from Eltham attending.

Friday, [May] 11. Prayed at Welling with a dying man, full of humility, and faith, and love.

Sunday, [May] 13. Enabled to discourse from the Prodigal [Luke 15:11-32] at Bexley.

Monday, May 14. At West's my mouth was opened to expound Rom. 8. Miss Raymond was among my hearers.

Tuesday, May 15. She was brought so strongly to my mind, that I was even constrained to pray for her with tears.

Wednesday, May 16. Preached with power and freedom in the Marshalsea. I prayed by Mrs Cameron, who owned herself convinced. She had been a deist, because it is so incredible the Almighty God should condescend to die for his creatures.

I attended George Whitefield to Blackheath. He preached in the rain to many listening sinners. At Fetter Lane a dispute arose about lay preaching. Many, particularly Bray and Fish, were very zealous for it. Mr Whitefield and I declared against it.

Saturday, May 19. At the Common, George preached from "The Holy Ghost shall come upon thee" [Luke 1:35]. In the evening I found my brother at Mr [Joseph] Hodges's.

---

43. Cf. Zech. 3:2.
44. MS has "April" for this and the next two days, in error.

Sunday, May 20. Received the Sacrament at St Paul's, with best part of our Society.

Monday, May 21. At Mrs Claggett's I found Miss Raymond, Rogers, John Cennick, [Howell] Harris, Whitefield, Piriam, Mason, the Delamottes. Mr Claggett was very friendly, and invited me to Broadoaks.[45]

Tuesday, May 22. Miss Raymond carried me in her coach to Islington. My friend Stonehouse was delighted to see me. We sang together and prayed, as in the months that are past.

Thursday, May 24. John Bray took upon him to reprove me for checking the course of the Spirit. I made him no answer; but I believe not every spirit,[46] nor any till I have tried it by the fruits and the written word.

Met Miss Raymond (as almost every day), and joined with her and our friends in prayer and singing. Mr Claggett pressed me now, with the utmost importunity, to go with him tomorrow.

Friday, May 25. At noon I set out on horseback; our sisters in the chaise. By two the next day we surprised Miss Betty at Broadoaks. Full of prayer that the Lord would gather a church in this place.

Sunday, May 27. Still Mr Claggett opposed my preaching. Went to church, where I preached "The New Birth."[47] We returned singing. Mr Claggett still more violent. I told him, he was doing the devil's work. Between jest and earnest he struck me; raged exceedingly to see the people come flocking to the word. God gave me utterance to make known the mystery of the gospel to four or five hundred listening souls.

Tuesday, May 29. Franklyn, a farmer, invited me to preach in his field. I did so, to about five hundred, on "Repent, for the kingdom of heaven is at hand" [Matt. 3:2]. I returned to the house rejoicing.

Wednesday, May 30. Convinced a sick man of unbelief. Another on his deathbed received forgiveness, and witnessed a good con-

---

45. Broadoaks Manor, the Claggetts' country home, is located just northwest of Thaxted, Essex. The school for the Moravian congregation in London was moved here in November 1742.
46. Cf. 1 John 4:1.
47. Likely on John 3:1-10.

fession. I invited near a thousand sinners (with whom the whole [place] was filled at night) to come weary and heavy-laden to Christ for rest.

Thursday, May 31. A Quaker sent me a pressing invitation to preach at Thaxted.[48] I scrupled preaching in another's parish, till I had been refused the church. Many Quakers, and near seven hundred others, attended, while I declared in the highways, "The Scripture hath concluded all under sin" [Gal. 3:22].

JUNE 1739

Friday, June 1. My subject, to above one thousand attentive sinners, was, "He shall save his people from their sins" [Matt. 1:21]. Many showed their emotion by their tears.

Saturday, June 2. At six set out for London, with a quiet mind, leaving my beloved friends in the hands of God. The first thing I heard in town was that my poor friend Stonehouse was actually married.[49] It is a satisfaction to me that I had no hand in it.

Sunday, June 3. George Whitefield advised me (I thank him for his love) to follow Mr Stonehouse's example. He preached in the morning in Moorfields, and in the evening at Kennington Common,[50] to an innumerable multitude.

Monday, June 4. Walked with a young Quaker to Islington church. Satan hindered me, so Mr Scott baptized him. He told me afterwards, "When the words were speaking, I sensibly found the Holy Ghost descend into my soul; the joy arose higher and higher, till at last I could neither speak nor move, but seemed rapt into the third heaven."[51]

I had some conversation with Mrs Stonehouse; surely a gracious, lovely soul! Then with him. We joined in prayer, and I was better reconciled to their sudden marriage.

---

48. Charles spells "Thackstead."
49. Stonehouse married Mary Crispe.
50. A large park in Kennington, Surrey, about one mile south of London, across the River Thames.
51. Cf. 2 Cor. 12:2.

Met Shaw, the self-ordained priest. He was brim-full of proud wrath and fierceness. His spirit suited to his principles. I could do him no good, but was kept calm and benevolent towards him. Therefore he could do me no harm.

I stood by George Whitefield while he preached on the mount in Blackheath. The cries of the wounded were heard on every side. What has Satan gained by turning him out of the churches?

Tuesday, June 5. With him at Blendon. Bowers and Bray followed us thither, drunk with the spirit of delusion. George honestly said they were two "grand enthusiasts."

Wednesday, June 6. Above sixty of the poor people had passed the night in Mr Delamotte's barn, singing, and rejoicing. I sang and prayed with them before the door. George's exhortation left them all in tears.

At the Society in the evening, Shaw pleaded for his spirit of prophecy; charged me with love of pre-eminence; with making my proselytes two-fold more children of the devil than before. Fish said he looked upon me as delivered over to Satan, etc. They declared themselves no longer members of the Church of England. We were kept tolerably meek, and parted at eleven. Now am I clear of them. By renouncing the Church, they have discharged me.

Thursday, June 7. Many of our friends have been pestered by the French prophets,[52] and such-like *pretenders* to inspiration. John Bray is the foremost to listen to them, and often carried away with their delusions. Today I had the happiness to find at his house the famous Prophetess [Mary] Lavington. She was sitting by Bowers and Mrs [Lydia] Sellers on the other side. The Prophet Wise asked, "Can a man attain perfection here?" I answered, "No." The prophetess began groaning. I turned and said, "If you have anything to speak, speak it." She lifted up her voice, like the lady on the tripod,[53] and cried out vehemently, "Look for perfection, I say, absolute perfection!" I was minded to rebuke her. But God gave me uncommon recollection, and command of spirit, so that I sat quiet, and replied not. I offered at last to sing, which she allowed, but did not join. Bray pressed me to stay, and hear her pray. They knelt, I

---

52. Cf. the December 11, 1738, entry above.
53. An allusion to the priestess at the Delphi Oracle, outside Corinth.

stood. She prayed most pompously, addressing to Bray with particular encomiums. I durst not say Amen. She concluded with a horrible, hellish laugh, and endeavoured to turn it off.

She showed violent displeasure against our baptized Quaker, saying, "God had showed her, he would destroy all outward things."

Friday and Saturday, June 8 and 9. I took the deposition of Anne Graham, Mrs Biddle, and Mrs Rigby concerning her lewd life and conversation, and warned our friends everywhere against her. Joined at West's with Hutchings and Miss [Molly] Kinchin, in earnest prayer for the promise of the Father.

Whitsunday, June 10. Read the Society my account of the prophetess.[54] All were shocked but poor John Bray. He had *appeared*, and strongly withstood me, and vindicated that Jezebel. I gave no place to him; no, not for a moment. My natural temper was kept down, and changed into a passionate concern for him, which I expressed in prayers and tears. All besides him were melted down. I kissed him, and testified my love, but could make no impression.

Monday, June 11. Expounded with great liberty of spirit, and found the blessing of opposition.

Tuesday, June 12. Heard more of my prophetess, who told a brother that she can command Christ to come to her in what shape she pleases—as a dove, an eagle, etc. The devil owed her a shame by bringing her again to Bray's. Wise, her gallant, came first; whom I urged with a plain question whether he had or had not cohabited with her. He was *forced* to confess he had. John Bray was vehement in her defence. When she came in, flew upon us like a tigress; tried to outface me; insisted that she was immediately inspired. I prayed. She cried the devil was in me. I was a fool, a blockhead, a blind leader of the blind, put out the people's eyes, etc. She roared outrageously. Said it was the lion in her (true, but not the Lion of Judah). She *would* come to the Society in spite of me. If not, they would all go down.

I asked, "Who is on God's side? Who for the old prophets rather than the new? Let them follow me." They followed me into the preaching-room. I prayed, and expounded the lesson with extraordinary power. The women, several of them, gave an account of

---

54. This manuscript has survived; it is located in MARC (ref. DDCW 8/12).

their conversion through my ministry. Our dear brother Bowers confessed himself convinced of his error. We rejoiced and triumphed in the name of the Lord our God.

Wednesday, June 13. My brother returned. Had over the prophetess's affair before the Society. Bray and Bowers much humbled. All agreed to disown the prophetess. Brother Hall proposed expelling Shaw and Wolfe.[55] We consented, *nem. con.*[56] that their names should be erased out of the Society-book, because they disowned themselves members of the Church of England.

Thursday, June 14. Heard my brother preach on Blackheath, "Christ our wisdom, righteousness, sanctification, and redemption" [1 Cor. 1:30]. We continued at the Green Man's,[57] singing and rejoicing. George Whitefield gave a lively exhortation to about thirty of us. I slept with Seward and my brother.

Friday, June 15. The last time I had met Mr Stonehouse and our opposers in the vestry, he astonished by telling me he had consented that I should preach no more. I thought in myself, "What is man? Or what is friendship?" and said nothing. Today, in company with my brother and him, I mentioned, without intending it, my exclusion through his consent. He pleaded that the Bishop of London had justified his churchwardens in their forcible expulsion of me; but at last was quite melted down, would do anything to repair his fault. Resolved no other should be excluded by him, as I had been.

Sunday, June 17. My brother preached to above ten thousand people (as was supposed) in Moorfields, and to a still larger congregation on Kennington Common. I preached twice in the prison.

Monday, June 18. Sang and prayed at Mrs Ewsters's[58]—a lively, gracious soul, but too apt to depend on her inward feelings.

Tuesday, June 19. At Lambeth[59] with Mr Piers. His Grace expressly forbade him to let any of us preach in his church—charged

---

55. Shepherd Wolfe. Charles spells "Wolf."
56. *Nemine contradicente:* with no one voting in opposition.
57. A public house at the top of Blackheath Hill.
58. This was apparently the mother of Mary Ewsters (b. 1723). Mary was a founding member of the London Congregation of the Moravian church when it organized in late 1742. Charles spells "Eusters."
59. Lambeth Palace, London residence of the Archbishop of Canterbury. Charles was meeting again with John Potter.

us with breach of the canon. I mentioned the Bishop of London's authorizing my forcible exclusion. He would not hear me, said he did not dispute. He asked me what call I had. I answered, "A dispensation of the gospel is committed to me" [1 Cor. 9:17]. "That is, to St Paul. But I do not dispute, and will not proceed to excommunication yet." "Your Grace has taught me in your book on church government,[60] that a man unjustly excommunicated is not thereby cut off from communion with Christ." "Of that I am the judge." I asked him, if Mr Whitefield's success was not a spiritual sign, and sufficient proof of his call; recommended Gamaliel's advice.[61] He dismissed us—Piers, with kind professions; me, with all the marks of his displeasure.

I felt nothing in my heart but peace. Prayed and sang at Bray's. But some hours after, at West's, sank down in great heaviness and discouragement. Found a little relief from the Scripture that first offered: Acts 17:3, "Opening and alleging that Christ must needs have suffered, and risen again from the dead, and that this Jesus whom I preach unto you is Christ."

Friday, June 22. The sower of tares[62] is beginning to trouble us with disputes about predestination. My brother was wonderfully owned at Wapping last week, while asserting the contrary truth. Tonight I asked in prayer that if God would have all men to be saved, he would show some token for good upon us. Three were justified in immediate answer to that prayer. We prayed again; several fell down under the power of God, present to witness his universal love.

Saturday, June 23. Some of the persons set at liberty came and called on me to return him thanks in their behalf. Twelve received forgiveness, it seems, last night; another in this hour. Dined at Mr Stonehouse's. My inward conflict continued. Perceived it was the fear of man; and that, by preaching in the field next Sunday, as George Whitefield urges me, I shall break down the bridge and become desperate. Retired, and prayed for particular direction, offering up my friends, my liberty, my life, for Christ's sake and the gospel's. Somewhat less burdened, yet could not be quite easy till I gave up all.

---

60. Cf. April 25, 1739, entry.
61. Cf. Acts 5:34-39.
62. Cf. Matt. 13:25.

Sunday, June 24. St John Baptist's day. The first Scripture I cast my eye upon was "Then came the servant unto him, and said, Master, what shall we do?" [Luke 3:12, alt.]. Prayed with West's, and went forth **in the name of Jesus Christ.**[63] Found near ten thousand helpless sinners waiting for the word in Moorfields. I invited them in my Master's words, as well as name: "Come unto me, all ye that travail, and are heavy laden, and I will give you rest" [Matt. 11:28]. The Lord was with me, even me, his meanest messenger, according to his promise. At St Paul's the psalms, lessons, etc., for the day put fresh life into me. So did the Sacrament. My load was gone, and all my doubts and scruples. God shone upon my path, and I knew this was his will concerning me.

At Newington the rector, Mr Motte, desired me to preach. My text was, "All have sinned, and come short of the glory of God; being justified freely, etc." [Rom. 3:23]. Walked on to the [Kennington] Common, and cried to multitudes upon multitudes, "Repent ye, and believe the gospel" [Mark 1:15]. The Lord was my strength, and my mouth, and my wisdom. Oh that all would therefore praise the Lord for his goodness!

Refreshed with the Society, at a primitive Love-feast.

Friday, June 29. At Wycombe heard of much disturbance and sin, occasioned by Bowers's preaching in the streets. Reached Oxford the next day.

Saturday, June 30. Waited upon the Dean, who spoke with unusual severity against field-preaching and Mr Whitefield; explained away all inward religion and union with God.

That the world, and their god, abhor our manner of acting, I have too sensible proof. This whole week has the messenger of Satan been buffeting me with uninterrupted temptation.

JULY 1739

Sunday, July 1. Preached my sermon on justification before the university with great boldness.[64] All were very attentive. One could not help weeping. At night received power to expound; several gownsmen were present, some mocked.

---

63. Charles printed these words and "St John Baptist's day" in block letters for emphasis.
64. On Rom. 3:23-25; cf. *Sermons*, 183–210.

Monday, July 2. Mr Gambold came. He had been with the Vice-Chancellor,[65] and well received. I visited the Vice-Chancellor, at his own desire. Gave him a full account of the Methodists, which he approved. But objected the irregularity of our doing good in other men's parishes; charged Mr Whitefield with insincerity, and breach of promise; appealed to the Dean, and appointed a second meeting there. All were against my sermon, as liable to be misunderstood.

Tuesday, July 3. Poor wild Bowers had been laid hold on for preaching in Oxford. Today the beadle brought him to me. I spoke to him very home.[66] He had nothing to reply, but promised to do so no more, and thereby obtained his liberty.

At night I had another conference with the Dean, who cited Mr Whitefield to judgment. I said, "Mr Dean, he shall be ready to answer your citation." He used his utmost address to bring me off from preaching abroad, from expounding in houses, from singing psalms. Denied justification by faith only, and all vital religion. Promised me, however, to read Law and Pascal.

Wednesday, July 4. Returned to London.

Sunday, July 8. Near ten thousand, by computation, gave diligent heed to the word preached in Moorfields: "Thou shalt call his name Jesus, for he shall save his people from their sins" [Matt. 1:21]. Numbers seemed greatly affected. Walking over an open field to Kennington Common, I was met by a man who threatened me for a trespass. I preached "Christ our wisdom, righteousness, sanctification, and redemption" [1 Cor. 1:30] to double my morning congregation, and the Lord Almighty bowed their hearts before him.

Monday, July 9. Corrected Mr Cennick's hymns[67] for the press.

Tuesday, July 10. Stopped Okely,[68] just going to Germany, and brought him quite off his design. Mrs H., a brand plucked out of the

---

65. Theophilus Leigh (1693–1784) was Vice-Chancellor of Oxford University, 1738–1740.
66. When used as an adverb, *home* may have the meaning of "direct" or "to the point."
67. These hymns did not go directly to print. John Cennick had only recently become involved with the revival, and in the coming months he would side with Whitefield and the predestinarians over against the Wesleys (cf. the November 4, 1740, entry below). This stance is reflected in the eventual published hymns: *Sacred Hymns for the Children of God, in the Days of Their Pilgrimage* (London: John Lewis, 1741).
68. If this was John Okely, he was only temporarily dissuaded by Charles. He went to Germany with Henry Cossart the following month.

burning through my brother's ministry, told me her wonderful history, which filled my heart with pity and love.

Saturday, July 14. Many were pierced through this evening with the sword of the Spirit, which is the word of God.[69]

Sunday, July 15. My subject in Moorfields, "God was in Christ, reconciling the world unto himself" [2 Cor. 5:19]; on the Common, "Blessed are the poor in spirit" [Matt. 5:3].

Sunday, July 22. Never knew till now the strength of temptation, and energy of sin. Who that conferred with flesh and blood would covet great success? I live in a continual storm. My soul is always in my hand. The enemy thrusts sore at me, that I may fall. And a worse enemy than the devil is my own heart. *Miror aliquem praedicatorem salvari!*[70] Received, I humbly hope, a fresh pardon in the Sacrament at St Paul's. Would have preached at the Fleet, but the warden forbade. Preached at the Marshalsea.

Monday, July 23. I talked in Newgate with five condemned malefactors.

Wednesday, July 25. Served with a writ by Mr Goter, for walking over his field to Kennington.[71] Sent Okely to the lawyer, who confessed he did not so much as know what his client sued me for.

Saw Dr [Philip] Doddridge at Mr Burnham's, but did not see much of him.

Thursday, July 26. The Lord applied his word at Bray's, so that one received forgiveness under it.

AUGUST 1739

Saturday, August 4. Dined with my friend George Whitefield at Mrs [Jane] Sparrow's in Lewisham. In the evening at Mrs Ewsters's, whom I visit most days for my own sake.

---

69. Cf. Eph. 6:17.
70. "I marvel that any preacher is saved!"
71. This writ, brought by Richard Goter, which instructed Wesley to appear at the Court of Common Bench to be held at Westminster on October 20, 1739, has survived and is in MARC (ref. DDCW 4/3). In Charles's hand is the annotation: "Thou shall answer for me, O Lord my God!" Cf. the October 18, 1739, entry below.

Sunday, August 5. In the fields I discoursed on the promise, "I will pray the Father, and he shall send you another Comforter" [John 14:16]. My subject was the same at Kennington. In the bands, one witnessed her having received her pardon. We gave thanks with her, whom the Lord hath redeemed.

Tuesday, August 7. I preached repentance and faith at Plaistow[72] and at night expounded in a private house, Lazarus dead and raised [John 11]. The next day I called with Hodges on Thomas Keen, a mild and candid Quaker; preached at Marylebone.[73] Too well pleased with my success, which brought upon me the buffetings of Satan. I preached on Kennington Common, "Repent ye, and believe the gospel" [Mark 1:15].

Friday, August 10. Gave George Whitefield some account both of my labours and my conflicts.

Dear George,
    I forgot to mention the most material occurrence at Plaistow; namely, that a clergyman was there convinced of sin. He stood under me, and appeared, throughout my discourse, under the strongest perturbation of mind. In our return we were much delighted with an old spiritual Quaker, who is clear in justification by faith only. At Marylebone a footman was convinced of more than sin, and now waits with confidence for all the power of faith. Friend Keen seems to have experience, and is right in the foundation.
    I cannot preach out on the weekdays for the expense of coach. Nor accept of dear Mr Seward's offer, to which I should be less backward, would he take my advice. But while he is so lavish of his Lord's goods, I cannot consent that this ruin should in any degree *seem* to be under my hand.
    I am continually tempted to leave off preaching, and hide myself like John Hutchings. I should then be freer from temptation, and at leisure to attend my own improvement. God continues to work *by* me, but not *in* me, that I can perceive. Do not reckon upon me, my brother, in the work God is doing, for I cannot expect he should long employ one who is ever longing and murmuring to be discharged. I rejoice in your success, and pray for its increase a thousand fold.

---

72. Most likely Plaistow, Essex, six miles east of London.
73. This area was largely open fields at the time, suitable for field preaching. Charles spells "Marybone."

Today I carried John Bray to Mr Law, who resolved all his feelings and experiences into fits or natural affections, and advised him to take no notice of his comforts, which he had better be without than with. He blamed Mr Whitefield's *Journals*, and way of proceeding; said he had had great hopes that the Methodists would have been dispersed by little and little into livings, and have leavened the whole lump. I told him my experience. "Then am I," said he, "far below you (if you are right), not worthy to bear your shoes." He agreed to our notion of faith, but would have it that all men held it; was fully against the laymen's expounding, as the very worst thing, both for themselves and others. I told him he was my schoolmaster to bring me to Christ,[74] but the reason why I did not come sooner to him was my seeking to be sanctified before I was justified. I disclaimed all expectation of becoming some great one.

Among other things, he said, "Was I so talked of as Mr Whitefield is, I should run away and hide myself entirely." "You might," I answered, "but God would bring you back like Jonah." Joy in the Holy Ghost, he told us, was the most dangerous thing God could give. I replied, "But cannot God guard his own gifts?" He often disclaimed advising, "seeing we had the Spirit of God," but mended upon our hands, and at last came almost quite over.

Sunday, August 12. Received power, great power, to explain the Good Samaritan [Luke 10:29-37]. Communicated at St Paul's, as every Sunday. I convinced multitudes at the Common from "Such were some of you, but ye are washed," etc. [1 Cor. 6:11]; and before the day was past felt my own sinfulness so great, that I wished I had never been born.

Monday, August 13. Wrote in a letter to Seward,

> I preached yesterday to more than ten thousand hearers. Am so buffeted, both before and after, that, was I not forcibly detained, I should fly from every human face. If God does not make a way for me to escape, I shall not easily be brought back again. I cannot like advertising. It looks like sounding a trumpet.
>
> I hope our brother Hutchings will come forth at last, and throw away, which he seems to have taken up, my mantle of reserve. But then he will no longer make Mr Broughton his counsellor.

---

74. Cf. Gal. 3:24.

Tuesday, August 14. Carried [Henry] Cossart, a Moravian, to Mr Law, and left them together. The whole congregation at Kennington seemed moved by my discourse on those words, "He shall reprove the world of sin, of righteousness, and of judgment" [John 16:8]. I could hardly get from them. We hear every day of more and more convinced or pardoned.

Wednesday, August 15. Wrote to George,

> Let not Cossart's opinion of your letter to the bishop[75] weaken your hands. *Abundans cautela nocet.*[76] It is the Moravian infirmity. Tomorrow I set out for Bristol. I pray you all a good voyage, and that many poor souls may be added to the church by your ministry, before we meet again. Meet again, I am confident we shall; perhaps both here and in America. The will of the Lord be done with us, and by us, in time and in eternity.

Called on our brother Bell, just as his wife received "like precious faith" [2 Pet. 1:1]. We were all partakers of her joy.

Thursday, August 16. Rode to Wycombe and, being refused the church, would have preached in an house. But Bowers's preaching here has shut the door against me, by confirming their natural aversion to the gospel. The next day we came to Oxford, and the day after that to Evesham.

Sent my brother and friends accounts of our going on from time to time. The following to my brother:

Bengeworth and Evesham,

> August 20, 1739
> Dear Brother,
> We have left the brethren at Oxford much edified, and two gownsmen, besides Charles Graves, thoroughly awakened. On Saturday afternoon God brought us hither. Mr [Benjamin] Seward being from home, there was no admittance for us, his wife being an opposer, and having refused to see George Whitefield before me. At seven Mr Seward found us at our inn, and carried us home. I expounded at eight in the schoolroom, which contains two hundred;

---

75. George Whitefield, *The Rev Mr Whitefield's Answer to the Bishop of London's Last Pastoral Letter* (London: W. Strahan, 1739).

76. "Abundant caution does harm." The inverse of a standard legal phrase: "*Abundans cautela non nocet.*"

and held out the promises from John 16[:7-11], "I will send the Comforter," etc. On Sunday morning I preached from George Whitefield's pulpit, the wall, "Repent ye, and believe the gospel" [Mark 1:15]. The notice being short, we had only a few hundreds, but such as those described in the morning lesson, "These were more noble than those of Thessalonica, in that they received the word with all readiness of mind" [Acts 17:11]. In the evening I showed to near two thousand their Saviour in the Good Samaritan [Luke 10:29-37]. Many, I am persuaded, found themselves stripped, and wounded, and half-dead, and are therefore ready for the oil and wine. Once more God strengthened me at nine to open the new covenant at the school-house, which was crowded with deeply attentive sinners.

Monday, August 20. Spoke from Acts 2:37 to two or three hundred market-people and soldiers, all as orderly and decent as could be desired.

I now heard that the mayor had come down on Sunday to take a view of us; and soon after an officer struck a countryman in the face, without any provocation. A serious woman besought the poor man not to resist evil, as the other only wanted to make a riot. He took patiently several repeated blows, telling the man he might beat him as long as he pleased.

Took a walk with Mr Seward, whose eyes it has pleased God to open, to see He would have all men to be saved. His wife, who refuses to see me, is miserably bigoted to the particular scheme.

We had the satisfaction of meeting with Mr Seward's cousin Molly, whom I had endeavoured to convince of sin at Islington. The Spirit has now convinced her of righteousness also. Today she told us a young lady here upon a visit had been deeply struck on Sunday night, under the word, seeing and feeling her need of a physician; and earnestly desired me to pray for her. We immediately joined in thanksgiving and intercession. After dinner I spoke with her. She burst into tears; told us she had come hither thoughtless and dead in pleasures and sin, but fully resolved against ever being a Methodist; that she was first alarmed at seeing us so happy and full of love; had gone to the Society, but never found herself out, till the word came with power to her soul; that all the following night she had been as in an agony; could not pray; could not bear our singing, nor have any rest in her spirit. We betook ourselves to prayer, and God hearkened. She received forgiveness in that instant, and triumphed in the name of the Lord *her* God. We were all of us upon the mount the rest of the day.

At six I explained the nature of faith from "Not I, but Christ liveth in me—Who loved *me*, and gave himself for *me*" [Gal. 2:20]. Afterwards showed them, in the school-house, their own case in dead Lazarus [John 11]. Some of those that were dead, I trust, begin to come forth. Several serious people from the neighbouring towns came home with us. We continued our rejoicings till midnight.

Tuesday, August 21. Besought my hearers to be reconciled unto God. I found Miss P. had been greatly strengthened by last night's expounding, and could scarce forbear crying out [that] she was that Lazarus; and if they would come to Christ, he would raise them as he had her. All night she continued singing in her heart, and discovers more and more of that genuine mark of his disciples' love.

Was prevailed upon to stay over this day. God soon showed us *his* design in it. Our singing in the garden drew two sincere women to us, who sought Christ sorrowing. After reading the promises in Isaiah, we prayed, and they received them accomplished in themselves. We were upon a mount, which reminded us of Tabor,[77] through the joy wherewith our Master filled us. How shall I be thankful enough for his bringing me hither! While we were singing, a poor drunken servant of Mr Seward's was struck. His master had last night given him warning, but now he seems effectually called. We spent the afternoon most delightfully in Isaiah. At seven the Society met, I could hardly speak through my cold, but it was suspended while I showed the natural man his picture in Blind Bartimeus [Mark 10:46-52]. Many were ready to cry after Jesus for mercy. The three that had lately received their sight were much strengthened. Miss P. declared her cure before two hundred witnesses, many of them gay young gentlewomen. They received her testimony, flocked round about her, and pressed her on all sides to come to see them. By this open confession, she purchased to herself great boldness in the faith.

Wednesday, August 22. This morning the work upon poor Robin[78] appeared to be God's work. The words that made the first impression were:

77. Mount Tabor is a traditional site for the Transfiguration of Jesus; cf. Mark 9:2.
78. Apparently the first name of the drunken servant of Benjamin Seward.

'Tis mercy all, immense and free,
For O! my God, it found out me![79]

He now seems full of sorrow, and joy, and astonishment, and love. The world, too, set to their seal that he belongs to Christ.

Here I cannot but observe the narrow spirit of those that hold particular redemption. I have had no disputes with them, yet they have me in abomination. Mrs Seward is irreconcilably angry with me, "for he offers Christ to all." Her maids are of the same spirit, and their Baptist teacher insists that I ought to have my gown stripped over my ears.

When Mr Seward, in my hearing, exhorted one of the maids to a concern for her salvation, she answered, "It was no purpose," she could do nothing. The same answer he received from his daughter of seven years old. See the genuine fruits of this blessed doctrine!

Gloucester, August 23
        By ten last night the Lord brought us hither through many dangers and difficulties. In mounting, I fell over my horse, and sprained my hand. Riding in the dark I bruised my foot. We lost our way as often as we *could*. Two horses we had between three, for Robin bore us company. Here we turned back from a friend's house by his wife's sickness. Last night my voice and strength wholly failed me. Today they are in some measure restored. At night I with difficulty got into the crowded Society; preached the law and the gospel from Rom. 3. They received it with all readiness. Three clergymen were present. Some without attempted to make a disturbance by setting on the dogs, but in vain. The *dumb* dogs rebuked the rioters.

Gloucester, August 24
        Before I went forth into the streets and highways, I sent, after my custom, to borrow the church. The minister (one of the better disposed) sent back a civil message: he would be glad to drink a glass of wine with me, but durst not lend me his pulpit for fifty guineas.
        Mr Whitefield durst lend me his field, which did just as well. For near an hour and [a] half God gave me voice and strength to exhort about two thousand sinners to repent and believe the gospel [Mark 1:15]. My voice and strength failed together; neither

---

79. "Free Grace," st. 3, *HSP* (1739), 118 (*Poetical Works*, 1:105).

do I want them when my work is done. Being invited to Painswick, I waited upon the Lord and renewed my strength. We found near one thousand gathered in the street. I have but one subject, on which I discoursed from 2 Cor. 5:19, "God was in Christ reconciling the world unto himself." I besought them earnestly to be reconciled, and the rebels seemed inclinable to lay down their arms. A young Presbyterian teacher clave to us.

I received fresh strength to expound the Good Samaritan [Luke 10:29-37] at a public-house, which was full above stairs and below.

Saturday, August 25. I showed them in the street that to them and to their children was the promise made [Acts 2:39]. Some are, I trust, on the point of receiving it. Three clergymen attended.

I prayed by a young woman, afraid of death, because it had not lost its sting.[80] I showed her the promise was to those that are afar off, even *before* they actually receive it, if they can but trust that they *shall* receive it. This revived her much, and we left her patiently waiting for the salvation of God.

At nine I exhorted and prayed with an house full of sincere souls, and took my leave, recommended by their affectionate prayers to the grace of God.

At Gloucester received an invitation from Friend Drummond. Dined with her and several of the Friends, particularly Josiah Martin, a spiritual man, as far as I can discern. My heart was enlarged, and knit to them in love.

Went to the field at five. An old intimate acquaintance (Mrs [Demaris] Kirkham) stood in my way, and challenged me, "What, Mr Wesley, is it you I see? Is it possible that you who can preach at Christ Church, St Mary's,[81] etc., should come hither after a mob?" I cut her short with, "The work which my Master giveth me, must I not do it?" and went to my mob, or (to put it in the Pharisees' phrase) this people which is accursed.[82] Thousands heard me gladly, while I told them their privilege of the Holy Ghost, the Comforter,[83] and exhorted them to come for him to Christ as poor lost sinners. I continued my discourse till night.

---

80. Cf. 1 Cor. 15:55-56.
81. Christ Church Cathedral and St Mary's Church, both in Oxford.
82. Cf. John 7:49.
83. I.e., his sermon on John 16:7-11.

Randwick,[84] August 26

The minister here lent me his pulpit. I stood at the window (which was taken down), and turned to the larger congregation of above two thousand in the churchyard. They appeared greedy to hear, while I testified, "God so loved the world, that he gave his only-begotten Son," etc. [John 3:16]. These are, I think, more noble than those at Evesham.

After the sermon a woman came to me who had received faith in hearing Mr Whitefield. She was terrified at having lost her comfort. I explained to her that wilderness-state into which the believer is *generally* led by the Spirit to be tempted, as soon as he is baptized by the Holy Ghost. This confirmed her in a patient looking for his return whom her soul loveth.

We dined at Mr Ellis's of Ebley.[85] Met our brother Ellis, who has the blessing of believing parents, two sisters awakened; one only brother continues an abandoned prodigal.

In the afternoon I preached again to a Kennington congregation.[86] The church was full as it could crowd. Thousands stood in the churchyard. It was the most beautiful sight I ever beheld. The people filled the gradually rising area, which was shut up on three sides by a vast perpendicular hill. On the top and bottom of this hill was a circular row of trees. In this amphitheatre they stood, deeply attentive, while I called upon them in Christ's words, "Come unto me, all that are weary" [Matt. 11:28]. The tears of many testified that they were ready to enter into that rest. God enabled me to lift up my voice like a trumpet, so that all distinctly heard me. I concluded with singing an Invitation to Sinners.[87]

It was with difficulty we made our way through this most loving people, and returned amidst their prayers and blessings to Ebley. Here I expounded the second lesson for two hours, and received strength and faith to plead the promise of the Father. A good old Baptist pressed me to preach at Stanley[88] in my way to Bristol.

Monday, August 27. Accordingly I set out at seven. The sky was overcast, and the Prince of the power of the air[89] wetted us to the

---

84. Randwick, Gloucestershire, just north of Ebley, and about seven miles from Gloucester (as John Wesley notes in his *Journal* [October 7, 1739], *Works* 19:102). Charles spells "Runwick."

85. Charles spells "Ebly."

86. Charles is speaking metaphorically here, implying that the congregation was as large as those that gathered in Kennington Common in London.

87. See note for February 14, 1739, entry above.

88. Likely Stanley Borough (=King's Stanley), Gloucestershire. John Wesley found a ready audience there a month later; cf. *Journal* (October 7, 1739), *Works* 19:102.

89. Cf. Eph. 2:2.

skin. This, I thought, portended good. We could not stay to dry ourselves, there being, contrary to our expectation, a company of near
one thousand waiting. I preached from a table (having been first
denied the pulpit), upon, "Repent, and believe the gospel" [Mark
1:15]. The hearers seemed so much affected that I appointed them to
meet me again in the evening. The minister was of my audience.

Rode back to Ebley, and was informed by brother Okely[90] that he
had fastened upon the poor prodigal, and spoke to his heart. His
convictions were heightened by the sermon. We prayed and sang
alternately, till faith came. God blew with his wind, and the waters
flowed. He struck the hard rock, and the waters gushed out,[91] and
the poor sinner, with joy and astonishment, believed the Son of
God loved him, and gave himself for him. Sing, ye heavens, for the
Lord hath done it; shout, ye lower parts of the earth![92]

In the morning I had told his mother the story of St Augustine's
conversion. Now I carried her the joyful news, "This thy son was
dead, and is alive again."[93] Expounded at a gentlewoman's house
in my way to Stanley, but could hardly speak through my cold.
Went forth in faith, and preached under a large elm tree, on the
Prodigal Son [Luke 15:11-32], and returned to Ebley rejoicing;
where I expounded the Woman of Samaria [John 4].

On *Tuesday evening, August 28,* I accompanied my brother to the
preaching-room, in the Horsefair, Bristol.[94] A drunken Quaker
(Benjamin Rutter) made a great disturbance by bawling out for his
wife. Some of the brethren hardly saved him from the mob.

Wednesday, August 29. At six o'clock prayers, with a large company of our brethren and sisters, who have learned of Christ to
come to the Temple[95] early in the morning. None of them as yet think
of it part of their Christian liberty to forsake the means of grace.

Spent the day with my brother in visiting several of the Society.

Thursday, August 30. My brother expounded and took leave of
them. His short absence cost them many tears.

---

90. Almost certainly Francis Okely, as his brother John had left for Germany.
91. Cf. Exod. 17:6.
92. Cf. Isa. 44:23.
93. Cf. Luke 15:24.
94. This is the meeting room that John Wesley had just built for Methodist gatherings in
central Bristol. Charles will repeatedly refer to it as "the Room" in subsequent entries.
95. Temple Church, just outside of Bristol proper, on the south side of the River Avon.

Friday, August 31. I entered upon my ministry at Weavers' Hall,[96] and began expounding Isaiah, with much freedom and power. They were melted into tears all around. So again at one, when the bands met to keep the church-fast. We were all of one heart and of one mind. I was much carried out in pleading the promises; forgot the contradiction wherewith they grieved my spirit at London; fell all at once into the strictest intimacy with these delightful souls; and could not forbear saying, "It is good for me to be here."[97]

I spoke to the poor colliers on "The blind receive their sight, the lame walk," etc. [Matt. 11:5]. Then began the gospel at Gloucester Lane, and preached with power on "Thou shalt call his name Jesus; for," etc. [Matt. 1:21]. I went home to Mrs Grevil's,[98] stronger in body than when I rose.

SEPTEMBER 1739

Saturday, September 1. At five I preached for the first time at the Bowling Green, in the heart of the city, and called all the weary and heavy-laden to Christ. None offered to go away, though it rained hard. The power of the Lord was in the midst, which forced one woman to cry out vehemently. Began the Romans at Weaver's Hall. The hearers appeared deeply affected.

Sunday, September 2. There was supposed to be above four thousand at the Bowling Green. My subject was, "To you and to your children is the promise made" [Acts 2:39]. Many experienced the great power of truth.

Received the Sacrament at St Nicholas.[99] Dined at Mrs Nichols's, full of faith and love. Prayed by Mr Coulston, desirous to be with Christ.

Preached at Rose Green,[100] to near five thousand souls, upon, "God so loved the world" [John 3:16]. They heard me patiently, and

---

96. Weavers' Hall, in the Temple Meads section of Bristol, became another regular preaching point for Charles and John Wesley.

97. Cf. Matt. 17:4.

98. Elizabeth Grevil (*née* Whitefield, b. 1713), recently widowed sister of George Whitefield.

99. St Nicholas's Church, in central Bristol near the River Avon.

100. Rose Green was a park in northeast Bristol, near Fishponds.

some gladly. Quite spent by the time I got to Weavers' Hall. The scoffers gave me new life. For two hours I preached the law, and then was fresh for the Love-feast. We could not depart before eleven.

Monday, September 3. Had some discourse with a gentleman who had been offended at the cryings out. My sermon upon the Holy Ghost had been blessed to his conviction, and stripped him of his outside Christianity. Found Weavers' Hall as full as it could hold, and proceeded in Isaiah.

Dined with the gentleman above mentioned, and spoke fully and strongly of the things of the kingdom. Then read him my own case. He laid down his arms, confessed he knew nothing yet as he ought to know, and is now looking for that faith which is the gift of God.

Preached at the Brick-yard, to upwards of five thousand, from 1 Cor. 6:9. I marvelled at their taking it so patiently, when I showed them they were all adulterers, thieves, idolaters, etc. Then expounded John 1, in Gloucester Lane, with demonstration of the Spirit.

Spent a delightful hour in prayer with a band, and were all melted into a sense of our deep poverty.

Tuesday, September 4. I talked with poor despairing Lucretia [Smith]. Never did I find greater faith in pleading the promises for any one; yet no answer, which convinces me that it is good for the choicest of God's children to receive (and that for a long time) the sentence of death in themselves. I have not found such depth of distress; no, not in Hetty Delamotte.

At four I preached over against the school in Kingswood to some thousands (colliers chiefly), and held out the promises from Isaiah 35: "The wilderness and the solitary place shall be glad for them and the desert shall rejoice, and blossom as a rose" [35:1]. I triumphed in God's mercy to these poor outcasts (for he hath called them a people who were not a people[101]), and in the accomplishment of that Scripture, "Then the eyes of the blind shall be opened, and the ears of the deaf shall be unstopped. Then shall the lame man leap as an hart, and the tongue of the dumb sing, for in the wilderness shall water break out, and streams in the desert" [Isa. 35:6]. O how gladly do the poor receive the gospel! We hardly knew how to part.

---

101. Cf. Hosea 2:23.

Just as I began in Weavers' Hall the devil set up his throat in Benjamin Rutter. I took that occasion to convince the hearers of sin, of the very sin of that poor reprobate. The chapter expounded was Rom. 2. To God be all the glory that I spoke convincingly.

Wednesday, September 5. I was much discouraged by a farther discovery of the disorderly walking of some, who have [given] the adversary occasion to blaspheme, by their rioting and their drunkenness. I am a poor creature on such occasions, being soon cast down, as in the case of Shaw and the Prophetess.[102] Yet I went and talked with them. God filled me with such love to their souls as I have not known before. They could not stand before it. I joined with Okely and Cennick in prayer for them. M——trembled exceedingly. The others gave us great cause to hope for their recovery.

The same power continued with me at the women's Society, whom I reproved in love and simplicity for their lightness, dress, self-indulgence. I then exhorted the men to self-denial and a constant use of the means *as* means. God greatly enlarged our hearts in prayer.

Thursday, September 6. Had my gentleman (now a little child) to breakfast, and surprised him much by Isaiah's promises. Dined at Mrs Ayers's, "sick of desire, if not of love."[103] Rode with [John] Deschamps to Publow, where I preached from, "God so loved the world" [John 3:16]. Spake with boldness at night on my favourite subject, Justification by Faith only [Rom. 3:23-24], and triumphed in the irresistible force of that everlasting truth.

Friday, September 7. At Weavers' Hall expounded Isaiah 3, where the prophet alike condemns notorious profligates, worldly-minded men, and well-dressed ladies.

God was with us in our meeting to keep the fast. I went to see one in her last agony, but throughly sensible of her dreadful condition. Preached Christ to her, and prayed in faith. She showed all imaginable signs of eager desire, and died within an hour. How comfortable it is that I can now hope for her, so often as I have disputed the possibility of a death-bed repentance!

---

102. Cf. the June 12, 1739, entry above.
103. "Longing After Christ," st. 3, *HSP* (1740), 62 (*Poetical Works*, 1:255).

The house and yards of sister England were crowded as usual. The Scripture from which I discoursed was John 1. God was with my mouth. I preached and prayed believing. I was led to ask a sign of God's universal love. He always answers that prayer. A poor ignorant man stood up, as God's witness, that in Christ he had redemption through his blood, the forgiveness of his sins; that he knew and felt it by such a love to every human soul, as he was hardly able to bear. He spoke with a simplicity which was irresistible. We all confessed that God was with him of a truth. Our prayers were answered on Mrs Ayers likewise, which she testified before us all.

Saturday, September 8. Two women came to me who had received the atonement last night, while the man was speaking, and were filled with unknown love to all mankind. We observed the thanksgiving-day at Mrs England's, and found the benefit of joint prayers and praises.

At the Bowling Green, I prayed God to direct me what to preach upon, and opened on Ezekiel's vision of the dry bones: "So I prophesied as I was commanded, and as I prophesied, there was a noise, and, behold, a shaking!" [Ezek. 37:7]. The breath of God attended his word. A man sunk down under it. A woman screamed for mercy, so as to drown my voice. Never did I see the like power among us. Coming home, I met Mrs Skinner, who told me she had found Christ at the expounding last Monday, and went home full of melting joy and love.

At the Room I preached from Rom. 4. God set to his seal. A woman testified she had then received the witnessing Spirit; was sure her sins were forgiven; full of love and joy in the Holy Ghost; knew Christ was hers; and could even, as she said, fly away to heaven.

Another declared she had never been able to apply the promises till last night, but then received the power; knew Christ died for her; said she had laboured many years to justify herself, and warned us earnestly not to do as she had done; not to mingle our own works with the blood of Christ.

Sunday, September 9. At the Bowling Green I preached on "When he is come, he shall convince the world of sin, and of righteousness," etc. [John 16:8]. The Green was quite full. I never spoke more searchingly. I would have passed on to the second office of the Spirit, convincing of righteousness, but was again and again brought back, and constrained to dwell upon the law. As often as I returned, some pharisees quitted the field, feeling the sharpness of the two-edged sword.[104]

Two thousand at Rose Green stood patient in the rain, while I explained how the Spirit convinces of righteousness and of judgment. After sermon, a poor collier afforded me matter of rejoicing (his wife received the atonement some days before). He had been with me before. Owned he was the wickedest fellow alive a month ago, but now finds no rest in his flesh by reason of his sin. Observing him much dejected yesterday at the thanksgiving, I asked him if he was sick. "No, no," he answered, "my sickness is of my soul." Here he informed me he had come home with such a weight upon him that he was ready to sink. It continued all night, but joy and deliverance came in the morning. He was lightened of his load, and now declared that he believed in Jesus.

The Room was excessively crowded. I spoke to their hearts from Rom. 5. Two who had been scoffing desired our prayers for them. For between two and three hours God strengthened me for his work.

Monday, September 10. At the Hall, while I was expounding Isaiah 4, a man perceived his filth purged away by the Spirit of judgment and burning. Sarah Norton, a Presbyterian, followed me home under strong convictions. We prayed and trembled before the face of God. She is not far from the kingdom of heaven. Two simple souls, Mary Fry and Jane Clansy, now informed me that God filled them on Friday evening with love and joy unspeakable. They expressed so much of it, and have been so tempted since, that I could not doubt of their being accepted.

Conversed and prayed with Mrs [Elizabeth] Hooper. I have a good hope that the sun of righteousness is risen upon her, with healing in his wings.[105]

Preached in the Brick-yard, where I think there could not be less than four thousand. It rained hard, yet none stirred. I spoke with great freedom and power. A woman cried out, and dropped down. I spoke to her at Mrs Norman's,[106] and found she had sunk under the weight of sin.

---

104. Cf. Heb. 4:12.
105. Cf. Mal. 4:2.
106. Mrs. Mary Norman, whose husband owned the Brick-yard and made it available for Methodist preaching.

At Gloucester Lane I discoursed two hours on John 3. A notorious drunkard gave glory to God, declaring he had found mercy last night, through faith in Jesus Christ. This stirred the pharisee in a woman's soul, and she cried out against him most vehemently. I took and turned her inside out, and showed her her spirit in those who murmured at Christ for receiving sinners. A woman of a broken spirit testified she had found redemption through his blood, when I preached last at Baptist Mills. We daily discover more and more who are begotten again by the word of God's power, or awakened to a sense of sin, or edified in the faith.

Tuesday, September 11. Took horse with Deschamps and Wigginton. The wind and rain almost confounded us. We got to Bradford[-on-Avon] by noon. Many were gone away, despairing of my coming. However, I found upward of a thousand, whom I called upon to repent, and believe the gospel [Mark 1:15]. I was forced to exert my voice to the utmost. They appeared much affected, especially a young woman and a very old man, who wept all the time like children.

We dined at Freshford in our return. I could scarce sit my horse, the wind and rain were so troublesome. Got, almost senseless, to Bristol, and to the Room, but could not stand. Yet spoke, I know not how, for an hour, and hastened to bed, utterly exhausted.

The pharisee, who protested last night against Christ's receiving sinners, sent tonight to desire our prayers, being in an agony of conviction. Some have since informed me that they observed her turn pale while I spoke. Her soul and body sympathize now. The Lord show himself the Physician of both!

The woman, I have just heard, whose soul and spirit were pierced and divided asunder last Sunday, was a stranger, wholly unawakened till that moment—an opposer, say some, and little better than an atheist. When they rebuked her that she should hold her peace, her answer was, "I am not mad, or out of my senses. But I must cry, and I will cry, to Christ for mercy, while I have any breath in me."

Wednesday, September 12. Rose half dead with the headache. I breakfasted at Mr [Henry] Page's, but could neither lift up my head nor speak. Went to a friend's, where I met poor Mr W—n, a sweet youth. I was much concerned for him. I cannot doubt his sincerity, or despair of his return. He was ready to hear, childlike and teachable, convinced of his fall. He thanked, and I believe loves, me. The world have taken the alarm, that he designs to desert them a second time.

This conference abated my headache. Expounding at the Hall gave me more strength.[107] After talking two hours with the poor people that came to me, and preaching at Baptist Mills, I was perfectly well.

Thursday, September 13. Breakfasted at Mrs Davis's,[108] a genius child of God, and stayed till noon, transcribing Isaiah. Providence threw me on Mr W—n, just as he was leaving Bristol. He cannot long hold out, without an alteration; is himself sensible of it, and the promises are not fulfilled in him; but trusts they shall before he goes hence. I have great love and faith for him.

Many were convinced at the Room this evening, by my exposition of Rom. 7.

Friday, September 14. Talked with two more women who lately received peace through my ministry. In the evening, while I was expounding the Woman of Samaria [John 4], Christ called forth two of his witnesses, who declared they now believed, because they had heard him of his own mouth.

Saturday, September 15. Having been provoked to speak unadvisedly with my lips, I preached on the Bowling Green in great weakness on "Lazarus, come forth!" [John 11:43]. Was surprised that any good should be done, but God quickens others by those who are dead themselves. A man came to me and declared he had now received the Spirit of life. So did a woman at the same time, which she openly confessed at Weavers' Hall. We had great power among us, while I displayed the believer's privileges, from Rom. 8. Another woman then stood forth and testified, "I have the witness of God's Spirit with my spirit, that I am a child of God." It was a most triumphant night indeed.

Sunday, September 16. Took coach at six with Mr and Mrs Wigginton,[109] Lucretia Smith, and Mrs Grevil, for Hanham Mount.

---

107. Almost certainly on Rom. 6, continuing his series.

108. This is most likely Elizabeth Davis, who was hosting the Bristol band meetings in her home at this time. She would die in January 1741. The other possibility is Anne Davis (d. 1775), who became in later years a great friend of Charles and his wife, Sally. See Charles's poetic reflection on her death in *Poetical Works*, 6:338–39.

109. Mrs. Anne Wigginton (d. 1757). See Charles's hymn on the occasion of her death in *Funeral Hymns* (1759), 31–34 (*Poetical Works*, 6:248–51).

I expounded the Good Samaritan [Luke 10:29-37] to between three and four thousand, with power. While I was repeating that in Jeremiah, "Is not my word like a fire, saith the Lord, and like a hammer that breaketh the rock in pieces?" [Jer. 23:29], a woman fell down under the stroke of it. I found afterwards that the good Samaritan had poured in his oil and made her whole. Another declared He had then bound up her wounds also. I heard on all sides the sighing of them that were in captivity, and trust more than I know of were set at liberty, for the Lord was among us of a truth.

Met between thirty and forty colliers with their wives at Mr [Thomas] Willis's, and administered the Sacrament to them. But found no comfort myself, in that or any ordinance. I always find strength for the work of the ministry, but when my work is over, my strength, both bodily and spiritual, leaves me. I can pray for others, not for myself. God by me strengthens the weak hands, and confirms the feeble knees, yet am I myself as a man in whom is no strength. I am weary and faint in my mind, longing continually to be discharged.

Today I found power to pray for myself. Confessed it good for me to be in desertion, and asked God to give me (if it was not tempting him) a sign from his word. The answer was from Isaiah 54:7, "For a small moment have I forsaken thee, but with great mercies will I gather thee. In a little wrath I hid my face from thee for a moment, but with everlasting kindness will I have mercy on thee, saith the Lord thy Redeemer."

At two I preached in the Bowling Green, by computation, to six thousand people. Before I began, and after, the enemy raged exceedingly. A troop of his children, soldiers and polite gentlemen, had taken possession of a corner of the Green, and roared like their brethren the two Gergesenes, before the devils were sent into the civiler swine.[110] They provoked the spirit of jealousy to lift up a standard against them. I never felt such a power before, and promised the people that they should feel it too. For I saw God had a great work to do among us by Satan's opposition. I lifted up my voice like a trumpet, and in a few minutes drove him out of the field. For above an hour I preached the gospel with extraordinary power, from blind Bartimeus [Mark 10:46-52], and am confident it could not fall to the ground.

---

110. Cf. Matt. 8:28.

Monday, September 17. This morning a woman received pardon through the word. The rain eased as I began, and began again as I left off.

Expounded the Prodigal Son [Luke 15:11-32] near the Brick-yard. Many, I hope, saw themselves. They come to me daily, who have found Christ, or rather are found by him, so that I lose count of them.

This afternoon I conferred with *Thomas Tucker* and *Elisabeth Shirdock*, both clearly justified. *Matthew Davis*, a notorious drunkard, etc., till last Saturday was sennight,[111] came then to the Green and was justified in a moment. *John Lewis* was filled with joy last night. *Prudence Nichols* knows that her Redeemer liveth. Several who had lost their peace are daily brought out of darkness, as was a woman this evening at Gloucester Lane. Another, while I was discoursing from John 5, received forgiveness, and testified it before us all. I did expect great things, for I was utterly exhausted *before* I began. "When I am weak, then I am strong," [2 Cor. 12:10]—for others, not myself. After preaching, the messenger of Satan came. He seldom fails me after success. But God, I knew, will avenge me of mine adversary.

Tuesday, September 18. Gave the Sacrament to a dying woman, who triumphed over death, disarmed of his sting.[112] I preached to above two thousand over against the schoolhouse, and pressed them to come to Christ weary and heavy-laden [Matt. 11:28]. I finished Rom. 8 at Weavers' Hall, which is always crowded within and without. Mr Rutter attempted to raise a disturbance, but none regarded him. Mrs Labbè[113] followed me to Mrs Grevil's, with a young gentlewoman, to whom the word had come with power. Upon Mr Okely's speaking to her the first serious word she had ever heard, she asked if the gentleman was not crazy. But now in the same hour God slew and revived her. She felt and made confession of her faith, being full of astonishment and love.

Wednesday, September 19. I breakfasted at Mrs Labbè's. The roaring lion had tried to tear her to pieces,[114] setting before her her

---

111. "Sennight" is a contraction of "seven-night." Thus, the transformation took place "a week ago last Saturday."
112. Cf. 1 Cor. 15:55-56.
113. Charles spells "Labu."
114. Cf. 1 Pet. 5:8.

sin (harmlessness) in all its aggravations, and persuading her she was lost, were it only for her telling me her sins were forgiven. She raised the family, not daring to be alone, and continued all night offering up prayers and supplications, with strong crying and tears, to Him that was able to save. Toward morning she was heard in that she feared, fell into a slumber, and waked in perfect peace. I spent an hour with her. She could do nothing but cry, and wonder, and rejoice.

At the Hall a poor man bore a noble testimony, that God had shed abroad his love in his heart last night, so that "I waked," said he, "this morning full of heaven." Another in the afternoon, formerly a Papist, declared himself set at liberty, after he had been hearing me expound. *Ann Bladworth* likewise informs me, that she has clear and strong evidence of her acceptance, ever since Sunday night.

I preached at Baptist Mills, on "The Son of man hath power to forgive sins upon earth" [Matt. 9:6]. I found him with my mouth, and knew he would set to his seal. Had great power in preaching, and greater in prayer. A woman sunk down with groaning that could not be uttered. I had not time to stay with her, but hastened to pray by Sally Murray, who lay a-dying and triumphing over death. I *felt* her spirit, and longed to be in her place.

Weak, spiritless, dead, among the men-bands, I wanted to get away without speaking or praying, because they were all as dead, it seemed, as I. Was overruled to stay and pray, and had the spirit of prayer as never before. We were all in a flame, prayed again and again, not knowing how to part.

Thursday, September 20. Was glad to be interrupted by *Anne Clayton*, who tells me that on Tuesday night, after expounding, she had had Jesus Christ evidently set forth before her eyes (of faith), as crucified.[115] This lasted from ten to twelve. At the same time, she saw herself inconceivably vile, and was filled with love and confidence of *her* Saviour. In that evening it was, that a man declared he had been seeking righteousness fourteen years, as it were by the works of the law, but never attained to it; and was now in despair of ever attaining it, unless by faith. One of the bands testified, "I feel the Spirit of Christ in me, continually springing up into everlasting life."

---

115. Cf. Gal. 3:1.

At the Hall I explained Rom. 9. Through mercy, we could none of us see aught of *the horrible decree*[116] there, but only his justice in rejecting them who had first rejected Him. Christ the Saviour of all men was in the midst of us. Two of his witnesses set to their seal, having received forgiveness yesterday at the Mills.

Friday, September 21. Appointed any who had been reconciled through my ministry, to call upon me after expounding. Among others, there came *Daniel Morris*, a gross sinner, till God awakened him by George Whitefield. On Saturday in the Bowling Green, faith came by hearing. "I was filled with joy," said he, "above what tongue can express. Went home leaping and rejoicing. I know my sins are forgiven. I hate them worse than death. Love every man, and particularly those who make a scoff at me."

Anne Cole declares that Monday was seven-night,[117] at Mrs England's, she was filled at once with inexpressible peace and comfort, "so that now I know I am forgiven. All my doubts and fears are vanished, and I could rejoice to die this moment."

John Quick was set at liberty from sin after many years of Egyptian bondage.

Elisabeth Parsons, while I was preaching at Baptist Mills that forgiveness is a present grace, experienced it such. "You said we must have our sins forgiven here, or not at all; upon which, I thought I have not forgiveness now, but believe God can, and will, give it me. Immediately I was as sure God had pardoned me as if he himself had spoken it to me, and have ever since been full of a comfort and peace which I never knew before."

Virtuous Whetman, long dead in sin, has now, she tells me, a full confidence that Christ died for her, and finds her whole dependence is on Him.

J. T. in a flood of tears, informed me Christ showed himself *her* Saviour at that word, "The *harlots* and publicans go into the kingdom of heaven before you" [Matt. 21:31]. Such was she till last night, but she is washed, but she is justified! And loves much, because much is forgiven her.

Richard Bourn, while I was speaking last Friday of the brazen serpent,[118] looked up to the Antitype, and was healed. The devil raged

---

116. That is, the decree of unconditional reprobation.
117. I.e., "a week ago Monday."
118. Cf. John 3:14.

exceedingly, and tore him with temptations, till Jesus about mid night got himself the victory, and filled his soul with love. All he desires now is to be with Christ.

Friday, September 21.[119] We had much of God with us in our general intercession. From Gloucester Lane I went to Mrs Labbè, and met with John Wilder's sermon.[120] While we were reading the blind man's protestation against colours (that is, the natural man's against any sensible operations of the Holy Ghost), Miss [Rachel] Godly, a girl of fifteen, helped us to a most convincing answer. She burst into tears, fell back in her chair, and discovered the strongest emotion of soul—but such as might well proceed from the God of order. I thought it was the accuser of the brethren troubled her. Inquired, but could not get an answer. We were greatly assisted in prayer for her. She took no notice till about half an hour after, when she waked, as out of a pleasant dream, and asked, "Where am I? Where have I been?" I returned her question, "Where have you been?" and she answered with loving simplicity, "In heaven, I think." Her every word, and sigh, and tear, evidenced the truth of what she told me, that it was grievous to her, after such communion with God, to find she must continue longer in the body.

Saturday, September 22. Mrs Esther Brook called, and told me she had been awakened (as others who now believe) by George Whitefield's ministry; convinced of sin by Mr Bray's; set at liberty under mine. That she believed, in general, while I repeated those words, "The promise is to all that are afar off" [Acts 2:39]; and had them strongly applied, while hearing me at Baptist Mills. In a moment she was assured that all her sins were forgiven, and filled with such joy that she could scarce live under it. It quite overpowered her body for two days. "But now, methinks," said she, "all the Scripture was written for me." I asked whether she was afraid to die. A visible joy in her face gave me the answer, which her tongue confirmed. Was I in her state, I should desire nothing so much as death.

In the afternoon spoke a word of caution to one who seems strong in the faith, and begins to be lifted up—the sure effect of her growing acquaintance with some of Calvin's followers.

---

119. This repetition of "Friday, September 21," comes at the turn of a page in the MS.

120. John Wilder (1680–1742), *The Trial of the Spirits; or, A Caution Against Enthusiasm or Religious Delusion* (Oxford: Sheldonian Theatre, 1739). Wilder was rector of St Aldate's in Oxford. Charles spelled his name "Wildair."

In the Bowling Green showed the nature and life of faith from Gal. 2:20; and then Justification by Faith alone [Rom. 3:23-24], at the Hall. Two clergymen were present. I proved from Scripture and our own Church, that all were Papists, pharisees, antichrists, and accursed, who brought any other doctrine. Some of my hearers were forced to turn their backs.

Sunday, September 23. I took coach for Hanham. A genteel Quaker was one of the company. Going and coming I laboured to convince her of sin, and spoke more closely than ever I did in my life, yet without convincing. Such power belongeth unto God.

Discoursed from 2 Cor. 5 to four thousand sinners, then gave the Sacrament at Mr Willis's. Among the communicants was Susanna Milsom, who has been oppressed by the devil. I prayed with a dying man, beyond Hanham. He was overjoyed to see me; had been awakened by field-preaching, but not yet found mercy.

Missed hearing a railing sermon at St James. Notwithstanding all opposition, we ride on because of the truth. So I found it at the Bowling Green, where I preached from Isaiah 61[:1], "The Spirit of the Lord God is upon me, because the Lord hath anointed me to preach good tidings unto the meek," etc. Near six thousand heard me, quietly at least. I spoke with uncommon power, especially to the unawakened.

The 11th of Romans led me unawares to speak of final perseverance, whereby some, I would hope, were cut off from their vain confidence.

Monday, September 24. Carried out at Weavers' Hall to speak to the blind guides, from Isaiah 29. Several followed me home; particularly *Charles Nichols* and *Betty Brown*, who were fully satisfied (at the Hall on Thursday night) of their pardon. So was Joseph Mountstevins, at the Bowling Green yesterday—confident, had he died before, he must have gone to hell; but that he should be saved, was he to die now.

Margaret Evans, in heaviness next to despair, found *the* comfort at eleven on Friday. The word applied was, "O Lord, our God, other lords besides thee have had dominion over us, but by thee only will we make mention of thy name" [Isa. 26:13]. The burden, she said, went off in a moment, and she has been full of joy ever since.

Sarah Rutter now informs me, that she first found power to believe while I was explaining Rom. 5.

I prayed, in my way to the Brick-yard, with a poor dying drunkard, who was glad to say, "Blessed is he that cometh in the name of the Lord" [Mark 11:9]. Whether I did not come too late, God only knows.

Cried from Isaiah 55, "Ho, everyone that thirsteth, come ye to the waters!" Between two and three thousand attended. I found great freedom in speaking to them, who *are* altogether such as I *was*. Had a weary walk to Nicholas-street Society, and thence to Mrs England's, where I discoursed for two hours on John 7.

Here Susanna Milsom made open confession of the faith, which had come to her by hearing yesterday. Her soul is delivered out of the snare of the fowler.[121] God hath avenged her of her adversary, and she now treads upon serpents and scorpions.[122]

Tuesday, September 25. Preached at Bradford[-on-Avon] to about two thousand. For an hour and half I described their state by nature and grace in the man that fell among thieves [Luke 10:29-37], and I did not spare them that were whole and had no need of a physician.[123] They bore it surprisingly. Received invitation to several neighboring towns. May I never run before God's call, or stay one moment after it.

Dined at a carnal Quaker's, who pleaded for a *moderate* pursuit of riches, and I was grieved to find no more of the spirit of religion among those who ought to have the most of it. But the desire of other things disproves their pretensions to the Spirit. "He that drinketh of the water shall thirst no more" [John 4:14].

We waited at a good Dissenter's near Bath, who seems to have the root of the matter in him. It was near eight before I reached the Hall. The chapter in course was Rom. 12, but I could not press particular duties till they had the foundation, and therefore exhorted them to get forgiveness *before* they could perform the best part of the law. The *brethren* I besought to present their bodies a living sacrifice, and pointed out the part of Acts 2 of this devotion.

Wednesday, September 26. Received much light and strength to expound Isaiah 30. A woman sunk down in deep distress. Several, who wait for faith, were affected greatly. From one to three more came that I was able to talk with, all seeking what many have found. In particular:

---

121. Cf. Ps. 91:3.
122. Cf. Luke 10:19.
123. Cf. Mark 2:17.

Anne Spanin was filled with joy in believing, while we were at prayers last Monday. So was *Mrs [Judith] Williams* in going home from church. *Susanna Trapman* likewise sees *her* interest in the blood of Jesus. *Elisabeth Parsons*, whom the evil spirit has often torn, is sensible now that he is cast out. 'Tis observable of the two last, that they have never been baptized. I now require no farther proof that one be an *inward* Christian without baptism. They are both desirous of it, and who can forbid water?[124]

Abraham Staples informs me that on Saturday was three weeks, while I was preaching "Lazarus, come forth" [John 11:43], he was called out of his natural state and raised to the life of faith. "I felt," said he, "that my sins were forgiven by a peace and warmth within me, which have continued ever since." "Then you know," said I, "that the Spirit of God is a Spirit of burning?"[125] "Yes," he answered, "and a Spirit of shaking too, for he turns me upside down. I am full of joy and life, and could be always a praying—should be glad to die this moment. What knowledge I have, I have given me of God, for I am no scholar, I can neither write nor read."

Sarah Pearce declares she received the first comfort in hearing Rom. 5 explained. She was then justified but did not draw nigh in full assurance of faith till last night. Every word I spoke came with power. She had the witness of her own spirit or conscience that all the marks I mentioned were in her. And the Spirit of God came in with his testimony, and put it beyond the possibility of doubt. Some of her words were: "I was once extremely bigoted against my brethren, the Dissenters, but am now enlarged toward them and all mankind in an inexpressible manner. I do not depend upon a start of comfort, but find it increase, ever since it began. I perceive a great change on myself, and expect a greater. I feel a divine attraction in my soul. Was once so afraid of death that I durst not sleep but now I do not fear it at all. I desire nothing upon earth. I dread nothing but sin. God suffers me to be strongly prompted. But I know, when he gives faith, he will try it."

See here the true assurance of faith! How consistent an humble, not doubting, a filial, not servile, fear of offending! I desire not *such* an assurance as blots out those Scriptures, "Be not high-minded, but fear" [Rom. 11:20]; "Work out your salvation with fear

---

124. Cf. Acts 10:47.
125. Cf. Isa. 44:4.

and trembling" [Phil. 2:12]; etc. God keep me in continual fear lest by any means, when I have preached to others, I myself should be a castaway.

At the Mills I preached upon "As Moses lifted up the serpent in the wilderness, even so, etc." [John 3:14]. Spoke plainly to the women's bands of their unadviseableness, their want of love, and bearing one another's burdens. We found an immediate effect in the enlargement of our hearts. Some were convinced they had thought too highly of themselves, and that their first love, like their first joy, was only a foretaste of that temper which continually rules in a new heart.

Thursday, September 27. Returning from early prayers, I met *Sarah Putnam,* the person that had been so wounded yesterday at the Hall. She informed me that Christ did then break off her yoke, and she felt herself at liberty from sin and sorrow. Soon after news was brought me that the man I had prayed by beyond Hanham was now in the full triumph of faith. On Sunday he desired longer life, but now he only longs, with an holy impatience, to depart and be with the Lord, which is far better.[126]

Gave offence at the Hall, by professing the doctrine of non-resistance from Rom. 12. What will they say to me tomorrow, when I come to the thirteenth?

Friday, September 28. Christianity flourishes under the cross. None who follow after Christ want that badge of discipleship. Wives and children are beaten, and turned out of doors; and the persecutors are the complainers. It is always the Lamb that troubles the water. Every Sunday damnation is denounced against all that hear us Papists, us Jesuits, us seducers, us bringers in of the Pretender.[127] The clergy murmur aloud at the number of communicants and threaten to repel them. Yet will not the world hear that we should talk of persecution. No! For the world is Christian now! And the offence of the cross ceased. Alas, what would they farther? Some lose their bread, some their habitations; one suffers stripes, another confinement; and yet we must not call this persecution. Doubtless they will find some other name for it, when they do God service by killing us.[128]

---

126. Cf. Phil. 1:23.
127. This is the accusation that the Wesleys are "Jacobites," or supporters of James Edward Stuart (1688–1766), exiled son of King James II (hence, the "Pretender"), who had tried to stage a return to power in 1715, with backing of the French.
128. Cf. John 16:2.

Today *Mary Hanney* was with me. While she continued a drunkard, a swearer, and company-keeper, it was very well; she and her father agreed entirely. But from the time of her turning to God, he has used her most inhumanly. Yesterday he beat her, and drove her out of doors, following her with imprecations and threatenings to murder her if ever she returned. When she was cast out, Jesus found her, and said unto her by his Spirit, "Be of good cheer, thy sins are forgiven thee" [Matt. 9:2]. She continued all the night in joy unspeakable, and can now with confidence call God her Father.

Preached at the Fishponds on "To as many as received him, to them gave he power to become the sons of God" [John 1:12].

Saturday, September 29. Breakfasted with six or eight awakened sinners, who are hourly waiting for the consolation of Israel.[129] I prayed by a dying woman, and cut off her confidence in the flesh. As sure as I ask the question, "Why do you hope to be saved?" I receive that woeful answer, "Because I have done no harm," or, "Because I have used my endeavours." This comes of our telling the people, "God, upon your sincere endeavours, will accept you." There were several present, whom I stripped of their filthy rags, and sent naked to Christ.

At noon, *Janet Clancy* gave me an account of her faith. It came as I was asking at Baptist Mills, "If Christ was now present, and said to you, 'Believest thou that I am able to do this, to forgive sins upon earth?' would you say, 'Lord, I believe, help thou my unbelief?'" The word was applied in that moment. "I went home," said she, "justified; in such peace, and joy, and love, as cannot be described; and I am still sure that the Son of God loved me, and gave himself for me."

At the Bowling [Green] I explained the first words that presented: "Now faith is the substance of things hoped for, the evidence of things not seen" [Heb. 11:1]. Afterwards I enforced obedience to the powers that be, from Rom. 13, and showed the scandalous inconsistency of your high-churchmen, who disclaim resistance, and yet practise it; continually speaking evil of dignities, nay, of the ruler of the people, as well as those who are put in authority under him. Fewer than I expected were offended at me.

---

129. Cf. Luke 2:25.

Sunday, September 30. Found my usual congregation at Hanham, and showed them their Saviour, from Isaiah 53. Many tears of love or desire were shed. At the Hall I expounded the Woman taken in Adultery [John 8:1-11]. Some, convicted by their own conscience, went out.

OCTOBER 1739

Monday, October 1. Expounded Isaiah 35 with great freedom and power. In the hours of conference, the following persons declared to me their faith in Him who justifies the ungodly:

Mary Brown, took with strong trembling last night at the Hall, was there set at liberty, both from fear and guilt. "I love all mankind," she said, (the best proof of faith) "and could die for my worst enemy."

Sarah Gough found the power of God present to heal her, while I repeated last Sunday night, "He hath sent me to bind up the broken-hearted" [Luke 4:18].

Sarah Norton was strongly tempted not to tell me that, on Wednesday in the Hall, she received forgiveness. I was bidding them "wait for the promise of the Father" [Acts 1:4]. She replied within herself, "Well, I will wait," and was immediately struck to the heart, and filled with joy unspeakable. This was greatly increased at the Sacrament.

The same good work was wrought in *William Spenser* on Saturday night, after hearing the word. He is now sure that his sins are blotted out, for the times of refreshment are come.

Eleanor Kitchinor, weak in faith before, received the full assurance last night.

Judith Williams (of whose being justified I heard last week) sends me word that her faith increases daily. Returning from the Hall in deep distress, God had opened her eye of faith to *discern her* Saviour.

Many find power to believe, either in or soon after hearing. So it was with *Joseph Black.* On Friday night in bed, he was suddenly taken ill, lost all strength, lay speechless. Soon after he found the power of God overshadow him, and a warmth and life spreading through soul and body. He revived in both, and was endued with power to apply Christ to himself in particular.

Satan strove hard to hinder *Francis Hud* from coming to inform me that he had been my constant hearer, and had always applied what I said of sinners to himself. "I saw," said he, "that I was in a damnable state, till I had forgiveness of sins, but was sure I should have it. The devil was very busy with me, especially in prayer. I told him, 'Satan, I am thy slave now, but thou canst not hold me long. Christ will soon come and deliver me.' He did come in my sleep. I was sure it was Christ himself. I waked in great triumph, knowing the devil's power was at an end. Since then I have been happy indeed."

In the afternoon I went out into the lanes and streets of the city, to call men in to the Great Supper (Luke 14). The power of the Lord accompanied me. So again at Gloucester Lane, while I discoursed on the man born blind (John 9). Three pharisees lay concealed at an house adjoining, and they could not have come at a more convenient season. God was with my mouth. They could not stand it, but made their escape in the middle of my discourse. The sincere were strengthened and comforted, as several testified at that time.

Tuesday, October 2. Dined at George the collier's, an happy soul; as full of joy and love as he can contain. I hope one day to be like him. I exhorted the colliers, by the example of the Syro-Phoenician woman [Mark 7:26-30], to pray always, till their requests are granted.

Wednesday, October 3. Sarah Townsend informed me that, on Sunday evening, while we were singing "Come to judgment, come away,"[130] she found and felt in herself that she *durst* come. The Spirit in that instant sealing her pardon upon her heart. She was filled all night with joy unspeakable.

Another testified that, at Kingswood yesterday, she caught hold of that word, "Be of good cheer, thy sins are forgiven thee" [Matt. 9:2], and knows she has apprehended Him, of whom she was first apprehended.

Sarah Stevens, aged seventy-three, confesses that a fortnight ago, she was first convinced of sin by my ministry, having been till then, as she and the world thought, a very good Christian. I have hardly known a soul under stronger convictions. Her expressions are full

---

130. This is the first line of every stanza of a hymn by George Herbert, which the Wesleys included under the title "Doomsday," in HSP (1739), 10–11 (*Poetical Works*, 1:11).

of self-abhorrence. She truly renounces her own, and hungers and thirsts after Christ's righteousness. We prayed and she received great comfort; whether *the* comfort, God will soon discover.

I look upon this instance as a peculiar blessing to me, for I had scarce any faith for old people. They are so strong in self-righteousness, so entrenched in their own works, so hardened by *the abuse of means.* Surely the weapons of our warfare are not carnal, but mighty through God, if they can pull down such strongholds.

Preached again from the Woman of Canaan [Matt. 15:22-28] with double power. I prayed by a dying man. Found him leaning on the broken reed of his own endeavours. I showed him that they could not bear his weight, but he must fall with violence into hell, unless he found a better support. I left him desirous to stay his soul on the Rock of Ages.

Friday, October 5. I had been often hindered from seeing Mrs Granil, the woman that cried out so vehemently in the Bowling Green. He that letteth[131] today was taken out of the way, and she came to me. She has had no rest for these three weeks; can neither eat nor drink as usual; believes Christ is able to deliver her. We betook ourselves to prayer and she screamed out as before. I broke off and let her pray, for I never heard any pray like her. We laid open the promises, sang, and prayed for her till the Comforter came. She now knows that her Redeemer liveth. She came afterwards to return me thanks for her deliverance through my ministry. Lord, not unto me!

The quickening Spirit was with us at Gloucester Lane, while I was discoursing on Lazarus raised [John 11]. Two women experienced Christ to be the resurrection and the life.[132] There was a great shaking among the dry bones,[133] and they that had life before, now had it more abundantly.[134]

Saturday, October 6. Averel Spenser, one that received faith last night, came today and declared it. While she was seeking Christ, she had several assurances in prayer that she should shortly find him. Last night she was pierced through with the sword of the Spirit,[135]

---

131. In the BCP and the AV, "letteth" is used in the sense of "hindering" or "preventing." Cf. 2 Thess. 2:7.
132. Cf. John 11:25.
133. Cf. Ezek. 37:1-14.
134. Cf. John 10:20.
135. Cf. Eph. 6:17.

and ascertained of her pardon, beyond the possibility of a doubt. Peace, joy, and love flowed in upon her soul. She is of that simple unopposing temper, which yields the freest passage to the grace of God.

My subject at the Bowling Green was, "Blessed are they which are persecuted for righteousness' sake" [Matt. 5:10]. Great need there is to prepare them for the gathering storm. Already it is come to that, that except a man forsake all that he hath (life only excepted), he cannot be Christ's disciple.[136]

Sunday, October 7. Declared the covenant of grace at Hanham. I never fail finding power among the colliers.

Received the Sacrament at St Phillip's.[137] I first earnestly asked that God would not send me empty away.[138] Returned to my pew, and was immediately overpowered, in a manner inexpressible, not with *the very thing*, but with the strongest assurance that I *should* receive ALL I wait for. God mollified my hardness, and I abhorred myself before him, as in dust and ashes. I asked (with all submission) some token from his word. I hardly remember to have read the passage—it came with power, and abased me to nothing: "Thou art my battle-axe, and weapons of war. For in thee I will break in pieces the nations, and with thee," etc. [Jer. 51:20].

I described the New Creature [2 Cor. 5:17] at the Bowling Green. Many (as they told me afterwards) were stripped of their vain religion.

Received still greater strength at night to expound Isaiah 43. Our souls did magnify the Lord, and our spirits rejoiced in God our Saviour.[139]

Monday, October 8. We found him applying his own promises, which we really believe belong to us, though delivered to the Jews some thousand years ago.

Sarah Stevens now finds they were made to her. She tells me, the moment she rose from prayer last Wednesday she felt her weight lessened and, before she got to the door, entirely removed. At seventy-three she is indeed converted, and become a little child; full as she can be of peace, and love, and joy. She feels the Spirit of God

---

136. Cf. Luke 14:33.
137. St Philip's Priory, Bristol.
138. Cf. Luke 1:53.
139. Cf. Luke 1:47.

within her, embraces Christ with the arms of faith, and cries out with old Simeon, "Lord, now lettest thou thy servant depart in peace, for mine eyes have seen thy salvation" [Luke 2:29].

Edward Hud testifies his faith in Christ, which came by hearing last week.

Mary Taylor witnesses the same good confession; and *Mary Haman*. The latter was justified in private prayer.

Called on the dying man with whom I prayed last night. I found him a new creature. He told me he now tasted the peace I spoke of, the joy and comfort of a living faith. I asked whether he was still afraid to die. "No, no," he replied, "I desire to die. I want to get away." "Why? Do you love Jesus Christ?" "Yes, dearly," said he with his voice and looks. I left him ready for the Bridegroom, and published the word of reconciliation [2 Cor. 5:19] at the Brick-yard. God in Christ was with us of a truth. I never spoke more clearly. The same power was in the Society. Mr Williams of Kidderminster was much edified among us. He followed a letter he wrote, inviting me thither. Of what denomination he is, I know not; nor is it material, for he has the mind which was in Jesus.[140]

Met my brother, just returned from London.

Tuesday, October 9. Received a letter from Holt, deterring me from coming again to Bearfield—upon which *invitation* I set out with my brother this morning. We called at Mr Cottle's and heard the people were much exasperated against me, it being everywhere reported that I am (*quem minus credere?*[141]) a strong predestinarian. Much pains had been taken to represent me as such. We judged this a call for me to *declare* myself, if the weavers, who were to rise, would suffer me.

We found about two thousand waiting. I let my brother pray, and then began abruptly, "If God be for us, who can be against us? He that spared not his own son, but delivered him up for us all, how shall he not *with him,* also freely give us all things?" [Rom. 8:31-32]. God opened my mouth so as seldom before. I felt what I spoke, while offering Christ to all. In much love I besought the Dissenters not to lose their charity for me because I was of opinion God would have *all* men to be saved. For an hour and a half, I strongly called

---

140. Cf. Phil. 2:5.
141. "Whom could you think less so?" Terence, *Self-Tormentor,* 192.

all sinners to the Saviour of the world. My strength do I ascribe unto Him. No one opened his mouth against me. The devil fled before us, and I believe he will no more slander me with being a predestinarian.

A Dissenting minister, who before clave to us, came to where we dined, and asked me with much passion *how I durst have the impudence to speak against the Dissenters.* I felt no emotion but pity and love. My brother was like-minded. We took notice of his hard speeches, but tried to pacify, and left him somewhat calmer. O that God would always give us that meekness which his cause deserves!

Thursday, October 11. Expounded the Prodigal Son [Luke 15:11-32] among the colliers. Many a one, if not most of them, is ready to say, "I will arise, and go to my Father" [15:18]. At six I began John 1, at the widow Jones's. It was the first time of my preaching by night in the open air. The yard contained about four hundred. The house was likewise full. Great power was in the midst. Satan blasphemed without, but durst not venture his children too near the gospel, when I offered Christ Jesus to them. The enemy hurried them away, and all we could do was to pray for them.

Saturday, October 13. I waited with my brother upon a minister, about baptizing some of his parish. He complained heavily of the multitude of our communicants, and produced the canon against strangers. He could not admit that as a reason for their coming to his church, that they had no Sacrament of their own. I offered my assistance to lessen his *trouble*, but he declined it. "There were a hundred of new communicants," he told us, "last Sunday; and I am credibly informed, some of them came out of spite to me."

We bless God for *this cause* of offence, and pray it may never be removed.

Sunday, October 14. Took horse for Bradford[-on-Avon], the minister having offered me his pulpit. But yesterday his heart failed. He feared his church would be pulled down. He feared the bishop would be displeased. I went to church, and thence to the common, where I preached forgiveness of sins to many serious hearers. In the evening returned to Bristol.

Monday, October 15. My brother being gone to Wales, I expounded at eleven, and was, with others, quite melted down;

especially in prayer. At the Brick-yard I discoursed on Matt. 11:5: "The blind receive their sight, and the lame walk," etc. In the midst of my discourse, Satan lift up his voice in his own children, which increased my boldness. I told the people Christ had a work to do, and they should find it so. The sons of Belial[142] soon quitted the field, but the power of the Lord continued with us. One man received a large increase of faith, and confessed it before many witnesses.

Prayed for a poor old woman, departing in the Lord. At the Society I met *Mrs [Mary] Thomas*, who testified her having received forgiveness while I spake to the rioters.

Dined at Rider's, a collier. *Elisabeth Hawkins* here told me that she received *the blessing* under the word some weeks since, but quickly lost it. While we were praying, our brother Rider found an unknown warmth and comfort. I told him, if it was the work of God begun, God would shine upon it and clearly convince him of righteousness.

In the school-house I preached the promise of the Comforter.[143] A woman fell to the ground with strong crying and tears. *Elisabeth Hawkins* received her faith, and rejoiced in the light of God's countenance.

In explaining Isaiah 50, I laid open the self-deceit of some, who rested short of the promises *because* they had a liking to the word, or me. Many were alarmed, and stirred up to a restless pursuit of Christ.

Wednesday, October 17. Elisabeth Field was with me, declaring she first found power to believe and love on Monday night, while I spoke from John 13, of our Lord's humility. "I was immediately lightened," she said, "assured my sins were forgiven, and so full of joy that I was ready to faint under it."

Mary Branker bore a like testimony, that she was then filled with unknown power and comfort.

Thursday, October 18. I would have visited the poor dying woman today, but the churchwarden, Mr Every, had been with her, and with threatenings declared if ever I came near her again he would turn her out into the street, sick or well.

Received notice from *Mrs Stonehouse* that her husband was ill of the smallpox and could not look after my affair with Goter; that I

---

142. Cf. 1 Sam. 2:12.
143. Cf. John 14:16.

must come, or send the writ, or be non-suited. I thought it too late (as the writ must be returned October 20) and rested quite content.[144]

Friday, October 19. Mrs Chad informs me she received remission of sins some time ago, in Isaiah 53, and has had continual joy ever since.

Many were comforted at the Hall, by Isaiah 53.

Abigail Savage says she found *the* comfort yesterday. She had long been in darkness, and could not lay hold on Christ; but is now fully persuaded of her redemption, and could not believe otherwise, if she would.

Read part of Mr Law on regeneration to our Society.[145] How promising the beginning, how lame the conclusion! *Sensi hominem!*[146] Christianity, he rightly tells us, is a recovery of the divine image. And a Christian is a fallen spirit restored and reinstated in paradise, a living mirror of the Father, Son, and Holy Ghost. After this, he supposes it *possible* for him to be *insensible* of *such* a change—to be happy and holy, translated into Eden, renewed in the likeness of God, one with Father, Son, and Holy Ghost, and *yet not know it.* Nay, we are not to expect, or bid others expect, any such consciousness, if we listen to one who too plainly demonstrates, by this wretched inconsistency, that his knowledge of the new birth is mostly in theory.

At Mr Labbè's I met Miss Jeffreys, the Quaker, whom I had so laboured to convince of sin. I did not perceive any impression my words made at the time. But now, it seems, they sunk deep. An horrible dread has overwhelmed her. Her flesh trembles for fear of God, and she is afraid of his judgments. She sees herself far worse than I described her, and thought at my last expounding she was every moment sinking into hell.

Saturday, October 20. Preached at Bradford[-on-Avon] in the townhall, with little power or effect.

---

144. Cf. the July 25, 1739, entry above. Jackson includes a footnote (p. 190) that states that Wesley was charged £10 for damages in this suit, and that Jackson had seen the bill for this amount minus taxes (£9.16s.8d.) among Wesley's family papers, with Charles's inscription: "I paid them the things I never took. To be re-judged in THAT DAY." The current whereabouts of this bill is unknown.

145. William Law, *The Grounds and Reason of Christian Regeneration: or, the New Birth* (London: W. Innys & R. Manby, 1739).

146. "I understood the man!" Charles perhaps intends the meaning: "I have seen his humanity (fallibility)."

Sunday, October 21. At the common, in the morning, I described the New Creature [2 Cor. 5:17] to above fifteen hundred; and in the afternoon, to thrice that number, I preached the word of reconciliation [2 Cor. 5:19]. They all followed me with their prayers. I trust my labour among them hath not been in vain.

Thursday, October 25. Called on one, who *did* run well, but is turned out of the way by an unbelieving parent. "Woe unto the world because of offences!" [Matt. 18:7]. Woe unto the man by whom the offence comes! It were better that a millstone were tied about his neck, and he cast into the depth of the sea, than that he should offend one of these little ones who believe in Jesus.[147]

Friday, October 26. I baptized Mr Wigginton in the river by Baptist Mills, and went on my way rejoicing to Frenchay.

The rain did not lessen our usual congregation at the Fishponds, to whom I spoke from Revelation 2:10: "Fear none of those things which thou shalt suffer. Behold, the devil shall cast some of you into prison," etc.

Saturday, October 27. I preached at the Green, on the strong man armed [Luke 11:21], and disturbed him in his palace.

Pressed the use of means, as means, from Isaiah 58, which is full of promises to those that walk in the ordinances with a sincere heart. I took occasion to show the degeneracy of our modern pharisees. Their predecessors fasted twice a week, but these maintain their character for holiness at a cheaper rate. In reverence to the Church, some keep their public day on Friday. None of them regard it, though enjoined, as a fast. As to prayer and Sacrament, their neglect is equally notorious. And yet these men cry out, "The Church, the Church!" when they will not hear the Church themselves; but despise her authority, trample upon her orders, teach contrary to her Articles and Homilies, and break her canons, *every man* of them, who *of late* pretend to press their observance.

Sunday, October 28. From Isaiah 57:15, "For thus saith the high and lofty One," etc., I spoke closely to the unawakened, and comfortably to the mourners.

---

147. Cf. Matt. 18:6.

In the hard rain I preached at the Bowling Green, from "Drop down, ye heavens, from above, and let the skies pour down righteousness" [Isa. 45:8].

Monday, October 29. Expounded, with extraordinary assistance, Isaiah 59, that dreadful description of national sin and punishment. While I was speaking, war with Spain was proclaimed,[148] which made us take the more notice of those words: "According to their deeds, accordingly he will repay; fury to his adversaries, recompense to his enemies. To the *islands* he will repay recompense. So shall they fear the name of the Lord from the *west,* and his glory from the rising of the sun. When the enemy shall come in like a flood, the Spirit of the Lord shall lift up a standard against him" [Isa. 59:18-19].

Tuesday, October 30. My brother preached his farewell sermon to the sorrowful colliers. I wrote as follows to the Bishop of Bristol:[149]

My Lord,
 Several persons, both Quakers and Baptists, have applied to me for baptism. Their names are W. Crease, Mary Crease, Mary Gregory, Rebecca Dickenson, Anne Spanin, Elisabeth Mills, Elisabeth Parsons. It has pleased God to make me instrumental in their conviction. This has given them such a prejudice for me that they desire to be received into the Church by my ministry. They choose likewise to be baptized by immersion, and have engaged me to give your Lordship notice, as the Church requires.

Today I talked with several who have lately found rest to their souls, particularly:

Joanna Nichols, justified on Sunday, in hearing the word. It was then she first said, "I have redemption in his blood."

Jane Connor, at Baptist Mills, found the power of the Lord present to heal her.

Jane Parker experienced the same, while we were singing.

Mary Connor on Thursday night recovered that unspeakable peace which she first received some weeks ago, but lost by keeping it to herself.

148. The British declared war after prolonged commercial disputes with Spain; it led into the War of Austrian Succession (1739–1748).
149. Joseph Butler (1692–1752) was Bishop of Bristol, 1738–1750.

John Hooper, at Baptist Mills, saw with the eye of faith our Lord as interceding for him with his Father. The word by which faith came was, "Behold, I have graven thee on the palms of my hands" [Isa. 49:16].

While my brother was praying among the bands, one attempted to run out. We stopped and found her in an angry despair, refusing to ask for mercy. Continued instant in prayer for her. God was with us of a truth. Several cried out and under strong convictions, others filled with peace and joy in believing.

A few stayed behind the rest, to comfort our despairing sister. God had hid his face from her, and she went on frowardly in the way of her own heart. Inordinate affection is the strong man's armour; and any unmortified desire, which a man allows himself in, will effectually drive and keep Christ out of the heart.

NOVEMBER 1739

Thursday, November 1. Met Miss [Sally (Suky)] Burdock at Mr Wigginton's, full of good desires, but kept down by the fear of a man. I told her plainly she would never find peace till she was deeply convinced of her having denied her Master. She now no longer justified herself, but confessed she had loved father and mother more than Christ.[150] I saw her in the toils, earnest for deliverance, but almost despairing. God enlarged my heart in prayer for her. She went away sorrowful, yet not without hope.

Friday, November 2. Our thanksgiving notes multiply greatly.

Received a summons from Oxford, to respond in divinity disputations; which, with other concurrent providences, is a plain call to that place.[151]

Saturday, November 3. Spent an hour with many of the Society, in *attempts* to thank God for all, and especially his late, mercies. I administered the Sacrament at Mrs Williams's. Began preaching with much reluctance on "Fight the good fight of faith" [1 Tim. 6:12].

---

150. Cf. Matt. 10:37.
151. Charles and John were both considering seeking B.D. degrees at Oxford (a degree subsequent to the M.A., requiring seven years in that rank—which Charles had earned in 1733). Cf. John's letter to Samuel Wesley, Jr. (Oct. 27, 1739), *Works* 25:692.

The Lord was with my mouth, when he had opened it. I trust many found he was.

Sunday, November 4. I preached in Kingswood on Isaiah 42:1, "Behold my servant, whom I uphold," etc. We found *that* Spirit was put upon him *for us*. Seldom have I perceived a greater power amongst us.

Gave the Sacrament to one whom I had left waiting for Christ. She was now full of his Spirit, ready for the Bridegroom.[152] No cloud interposed between her Beloved and her on the thin veil of flesh and blood, which was well nigh rent asunder. What would I give to be on that death-bed!

Met Miss Burdock once more with her sister, and spent two hours in awakening and exhorting them. I doubt not but they will yet break through the host of the Philistines, and draw water out of the well of Bethlehem.[153]

Expounded the Parable of the Sower [Matt. 13:3-23]; and in the evening our Lord's divine prayer, John 17. Many, I trust, found him *then* interceding for them.

Monday, November 5. Met some of the bands at our sister Linford's. In prayer one received forgiveness.

We had a greater blessing at the [Weavers'] Hall than ever before. I summed up all I had said, either to publicans or pharisees, to the comfort or discomfort of every one present.

I spent the time of conference with the candidates for baptism. All seem prepared for that holy ordinance.

In the Brick-yard I discoursed on the Woman with the Issue of Blood.[154] God magnified his strength in my weakness.[155] Several cried out they were healed! Virtue was gone out of him. They heard his voice, "Thy faith hath made thee whole. Go in peace" [Mark 5:34].

Many had fellowship with Christ in his sufferings, while I spoke of them in the words of St John. He melted me into tears of love. I knew not how to leave them, so many testified that they then tasted the good word of God, and the powers of the world to come.

152. Cf. Matt. 25:1-13.
153. Cf. 2 Sam. 23:15.
154. It is clear in the June 28, 1738, entry that Charles was there looking at the account in Matt. 9:20-22. But this and later sermons on this topic may have focused as well on the parallel passages in Mark 5:25-34 and Luke 8:40-56.
155. Cf. 2 Cor. 12:9.

Tuesday, November 6.[156] I was called to a woman at Bedminster. I have seldom seen a soul more deeply plunged into the spirit of bondage, or under stronger pangs of the new birth. She received immediate relief in prayer, and came at noon to tell me that her yoke was wholly broken off.

MARCH 1740

Friday, March 14. By eleven I reached Gloucester, where the very last spark, I think, is gone out. In the evening I preached to a few people in Mr Whitefield's field, on Isaiah 53:1: "Who hath believed our report?" I was a little revived just before by Mrs Wynn of Painswick telling me she and two more of her family had lately received forgiveness. There was more stirring among the dry bones than I expected.[1]

Saturday, March 15. Between two and three we came to Bengeworth. I sent for Mr [Benjamin] Seward. Answer was returned that he had taken physic, but would send his brother Henry to me. Mr Henry [Seward][2] followed me to Mr Canning's, and fell upon me without preface or ceremony: I was the downfall of his brother, had picked his pocket, ruined his family, come now to get more money, was a scoundrel, rascal, and so forth, and deserved to have my gown stripped over my ears. He concluded with threatening how he would beat me, if he could catch me on Bengeworth Commons. I spoke little, and with temper.

All letters, I find, have been intercepted since Mr Seward's illness; his fever called madness; his servants set over him as spies, etc. Be sure he is to know nothing of my being here! But I mean to give him an hint of it tomorrow, by shouting from the top of the wall.

Sunday, March 16. I preached the law and gospel last night, from Isaiah 40, with much freedom and power. Appointed the usual place for preaching. Mr Henry [Seward] came to dissuade me. Said, "Four constables ordered to apprehend you, if you come near my brother's wall. So come at your peril."

---

156. This was the day that Charles's older brother, Samuel Wesley, Jr., died. This helps account for why the MS Journal breaks off at this point for four months.

1. Cf. Ezek. 37:1-14.

2. Charles uses only the first name of Mr. Seward's brother in the next few entries, which can be confusing. We have added the last name in brackets for clarity.

I walked toward the place. An officer from the mayor met and desired me to come to him. I said I would first wait upon my Lord, and then upon him, whom I reverenced for his office's sake. Went on. Mr Henry [Seward] met me with threats and revilings. I began singing,

> Shall I, for fear of feeble man,
> Thy Spirit's course in me restrain?[3]

He ran about raving like a madman, and quickly got some men for his purpose, who laid hold on me. I asked by what authority? Where was their warrant? Let them show that, I would save them the trouble of using violence. They said they had none, but I should not preach there, and hurried me away amid the cries of the people. Truly their tongues were set on fire of hell. Henry [Seward] cried, "Take him away, and duck him." Broke out into singing with Thomas Maxfield, and let them carry me whither they would. At the bridge in the lane they left me. There I stood, out of the liberty of the corporation, and gave out,

> Angel of God, whate'er betide,
> Thy summons I obey.[4]

Some hundreds they could not frighten from hearing me, on "If God be for us, who can be against us?" [Rom. 8:31-32]. Never did I feel so much what I spoke. The word did not return empty,[5] as the tears on all sides testified.

Then I waited upon Mr Mayor. The poor sincere ones followed me trembling. He was a little warm at my not coming before. I gave him the reason, and added that I knew no law of God or man which I had transgressed. If there was any such, desired no favour. He said he should not have denied me leave to preach, even in his own yard. But Mr Henry Seward and the apothecary had assured him it would quite cast his brother down again. I said it would rather restore him, for our gospel was life from the dead.

---

3. "From the German," st. 1, *CPH* (1738), 65. John Wesley's translation of Johann Joseph Winckler's hymn "Sollt ich, aus Furcht für Menschenkinder."

4. "At Setting out to Preach the Gospel," st. 1, *HSP* (1740), 113 (*Poetical Works*, 1:294).

5. Cf. Isa. 55:11.

A lawyer began declaiming against my making the poor gentleman mad. I granted, "You fools must count his life madness." Here a clergyman spoke much—and nothing. As near as I could pick out his meaning, he grumbled at Mr Whitefield's speaking against the clergy in his *Journal*. I told [him], if he himself was a carnal, worldly-minded clergyman, *I* might do what he would call railing: warn God's people to beware of false prophets.[6] I did not *say* (because I did not know) that he *was* one of those shepherds that fed themselves, not the flock; of those dumb dogs that could not bark; of those greedy dogs that could never have enough. If he was, I was sorry for him, and must leave that sentence of Chrysostom with him, "Hell is paved with the skulls of Christian priests."[7]

He charged me with making a division in Mr Seward's family. I asked, "Are you a preacher of the gospel, and do not know the effect it has among men? 'There shall be five in an house, two against three, and three against two'" [Luke 12:52]. He laughed, and cried to his companion, "Did not I tell you he would bring that?" I urged the necessity of persecution, if one of a family was first awakened. "Awakened!" said he, "I don't know what you mean by that." "I mean, your speaking truth, when you tell God the remembrance of your sins is grievous to you, the burden intolerable."[8]

I turned from him, and asked the mayor whether he approved the treatment I had met with. He said, "By no means"; and if I complained, he would bind the men over to answer it at the sessions. I told him I did not complain, neither would I prosecute them, as they well knew. I assured him I had waited upon him, not out of interest, for I wanted nothing of him; not out of fear, for I had done no wrong, and wanted no human support; but out of true respect, and to show him I believed the powers that be are ordained by God.[9]

In church the minister I had talked with, Mr Pr., seemed utterly confounded at the second lesson, John 3. That saying in the epistle, likewise, was sadly inconsistent with some of his: "But as then he that was born after the flesh persecuted him that was born after the Spirit, *even so it is now*" [Gal. 4:29]. In his pulpit (Nicodemus's

6. Cf. Matt. 7:15.
7. This quotation was apparently attributed broadly to St John Chrysostom. John Wesley cites it too: Letter to "John Smith" (March 25, 1747), §12, *Works* 26:237; and Sermon 125, "On a Single Eye," §5, *Works* 4:129. However, it has not been located in the works of Chrysostom.
8. Cf. BCP, Holy Communion, general confession.
9. Cf. Rom. 13:1.

stronghold), he strained hard to draw a parallel between the Pharisees and Methodists. I suppose because we preach self-justification. In the evening I preached without interruption, "The blind receive their sight," etc. [Matt. 11:5]. Our Lord was present. None stirred for the rain. The schoolhouse was crowded at seven. I spoke convincingly, to some scoffers in particular, who could not long stand it.

> Sing ye to our God above
> Praise eternal as his love![10]

We have seen wonderful things today.

Monday, March 17. My yesterday's treatment has provoked many to love. They receive me the more gladly into their houses, because Mr Seward's is shut against me.

Breakfasted at a loving Quaker's. Preached at three by the river's side, on "Blow ye the trumpet in Sion, sound an alarm in my holy mountain," etc., Joel 2:1. God put strong words into my mouth, and inclined the people's hearts to hearken.

Mr Henry Seward, mad with passion at my stay, spreads the news of it everywhere, and much increases my audience. Tonight I proceeded in the Beatitudes. When I came to the last, "Blessed are they which are persecuted" [Matt. 5:10], our enemies, not knowing the Scriptures, fulfilled them. A troop poured in from a neighbouring alehouse, and set up their champion, a schoolmaster, upon a bench over against me. For near an hour he spake for his master, and I for mine. But my voice prevailed. Sometimes we prayed, sometimes sang and gave thanks. The Lord our God was with us and the shout of a king was amongst us.[11] In the midst [of] tumult, reproach, and blasphemy, I enjoyed a sweet calm within, even while I preached the gospel with most contention. These slighter conflicts must fit me for greater.

Tuesday, March 18. Last night's disturbance, we now hear, was contrived at the alehouse by the squire and rector.

Preached at the usual place, from Isaiah 11[:6], "The wolf also shall dwell with the lamb," etc. Set my eyes on the man that had

---

10. "Hymn to the Trinity," *HSP* (1740), 101 (*Poetical Works*, 3:345).
11. Cf. Num. 23:21.

been most violent with me on Sunday, and testified my love. He thanked me, and seemed melted.

While I was concluding, my friend the schoolmaster set up his throat. We had recourse to singing, which quite spoiled his oration. Henry [Seward] had kept him in town, warm with drink, for this purpose. I could hardly restrain the people from falling upon him.

Went up to my other rough friend, the sergeant, and shook him by the hand with hearty good-will. He could not well tell how to take it. Said he had only done what he was ordered, and seemed glad to get out of my hands.

Some had come merely to make a riot, but my God was stronger than theirs.

I had a message before preaching from Mr Price,[12] the minister, that if I did not immediately quit the town, Mr Henry Seward could easily raise a mob; and then let me look to myself.

Mr Canning and others dissuaded me from going to the Society, for my enemies were resolved to do me a mischief, which I ought to avoid by going out of the way for a while. I answered in the words of Nehemiah [6:11], "Should such a man as I flee?" Not in self-confidence (for I am naturally afraid of everything), but I was told in the morning psalms, "Whoso dwelleth under the shadow of the Most High, shall abide under the defence of the Almighty," etc. [Ps. 91:1, BCP alt.].

I went, and set upon the opposers. Bade them glory of me, for they had terrified me now. I was really afraid—to leave Evesham. I durst no more do it, ~~till~~ than forsake my Captain, or deny my Master, while any one of them opened his mouth against the truth. No man answered a word, or offered to disturb me in my following exhortation. Many were convinced. Mrs Canning was in the depth of mourning. We spent an hour in songs of triumph. Some Quakers joined us, and found their giving God praises with their lips did not at all obstruct the melody of the heart.

I received great comfort from those words in the first lesson, "The men of the city said to Joash, Bring out thy son that he may die, because he hath cast down the altar of Baal. And Joash said unto all that stood against him, Will ye plead for Baal? Will ye save him? If he be a god, let him plead for himself, because one hath cast down his altar" [Judg. 6:30].

---

12. Rev. John Price, vicar of All Saints Church and St Lawrence's Church, Evesham.

In the afternoon there was none to plead for him, or to molest me in the work of God, while I showed God's method of saving souls: "For he maketh sore, and bindeth up; he woundeth, and his hands make whole" [Job 5:18]. The tears that were shed gave comfortable evidence that my labour had not been in vain.

Wednesday, March [19].[13] Laboured to convince my many hearers of sin, from the law, as interpreted by our Lord. The floods began to lift up their voice. I went and stood by the door. The enemy still murmured without, and attempted to force their way in. I turned upon them, and invited them to Christ, till all their opposition ceased. I then took my leave of the little flock, but for no long season.

After much wandering, by three we found out Mr Morgan's. They received us very affectionately. Mrs Morgan was very open. God gave her a kind prejudice in my behalf. She related what passed the week they spent at Mr Bray's. He urged her to cast off all the means of grace—not to go to church, or Sacrament; not to read the Scriptures; not to pray in private, but *be still*; and the "*New Light*," as he called it, would come of itself. She would very soon have it, he promised her, *for he felt her spirit*. The effect of his discourse was, it made her utterly regardless of religion. For the new light would come, she thought, when it would. Mr Morgan they dissuaded from family prayer, or preaching, till he should receive it. George Whitefield, they told her, was quite in the dark, and had done great mischief by preaching. So had my brother and I, but of me they had great hopes. Mrs Ewsters and Mrs Vaughan were also brought to bear their testimony against the ordinances, and spoke much concerning the *pernicious* use of them.

---

13. Starting with the date of Wednesday, March 19, Wesley's chronology of days and dates is incorrect.

Manuscript sequence of days and dates	*Probable sequence of days and dates*
Wednesday, March 20	Wednesday, March 19
Saturday, March 23	Saturday, March 22
Sunday, March 24	Sunday, March 23
Monday, March 25	Monday, March 24
Tuesday, March 26	Tuesday, March 25
Tuesday, March 25	Wednesday, March 26
Wednesday, March 26	Thursday, March 27
Thursday, March 27	Friday, March 28

The MS sequence is correct from Saturday, March 29.

Great was the offence which these two poor souls took at [the hands of] our London friends. Mrs Morgan they dealt with apart, and would have her go to Germany, setting her against her husband. He complains that since she came under their teaching she has lost all desire of being a Christian. I can never enough thank God for this unexpected warning against their diabolical stillness. Was I engaged in the devil's service to turn back an awakened soul, I would send him to them for instruction.

We spent the evening in defacing bad impressions, and mutual unmystical exhortation. Next morning we left our weaker friend, delivered out of the snare of the devil, we trust, and again resolved to work out her salvation.

Mr Morgan attended us as far as Woodstock, and was astonished at Thomas Maxfield's experience. By three we got to Oxford, where the little flock is kept together by our brother [Richard] Viney, whose stillness does not yet consist in trampling upon God's ordinances.

Saturday, March [22]. We returned to Mr Morgan, having before agreed that I should preach in his churches, and then once more look the world in the face at Evesham. He now told me more of John Bray, and his new guides. John advised him first to get preferment, and then declare himself. They caressed all his natural inclinations, on condition he would come into their notion of stillness. They taught him a Christianity which had no cross in it, no work of faith, no patience of hope, no labour of love.

Sunday, March [23]. I read prayers and preached once more in a church at Westcote.[14] It was full of attentive hearers. My text, "What must I do to be saved?" [Acts 16:30], I never spoke with greater plainness. Many seemed pricked at the heart. Mrs Morgan cried all sermon-time. I went home full of comfort. Preached at Idbury, to a much larger congregation, from our Lord's invitation, "Come unto me, all that labour," etc. [Matt. 11:28]. Never preached more closely. I returned to Westcott, and showed the legal and evangelical states from 2 Tim. 1:7, "God hath not given us the spirit of fear, but of power, and of love, and of a sound mind." Still our Lord was faithful to his promise, "Lo, I am with you" [Matt. 28:20].

---

14. Charles spells "Westcott."

227

Monday, March **[24]**. Returned to Evesham, and met Mr [Seward] Henry. He asked me to step into the Crown. I answered, I did not frequent taverns.

[*Henry:*] "What business have you with my brother?"

[*Wesley:*] "Can you imagine, if I have any business with him, as a Christian, I shall communicate it to you?"

[*Henry:*] "Why not to me?"

[*Wesley:*] "Because you are a natural man."

[*Henry:*] "Why, are not you a natural man as well as I?"

[*Wesley:*] "You are a *mere* natural man, in your sins and in your blood."

[*Henry:*] "What do you mean by that? I say, have you any particular business?"

[*Wesley:*] "I have business at present, somewhat different from talking with you."

Tuesday, March **[25]**. News was brought us that Mr Benjamin Seward was carrying out to Badsey, to be secured, no doubt, till I turn my back on Evesham. I walked out that way, and met Henry. He excused his past behaviour, said anger was rooted in his nature.

[*Henry:*] "But, indeed, Sir, you are the downfall of my brother Benjamin. He has certainly been out of his senses."

[*Wesley:*] "Yes; and so have I been before now in a fever."

[*Henry:*] "O, but we all really think him mad through means of you gentlemen."

[*Wesley:*] "Very likely you may. And if it should ever please God to make *you* a Christian, you will be thought mad too."

[*Henry:*] "God make me a Christian! I am a better Christian than you are."

[*Wesley:*] "You was once in the way of being one, but you have stifled your convictions."

[*Henry:*] "I say, I am a better Christian than you are. I have good ministers and the Scriptures to teach me."

[*Wesley:*] "Yes; and those Scriptures say, a man that loves money is no more a Christian than an adulterer."

[*Henry:*] "What, Sir! Must not a man love money? How shall he go to market without it? Not that I value it, not I.—But what do you mean by making divisions in our family? You come now to get money."

[*Wesley:*] "Indeed, sir, you know not what I come for. You cannot tell what to make of me. You have no standard to measure me by but yourself. I don't wonder at your outcries. Micah cried after them that ran away with his gods, and should they ask him what ailed him? Money is your god, and you think I come to rob you of it."

He rode to a good convenient distance, then, turning back, cried out, "You are a rascal, and a villain, and a pickpocket!" and, setting spurs to his horse, rode off as fast as he could. Brother Maxfield and I walked on, calmly praising God.

Mr Canning's little daughter told us she had watched in the lane, and put a note into Mr Benjamin [Seward]'s hand. Soon after his chariot stopped at our door, and I went out and found my friend. He invited me to his house. Henry was upon the coach-box, a place he full well became, and which nothing could make uneasy to him but my presence. Yesterday he told me I should never see his brother, and today he himself brings him to me.

Dined at Mr Keech's, who is somewhat awakened, his daughter more so, his wife a true mourner. Drank tea with one that *was* a sinner, but now looks unto Jesus. Walked out with brother Maxfield to the riverside, and spent a comfortable hour in prayer and singing. Then we went to Mr Benjamin Seward's. Found Henry and his wife with him, both surprisingly civil and full of apology. Henry begged my pardon, and waited upon me to the gate.

I finished Matthew 5 with the Society. All was quiet till the last hymn. Then I heard the enemy roaring, and gave out another. They left off first, and the people departed. Not all, I hope, in peace, for the strong man armed is disturbed in many.[15]

Wednesday, March [26]. Breakfasted at Mr Seward's. We were all diverted at Mr Henry [Seward]'s making, and continually breaking, his promise not to be angry. Who maketh me to differ?

Expounded John 3, and was much assisted in the application. A poor harlot spoke out, after her manner, but the devil durst not let her stay. He soon hurried her out of the reach of the gospel, as he did two or three more who, as soon as they had spoken a word for him, made off.

Thursday, March [27]. Finished John 3 in as strong words as I could speak. What a stony heart has the natural man, till the hammer of God's word breaks the rock in pieces![16]

---

15. Cf. Matt. 12:29.
16. Cf. Jer. 23:29.

Friday, March [28]. Met Mr Henry [Seward] at his brother's, and with all plainness of love endeavoured to convince him of sin. Never have I found a man of so little sense, with so many evasions. I simply told him that if he died in his present condition, he must die eternally; that he raged in vain, my hook was within him; I had warned the sinner, and delivered my own soul. "Your hook!" cried he; "what do you mean by your hook?" Benjamin [Seward] answered, smiling, "You know, brother, Mr Wesley is a fisher of men." As a minister, I added, I now showed him *his* lost estate, and that whether he would hear, or whether he would forbear.

In the school-house I summed up all I had said, and encouraged them to build up one another, promising to see them again, when the Lord directed my way to them. We had a few noisy ἀγοραῖοι[17] to quicken us. Our parting was as it ought to be.

Saturday, March 29. Took my leave of Mr Seward. Henry [Seward] fell upon me, for advising his brother to keep up the Society. "Rogue, rascal, villain, pickpocket," were the best titles he could afford me. Mr Benjamin [Seward] interposed. I begged him not then to answer a fool according to his folly.[18] Henry started up, and courageously took me by the nose. The cries of Mrs Seward stopped any farther violence. I was filled with comfort, felt the hand of God upon me, and sat still. Said to Mrs Seward, "Be not disquieted, Madam. I have learned to turn the other cheek." Henry was as the troubled sea. Benjamin, perfectly composed, said to me, "You have now received one mark of Christ"; to his brother, "Was I what you are, I should turn you out of my house this moment." I would not let him proceed. Begged pardon for the disturbance I had been the innocent occasion of, and departed, rejoicing that I was counted worthy to suffer shame for the name of Christ.

Came to Westcott. Found Mrs Morgan hungering and thirsting for righteousness.[19] The last was become the first.[20] They desired me to expound the lesson, St Paul's Epistle to Philemon. In speak-

---

17. ἀγοραῖος means literally one "in, of, or belonging to the market place," and often in the plural has the connotation of "noisy rabble." Cf. its only biblical use in Acts 19:38.
18. Cf. Prov. 26:5.
19. Cf. Matt. 5:6.
20. Cf. Matt. 19:30.

ing to the fifteenth verse, "For perhaps he therefore departed for a season, that thou shouldest receive him for ever," the Spirit was present in his demonstration. Brother Maxfield felt it, and told me, he *knew* Mrs Morgan had received the blessing. She retired to prayer; informed us (afterwards) that she had been filled with inexpressible comfort, from an assured sense of pardon; that, while she was praying, a sudden damp came over her, for having *blasphemously* thought her sins forgiven. She knew not then, though we did, from whence this fear proceeded.

Sunday, March 30. My late discourses have worked differently. Some are wounded, some hardened. I hear of no neuters. The word has turned them upside down.

In the pulpit I opened the book on "The Spirit of the Lord is upon me, because the Lord hath anointed me to preach the gospel to the poor" [Luke 4:18]. I described our Lord's prophetic office, and the persons on whom *alone* he could perform it. We returned from the altar with the voice of praise and thanksgiving, among such as keep holiday. Mrs Morgan felt every word we sang.

From hence we hasted to the meat which the world knoweth not of.[21] Idbury church and churchyard were full. I showed them wherein holiness consisted; answered their objections, dividing to them the word of truth, both law and gospel. Many were pierced to the dividing asunder their soul and spirit. One woman the commandment plainly slew, and she was carried off in a fit. O that all hardened sinners were so wounded in spirit!

We hasted back to Westcott, where I preached the pure gospel from the Good Samaritan [Luke 10:29-37]. Surely he was in the midst, pouring in his oil and wine.

Adjourned to Mr Morgan's. His house was crowded as a minister's ought to be. In the morning I had thoughts of expounding Rom. 7. And now a woman told me she had read that Mr William Seward had been convinced by my explaining Rom. 7, and therefore begged me to expound it now. I did so, with great assistance. The woman heard (as her tears confessed) her own state, not St Paul's, described. Another serious Dissenter was equally moved.

Monday, March 31. Got, well weary, to Oxford.

---

21. Cf. John 4:32.

APRIL 1740

Tuesday, April 1. Encouraged Charles Graves against the fear of man, which had almost separated him from the despised followers of Christ. Preached to the Society "Christ, our wisdom, righteousness, sanctification, and redemption" [1 Cor. 1:30]. Brother Viney allows we speak the same words with him—if he disallowed it, it makes no matter with me.

Thursday, April 3. Reached London by two. Found my brother [Westley] Hall quite cold and unconcerned. He seems never to have heard of the gospel, or that God is reviving his work in these latter days.

At the Foundery[22] preached on "The kingdom of God is not meat and drink, but righteousness, and peace, and joy in the Holy Ghost" [Rom. 14:17]. We joined to meet in the name of Jesus. My heart was enlarged in prayer for the infant Society.

Talked with poor perverted Mr [John] Simpson. The *still ones* have carried their point. He said some were prejudiced against the Moravian brethren, and particularly against [Philipp] Molther, but that he had received great benefit from them. I asked whether he was *still in* the means of grace, or *out* of them. "Means of grace!" he answered, "there are none. Neither is there any good to be got by those you call such or any obligation upon us to use them. Sometimes I go to church and Sacrament for example sake, but it is a thing of mere indifference. Most of us have cast them off. You must not speak a word in recommendation of them. That is setting people upon working."

What shall we say to these things? I then *said* little, but thought, "Ah, my brother! You have set the wolf to keep the sheep."

Good Friday, April 4. Called on a multitude of sinners at the Foundery, "Behold the Lamb of God, which taketh away the sin of the world" [John 1:29]. Many were melted into tears. But their tears, our brother Simpson observed, were a sign that they were *not* affected.

---

22. A former factory for making cannons, in Moorfields, which John Wesley acquired early in 1740 (having preached there in November 1739), in anticipation of the split in the Fetter Lane Society. He converted it into the London headquarters for the Wesleyan movement.

After preaching, James Hutton came to fetch me to Molther, at John Bray's. I chose rather to fast, than eat; and to pray in God's house, than dispute in another's.

Called with Maxfield on Molther in the afternoon. He did not much open himself, only talked in general against *running after ordinances*. We parted as we met, without either prayer or singing. The time for these poor exercises is past. Brother Maxfield was scandalized at their trifling, which is perfectly consistent with stillness, though Christian exhortation is not.

At six read several bills of thanksgiving for comforts received under the word in the morning. Our Lord was powerfully with me, while I described his sufferings (Isa. 53).

Saturday, April 5. Spent an hour with Charles Delamotte. The Philistines have been upon him, and prevailed. He has given up the ordinances, as to their being matter of duty. Only his practice lies a little behind his faith. He uses them still.

He would not have me plead for them. "They are mere outward things. Our brethren have left them off. It would only cause divisions to bring them up again. Let them drop, and speak of the weightier matters of the law." I told him I would hear them of their own mouth, who talked against the ordinances; first have my full evidence, and then speak and not spare.

Breakfasted with my mother, who has been dealt with, but in vain. Bishop Beveridge would as soon have given up the ordinances.[23]

I disturbed Mr Stonehouse before his time. It was but eight o'clock. However, he rose and came to me.

"If thou art he! But O, how changed! how fallen!"[24] How a mere, mere Moravian all over! He is now taught to teach that there are no degrees of faith, no forgiveness of faith where any unbelief remains; any doubt, or fear, or sorrow. He himself was never justified, is going to leave his parish, and *transport* himself— to Germany!

I have given an account of his wife in him.

---

23. A reference to William Beveridge (1637–1708), and particularly his book *The Great Necessity and Advantage of Public Prayer and Frequent Communion* (London: R. Smith, 1708). Beveridge was Bishop of St. Asaph, 1704–1708.

24. Compare Satan's reaction to first seeing the effects of the angelic fall upon one of his followers in John Dryden, *The State of Innocence and the Fall of Man, an Opera* (London: Herringman, 1677), 2:

If thou art he. But ah! how changed from him,
Companion of my Arms! how wan! how dim!

From eleven to one is devoted to conference. The first that came was *Stephen Dupee*, a soldier, who informs me he received forgiveness this week *in* hearing the word, and could lay down his life for the truth of it. But forasmuch as faith came not by hearing the Moravians, I suppose in his first temptation they will remand him to the prison of Satan, and not allow him to have faith till he subscribes to theirs.

Margaret Austin tells me she has longed for my coming as a child for the breast. "I was justified," she said, "the first Friday you was at Wapping, with those many others; saw my Saviour bringing me a pardon written in his blood. But their telling me I had no faith if I had any doubt, brought me again into darkness. I have been in an agony ever since. But last night my Saviour returned. I received your words as coming from his mouth, and with the eye of faith I again saw my pardon, written in his blood."

Walked with brother Maxfield, praying and praising God. A sweet confidence he gave us that he would not leave us alone, but by us weak things confound the things that are strong.

Sister [Jane] Jackson called, and much strengthened my hands. Most of the women have renounced the ordinances. Our sister Muncy[25] has left their Society, for their treatment of *her* ministers.

A separation I foresee unavoidable. All means have been taken to wean our friends of their esteem for us. God never used us, say they, as instruments to convert one soul. Indeed, I have just received a noble testimony of William Seward's to the contrary. But he and George Whitefield are reprobated for unbelievers. In a letter now received, George writes, "Remember what Luther says, 'Rather let heaven and earth come together, than one tittle of truth perish.'"[26] I preached at Bowers's Society. Many *still* ones were there, watching for my halting. As yet I fight in the cloud, and think it safest not to converse with such of our misled, mis-leading brethren as I love best—particularly Mr Stonehouse and Mr Claggett.

Easter Day, April 6. At the Foundery I strongly preached Christ, and the power of his resurrection, from Phil. 3:9-10. My intention was, not to mention one word of the controverted points till I had

---

25. Jane Muncy went with the Wesleys when Fetter Lane divided. Charles spells "Munsy."
26. This appears to be a hazy memory of Luther's comment on Gal. 5:12 in his *Commentary on Galatians*, where he defends the truth of Scripture, insisting "every tittle thereof is greater than heaven and earth."

spoke with each of the seducers. But God ordered it better, and led me, I know not how, *in ipsam aciem et certamen.*[27] My mouth was opened to ask, "Who hath bewitched you, that you should let go your Saviour?[28] That you should cast away your shield and your confidence, and deny you ever knew him?"[29] More to this purpose I said, and then followed a burst of general sorrow. The whole congregation was in tears. I called them back to their Saviour, even *theirs,* in words which were not mine. Pressed obedience to the divine ordinances, and prayed my Lord to stay his hand, and not set to his seal, unless I spake as the oracles of God.

After preaching, he sent me a witness of his truth which I had delivered. A sister, long in darkness through doubtful disputations, came and declared Christ has again appeared unto her and imprinted forgiveness on her heart. My heart, for the time, was as hers. Brother Maxfield was in full triumph of faith.

Dined at Hilland's,[30] halting between two.[31] Bell, Simpson, and others, when the bell rung for church, said, "It is good for us to be here." "Well, then," said I, "I will go myself, and leave you to your antichristian liberty." Upon this they started up and bore me company.

One of them told a poor man in my hearing, "That comfort you received at the Sacrament, was given you by the devil." I should less blasphemously have called it, the drawing of the Father,[32] or preventing grace.

The Foundery at night was filled, both within and without. I showed them their natural estate, and the way to come out of it, in Blind Bartimeus [Mark 10:46-52], who sat by the wayside begging. I could not have *so spoken* of the ordinances, had not God instituted them. Every word brought its own evidence to their hearts.

Walked with Maxfield to Bowers's, where the bands were to meet, the door was shut against us. I carried the few sisters to John Bray's. More joined us in prayer and praise. God blessed my words,

---

27. "in the very line of battle and [in the] contest." Cf. Cicero, *Epistulae ad Familiares,* XV.iv.16, which has *"in ipsam aciem,"* but not the words *"et certamen."*

28. Cf. Gal. 3:1.

29. Cf. Luke 22:57.

30. John Hilland (or Hyland, d. 1749), a hog butcher, of Old Street; and his wife, Martha (d. 1767). Charles spells "Hiland."

31. Cf. 1 Kings 18:21: "How long halt ye between two opinions?" See also Charles's sermon on this text, *Sermons,* 110–22.

32. Cf. John 6:44.

and enlarged our hearts in love to each other. The poor scattered sheep *knew my voice*. A stranger they will not follow.[33]

John Bray came with Edmonds, took me aside, and desired brother Maxfield might be turned out. I submitted it to the sisters, who all desired he might stay. Then, without losing an hour in dumb show, I gave out an hymn, and prayed according to God. For an hour I spoke freely, no one forbidding me. Avowed my love to them, my disinterestedness, my success. Told them what God had done for my soul, and others through me. Gloried in the cross of Christ. Lamented their having been so troubled. Exhorted them to hold fast whereunto they had attained, and never to forsake the holy ordinances; to avoid all reasonings and disputes about their faith; and to go on to perfection.

Many close things God enabled me to speak, concerning those that troubled them, and would exclude us, that they might affect them; yet all in the spirit of meekness.

I asked Bray whether he denied the ordinances to be commands. He answered directly, "I grant them to be great privileges." (Edmonds confessed more honestly that he had cast them off.) Whether he had not denied George Whitefield to have faith? This question he answered by begging to be excused it. He denounced grievous woes against the women for suffering Maxfield to be present, contrary to order. That order, they said, had been imposed upon them when no minister was present, and they were threatened to be turned out unless they consented to it. I put my brother Bray in mind of his respect for the Prophetess Lavington,[34] to show he was not infallible.

We plainly saw his stillness was ruffled. He *showed* it by threatening to renounce all care of the bands till they refused Maxfield admittance. I told him I did not see what good he had done them since our leaving London. Asked if he could charge us with preaching another gospel,[35] preferred Molther to myself. Yet declared I would not give place to him by subjection; no, not for an hour. But whosoever cast off the ordinances, I would cast off him, although it was my own brother.

Concluded our conference with thanksgiving.

Below, John Bray asked me whether I should come to my band on Monday. I answered, "No." He modestly replied, "Then you shall be expelled."

---

33. Cf. John 10:4-5.
34. See the June 12, 1739, entry above.
35. Cf. Gal. 1:6.

Monday, April 7. Cried above five thousand at Kennington Common, "Ho every one that thirsteth, come ye to the waters" [Isa. 55:1]. The love this people bear me requires the counterbalance of our stronger brethren's contempt.

My companions in the coach had been Quakers, but left them for their worldly-mindedness, and clave to us. They begin to feel themselves sinners.

Came to brother Maxfield's assistance, who was engaged in dispute with Bell, but an over-match for him, and much wiser in the things of God than his teacher. Bell graciously allows him to be a child of God, although never brought into confusion by the still brethren.

Tuesday, April 8. Met Simpson and [William] Oxlee[36] at the Foundery. The former told me plainly, if I recommended the ordinances, he must preach against me. I avowed my resolution never to give them up, as he and our poor deluded brethren had done. He tried all his Moravian questions upon Maxfield: *illidens solido.*[37]

Preached on Mark 2:10, "The Son of man hath power on earth to forgive sins." *Anne Young,* one who has been brought into confusion, testified that power, having now received the witness into herself. Several others come out of darkness daily, and recover their comfort.

Many poor sinners came to confer with me today about their souls. Two hours is full little for this work.

At one the woman bands met by my appointment. I began praying and we were all overwhelmed. I spoke largely of their being brought into the wilderness, of their folly and ingratitude in giving up not his ministers only but their Saviour himself. My love and sorrow ran through them all. I told them that their forsaking the ordinances sufficiently accounted for their being forsaken by Christ. Warned them against disputing; against vindicating *me,* or saying, "I am of Paul, and I of Apollos" [1 Cor. 1:12]; against the double extreme of resting in the means, of slighting them; but, above all, against stopping short of the glorious image of God.

Jane Jackson and others witnessed what God had done for their souls, through our ministry. If Christ be not with us, who hath begotten us these? His power overshadowed us at this time. Therefore our heart danced for joy, and in our song did we praise him.

---

36. Charles spells "Oxley."
37. "Remained resolute under the attack."

I drank tea at Mr Hawthorn's, who seems, with his wife and sisters, not far from the kingdom of God. I spoke of the love of Christ crucified to the Misses of the school, and melted them into tears. How easily might children receive their Saviour, if he were tendered to them!

Preached at the Common to six thousand poor, maimed, halt, and blind. Glory to Him, who is with his messengers *always!*

At Mr Crouch's I opened the book upon Phil. 1:25, "And having this confidence, I know that I shall abide and continue with you all, for your furtherance and joy of faith," etc. I gave some account of our colliers, and prayed that their spirit might be with us. He was so, indeed. One received his testimony in her heart; all some spiritual gift.

Wednesday, April 9. I began Isaiah. At one, I met the women. Prayed in faith that some might receive a second gift. Sister Hinsom recovered the sight of *her* Saviour. So did sister Barber. He was with us of a truth. How vainly does man deny, when God confirms!

Dined at Mr Dawson's, a sincere soul, his wife unawakened. As we were going, two gentlewomen came in. One was seeking Christ. We prayed, and had free access. We prayed again, and wrestled for an answer. The work went visibly forward in her soul. She trembled exceedingly. The Spirit cried and groaned from her heart. Her sighs shook my soul, till deliverance came. The clouds were scattered more and more. Her doubts and fears died away, and at last she confidently laid claim to Jesus *her* Saviour.

I never saw a soul so sweetly rising to the assurance of faith. In our thanksgiving she triumphed. Full of the spirit of love and supplication. I lent words to her faith. Mrs Dawson trembled. Her husband mourned. I was filled with confidence. Brother Maxfield was almost out of the body.

This was to prepare us for Fetter Lane, whither I carried brother Maxfield. I was in a mild, open, loving frame. The brethren could not contain long. Hutton began with objecting to Maxfield's presence at the women's Love-feast. I spoke as reconciling as I could (but the strong cannot bear with the weak). Desired their prayers that what I knew not, the Lord would show me.

James welcomed Maxfield by telling him, "If ever you speak to any of the women as you used to do at Bristol, you must not come here." Maxfield was the only *still* person among us. The old man rose in me,[38] but my Lord kept me within bounds.

Simpson took upon him next to reprove me for mentioning myself in preaching, and showing such vehemence, which was all animal spirits. I took him up short, that I should not ask him, or any of the brethren, how an ambassador of Christ should speak.

The strong ones were now brim full of dispute. I was to declare my success at Bristol, but they would not permit me. After much thwarting, I told them they did not deserve a true minister of Christ. James began giving me good words, but Simpson spoiled all again by accusing me with "preaching up the ordinances." Got home, weary, wounded, and bruised, and faint, through the contradiction of sinners. *Poor* sinners, as they call themselves, these heady, violent, fierce contenders for stillness. I could not bear the thought of meeting them again.

Finished Isaiah 1 at the Foundery, which led me to speak explicitly on the ordinances. God gave me great power—or, as our brethren will have it, animal spirits—sealing my words upon many hearts.

Mrs Seaton's in particular. The hammer had broke the rock.[39] "*I had so built her up in ordinances*," as they phrase it, that she saw herself a damned sinner, a Pharisee, and hypocrite, trusting in a form of godliness all her life, but not knowing the power.[40] She now felt her heart-sins, and that she was capable of all manner of wickedness.

Prayed by a faithful soul, whom Simpson had buffeted. But she would not quite let go her Saviour. She was greatly confirmed. And Mrs Seaton, too, was fully set at liberty, and rejoiced, believing with all her heart.

Simpson and the rest have dissuaded them, and indeed all our friends, from ever hearing my brother or me, or using any of the means. They condemn all doing good, whether to soul or body. "For, unless you *trust* in them," say they, "you would not do good works, so called."

Yesterday Simpson declared, "No soul can be washed in the blood of Christ, unless it be first brought to a true believer, or one in whom Christ is fully formed. But there are only *two such ministers* in London, which are Molther and Bell." If this is not calling

38. Cf. Rom. 6:6.
39. Cf. Jer. 23:29.
40. Cf. 2 Tim. 3:5.

man Rabbi,[41] what is? Nay, it is worse. It is making the excellency of the power to be of man, and not of God.[42] It is robbing Christ of his glory, and making his creature *necessary* to Him in his peculiar work of salvation. First perish Molther, Bell, and all mankind, and sink into nothing, that Christ may be all in all.

I am astonished at the divine goodness. How seasonably did it bring us hither, and lead us since! The adversary roared in the midst of the congregation, and set up his banners for tokens. A new commandment, called "stillness," had repealed all God's commandments, and given a full indulgence to lazy, corrupt nature. The *still* ones rage above measure against *me*, for my brother, they *say*, had consented to their pulling down the ordinances, and here come I, and build them up again.

God overruled me to declare myself *before the time* I intended, which cut off their πιθανολογία.[43] O what a deliverance was this! For they would deceive the very elect. Satan has transformed himself into an angel of light.[44] What havoc would these "dogs of hell" have made, had not our Lord arose to maintain his own cause! But, glory be to Him, when the enemy was come in like a flood, then the Spirit of the Lord lifted up a standard against him.

Met such of the sisters as have not forsook the ordinances. Our Lord divides the spoil with the mighty, and I doubt not but a little one will become a thousand. Some or other continually recover their comfort.

Received the following letter from him we dined with yesterday:

> O praise the Lord with me, and let us magnify his name together! Reverend Sir, I cannot forbear acquainting you how mercifully God heard your prayers for me. After you left me, I was deeply depressed, and went mourning all the evening, as I had done for months before; my prayers seldom reaching farther than sighs and groans. At waking, I offered up my first thoughts, and was presently answered with a comfortable power to say, "I know that my Redeemer liveth."[45] My heavy load is vanished. Blessed be his eternal goodness! Now can I praise him with joyful lips. O pray

41. Cf. Matt. 23:8.
42. Cf. 2 Cor. 4:7.
43. "Persuasive speech" or "art of persuasion." It is used here, as in its only biblical occurrence (Col. 2:4), with a negative sense of "false but persuasive words."
44. Cf. 2 Cor. 11:14.
45. Cf. Job 19:25.

for me, my dear pastor, for to you and your brother I am a debtor more than I can pay. But my Lord will pay it for me. And now I *know* he has paid all my debts above, he will not forget these below.

From your young son in Christ,
Robert Dawson

At six I began St John's Gospel. The true Light shone in our darkness. Several saw his glory. Some testified it in the Society, and more in their notes of thanksgiving. I prayed in confidence. Bell was present. God called forth his witnesses. Four made confession of the faith then given, or restored. I carried Bell to each. He had nothing to object to their strong and full testimony. Two declared they had apprehended Christ before, but on their forsaking his ordinances he had forsook them. I warned them all from hence not to trust in the ordinances, lest God in judgment should suffer them to cast them off. Spoke strongly and mildly of those who had turned the lame out of the way. Prayed for their return, and for the increase of this little flock. God himself could not convince one who *would* not be convinced; no, not though he made bare his arm before us.[46] "Christ commands me to say," said Bell, if we would believe him, "that the ordinances are no commands." I forbade all dispute, telling him it should rest here—he said they were no commands, I said they were; let the word of God determine. In Fetter Lane none durst speak for them. Here none should speak against them. If he could forbear, he should be welcome here; otherwise, not.

Friday, April [11].[47] The still brethren confront me with my brother's authority, pretending that he consented not to speak of the ordinances (i.e., in effect to give them up), but leave it to every one's choice whether they would use them or not. That necessity is laid upon us to walk in them, that "Do this in remembrance of me" [Luke 22:19] has the nature of a command, they absolutely deny. From "Woe unto the world because of offences," etc. [Matt. 18:7], I argued that their having offended or stumbled one of these little ones was no proof that he did not believe in Jesus, but a dreadful proof that the offender had better never have been born.[48]

---

46. Cf. Isa. 52:10.
47. MS has April "10," which is in error.
48. This reflects the Matt. 18:6-7 quotation, but the words echo Matt. 26:24.

Poor Simpson was present, but could not stand it. He withdrew dejected; I hope, shaken, for a mighty power accompanied the word.

Anne Parker, in conference, told me, they had darkened, but could not quite destroy, the work of God in her soul. Her faith she would not give up, though she lost the comfort of it through their doubtful disputations. But on Thursday, while we were praying, she recovered it with large increase.

Hannah Kent declares she felt Christ's blood applied last night. So did *Elisabeth Morison* upon my asking, "Believest thou that he is able to do this? That the Son of man can forgive you this moment?" *Elisabeth Bowen*, likewise, received her pardon last night in hearing.

I am forced to allow more time for conference. Today the weak ones found me full employment from three to eleven.

At Wapping I was directed to, "Go, wash in the pool of Siloam," John 9:7. Well is the Spirit compared to a mighty rushing wind. We heard the sound of it now, and the flame was kindled. Many felt the pangs of the new birth. Behold, a cry, "The Bridegroom cometh!"[49] I knew not when to leave off preaching, praying, singing. Four witnesses stood forth and testified, "A man that is called Jesus hath opened mine eyes."[50] From Him they received power to believe, and they worshipped Him.

Mr Simpson called, and laid down his two postulatums that 1) The ordinances are no commands; 2) It is impossible to doubt after justification. I maintained the contradictory; plainly told him they were fighting against God, robbing him of his glory, offending his little ones, and were under a strong delusion.

While I was going to bed, he came again with Bell and disputed against the ordinances and degrees of faith. He often repeated to himself, "O my Jesus!" I asked him, "Have you a new heart?"

[*Simpson:*] "No."

[*Wesley:*] "Have you faith?"

[*Simpson:*] "No."

[*Wesley:*] "Would you not be damned, if you died this moment?"

[*Simpson:*] "Yes."

[*Wesley:*] "Then how dare you, a damned unbeliever, say, 'My Jesus'?"

He was struck, and had nothing to answer.

---

49. Cf. Matt. 25:6.
50. Cf. John 9:11.

Sunday, April 13. Spoke strong words of waiting for Christ *in* the use of means. In vain do our brethren dissuade. They have set the house on fire, and now say they will be quiet if I will.

Before preaching, a woman came to me in the agony of despair. After preaching, I saw her rejoicing in Christ *her* Saviour. Such seals he gives me, as often as I speak in his name. And while he does so, I am content that man should withhold his testimony.

Received the Sacrament at St Paul's. The last time I communicated there was in company with our whole Society. Who hath bewitched them,[51] that they should not obey their Saviour? A Moravian, by declaring some months ago, he had long sought Christ in the ordinances in vain; but on his leaving them off, immediately found him. Nature caught the word, and our brethren cast off all means at once.

I am now informed that Mrs Sutherland was to hear me on Thursday evening, and when she got home was filled with all peace and joy in believing.

My soul was exceeding sorrowful at the Love-feast to find so little love, and so much dispute. I spoke as healingly as I could. Declared what God had done for the colliers. Put them in remembrance of his work begun in *them* by our ministry, and what manner of entrance in we had among them. Concluded with expostulation how injuriously our brethren had dealt with us, by dissuading all from hearing us, and hindering, as much as in them lay, the farther course of our ministry. Clark (another Shaw) denied the fact. I appealed to Simpson, who had confessed to me that he had dissuaded such and such persons from either hearing or seeing me. Our brother Hodges next began talking at random against peace, and joy, and love, as if they were any marks of faith. He had much of them before he had any faith at all—i.e., any stillness. The women stopped his mouth. Many bore testimony to the truth of our doctrine, and that the Moravians, since Peter Böhler, had added nothing to us. In singing and prayer my spirit revived. We praised the Lord with *supernatural* joy, and magnified his name together.

Tuesday, April [15]. Received the following letters:

My friend in Christ,
    I cannot help letting you know that the Lord carries on the work he began in me. He has showed me you are a minister of his

---

51. Cf. Gal. 3:1.

own sending. He hath taken the scales from my eyes. I was lame; he has made me walk. I was bound as with chains of darkness; he has burst my bonds in sunder. He has plucked me as a brand out of hell, and shall I dare to hide this? Shall I not declare what he hath done for my soul? I am not ashamed to say I sat by the way-side begging, and, as Jesus passed by, I received my sight. I am not afraid to say a servant of Christ uncovered the roof, and Jesus saw me brought unto him, poor and helpless. He looked on me, and said, "Thy sins are forgiven thee; thy faith hath made thee whole."

O, this small grain of faith is of matchless value! "Thy sins are forgiven thee!" O, that word was Christ! Christ was the word that spoke it. Behold a miracle indeed! A greater one than if a dead body had been raised out of the earth. I was dead in sin, and Jesus raised me. He brought me from the pit of hell into the kingdom of light. Flesh and blood could not have revealed this, but the Spirit of God, which dwelleth in me. O, Jesus, make this light a continuing spring of life!

The Lord confirmed the word you delivered on Friday concerning Satan's devices. He regards the low estate of his handmaid. I have some strivings, but he that keepeth me neither slumbers nor sleeps. I lean on him. I am as a new-born babe. He gently leads me. My Lord has brought me into his banqueting-house, and his banner over me is love. That the Lord may bless your ministry, and that there may never be wanting a constant supply of faithful labourers, is the most earnest prayer of

Yours in Christ,
E. Bristow

Sir,

I beg leave to ask your opinion about my state. I do not doubt myself. For through the grace given me, I am confident God for Christ's sake hath forgiven and made me free. But it has been questioned by a believer, whether I have received faith or not.

I was brought up an heathen in a D.D.'s house. After that I went to the Lord's table, and then thought myself a good Christian. But, blessed be God, I now see that I was an abominable Pharisee. For my pride God cast me out of his house, and I fell into the foulest crimes I could commit.

After some time, I had a sight of my damnable estate, and that I was nothing but sin. I daily dreaded God's vengeance. I durst not offer to pray, knowing my prayer was an abomination to that God who is of purer eyes than to behold iniquity. I could not think it possible there should be forgiveness for me.

I had my punishment in view.
I felt a thousand hells my due.[52]

I went twice to hear Mr Whitefield, but thought it did not signify. My misery still increased. But it pleased God, the last time
you, his faithful minister, preached at Kennington, from [2] Cor.
6:9, my blessed Saviour was revealed in me, in so glorious a manner, that I rather thought myself in heaven than upon earth. I
thought I could meet death with boldness. I was ready to cry out
to every one, "O taste and see how good the Lord is!" I would not
for a thousand worlds be in my former state again.

May God prolong your life and health in his service and
kingdom!

Dined at Mr Crouch's, with Mrs Seaton. Young West came in. I
asked him abruptly, "Should you be as glad to see me at your
house now as before I left London?" He was honest not to answer
in the affirmative.

Our brethren have set themselves to take off all the authority
with our friends, even before they knew we should not come in to
their notions. It was best to make all sure, for fear we should not
call them Rabbi.[53] West would not believe they had warned any
against hearing us, till Mrs Seaton declared they had absolutely
forbade her running after my brother, and gave this reason, "He
owned to us that he had not the Spirit of God. Why, then, should
you go to hear him?" Which shall I most admire, his simplicity in
making such a confession, or their baseness in making *such* an use
of it?

From our Lord's temptation I reasoned, that our being immediately tempted is no proof of our not being baptized with the Holy
Ghost; that the devil's questioning our sonship is no disproof of
it; that we may be in heaviness through manifold temptations,
and yet have faith; that we are not to tempt God by neglecting the
use of means, etc. The words reached many hearts, particularly
Mrs West's.

Wednesday, April [16]. Breakfasted with two sisters who, I think,
from their own relation, were justified on Sunday last. Hear of fresh

52. "Hymn on Gal. 3:22," st. 11, HSP (1739), 94 (*Poetical Works*, 1:85). The original couplet
is in the present tense.
53. Cf. Matt. 23:8.

seals at all the times of conference. Went to Deptford with Mrs Ewsters. Bray had lately been with her, and tried to bring her *into confusion*, telling her if she still heard me she never could be justified, but would have all her work to begin again. Simpson, too, draws away all he can, bidding them to go to Molther, or they cannot come to Christ.

Their behaviour is all of a piece, and perfectly consistent with that charitable assertion of John Bray's that it is impossible for any one to be a true Christian *out* of the Moravian church.

Expounded with great enlargement at a Society in Whitechapel. Some were deeply wounded. I lost count of them that are cured. Let God have all the glory.

Met the Society at the Foundery. Recommended true stillness *in* the use of means. Sang, prayed, and exhorted with much freedom and love, till Mr Simpson declared against the Sacrament, and asserted that no unjustified person ought to receive it; for if he did, he ate and drank his own damnation.[54] I replied, it was not fitting for *us* to dispute there. I would leave him to speak what he thought good to the Society. I retired, but returned unseen, that I might undo any mischief he might occasion. A few of the women cried, "Let him go. We will hear Mr Simpson." Poor Mrs Hamilton extolled him for contradicting me, and protested against those who had snatched her as a brand out of the fire. The far greater part were filled with grief and love.

After Mr Simpson had spoke all he had to say, I appeared, and concluded with the hymn on the means of grace.[55]

In conference heard of more who have tasted the word of life by our ministry.

Expounded in Rotherhithe. The people are quite untamed, but there was power among us, which drove out several. At Wapping I preached the pure gospel from the Woman washing her Saviour's Feet [Luke 7:36-50]. Many joined their tears with hers.

At Mr Mason's found an old believer, who had never been taught by Molther. I met Mrs Macune, who is now wholly perverted (our brethren would judge) and wants unsettling and confounding, as much as if she had never heard the new Gospel of Stillness.

---

54. Cf. 2 Cor. 11:29.

55. Charles had just published "The Means of Grace" as a broadsheet, in response to the controversy at Fetter Lane. He and John then included it in *HSP* (1740), 35–39 (*Poetical Works*, 1:233–36), which was published in July.

Was informed that our brothers Parker and Fish had been in quest of me. How applicable the Scripture I last expounded: "They all lie in wait. They hunt every man his brother with a net. The best of them is as a briar, the most upright is sharper than a thorn-hedge. Trust ye not in a friend, put ye not confidence in a guide" (Mic. 7[:2-5]).

Sunday, April 20. God confirmed his word, "If we confess our sins (unto God), he is faithful," etc. [1 John 1:9]. And while he does so, let who will despise prophesyings.

Preached at the Marshalsea forgiveness by Christ Jesus, from Acts 13:38. Thence Mrs Sparrow carried me to Kennington Common, where I divided the word of truth[56] to upward of seven thousand hearers.

At the Foundery I discoursed on Lazarus raised [John 11]. The sons of Belial[57] blasphemed. I *invited* them, till they were quiet as lambs. Then I strongly recommended the use of means from those words, "Take ye away the stone" [11:39]; and showed the weakness of faith from those [words], "He that was dead came forth, *bound hand and foot*" [11:44]. The word came with *divine* evidence. We rode triumphantly. Mrs Sparrow thankfully acknowledged she was now delivered out of the snare of stillness, which they had laid for her. Mrs Macune was very full of what they call *animal spirits*!

I was greatly refreshed in the Society, who are all of one heart, and of one mind. Two orders were now agreed upon: 1) That no order shall be valid, unless the minister be present at the making of it; 2) That whosoever denies the ordinances to be commands shall be expelled [from] the Society.

Tuesday, April 22. Met Molther at Mr Ibison's. He expressly denies that grace, or the Spirit, is transmitted through the means, particularly through the Sacrament. This, he insists, is no command; is for believers *only*, that is, for such as *are* sanctified, have Christ fully formed in their hearts. Faith, he teaches, is inconsistent with any following doubt, or selfish thought. Forgiveness, and the witness of the Spirit, the indwelling, the seal, are *always* given *together*. Faith, *in this sense*, is a pre-requisite of baptism. That is, the

---

56. Cf. 2 Tim. 2:15; this was likely the text of Charles's sermon, as he had been preaching from 2 Tim. 1 earlier (see March 23, 1740, entry above).

57. Cf. 1 Sam. 2:12.

candidate must have received the Holy Ghost, must have Christ living in him, must be justified, and sanctified, must be born of God—*in order* to—his being born of God.

He mentioned it as a sign of my carnal state that I complained of our brethren for withdrawing the people's love from me and my brother. I answered, "So did St Paul on the like occasion. 'They zealously affect you, but not well; yea, they would exclude *us*,[58] that ye might affect *them*' [Gal. 4:17]. If I desired their love for my own sake, it was wrong and carnal; if for theirs, it was right and apostolical."

Dined at Islington with Mr Wild and others, who cannot yet to be prevailed upon to throw away either their weak faith, or the ordinances. They pressed me much to expound. I answered, "When Mr Stonehouse (whom they ought still to reverence) desired it, then I would."

At Crouch's Society many were wounded. I left among them the hymn entitled "The Means of Grace," which I have printed as an antidote to stillness.[59]

Found my brother at the Foundery and praised God for his seasonable return. Mr Simpson, etc., had sent for him, to stop my "preaching up the ordinances."

Attended my brother to Fetter Lane. The first hour passed in dumb show, as usual; the next in trifles not worth naming. John Bray, who seems to be a pillar, if not the main one, expelled one brother, and reproved me for not attending my band. We parted as we met, with little of singing, less of prayer, and nothing of love. However, they carried their point, which was to divert my brother from speaking.

Thursday, April 24. My brother spoke after my own heart. His text, "Thou fool, that which thou sowest is not quickened, except it die" [1 Cor. 15:36]. Simpson and other disputers heard him describe that wilderness-state. They will not now say that my brother and I preach different gospels.

To the Society he demonstrated the ordinances to be both means of grace and commands of God. His power rested on us. None opened their mouth against the truth. We trust the little flock, who were following their new leaders into ruin, will now, through grace, come back again.

58. Note that Wesley has changed "exclude you" to "exclude *us*."
59. See *HSP* (1740), 35–39 (*Poetical Works*, 1:233–36).

Friday, April 25. Had a conference with Molther and our still brethren, but could come to no agreement. They contend for the impossibility of doubting after justification, and an absolute liberty from the means of grace, as we falsely call them, when they are neither means nor commands. We could not consent to say nothing, and so parted. Talked in the evening with James Hutton concerning the division which must soon ensue. I asked, "Have you the witness in yourself?" "No." "How then can you have faith?" "I have it not in the full proper sense. But I am in no fear. I have the full assurance of hope, and know my Saviour will give it me."

This, in my opinion, is giving up the point. Here is a lower faith, where the abiding, indwelling Spirit is *not yet*. And I see no necessity of denying the imperfect faith, in order to gain the perfect.

Sent a friend at Bristol the following account:

> My brother came most critically. The snare, we trust, will now be broken and many simple souls delivered. Many here insist that a part of their Christian calling is liberty *from* obeying, not liberty *to* obey. The unjustified, say they, are *to be still*; that is, not to search the Scriptures, not to pray, not to communicate, not to do good, not to endeavour, not to desire; for it is impossible to use means without trusting in them. Their practice is agreeable to their principles. Lazy and proud themselves, bitter and sensorious toward others, they trample upon the ordinances, and despise the commands, of Christ. I see no middle point wherein we can meet.

Saturday, April 26. Received a most insolent letter from [Richard] Ridley, threatening my downfall and destruction!

Sunday, April 27. Heard my brother preach at the Common, to a multitude of ten thousand. The still brethren at the Love-feast were kept down.

Monday, April 28. Brother Ibison declared his having found peace through my ministry. Likewise my sister [Patty] Hall gave me reason to hope she is accepted in the Beloved.

Wednesday, April 30. At Fetter Lane I read Ridley's letter. James strove to palliate it. Ridley himself justified it. They fell upon me about the women reading *their* rule for the exclusion of the brethren. We answered, "Whence had you your authority over them? We will save you any farther trouble, and *do now take them out of your hands."* They would fain have kept them still. I insisted that they should not. Much dispute ensued. The question about the ordinances was debated. My brother exhorted to love, in vain. We left them daunted and overawed, having rescued our lambs out of their hands.

MAY 1740

Thursday, May 1. Met sister [Martha] Soane's[60] band, full of love, and longing for the Lord's appearing. Conferred with more who were lately justified. Visited a sick man, just sent forth out of the pit by the blood of the covenant.[61]

Friday, May 2. Prayed at Islington with *Anne Gates*, believing we had the petitions we asked. Then baptized a child and her. We all felt the descent of the Holy Ghost. Before, she was in the spirit of heaviness and bondage. The moment the water touched her, she declares she felt her load removed, and sensibly received forgiveness. Sorrow and sighing fled away. The Spirit bore witness with the water, and she longed to be with Christ. We gave glory to God, who so magnified his ordinance.

Began observing the weekly church-fast with a few at the Foundery. I rebuked one of the bands, who was fallen asleep. Instead of spending the Sunday in carnal ordinances, she passed it partly in idleness, partly in her common business. For what signified her endeavours to keep the commandments before she had faith?

Preached the gospel at Wapping to the poor. Their groans and tears testified their inward affection.

Received the following simple letter. Let our brethren of Fetter Lane answer it.

My Rev Father in Christ,
    My heart being now open before God, I write as in his presence.
    The first gift of faith I received after I had seen myself a lost sinner, bound with 1,000 chains, and dropping into hell. Then I heard his voice, "Be of good cheer, thy sins are forgiven thee" and

---

60. Charles spells "Soan."
61. Cf. Heb. 13:20.

could say, "The Son of God loved me, and gave himself for me." I thought I saw him at the right hand of his Father, making intercession for me. I went on in great joy for four months. Then pride crept in, and I thought the work was finished, when it was but just begun. There I rested, and in a little time fell into doubts and fears whether my sins were really forgiven me, till I plunged myself into the depth of misery. I could not pray; neither had I any desire to do it, or to read, or hear the word. My soul was like the troubled sea. Then did I see my own evil heart, my cursed, devilish nature, and feel my helplessness, that I could not so much as think a good thought. My love was turned into hatred, passion, envy, and "I felt a thousand hells my due,"[62] and cried out in bitter anguish of spirit, "Save, Lord, or I perish."

In my last extremity, I saw my Saviour full of grace and truth for me, and heard his voice again whispering, "Peace, be still." My peace returned, and greater sweetness of love than ever before.

Now my joy is calm and solid, my heart drawn out to the Lord continually. I know that my Redeemer liveth for me. He is my strength and my rock, and will carry on his work in my soul, to the day of redemption.

Dear Sir, I have spoke the state of my heart, as before the Lord. I beg your prayers, that I may go on from strength to strength, from conquering to conquer, till death is swallowed up in victory.

Grace Murray[63]

Saturday, May 3. My spirit revived at the sight of the scoffers in the Foundery. I was directed to Heb. 12:18, "For ye are not come to the mount that might be touched, and that burned with fire, nor unto blackness," etc. God put strong words in my mouth, and in battles of shaking did he fight with them. The effect was both seen and heard—therefore would our still brethren say it had no effect at all.

Sunday, May 4. I dwelled on that word, "Thou art a God that hidest thyself, O God of Israel the Saviour" [Isa. 45:15], and spoke, with much liberty and power, of the wilderness state and the means of grace.

62. Hymn on Gal. 3:22, st. 11, ln. 4, *HSP* (1739), 94 (*Poetical Works*, 1:84).
63. This is the woman to whom John Wesley later made a marriage proposal. Charles then intervened and persuaded her to marry John Bennet (1715–1759) instead.

After sermon I was accosted by Howell Harris, whom God sent to my assistance. He had first called on James Hutton, who directed him to go hear Viney preach. But he blundered to the Foundery. "His conscience in the Holy Ghost," he said, "bore witness to the truth I spoke, and he found his heart immediately knit to me." We took sweet counsel together, and went to the altar of God as friends.

In the evening I opened the book on "And as ye go, preach, saying, 'The kingdom of heaven is at hand'" [Matt. 10:7]. He who sent was with me, in his promised power. The fire was kindled in many hearts. "Ascribe unto the Lord the honour due unto his name" [Ps. 96:8, BCP].

Carried Howell to the bands. He spoke in simplicity concerning Satan's devices, and repeated the very words which the tempter has so often spoke to us by the mouth of our still brethren. All his arguments touching false joy, animal spirits, presumption, etc., had been tried upon our brother, to make him let go his shield.

Monday, May 5. Carried him to sister Anderson's, to whom he spoke in words which man's wisdom doth not teach. The Spirit of love and supplication was poured out. There was as in us all one soul.

We met the bands at five. I bear them witness that their love abounds yet more and more in knowledge and in all judgment.

I preached from John 3. The word made great havoc. They cried out on all sides, and fell down under it. I spoke afterwards to two or three of them. In the same hour God had made them sore, and bound them up; he had wounded, and his hands made them whole.

Tuesday, May 6. In the hours of conference *Elizabeth Holmes* informed me she had been filled with the Spirit of love while we were praying at sister Anderson's. *Cordelia Critchet*, a Papist till convinced by us, appeared not far from the kingdom of heaven. I want time to take a particular account of them who are daily convinced of sin or of righteousness. Our brethren, I bless God, are mistaken in saying He no longer works by our hands.

I heard Howell Harris expound at Crouch's. He is indeed a son of thunder[64] and of consolation.[65]

---

64. Cf. Mark 3:17.
65. Cf. Acts 4:36.

Wednesday, May 7. Was much enlarged to expound and plead the promise Isaiah 50:10, "Who among you is there that feareth the Lord, that obeyeth the voice of his servant, that walketh in darkness, and hath no light? Let him trust in the name of the Lord, and stay upon his God." Here the fear of the Lord, which is the beginning of wisdom,[66] and obedience which is the fruit of faith, are attributed to one that walketh in darkness and hath no light. Nay and the Spirit saith expressly that this *dark* disconsolate soul *may* be a believer. "Let him trust in the name of the Lord, and stay upon his God"—even while he walketh in darkness and hath no light. Therefore a believer *can* doubt.[67]

God put it into our hearts to pray for the poor malefactors passing to execution, and his Spirit made intercession. I am sure (how much more the rest of us!) that our prayer was heard, and answered, upon some of our dying brethren.

At eleven *Cordelia Critchet* came to let me know she received the atonement yesterday, while we were at prayers. The work, as far as I can discern, is real.

Another who, after justification, had fallen into gross sin, informs me God has again received him to his mercy in Christ Jesus. His deep humility and abundant love are good evidences for him.

Lucy Spring, who, on Monday night, fell into the pangs of the new birth, came today, full of peace and comfort.

Howell Harris, whom I carried to the still bands, delivered a full and noble testimony that "he had been drawn to the Sacrament while dead in sin, and received forgiveness there. *Afterwards* the love of God was shed abroad in his heart by the Holy Ghost, then given him. From *thence* commenced the fight of faith. Fears, doubts, darkness returned, and he was brought through fire and water into a wealthy place."

His words were contradictory to all our still brethren have been teaching this half year. They were scandalized and confounded; the weak comforted. Much caviling followed. Howell, be sure, had no faith. Bray attempted to explain away what he said; Bell and Oxlee to confute it. The latter compared him to Cain, when God lightened

---

66. Cf. Prov. 1:7.
67. This paragraph is omitted in Jackson. In the MS Journal two vertical lines are drawn through the entire paragraph. The origin of the lines is unknown.

his burden, upon his complaining it was too heavy for him to bear. All agreed that he had not seen his heart, and because he had some strivings, had no faith. I invited them to hear more of him on Thursday evening.

Thursday, May 8. He declared his experience before our Society. O what a flame was kindled! Never man spake, in my hearing, as this man spake. What a nursing-father has God sent us! He has indeed learned of the good Shepherd to carry the lambs in his bosom. Such love, such power, such simplicity was irresistible. The lambs dropped down on all sides into their shepherd's arms. Those words broke out like thunder, "I now find a commission from God to invite all poor sinners, justified or unjustified, to his altar; and I would not for ten thousand worlds be the man that should keep any from it. There I first found Him myself. That is the place of meeting." He went on in the power of the Most High. God called forth his witnesses. Several declared they had found Christ *in* the ordinances.

Poor Simpson stood by, hardening his heart. I suppose now he will call Howell, as he does my brother, "a subtle deceiver of the people." Scarce any from Fetter Lane were present; too good care had been taken to prevent them.

Friday, May 9. Went to Islington, intending to baptize Bridget Armstead. Satan hindered, by *his* churchwardens. But can anyone forbid water? Not unless they can dry up the Thames.

In conference Mrs Dupee informed me she had received forgiveness last week while I was preaching it. Is His hand shortened at all, that He cannot save?[68] Or, because we are weak, hath He no power to deliver![69]

Met about one hundred of the Society to keep the fast. Christ owned *his* ordinance and melted us into prayer, through his Spirit helping our infirmities.

Went to give the Sacrament to a dying woman. I found her an old, subtle Pharisee. Could have no access in speaking, and betook myself to prayer. The sin-convincing Spirit came mightily upon her, so that she roared for the very disquietness of her heart. The strong man who had peaceably kept his palace for above seventy

---

68. Cf. Isa. 59:1.
69. Cf. Isa. 50:2.

years, was now disturbed, tormented, bound, cast out.[70] She broke forth into strong cryings, and soon after into blessings and thanksgivings. As far as I can discern, she is quite delivered. We showed forth our Lord's death, and he was with us of a truth.

Saturday, May 10. Spoke closely to those who trusted to their faith of adherence, and insisted on that *lowest mark* of ~~the new birth~~ forgiveness of sins.

My back was scarcely turned, when Oxlee took his opportunity to draw away Howell Harris to deaf Bell's. I came time enough to break off their conference with my unwary friend. He now, without distrusting God, resolves to go nowhere without me. Two are better than one. Their word doth eat as a canker; especially Oxlee's, ~~the viper~~, whom we have cherished in our bosom. God help me to love *him*! I abhor both his principles and practices.

At Bowe's Society I found Bell, Bray, Hutton, Oxlee, Holland, Ridley, and others of the same class. I withstood them to the face, and appealed to the God that answered by fire[71] for the truth of my doctrine, that the ordinances bind all, both justified and unjustified. A woman testified that the last time I expounded here, and bade them who had been confounded ask Jesus Christ *alone* whether they had faith, she did ask in our prayer, and immediately the love of God overflowed her heart.

I preached at the Foundery on 1 John 2:12, "I write unto you, little children," etc. Hence, I showed the three particulars which difference a *child* from a *young* man. The young man is *strong*, the child *weak*. The young man *hath* overcome the wicked one, the child is *overcoming* him. In the young man the word of God *abideth*; that is, he hath the *constant* witness of the Spirit. In the child the word *abideth not*; i.e., he hath not the *abiding witness*, but only visits now and then, as pledges and tokens that he *will* shortly come and make his abode with him forever. I never spoke with greater strength.[72]

In the Society Howell spoke excellently of good works, searching the Scripture, and loving one another.

Sunday, May 11. Met the women leaders for the first time and, after a lively prayer, led them to the Lord's table at St Paul's.

70. Cf. Matt. 12:29.
71. Cf. 1 Kings 18:37-38.
72. The last sentence of this paragraph is omitted in Jackson.

Went forth to Kennington Common. The hand of the Lord was upon me, and I prophesied, "O ye dry bones, hear the word of the Lord" [Ezek. 37:4]. Truly there were very many in the open valley, and lo, they were very dry. But as I prophesied there was a noise, and, behold, a shaking, which we both saw and heard. Into some, I am confident, the breath came, and they lived.

Monday, May 12. Employed three hours most profitably in conferring with the poor people, more of whom daily receive forgiveness, or the witness of the Spirit. Three or four were now set at liberty, in immediate answer to prayer.

With Miss Branford, who has been in darkness ever since her eyes were first opened (two years ago, at St Helen's) to see her sins forgiven. In prayer, the love of God was now shed abroad in her heart, and she was translated into his marvelous light.[73]

An aged gentlewoman here testified that she had long denied that article of her creed, "forgiveness of sins," but was yesterday experimentally convinced of it under Mr Hall's ministry. Others I meet with, who have passed from death unto life in hearing our brother Whitefield. Our brethren of Fetter Lane deny the fact that any soul has been justified by our ministry, since "no one gives what he has not himself."

Tuesday, May 13. Sarah Redford, justified under the word last Sunday; *Mary Barraby* and *Anne Broad*, a few days ago; and others were with me today, testifying the work of God in their souls.

Mrs Ricard told me at sister [Elizabeth] Witham's that in the depth of despair Christ had given her rest, but Satan came in with the still brethren and gained such advantage over her; that she even denied the faith, and its Author. Our Lord again confirmed his love to her—through a worm, the very scorn of men, and outcast of the still ones.

Met the men leaders at Bray's, and was surprised to find about twenty of the still brethren there; and more, to hear they constantly meet on Thursday and Sunday, while I am preaching at the Foundery. The reason is obvious.

I bore my testimony for the ordinances and weak faith.[74] Asked whether they did not hold 1) that the means of grace are neither

---

73. Cf. Rom. 5:5 and 1 Pet. 2:9.
74. Charles's concern to defend the validity of *degrees* of faith led to publishing another

commands nor means; 2) that forgiveness is never given but together with the abiding witness of the Spirit? James Hutton would not have them give me any answer. I said, if they durst not avow their principles I should take their silence for confession, and warn God's people against them.

Wednesday, May 14. Talked with a woman to whom Jesus lately appeared, but immediately vanished out of her sight. Never did I see a soul more inconsolable.

Esther Owen was with me, pierced, melted, overpowered with love.

At Blackheath I preached redemption in the blood of Jesus [Eph. 1:17]. He gave me power "to sound the unbelieving heart."[75] A woman screamed out so loud that I could not be heard and therefore had her removed, but not out of hearing. To the scoffers I spoke with much contention. Many were driven off, and others constrained to stay. I am sure the word did not return void.

Found Mr Hall at Fetter Lane, asking them whether they would try their spirits by the word, or the word by their spirits.[76] I enforced the question, which they strove to evade. Rabbi Hutton forbade their answering me. I warned the few remaining brethren to beware of the leaven of stillness; showed them the delusion of those who had cast off the ordinances, and confined the faith to *themselves only*; foretold the dreadful consequences of their enthusiasm; set the case of Greger[77] before their eyes; besought, entreated, conjured them not to renounce the means, or deny the Lord that bought them; read a letter from one who had been strongly tempted to leave off the Sacrament, but, in receiving, powerfully convinced that her dissuader was the devil. Hodges, Hall, and Howell Harris confirmed my words. Others were hereby emboldened to bear their testimony to the divine ordinances. By the

---

hymn as a tract, a paraphrase of Heb. 11 titled *The Life of Faith* (published by William Strahan on May 24). This hymn was also included subsequently in *HSP* (1740), 6–20 (*Poetical Works,* 1:209–21).

75. Cf. "Hymn on the Descent of the Holy Ghost at Pentecost (altered from Henry More)," st. 8, *HSP* (1739), 186 (*Poetical Works*, 1:166):

> The Spirit of convincing speech,
> Of power demonstrative impart,
> Such as may every conscience reach,
> And sound the unbelieving heart.

76. Cf. 1 John 4:1.
77. This spelling is clear in the MS, but the referent is unknown.

strength of the Lord we have stood between the living and the dead, and the plague, we trust, is stayed.

Poor James was all tergiversation.[78] O how unlike himself! The honest, plain, undesigning Jacob, is now turned a subtle, close, ambiguous Loyola.[79] Bell was more frank, and I therefore put him upon speaking. He expressly denied the Sacrament to the unjustified—that is, in effect, to all but Molther, Mary Ewsters,[80] and himself; for these three are all the church Christ has in England.

I mentioned Simpson's advice to Mrs Seaton, that if she would but leave off the Sacrament, prayer, and reading the Scriptures for *one week*, she should then find what she never found before in her life. He justified his advising her, and several others, to lay aside their Bibles, *because they trusted in them*. The rest abated somewhat of their stiffness, and much pressed me "to preach Christ the foundation"—meaning, that I should not recommend the ordinances, but let them trample on them undisturbed. I did not *say* that I *understood* them.

Ascension Day, May 15. I preached from Rom. 8:33-34. Great power accompanied the word; but greater still, while I exhorted the Society to wait for the promise of the Father. Many cried out in the birthpangs. After a long and violent struggle, *Eleanor Tubbs* testified that God had now showed her her heart, and broke it in pieces, and bound it up.

Sarah Church informed me she had received forgiveness the night Mr Simpson expounded at Rag Fair;[81] not under his preaching, which was quite dead to her, but in singing an hymn which I gave out. So did Anne Roberts, after hearing the word in the same carnal ordinance of singing.

Mary Shrievely, who has been groaning under the burden of sin from the time she first heard me preach, was last night relieved by the coming of Jesus, and now goes on her way rejoicing.[82] Jane Bourn also informs me that she received forgiveness in the Society, and was sprinkled from her idols.

---

78. *OED* defines "tergiversation" as the act of being evasive or ambiguous.
79. I.e., Ignatius Loyola (1491–1556), founder of the Jesuit order.
80. Mary Ewsters (b. 1723), who was made Warden of the Single Sisters' Choir when the London Congregation of the Moravians organized in 1742. Charles spells "M. Eusters."
81. A clothing market area in London.
82. Cf. Acts 8:39.

Friday, May 16. Almost the whole Society met at one. A spirit of contrition ran through all.

Received the following letter:

My friend,

I hear there are divisions among you. For some say "I am of Wesley," and others, "I am of Molther."[83] But I say, I am of Christ, and what he bids me do, I will do, and not trust in any man.

Here some will say, "What Christ bids you do, is to believe and be still." True, but does he bid me do nothing else? He bids me let my light so shine before men, that they may see my good works, and glorify my Father which is in heaven [Matt. 5:16].

He likewise says, "The scribes and Pharisees sit in Moses' chair. All therefore whatsoever *they bid you* to observe, that observe and do" [Matt. 23:2-3]. But how can I know what they bid me do, except I go to hear them?

Again, Christ bids me observe all things which he commands the Apostles, and with such he will be to the end of the world.[84] But if I do not observe and do his commands, he will not be with me.

He bids me "do this in remembrance of" Him [Luke 22:19]. Now, if any man can prove this is not a command, I will obey it no longer. "But whosoever breaketh one of these least commandments, and teacheth men so, shall be called least in the kingdom of heaven" [Matt. 5:19].

As to stillness, our Saviour saith, "The kingdom of heaven suffereth violence, and the violent take it by force" [Matt. 11:12]; and "strive to enter in at the straight gate" [Luke 13:24]. And St Paul saith, "Work out your salvation with fear and trembling" [Phil. 2:12]. And, "God is a rewarder of them that *diligently seek him*" [Heb. 11:6]. Now these Scriptures imply somewhat more than barely sitting still.

Some deny that there are any means of grace. But I will be thankful for them, since it was in them I first heard you preach faith in Christ; and had I not been there, I might have been without faith unto this day.

One told me, when you preached you had nature in your face. So will every one have who speaks with zeal. But no matter for that, if he has but grace in his heart.

My friend, there are many teachers, but few fathers. But you are my father, who begot me in the gospel, and, I trust, many more.

May the Lord lead you into all truth!

83. Cf. 1 Cor. 1:12.
84. Cf. Matt. 28:20.

Saturday, May 17. Expounded the chapter in course, Isaiah 53. One could not bear my enlarging on that "The Lord hath laid on Him the iniquity of us all," but often interrupted me with "Stop his mouth." Alas! thought I, if meekness be the mark of the elect, I fear thou art still a reprobate.

Dined at Mr Williams's. His wife had formerly found favour with God under the word, but Satan reasoned her out of it. After our praying, she said she had an answer in herself at every word. All doubt and unbelief fled away, and she clearly saw *her* interest in the Saviour of all men.

Sunday, May 18. Preached to near ten thousand at the Common, from 1 Cor. 6:9, etc. The Lord was with us in his convincing power. I *would* give Him the glory.

Monday, May 19. Our brethren complain that we unjustly charge them with speaking against the ordinances. Yet they teach that your using them *before* faith *necessarily* keeps you out of it, and your using them *after* faith necessarily makes you lose it. Particularly when you find comfort, by no means offer to pray (they say); if you pray then, you will forfeit it immediately.

Ridley is famous for saying, "You may as well go to hell in praying as in thieving."[85] Mr Brown's words are, "If we read, the devil reads with us. If we pray, he prays with us. If we go to church or Sacrament, he goes with us."

In the time of conference *Mary Benham* declared her faith, which she has lately received. *Anne Judge* found power to believe under the word last Monday; Thomas Boreman, while we were at prayers.

While I expounded the Woman of Samaria [John 4], the word reached many hearts, particularly Mrs Ash the Quaker's, a great enemy to crying out. However, she could not now forbear, for the love of Christ constrained her.[86] Jesus had said, "I that speak unto thee am He!" [4:26]. Her sister appeared under strong convictions at the sight of her. O that the flame might spread throughout all the earth!

---

85. John Wesley quotes the same saying by Richard Ridley in his letter to Zinzendorf summarizing concerns about the Moravian community in England (see *Works* 19:281).
86. Cf. 2 Cor. 5:14.

Tuesday, May 20. Poor desperate John Dickinson received the word of reconciliation, Isaiah 54[:7], "For a small moment have I forsaken thee, but with great mercies will I gather thee," etc. After having been long afflicted, tossed with tempests and not comforted, in this hour he found rest to his soul.

At eleven, *Elizabeth Bird* testified her having lately felt the atoning blood; as likewise *Astrea Edzard* and *Thomas Haddock*; all by the ministry of the word. *Mary Wotlen* too can set to her seal that God is true.

Found sister Sutherland strong in the Lord. Several others were present, whom I took knowledge of that they have been with Jesus.

Went with Maxfield to Bray's, as a fool to the correction of the stocks.[87] I laboured for peace, but only the Almighty can root out those cursed tares of pride, contempt, and self-sufficiency with which our Moravianized brethren are overrun.

Wednesday, May 21. Carried Bridget Armstead to Bloomsbury church,[88] where the minister baptized her. She had been bred a Quaker. I was one of the witnesses. We were all in great heaviness before, but perceived that Christ was always with us in his ordinances. The Spirit infallibly bears witness on this occasion. Our youngest sister assuredly knows that she is born of water and of the Spirit.[89]

Thursday, May 22. Found our dear brother Ingham at Mrs West's. He is clear in that truth that forgiveness and the witness of the Spirit are distinct gifts and generally given at different times.[90] The holiday mob was very outrageous at the Foundery. God filled my mouth with threatenings and promises. Both, I believe, took place; for at last we got the victory, and the fiercest rioters were overawed into silence.

The Day of Pentecost, May 25. Discoursed on the first pouring out of the Spirit, Acts 2. He gave me utterance. Many felt his descent in an invisible power; and even trembled at his presence.

At the Common I again declared *the promise* [Acts 2:37-39] to many thousands. At the Love-feast I was overwhelmed with the burden of our brethren, with such visible signs of dejection, that

---

87. Cf. Prov. 7:22.
88. St George's Church, Bloomsbury, London. Edward Vernon (1695–1761) was rector.
89. Cf. John 3:5.
90. This sentence is omitted in Jackson.

several, I was since informed, were in great hopes that I was now coming down in my pride, or unsettling, and coming into confusion. Indeed, my faith did well nigh fail me, for in spite of the seeming reconciliation which brother Ingham *forces* them into, it is impossible we should ever be of one mind, unless they were convinced of their abrogating the law of *Christian* ordinances, and taking away the children's bread.[91]

Monday, May 26. A woman from Islington complained to me that she had brought Mr Stonehouse to her mother, who lay a-dying, but waiting for redemption. Her minister told her, "it signified nothing to pray either publicly or privately. Reading the Scriptures, or taking the Sacrament, were equally useless. These outward things must all be laid aside." She had nothing to do but to be still. He refused to pray for her, and *so* left her.

The work of grace goes on in several that were with me today, and God still gives fresh seals to my ministry.

Tuesday, May 27. Rejoiced to find no difference betwixt my brother Ingham and me. He has honestly withstood the deluded brethren, contradicted their favourite errors, and constrained them to be *still*. That blot he easily hit: "You say no man must speak of what he has not experienced. You, Oxlee and Simpson, say, that one in gospel-liberty can have no stirrings of sin." "Yes." "Are you in gospel-liberty?" "No." "Then out of your own mouth I judge you: you speak of the things which you know not of."

Expounded in Snowsfields, and met the bands at the Foundery. An extraordinary power overshadowed us. Sister Hunting received the witness in herself. Richard Ridley was even lost in love.

Wednesday, May 28. At Blackheath discoursed from Matt. 21[:44], "He that falleth on this stone shall be broken," etc. There were a multitude of scoffers, but all forced to fly before the sword of the Spirit.[92]

Talked once more with our wild brethren, and laboured heartily for peace and union. But it cannot be, while they are so full of bitter, proud contempt of all except themselves.

Thursday, May 29. I expounded Isaiah 57, a chapter most contradictory to the doctrine of our brethren.

---

91. Cf. Matt. 15:26.
92. Cf. Eph. 6:17.

Dined at Friend [Thomas] Keen's, a Quaker and a Christian, and read George Whitefield's account of God's dealings with him.[93] The love and esteem he expresses for me, filled me with confusion, and brought back my fear, lest, after having preached to others, I should be myself a castaway.

At Marylebone the scoffers fulfilled the Scripture I explained: "The wicked are like the troubled sea, when it cannot rest, whose waters cast up mire and dirt" [Isa. 57:20]. I addressed myself to one of them after another, and silenced them on whatever side I turned. Sometimes a stray coach would stop, but my doctrine did not suit them. Our Lord vouchsafed us much of his presence at the Society. We find him daily uncovering our hearts, casting down imaginations, and bringing every thought into captivity. The souls of many were smitten asunder as with a sword; and I am sure, if God wounds, he will bind up again.

Friday, May 30. Had yet another conference, but could not convince our dear brother Simpson. He cannot allow there are more than four Christians in London, which are Molther, Mary Ewsters, Wheeler's maid, and Bell. Of the last he roundly affirms, that he is holier than Moses, the meekest of men; than Abraham, the friend of God; than David, the man after God's own heart; than Elijah and Enoch, who walked with God, and were translated. As to our father Abraham, he denies him to have had any right faith at all.

Saturday, May 31. Took sweet counsel with Benjamin Ingham and Howell Harris. A threefold cord cannot easily be broken.

Heard that the Foundery was lately presented at Hick's Hall[94] for a seditious assembly. Sir John Ganson interposed, and objected that no persons were named in the presentment. Upon this they presented Charles Wesley, clerk; James Hutton, bookseller; Timothy Lewis, printer; and Howell Harris, *alias* the Welsh Apostle. But our friend Sir John quashed the whole.

JUNE 1740

Sunday, June 1. I was much refreshed in spirit among the women bands. They have rest, and walk in the comfort of the Holy Ghost, and are edified.

---

93. George Whitefield, *A Short Account of God's Dealings with the Reverend Mr George Whitefield* (London: W. Strahan, 1740).
94. A courthouse in London.

Monday, June 2. Preached up the ordinances, as they call it, from Isaiah 58, but first with the prophet I preached them *down.* Töltschig, Ingham, etc., were present, which made me use greater plainness, that they might set me right, if I mistook.

Talked with several in whom the work of conversion is effectually begun; particularly *Mary Russel,* convinced and deeply wounded by my last discourse at Kennington; *Mary Peck,* whom God showed her heart in singing; *Sarah Redford,* to whom faith lately came by hearing; and Mary Litchfield, who, by all I can yet discern, was justified the last time I preached at Blackheath.

Preached on Job 23:8[-10], I would hope, to the comfort of many whose hearts God is directing into the love of Christ, and into the patient waiting for him.

Tuesday, June 3. Met with Amos Comenius's moving exhortation of the Bohemian churches to the Church of England.[95] O that we might see, at least in this our day! Who knows but *our* eyes may behold "the last surviving bishop of the Church of England!"

Wednesday, June 4. Preached at Marylebone on "What must I do to be saved?" [Acts 16:30]. The opposers had threatened me hard, but all they now could do was to curse and swear. I only *invited* them to Christ. But I am more and more persuaded that the law has its use, and Moses must bring us to Christ.[96] The promises to the unawakened are pearls before swine.[97] First the hammer must break the rocks,[98] then we *may* preach Christ crucified.[99]

Thursday, June 5. My brother returned from Bristol.

Friday, June 6. I spoke with Bilhah Aspernell,[100] who had lately been with me in the depth of mourning. A still brother had been troubling her, and deterring from the word and Sacrament. Last night it pleased our Lord to lift up her head above all her enemies.

95. Johann Amos Comenius (1592–1670), *An Exhortation of the Churches of Bohemia to the Church of England, Wherein is set forth the Good of Unity, Order, Discipline, and Obedience in Churches . . .* (London: Thomas Parkhurst, 1661). Comenius was the last surviving bishop of the Bohemian branch of the Unity of the Brethren church.
96. Cf. Gal. 3:24.
97. Cf. Matt. 7:6.
98. Cf. Jer. 23:29.
99. Cf. 1 Cor. 1:23.
100. Charles spells "Billal Aspernel."

He spoke to her in the word, and she had joy again, and her joy shall no man take from her.

Martin Chow and *Margaret Martin* at the same time found the power of the Lord present to heal them; as did *Eleanor Gambel* the Thursday before.

Went with my brother, and Howell Harris, and John Purdy, to see Molther at Islington. Wished George Stonehouse joy of his good bargain, and left him to justify ~~the selling his living~~ to my brother the selling of his living.

Half persuaded a Dissenter out of her faith of adherence.

Explained the progress of grace by our Lord's comparison of the grain of mustard-seed, and the little leaven [Matt. 13:31-33].

Saturday, June 7. Recommended the Woman of Canaan [Matt. 15:22-28] as a pattern of triumphant importunity. (It is plain she had not heard of the doctrine of stillness.)

Monday, June 9. Dined at Mr Wild's in Islington and rejoiced over a few *unperverted* souls. The shepherd, alas, is smitten, and the sheep are scattered.[101] But not all, God has left himself a very small remnant.[102]

Tuesday, June 10. Rode with Maxfield to Bexley and was greatly comforted with my brother [Henry] Piers. The weak stand when the strong fall. In spite of all the *still* ones, he had held fast the truth, neither forsaking the ordinances nor denying his *weak* faith.

Went thence to Blendon, no longer Blendon to me. They could hardly force themselves to be barely civil. I took an hasty leave, and with an heavy heart, weighed down by their ingratitude, returned to Bexley.

Here I preached the gospel to a little flock, among whom the grievous wolves are not entered.

Wednesday, June 11. Was constrained to bear my testimony for the last time at Blendon. Maxfield accompanied me. I desired to speak with Mrs Delamotte alone. She did not well know how to refuse, and walked with me into the hall. I began, "Three years ago God sent me to call you from the form to the power of godliness.[103]

---

101. Cf. Matt. 26:31; Zech. 13:7.
102. Cf. Isa. 1:9.
103. Cf. 2 Tim. 3:5.

I told you what true religion was, a new birth, a participation of the divine nature. The way to this I did not know myself till a year after. Then I showed it to you, preaching Jesus Christ, and faith in his blood. You know how you treated me. God soon after called you to a living faith by my ministry. Then you received me as an angel of God. Where is now the blessedness you spake of? Whence is this change? This jealousy, and fear, and coldness? Why are you thus impatient to hear me speak?" She offered several times to leave me; said "She did not know what I meant," "did not want to dispute," etc. "I do not come to dispute. Why are you afraid of me? What have I done? You gave as a reason for not seeing me in town that you did not care to be unsettled. Once I unsettled you through the strength of the Almighty, stirred you up from your lees, took you off your own works, and grounded you upon Christ. Other foundation than this can no man lay.[104] I only desire to settle you more firmly upon Him, to warn you against the danger of being removed from the hope of the gospel. Our brethren, whom now you follow, are making a schism in the church. Follow them not in this." She would not bear any more, but hurried into the parlour. When I came in, Betty left it, but afterwards returned. She has not been at the Sacrament for several months. I warned them against casting off the ordinances, which were divine commands, binding all, whether justified or unjustified.

They continually interrupted me asking why I talked to them. I answered, because I durst not forbear but must deliver my own soul. Betty said she had received great benefit from Molther and should therefore hear none but him. I told her I had nothing to say against her hearing him, unless he spoke against the ordinances.[105]

Upon their again and again bidding me silence, I asked, "Do you, therefore, at this time, in the presence of Jesus Christ, acquit, release, and discharge me from any farther care, concern, or regard for your souls? Do you desire I would never more speak unto you in His name?" Betty frankly answered, "Yes." Mrs Delamotte assented by her silence. "Then here," said I, "I take my leave of you, till we meet ~~in the day of judgment~~ at the judgment-seat." With these words I rendered up my charge to God.

104. Cf. 1 Cor. 3:11.
105. This paragraph is omitted in Jackson.

Then said I, after leaving them, "I have laboured in vain. I have spent my strength for nought. Yet surely my judgment is with the Lord, and my work with God." Surely this is enough to wean and make me cease from man. With Blendon I give up all expectation of gratitude upon earth. Vanity of vanities, all is vanity,[106] even friendship itself.

I rode on softly to Eltham, cast out by my dearest friends. I pray God it may not be laid to theirs or their seducers' charge! Piety and grief for them was uppermost in my heart, and these were much relieved by the Scripture that first offered: "And Paul went down, and fell on him, and, embracing him, said, Trouble not yourselves, for his life is in him" [Acts 20:10].

Returned to be exercised by our *still* brethren's contradiction. My brother proposed new-modelling the bands and setting by themselves those few who were still for the ordinances. Great clamour was raised by this proposal. The noisy *still*-ones well knew that they carried their point by wearying out the sincere ones, scattered among them, one or two in a band of disputers, who had harassed and sawn them asunder, so that a remnant is scarcely left. They grudged us even this remnant, which would soon be all their own, unless immediately rescued out of their hands. Benjamin Ingham seconded us, and obtained that the names should be called over, and as many as were aggrieved put into new bands.

We gathered up our wreck—"*raros nantes in gurgite vasto*,"[107] for nine out of ten are swallowed up in the dead sea of stillness. O, why was not this done six months ago? How fatal was our delay and false moderation? "Let them alone, and they will be soon weary, and come to themselves of course," said one—"*unus qui nobis* cunctando *restituit rem!*"[108]

I tremble at the consequence. Will they submit themselves to every ordinance of man, who refuse subjection to the ordinances of God?—"*Hic fiunt homines!*"[109] The Ziscas, Olivers, and Munsters.[110]—

---

106. Cf. Eccles. 1:2.

107. "Swirling about in the vast abyss." Virgil, *Aeneid*, i.118.

108. "One who by *delaying* would restore the state." Virgil, *Aeneid*, vi.846.

109. "Here they will become men!" Juvenal, *Satires*, ii.167. It is crucial to note the satirical tone of this quotation. Juvenal is mocking the claim that bringing boys from conquered countries to Rome will facilitate their development as soldiers and statesmen, suggesting instead that degenerate Roman culture leads to their debauchery. Charles is implying that those who claim the superiority of avoiding ordinances are similarly creating something other than spiritual maturity.

110. Charles lists three religiously motivated revolutionaries that he clearly considers to

O that I may be a false prophet and disappointed of Luther's Anabaptists.[111] I told them plainly **I should only continue with them so long as they continued in the Church of England.**[112] My every word was grievous to them. I am a thorn in their sides, and they cannot bear me.

They *modestly* denied that we had any but hearsay proof of their denying the ordinances. I asked them all and every one, particularly Bray, Bell, etc., whether they would now acknowledge them to be commands or duties; whether they sinned in omitting them; whether they did not leave it to every man's fancy to use them or not; whether they did not exclude all from the Lord's table, excepting those whom *they* called believers. These questions I put too close to be evaded, though better dodgers never came out of the school of Loyola. Honest Bell and some others spoke out, and insisted upon their antichristian liberty. The rest put by their stillness, and delivered me over to Satan for a blasphemer, a very Saul (for to him they compare me) out of blind zeal persecuting the church of Christ.[113]

Thursday, June 12. The power of the Lord was present in his word, both to wound and heal. The adversary roared in the midst of the congregation; for to him, and not to the God of order, do I impute those horrible outcries which almost drowned my voice and kept back the glad tidings from sinners.

Friday, June 13. At Wapping some so disturbed us by their outcries that my preaching was vain. Those who cried "Away with them," I rebuked, but wish for the sake of all, and myself also, that, if it be the will of God, this stumbling block may be removed.

At the time of intercession we were carried out for all mankind, especially for our own Church and nation, and the little flock which God is gathering. I prayed believing that Satan might not destroy his work, as in the last age, by that spirit of rebellion and enthusiasm which is so visible in our deluded brethren.

---

have been misguided: John Zisca (d. 1424), who led a Hussite rebellion in Bohemia; Oliver Cromwell (1599–1658), leader of the Puritan forces in England; and (confusing the spelling) Thomas Müntzer (1489–1525), who led the peasants' rebellion in Germany. As an alternative, the third reference may be to the revolt in Münster in 1533.

111. The preceding two sentences are omitted in Jackson.

112. These words are printed by Charles in block letters, rather than in longhand, with a clear intention of emphasis.

113. Cf. Acts 22:4, etc.

Monday, June 16. Mrs Sparrow carried me to Eltham, where I called to many, in King John's chapel,[114] "Ho, every one that thirsteth, come ye to the waters" [Isa. 55:1]. It was indeed a solemn assembly. We found God had formerly recorded his name there, and that was one place of meeting Him. Several of the assembly-ladies heard me patiently while I showed them they were in no wise better than the harlots and publicans.

Tuesday, June 17. Had an extraordinary meeting of the Society, now increased from twelve to three hundred, most of them justi-fied, and took my leave of them with hearty prayer.

Wednesday, June 18. Set out at two for Oxford, with brother Maxfield, and an nephew[115] I was going to prentice at Bristol. We stopped half-an-hour at brother Hodges's. Lost our way through Kensington. Baited[116] an hour at Gerrard's Cross. Three miles short of Wycombe, several people met and asked us if we had seen an highwayman, who had shot a man on the road not an hour ago. In a mile's riding, we found the poor man weltering in his blood. The minister of Wycombe informed us that he was a little behind, and heard the highwayman threaten to shoot him if he did not deliver his money that instant. He answered, "You shall have all the money I have, but it is not much," and the other, without any more words, shot him through the head.

I could not but observe the particular providence of God over us. Had we not delayed in the morning, had we not called on Hodges, had we not stopped at Gerard's Cross, we had just met the murderer.

Thursday, June 19. Hearing he was apprehended at a farrier's, his horse having cast a shoe, I went this morning to tell him Christ died to save murderers. But his heart was harder than the nether millstone.

By noon we came to Oxford. Called on Mrs Ford and found her shut up. She besought me *not to speak* in the Society, not to make disturbances and divisions, etc. I told her, I spoke no other words than I had from the beginning, whence then her unusual apprehen-sions? Mr Simpson's presence accounted for it. Wherever he comes,

---

114. The chapel in Eltham Palace.
115. John Lambert, the son of Charles's sister Anne and her husband, John. He was apprenticed to Felix Farley, the printer, in Bristol (cf. Charles's letter of June 28, 1740, to John Wesley; *Works* 26:17).
116. *OED:* (of travelers) "to stop at an inn for food."

his first business is to supplant us, which he does by insinuating himself, under the appearance of our friend.

To the Society I described the stillness of the first Christians (Acts 2:42), who continued *in* the Apostles' doctrine, and *in* fellowship, and *in* breaking of bread, and *in* prayers.

Friday, June 20. At the desire of some Baptists in Malmesbury I expounded Rom. 7, but not at all to their satisfaction. They could not see any higher state of perfection than what is there described.

Saturday, June 21. Such an unaccountable heaviness came over me on the road that I was forced to light and lied down for a quarter of an hour. I rose refreshed with this little sleep, and rode forward till we met a poor old man of eighty; was enabled to preach the gospel to his heart. We left him looking up to Jesus, and went on praising God.

My first greeting in Kingswood was by one of our colliers' daughters. I then rejoiced with William Hooper and Hannah Cennick. In the evening at the Malt-room[117] I addressed myself to those in the wilderness. O what simplicity is this childlike people! A spirit of contrition and love ran through them. Here the seed has fallen upon good ground.

Sunday, June 22. Went to learn Christ among our colliers, and drank into their spirit. We rejoiced for this consolation. O that our London brethren would come to school to Kingswood! These *are* what they *pretend* to be. God knows their poverty, but they are rich,[118] and daily entering into rest,[119] without being first brought into confusion. They do not hold it necessary to deny the weak faith in order to get the strong. Their soul truly waiteth still upon God, in the way of his ordinances. Ye many masters, come learn Christ of these outcasts; for know, except ye be converted, and become like these little children, ye cannot enter into the kingdom of heaven.[120]

Met several of those whom I had baptized, and found them grown in grace. Some thousands waited for me at Rose Green, to whom I expounded Ezekiel 16. And surely the Lord passed by, and said to some in their blood, "Live" [16:6]. Concluded the day at the

---

117. This was a large room near Weavers' Hall that the Wesleys used for meetings when they could not meet in the latter. Charles also calls it the "Malt-house."
118. Cf. 2 Cor. 8:9.
119. Cf. Heb. 4:1.
120. Cf. Matt. 18:3.

men's Love-feast. Peace, unity, and love are here. We did not forget our poor distracted brethren (that were, till the Moravians came).

How ought I to rejoice at my deliverance out of their hands and spirit! My soul is escaped as a bird out of the snare of the fowler. *Abii, erupi, evasi.*[121] And did I not love the lambs of Christ, indeed, the grievous wolves, I would see your face no more.

I am no longer a debtor of the gospel to *you*. Me ye have fairly discharged. But if you reject my testimony, others receive it gladly and say, "Blessed be he that cometh in the name of the Lord" [Matt. 21:9].

Tuesday, June 24. Preached Christ, the Way, the Truth, and the Life [John 14:6], to one thousand little children at Kingswood. At the Room I proceeded in St John. Some were present who fancy themselves elect, and therefore sink back into their old tempers. Without meddling in the dispute, I rebuked them sharply, yet in much love.

Read my journal to the bands, as an antidote to stillness.

Thursday, June 26. Saw Mrs Turner under the buffetings of Satan, to whom she is plainly delivered over, for her pride and envy. O that she may learn hence not to blaspheme, or mimic the Spirit of God with her imaginary experiences!

In my farther exposition of Ezekiel 16, the secrets of many hearts were revealed. When some cried out, I bade the people be quiet, that Satan might lose his end. Those noisy souls I believed sincere, but he tormented them to make them confound the work and hinder the word of God. Immediately, as if his device was discovered, the enemy withdrew and the outcries ceased.

Saturday, June 28. Met the bands in Kingswood, and reproved Hannah Barrow before them all. She would not be convinced of her pride, but was *sure* she had the witness of the Spirit, and the seal, and what not. I tremble to think what will be the end.

Sunday, June 29. Found the spirit of the colliers before I began to speak. Then my mouth was opened to declare the promise of sanctification, Ezekiel [36:24-30]. Gave the Sacrament to about eighty colliers, exhorted the last-baptized, met the men-Leaders, preached to the usual congregation at Rose Green, and returned without strength to the Horsefair.

---

121. Cf. Cicero, *In L. Catilinum Oratio* ii.1.1: "*Abiit, excessit, evasit, erupit*" ("He has left, absconded, escaped, disappeared"). Charles is rendering in first person, and forgets *excessit*.

When I am weak, then I am strong; and was never more enlarged, nor I think so much, as in speaking from that Scripture: "Holding forth the word of life, that I may rejoice in the day of Christ, that I have not run in vain, neither laboured in vain" [Phil. 2:16]. Many in that hour found heaven begun upon earth.

Monday, June 30. Spent a week at Oxford to little purpose but that of obedience to man for the Lord's sake. In the Hall I read my two lectures on Psalm 130, preaching repentance towards God and faith in Jesus Christ. But learned Gallio cared for none of these things.[122]

Yet even in this place God did not leave himself without witnesses. He *began* to call them forth, but where are they now? All scattered by those refiners on Christianity who make the cross of none effect,[123] and forbid men to remember God in *his* ways. Therefore, when I came in the name of the Lord Jesus, there was no man. When I called them to Him, there was none to answer, or at most a score, out of the multitude which Mr Viney found.

JULY 1740

Sunday, July 6. Preached at Stanton Harcourt in the morning, at South Leigh in the afternoon, then expounded Blind Bartimeus [Mark 10:46-52] at Mr Gambold's. The next evening I discoursed on the Good Samaritan [Luke 10:29-37].

Tuesday, July 8. Came to Malmesbury with Mr Robson, and the next day to Bristol. Met the Lord among the people. Brother Robson said, "It is good for me to be here"[124] and that the half had not been told him[125] of God's goodness to this little flock.

Friday, July 11. This morning he preached on Lazarus raised, with the demonstration of the Spirit. I carried him to Kingswood. He was in love with our colliers.

---

122. Cf. Acts 18:17. These lectures would have been part of the process toward the B.D. degree (cf. the November 2, 1739, entry above). Both Charles and John soon abandoned their pursuit of this degree.
123. Cf. 1 Cor. 1:17.
124. Cf. Matt. 17:4.
125. Cf. 1 Kings 10:7.

Saturday, July 12. Passed the afternoon with them. They grow in grace, and in the knowledge of our Lord Jesus Christ. We cannot be among them, and not perceive the divine presence.

Sunday, July 13. Gave the Sacrament to above seventy of them, different from those who received the last time. Preached at Rose Green on the fall of man, Gen. 3. I dare not depart from the work, while God so strengthens me therein. We walked over the waste to the school, singing and rejoicing. It was their Love-feast. Two hundred were assembled in the Spirit of Jesus. Never have I seen and *felt* such a congregation of faithful souls! I question whether Hernnhuth can now afford the like.

Tuesday, July 15. To the colliers I described what many of them have experienced, religion, a participation of the divine nature [2 Pet. 1:4]. At Bristol I pressed the example of the primitive Christian, Acts 2, and tasted something of their spirit.

Wednesday, July 16. I was convincing the natural man of sin, when a poor sinner cried out vehemently, "What do you mean by looking at *me,* and directing yourself to *me,* and telling *me* I shall be damned?" I did then address myself to him, but he hurried away with the utmost precipitation.

At the time of intercession the Spirit greatly helped our infirmities. We began with particulars, but at last were enlarged in prayer for all mankind.

Dissuaded one who was strongly tempted to leave the fellowship. The devil knows what he does: *Divide et impera,*[126] will carry the world before him.

While I was meeting the bands, my mouth was opened to rebuke, reprove, exhort, in words not my own. All trembled before the presence of God. I was forced to cut off a rotten member. But I felt such love and pity at the time, as humbled me into the dust. It was as if one criminal was made to execute another. We betook ourselves to fervent prayer for him, and the Society. The Spirit was poured out, and we returned unto the Lord in weeping, and mourning, and praying.

Thursday, July 17. We have had put up dismal, sick notes as the following: "A person declares before the congregation that while the minister was appealing to God for the truth of universal redemption

---

126. "Divide and rule."

and desiring a token thereof on some sort present, the Spirit of the Lord did then bear witness with his spirit that the doctrine there delivered was the truth of God, and she would have staked her eternal salvation thereupon."[127]

Admitted near thirty new members into the Society.

Sunday, July 20. Our poor colliers being repelled from the Lord's table by most of the Bristol ministers, I exhorted them, notwithstanding, to continue daily with one accord in the Temple, where the wickedest administrator can neither spoil the prayers nor poison the Sacrament. *These* poor sinners *have* ears to hear.

Wednesday, July 23. Talked with Mrs Turner, who justifies God, and the wisdom of his children, taking shame to herself, and confessing that spiritual pride was the sole occasion of her fall.

In the bands I reproved one who was fallen asleep again, and yet horribly confident she was in a good way, and should go to heaven if she died that moment. I tried the weapons of our warfare upon her strong-holds, and pulled them down, to the conviction of all but herself. At last she raged and tore like a mad woman—this child of God, with her full assurance of faith! I showed the rest, through her, the deceitfulness of the heart, and the blinding power of Satan.

Thursday, July 24. I went to see her, lest Satan should get irrecoverable advantage over her. She was more moderate, but still in the false assurance of unbelief, in the spirit of self-delusion. What an exertion of omnipotence does such a soul require to reawaken it!

Friday, July 25. Began examining each member of the Society. One came crying out, "I am born of God. I have the indwelling Spirit. I have a new heart," and she could give no account of her faith, no proof of her pretensions; only she was sure of it and all the world should not persuade her to the contrary. I fear nothing less than her falling into gross sin will be sufficient to open her eyes.

How exceeding cautious ought we to be in receiving people's testimony of themselves. "*Nil admirari*"[128] should be our rule, and not to take much notice of such as think themselves justified, till self be brought into subjection and they have seen their hearts, which lie hid under that first joy.

---

127. This paragraph is not included in Jackson.
128. "Marvel at nothing." Horace, *Epistles*, I.vi.1.

Spake with another who much wants to be *unsettled* from her ties. I plainly see why almost all lose their first comfort. It is expedient for them that it go away. Till nature is quite dead, it will feed upon the gift, instead of the giver; the grace which is in itself, instead of that which is in Christ Jesus.[129]

At night I took occasion, from Acts 7, to discourse on the sin of resisting the Holy Ghost. He sent the word home to many souls.

Sunday, July 27. Heard a miserable sermon at Temple church, recommending religion as the most likely way to raise a fortune. After it, proclamation was made "that all should depart who were not of the parish." While the shepherd was driving away the lambs, I stayed, suspecting nothing, till the clerk came to me and said, "Mr Beacher[130] bids you go away, for he will not give you the Sacrament." I went to the vestry door and mildly desired Mr Beacher to admit me. He asked, "Are you of this parish?" I answered, "Sir, you *see* I am a clergyman." Dropping his first pretence, he charged me with rebellion in expounding the Scriptures without authority, and said in express words, "I repel you from the Sacrament." I replied, "I cite you to answer this before Jesus Christ at the day of judgment." This enraged him above measure. He called out, *"Here, take away this man!"* The constables were ordered to attend (I suppose, lest the furious colliers should take the Sacrament by force), but I saved them the trouble of taking away this man, and quietly retired.

I preached the gospel in Kingswood with double power, from Isaiah 40[:1], "Comfort ye, comfort ye my people, saith your God." Before sermon I declared our brother Cennick's entire agreement with me in the belief of universal redemption, and he confirmed my saying with an hymn of his own. Never did I find my spirit more knit to him.

At Rose Green, though my bodily strength was gone, I was carried out beyond myself in speaking of God's free grace to sinners.

Monday, July 28. Spoke searchingly on those words of our Lord: "Nevertheless, I tell you the truth; it is expedient for you that I go away. For if I go not away, the Comforter will not come," etc. [John 16:7].

---

129. With the exception of the following two sentences, the entire entry for July 25 is crossed through in the MS Journal, and omitted by Jackson.

130. Rev. Henry Beacher was rector of Temple church, Bristol.

Tuesday, July 29. One, pestered with the predestinarians, desired me to expound Rom. 9. I did, through Christ strengthening me, in an extraordinary manner. The poor creature [Jonathan] Wildboar contradicted and blasphemed, and even *called for damnation upon his own soul, if Christ died for all, and if God was willing that all men should be saved.* The power of the Lord was present so much the more. Many believed with their heart, and made confession with their mouth, of Jesus Christ the Saviour of all men.[131] I have not known a more triumphant night since I knew Bristol.

AUGUST 1740

Sunday, August 3. Preached Jesus Christ to the colliers from Isaiah 63[:1], "Who is this that cometh from Edom, with dyed garments from Bosrah?" Great power was in the midst. Many wept. I myself was much affected. At Rose Green my text was, "Drop down, ye heavens, from above, and let the skies pour down righteousness" [Isa. 45:8]. It rained hard, but that did not interrupt their attention. I was comforted at the women's Love-feast.

Tuesday, August 5. I talked sharply to Jenny Deschamps, a girl of twelve years old, who now confessed that her fits and cryings out (above thirty of them) were all feigned, that Mr Wesley might take notice of her.

Wednesday, August 6. In great heaviness I spoke to the women-bands, as taking my farewell. Sang the hymn which begins—

> While sickness shakes the house of clay,
>   And, sapp'd by pain's continued course,
> My nature hastens to decay,
>   And waits the fever's friendly force.[132]

After speaking a few faint words to the brethren, I was immediately taken with a shivering; and then the fever came.

The next morning I was bled and carried by Mrs [Elizabeth] Hooper to her house. There I looked into the Bible, and met with, "The Lord will strengthen him upon the bed of languishing, thou

---

131. Cf. Rom. 10:9.
132. "Written in Sickness," st. 1, HSP (1740), 47 (*Poetical Works*, 1:242).

wilt make all his bed in his sickness" [Ps. 41:3]. My pain and disease increased for ten days, so that there was no hope of my life. But then Jesus touched my hand, and rebuked the fever, and it left me. I had no apprehension of death myself. It was reported I was dead, and published in the papers. But God had not finished (O that he had effectually begun) his work in me. Therefore, he held my soul in life and made all things work together for my recovery.

Dr Middleton,[133] an utter stranger to me, God raised up, and sent to my assistance. He refused taking any fees, and told the apothecary he would pay for my physic, if I could not. He attended me constantly, as the divine blessing did his prescriptions, so that in less than a fortnight the danger was over.

For the next fortnight I recovered slowly, but had little use of my legs, and none of my head. One of our colliers, taken ill of the same fever since me, has died in full triumph of faith.

When I was just able to stand, my brother came from London. We rode out most days in Mr Wane's, or an hired, chariot, comparing our dangers, temptations, and deliverances.

I found myself, after this gracious visitation, more desirous and able to pray, more afraid of sin, more earnestly longing for deliverance and the fullness of Christian salvation.

SEPTEMBER 1740

Sunday, September 7. As soon as my bodily weakness would permit, I returned to my old hours of retirement; but with fear, and earnest prayer that I might not rest in my own works or endeavours.

Mr Cary's curate informed us that Mr Cary had ordered him to repel my brother and me from the Sacrament.

Wednesday, September 10. It rained all day, but cleared up when I went to the bands. A few words I spoke in great weakness; and they seemed not spoken in vain.

Monday, September 15. Passed two or three days at Mr Arthur's in Kingswood, and, by the blessing of God, recovered the use of my understanding, which was so clouded, that I could neither read nor think.

---

133. Dr. John Middleton (d. 1760) became a close friend and physician for Charles. The poem that Charles composed at his death can be found in *Poetical Works*, 6:300–306.

Thursday, September 18. Out of weakness I was made strong to preach at the Room tonight, not for a quarter of an hour, as I proposed, but for an hour and an half.

Friday, September 19. "They that wait upon the Lord shall renew their strength" [Isa. 40:31]. So I found it this morning, both in soul and body. At night I was enabled to preach Anne Hodges's funeral sermon.

Monday, September 22. I was setting out for the Downs,[134] when one asked me to ride out toward Mr [Thomas] Willis's. At the end of the town I was informed the colliers were risen. Above one thousand of them I met at Lawrence Hill. They came about me, and saluted me very affectionately, not having seen my sickness. The occasion of their rising, they told me, was the dearness of corn. I got [up on] an eminence, and began speaking to them. Many seemed inclined to go back with me to the school, but the devil stirred up his oldest servants, who violently rushed upon the others, beating, and tearing, and driving them away from me. I rode up to a ruffian who was striking one of our colliers, and prayed him rather to strike me. He would not, he said, for all the world, and was quite overcome. I turned upon one who struck my horse, and he also sank into a lamb. Wherever I turned, Satan lost ground, so that he was obliged to make one general assault, and—by the few violent colliers—forced on the quiet ones into the town.

I seized on one of the tallest, and earnestly besought him to follow me. That he would, he said, all the world over. About six more I pressed into Christ's service. We met several parties, stopped and exhorted them to join us. We gleaned a few from every company, and grew as we marched along singing to the school. From one till three we spent in prayer that evil might be prevented, and the lion chained. Then news was brought us that the colliers were returned in peace. They had quietly walked into the city without sticks or the least violence. A few of the bitter sort went to the mayor, and told their grievance. Then they all returned as they came, without noise or disturbance. All who saw were amazed, for the leopards were laid down.[135] Nothing could have more shown the change wrought in them than this rising.

---

134. A flat limestone area on the northeast outskirts of Bristol.
135. Cf. Isa. 11:6.

I found afterwards that all our colliers to a man had been forced into it. Having learned of Christ not to resist evil, they went a mile with those that compelled them rather than free themselves by violence.[136] One the rioters dragged out [of] his sick-bed, and threw him into the Fishponds. Near twenty of Mr Willis's men they got by threatening to fill up their pits, and bury them alive, if they did not come up and bear them company.

Tuesday, September 23. Mr William Seward came, and was very cordial. We prayed, rejoiced, and gave thanks. If I did not love him the better for his opinion, I am sure it made me more industrious to confirm my old love towards him.

I carried him to Mr Wane's, and then to our colliers, before whom I set the things they would have done in the late rising, had not grace restrained them. One poor man declared, when they forced him away, he would much more willingly have gone to the gallows.

Mr Seward spoke a few words to them, which did not convince me of his call to preach. In our return he told me Mrs Grevil and others had urged him to claim the Room in the Horsefair, but he abhorred their baseness.

Wednesday, September 24. He told me he was in a mist, the Baptists last night having laboured hard to make him oppose me publicly. Before we parted all was set right again.

Yet a few hours after, he came from them and utterly renounced both me and my brother, in bitter words of hatred which they had put in his mouth. I pray God lay not this sin to their charge, neither all the weakness of word and action when ensued for the following days.

God endues my soul and body also with much strength. This day he has comforted me on every side. To Him be all the glory.

Friday, September 26. Was greatly assisted in the evening to preach the Christian perfection—that is, utter dominion over sin; constant peace, and love, and joy in the Holy Ghost; the full assurance of faith, righteousness, and true holiness. I see more and more into the height of our privileges, and that God will give them to me.

Sunday, September 28. At the Sacrament I received power to believe sin shall not have dominion over me. Reached many hearts in expounding Blind Bartimeus [Mark 10:46-52].

---

136. Cf. Matt. 5:41.

Our Love-feast was such as deserved the name. We all rejoiced in hope of the glory of God.

Monday, September 29. God was wonderfully with our assembly, and opened my eyes to see the promise of holiness or perfection, not in some, but in almost every Scripture.

OCTOBER 1740

Thursday, October 2. Rejoiced to hear that Mrs Purnell was on Sunday morning, under the word, taken into the very borders of Canaan. The patient abiding of the meek shall not perish for ever.

Sunday, October 5. Offered myself at the Sacrament, and was not refused, though Mr Cary himself administered. I received it with comfort.

Monday, October 6. Prayed by Margaret Thomas. At my first visit, she *hoped* her sins were forgiven. Now she more than hoped it, having received the faith which works by love,[137] and filial fear of offending.

Met the leaders and endeavoured to humble one who begins to grow rich, not by denying what God has done for his soul, but by showing him he could no more trust to his graces than his works, but must still come to Christ as a poor sinner that has need of all things.

Wednesday, October 8. Took down the case of Catherine Hyfield. She was charged with robbing her master (one Townsend) of £300, whose dying wife my brother had visited. Alderman Day, etc., threatened to put her in irons, etc., if she would not confess she had given the money to my brother. When no proof could be brought against her, they were forced to discharge her; and soon after, her master found the money where [he] himself had lodged it.

Thursday, October 9. Was much revived by the sight of Margaret Thomas, dying in the highest triumph of faith. I could not help asking,

> Is this the soul so late weigh'd down
> By cares and sins, by griefs and pains?
> Whither are all thy terrors gone?
> Jesus for thee the victory gains,

---

137. Cf. Gal. 5:6.

And death, and sin, and Satan yield
To faith's unconquerable shield.[138]

Her hope was now full of immortality. She had no desire of life or death, or ease in her great pain. God had finished his work, and her will was quite swallowed up in his. This is that holiness without which no one shall see the Lord.

Friday, October 10. Prayed by Mrs Purnell, who patiently waits for the seal of her pardon. At night I spoke strongly to the unawakened; and, behold a cry! But such as became poor lost sinners. Great was the stirring among the dry bones.[139]

Sunday, October 12. From Isaiah 54 I was assisted to stir up those who had settled upon their lees since they were justified. I visited Margaret, now at the haven where she would be, and only waiting the word, "Come up hither!"[140] Her spirit helped me wonderfully in prayer. She told me she had been heard in my behalf, and God would give me an humble heart.

Monday, October 13. Breakfasted and gave an exhortation to some of our friends. One *seemed* so deeply affected that her outcries much interrupted me. I took no notice of her, seeing she *could not help it*, only said at last, "I do not think the better of you for this," and immediately her trouble was over, and she hushed, and unconcerned as before.

Wednesday, October 15. At the intercession, our casting down was in the midst of us. O that I was always as I am sometimes! But a fit or start of humility is not to be depended on.

Thursday, October 16. Rejoiced in an opportunity of heaping coals of fire upon the head of an enemy.[141] Poor Mitchel, arrested by Charles Martin, sent me first a reproaching, and then a begging, letter. I paid his debt, and won him a very moderate price.

---

138. "Congratulations to a Friend, Upon Believing in Christ," st. 12, *HSP* (1739), 206 (*Poetical Works*, 1:182). It has been suggested that Charles wrote this thirteen-stanza poem to his brother John on the occasion of his "finding peace."
139. Cf. Ezek. 37:1-14.
140. Cf. Rev. 4:1.
141. Cf. Rom. 12:20; Prov. 25:22.

Friday, October 17. I prayed by Mrs Purnell, near death. She had no fear and no assurance of pardon, but believed she should know her sins forgiven before she went hence. I called again at noon, and then the Lord had showed her his salvation, and she could confidently testify, "God for Christ's sake hath forgiven me."

Sunday, October 19. Called on a dying man, who told me he hoped to be saved through Christ, because he was none of the worst of sinners. "If that be your plea," said I, "you must be damned without all remedy." Proceeded to set before him the spirituality of the law, and the terrors of the Lord. He fought hard against God, often repeating the words of his predecessor, "I am not like other men" [Luke 18:11], reproaching my Master, not me, and refusing to humble himself under the mighty hand of God. He told me he never desired to see me more. Yet when I offered to go, he desired me to pray by him. I did, in faith, that God might open his eyes to see himself the chief of sinners. He begged me to call again.

Gave the Sacrament to Mrs Purnell, who, after receiving the cup, cried, "It is finished!" [John 19:30]. Visited her once more in her last conflict—yet, even then, by plain signs expressing her confidence. She held out till Wednesday morning, October 22, and then departed to the church triumphant.

Met the leaders, and removed one (Jenny Worlock), who was much lifted up, but lay concealed from herself by a voluntary humility. She cheerfully resigned an office which she owned herself so unfit for; yet, afterwards, I heard, complained, with many tears, that I should think ill of her from the report of others. The next day she was taken with a fit of humility, and bade a sister go and tell it me. "Anybody now," she said, "might trample upon me. Do you, pray trample upon me. But tell Mr Wesley." Verily, "the heart is deceitful above all things. Who can know it?" [Jer. 17:9].

Thursday, October 23. Met several of the bands at the house of our departed sister Purnell, and solemnly rejoiced over her, with singing. Walked with the funeral as far as the church, then hastened back to the Room, where lay the corpse of Margaret. Her spirit was, with the other's, returned to God. A wonderful power accompanied the word preached, 1 Cor. 15. O what triumph did we find in the house of mourning! Many strangers were convinced.

The Society attended her to the grave, and praised God with joyful lips for her translation.

Friday, October 24. Was greatly enlarged in enforcing that promise, "The Lord knoweth how to deliver [the godly] out of temptation" [2 Pet. 2:9]. Showed them the only infallible way to conquer sin, namely, "Sin shall not have dominion over me, because I believe in Jesus Christ that it shall not." A poor drunkard believed, and had a witness that he shall no more turn back to his own wickedness.

Sunday, October 26. Heard Mr Tucker's[142] (not railing) accusation against the Methodists, "that they went contrary to custom, did not catechise their children, did not reform men in the regular way." He told us farther what Mr Whitefield would say when he returned from Georgia, and concluded with an excellent quotation out of Mr Law. I offered my assistance at the Sacrament, which he civilly declined.

Monday, October 27. Met a young gentlewoman who was never under the word till the night of our triumphant funeral. Then it laid hold on her heart. Yet I could not persuade her to expect the promise till she had endeavoured, and mourned, and waited *longer.*

In the evening I set the terrors of the Lord in array against sinners, and an horrible dread overwhelmed some of them. May the law be their schoolmaster to bring them to Christ.[143]

Tuesday, October 28. Was exceedingly shocked with the news of Mr [William] Seward's death, but he is taken from the evil, rescued out of the hands of wicked men.

Calling on the pharisee whom I had visited last week. I found him dead, but at the last hour he had cried unto Jesus as a poor, undone sinner, who *was* like other men.[144]

Led in the evening to preach universal redemption from those words, "The Lord is not willing that any should perish, but that all should come to repentance" [2 Pet. 3:9]. The Spirit mightily confirmed that irresistible truth. I then spoke with unfeigned concern of our dear departed brother, and with just abhorrence of those unhappy bigots whose headlong zeal had robbed us of him. We sang

---

142. Josiah Tucker (1712–1799), rector of All Saints church, Bristol.
143. Cf. Gal. 3:24.
144. Cf. Luke 18:11.

a funeral hymn over him, and were comforted in the hope of soon meeting him again, where no sower of tares,[145] no reprobating pharisee, shall ever part us more.

Friday, October 31. The time for my going to Wales is now come. Today Captain Philips challenged me—said he came to fetch me, and Mr [Nathaniel] Wells invited me to preach in his churches.

Passed an hour with two very wise Quakers, who were for inverting the order of God, and making Christ our sanctification before he is our righteousness. The true Light, I trust, will one day teach them better.

NOVEMBER 1740

Tuesday, November 4. At Kingswood Mr Cennick showed me a letter from Howell Harris, wherein he justified poor Mr Seward, and talked of declaring against us himself. With the loss of him and all things, I am commanded to preach the gospel to every creature. I did so to the colliers, from Titus 2:11, and was carried out more than ever before, till all were drowned in tears of love. While I was testifying Christ died for all, Mr Cennick, in the hearing of many, gave me the lie. I calmly told him afterwards, "If I speak not the truth as it is in Jesus, may I decrease, and you increase."[146]

Thursday, November 6. At six took boat for Cardiff, and at six in the evening landed on Welsh ground with the voice of praise and thanksgiving. Mr Wells, who invited me over, waited to give me the first greeting. From his house we went to the Society, where God opened my mouth to call, "Ho, every one that thirsteth, come ye to the waters" [Isa. 55:1]. They received the word with all readiness. I lodged at Mr [Thomas] Glascott's.

Friday, November 7. Rode with Mr Williams[147] to St Andrews,[148] a little town four Welsh miles from Cardiff. Mr Wells was not afraid

---

145. Cf. Matt. 13:25.
146. Cf. John 3:30.
147. This is likely Thomas Williams (c. 1697–1783), a prominent farmer from Llanishen (where Charles would preach five days later), who became a Methodist exhorter. John Wesley stayed with Williams on his trip to Wales the following year, October 1, 1741 (cf. *Works* 19:222).
148. St Andrews Major, Glamorgan.

to trust me in his pulpit. I was greatly assisted to invite many poor sinners to come weary and heavy laden to Christ [Matt. 11:28]. They gladly received my saying. Mr [John] Hodges desired me to preach next Tuesday in his church in Wenvoe.[149] Returned to Cardiff rejoicing; and expounded 1 John 1, to the conviction, I hope, of many.

Saturday, November 8. Had an opportunity to moderate the spirits of some who were greatly exasperated against Howell Harris for preaching predestination among them.

After church I waited with Mr Wells on the sick minister; who was extremely civil, invited me to dinner, and to preach in his pulpit morning and evening.

Spent the day in singing and close conference with some who would fain persuade themselves they had faith, without forgiveness. My Master, I trust, will soon persuade them that they have both together.

Sunday, November 9. At six I explained the legal state, from Rom. 7. Read prayers, and preached to a large congregation, "All have sinned and come short of the glory of God" [Rom. 3:23]. Administered the Sacrament to many strangers. Read prayers in the afternoon, baptized a child, and preached both law and gospel with great plainness. My hearers were surprisingly patient. Only one went out. I continued my discourse till it was dark, and had much comfort in having delivered my message.

The Scripture to be expounded at night was, 1 John 2[:1], "If any man sin, we have an advocate with the Father," etc. God opened my mouth to declare the truth of his everlasting love to all mankind. At the same time he enlarged my heart to its opposers. I took the occasion to speak of Howell Harris. Bore such a testimony of him as he deserves, and mildly upbraided them for their ingratitude toward the greatest benefactor their country ever had. We all expressed our love by joining in hearty prayer for him.

Monday, November 10. Set out for St Nicholas. Called at Llandaff on the then officiating minister, to ask the pulpit. He referred me to the chapter, but I do not mean to trouble them. The church at St Nicholas also was shut against me, but we met at a neighbouring

---

149. Charles spells "Wenvo."

285

Mr Deer's, where I offered Christ to all sinners, with much freedom and power.

At Cardiff spoke a word in season to one (Susan Young) who was puffed up, and boasted of her graces, and took upon her to teach others. I told her she had deceived her own soul and brought a scandal of religion. She flew out into self-justification: God knew her heart, would not quench the smoking flax, etc. But I cut her short and with six plain words, God accompanying them with his power, struck her down into the deep. She cried out, "I am damned, I am damned," and was stripped of all, as in one moment.

Sent a messenger to Howell Harris, with the following letter:

> My dearest friend and brother,
>   In the name of Jesus Christ I beseech you, if you have his glory and the good of souls at heart, come immediately, and meet me here. I trust we shall never be two in time or eternity. O my brother, I am grieved that Satan should get a moment's advantage over us, and am ready to lay my neck under your feet for Christ's sake. If your heart is as my heart, hasten, in the name of our dear Lord, to your second self.
>
> C. W.

Tuesday, November 11. The church at Wenvoe was full as it could hold, while I preached the gospel from the Good Samaritan [Luke 10:29-37]. All were visibly affected. Went to Mr Hodges. Took sweet counsel with him and Mr Wells. The former, at parting, in great simplicity desired my prayers and a kiss.

Wednesday, November 12. In Llanishen[150] church preached on "Repent, and believe the gospel" [Mark 1:15]. Our Lord was never more with me than at this time. I concluded with earnest prayer for the curate.

Dined at Mr Well's with several of the brethren, and Mr [Philip] Thomas, a neighbouring curate of great simplicity, who preaches not himself, but Christ Jesus the Lord.

Thursday, November 13. Went with reluctance to the prisoners, almost despairing to do any good, when I received faith to believe Christ would be with me. I looked up to him, and never preached

---

150. Charles spells "Lanissan."

the gospel with greater freedom. Two women fell down as dead. The infection ran through us all, and we felt that the gospel was indeed the power of God.

The three ministers, Mr Wells, Hodges, and Thomas, made part of my evening congregation, to whom I showed in strong words the blessedness of persecution.

Friday, November 14. Rode with Mr Wells, Hodges, to Michaelston le-pit.[151] He read prayers. I preached Christ from, "Who is this that cometh from Edom with dyed garments?" etc. [Isa. 63:1]. He was evidently set forth before our eyes as crucified.[152] Rode back in the spirit of triumph. Heard the players had sent me a challenge—that is, a ticket and invitation to their play. Suffice for the time past. I now serve another Master.

Saturday, November 15. At Mr [Thomas] Price's, in Watford, preached "Christ our wisdom, righteousness, sanctification, and redemption" [1 Cor. 1:30]; and again at five with double power. An Arian minister of our own Church, and a Baptist teacher, were present. The latter could not allow either justification or sanctification necessary to salvation.

Sunday, November 16. Mr Williams informed me that many had bound themselves with a curse to make a disturbance in the church, and not suffer me to preach. Then the clerk told me I was not to preach in the afternoon. I answered, "I had not expected to preach there in the morning, or indeed, a second time."

The psalms began, "O God, the heathen are come into thine inheritance. Thy holy temple have they defiled" [Ps. 79:1]. The second lesson was very animating, being John 8, that earnest contention of our Lord with the Pharisees.

My text was, "If God be for us, who can be against us?" [Rom. 8:31-32]. I began abruptly with the opposers, and defied them in the name of the Lord Jesus. The Spirit of power was with me. But I soon perceived him as the Spirit of love, and besought those unhappy sinners to be reconciled unto God. Their master durst not hazard their staying any longer but, in the midst of my discourse, hurried them out of church.

---

151. Charles spells "Michelston-Lepit."
152. Cf. Gal. 3:1.

I went on convincing and entreating the Pharisees to submit to the righteousness of God. Never was my mouth and heart more enlarged. Upon my repeating, "It pleased God by the foolishness of preaching to save all them that believe" [1 Cor. 1:21], a gentleman rose, and turned his back on the gospel of salvation. I called after him in vain, then earnestly prayed for him and the rest, the Spirit helping my infirmity.

Read prayers in the afternoon. Many hungry souls were disappointed through my not preaching. I sent them to the Society. Several players were present, but quickly fled before the sword of the Spirit.[153] When were departing, Mr Wells stopped us to hear his unexpected apology for me. He strongly enforced the truths I had delivered and, with great humility, asked me to set him right, if had spoken aught contrary to sound doctrine.

Monday, November 17. Again my mouth was opened to preach the law and the gospel[154] at Llantrisant.[155] Mr [Richard] Harris, the minister, was exceeding civil. He had been dealt with to refuse me the pulpit, but would not break his word.

Tuesday, November 18. Preached at St Bride's,[156] "Thou shalt call his name Jesus," etc. [Matt. 1:21]. Here, too, I cast my net to catch the fisher. We were setting out from the public-house when God brought Howell Harris to us. All misunderstandings vanished at sight of each other, and our hearts were knit together as at the beginning. Alas poor world, poor devil, poor Baptists! —*ibi omnis Effusus labor.*[157] We sang an hymn of triumph. God had prepared his heart for this meeting. At the Sacrament he had found the spirit of martyrdom falling upon him, and immediately I was brought to his remembrance. His heart overflowed with love, and he thought we were going hand in hand to the stake.

Before the Society several were with me, desiring me, now I had gotten him, to reprove him openly. Some wanted me to preach against lay preaching; some against predestination, etc. In my discourse on Isaiah 60, a gentleman, who had come thither on purpose, interrupted me, by desiring I would now speak to Mr Harris,

---

153. Cf. Eph. 6:17.
154. Likely from Rom. 3; cf. the August 23, 1739, entry above.
155. Charles spells "Lantrissent."
156. St Bride's-super-Ely, Glamorgan.
157. "At that moment all his toil was spent," Virgil, *Georgics*, iv.492.

since I was sent for to disprove his errors, and Mr Wells, an experienced clergyman, sat by to moderate between us. God gave me immediate recollection. I smiled at Satan's imprudence, but turned aside the question with mildness, and thanks to the proposer. In vain he urged me to enter the lists with my friend. I quashed all farther importunity by declaring, "I am unwilling to speak of my brother Howell Harris, because, when I begin, I know not how to leave off, and should say so much good of him as some of you could not bear." The gentleman, disappointed of his hope, immediately departed.

After this victory over Satan, I proceeded with double power, addressing myself particularly to the ladies, whose company we were favoured with because there was no play tonight. I showed them they were no better than common harlots, if they outwardly differed from them through pride, not virtue. The Lord open their hearts to receive my hard saying.

The captain giving me notice that he should sail the next day, I determined to spend the night in taking leave. We supped at the friendly Mr Well's, and then called at Captain Philip's. Between ten and eleven, just as I was going, Satan began to show his wrath at the many sore disappointments he has met with this very day. He could not set the children of God against each other, and was therefore forced to make use of his own. The physician, who had gone out of church on Sunday, stirred up his companions, and unusually heated with wine, came and demanded satisfaction of me for calling him Pharisee. I said I was ready to acknowledge my mistake, if he would assure me he had gone out of church to visit his patients. He replied he had gone out because he disliked my discourse.

[*Wesley:*] "Then, Sir," said I, "I cannot ask pardon for telling you the truth."

[*Physician:*] "But you must for calling me a Pharisee."

[*Wesley:*] "I still insist you are a Pharisee, and cannot endure sound doctrine. My commission is to show you your sins, and I shall make no apology for so doing, to you or any man living. You are a damned sinner by nature, and a Pharisee, like me; and this testimony I should bear before rulers and kings. You are a rebel against God, and must bow your stiff neck to Him before you can be forgiven?"

[*Physician:*] "How do you know my heart?"

[*Wesley:*] "My heart showeth me the wickedness of the ungodly."

[*Physician:*] "Sir, I am as good a Christian as yourself."

[*Wesley:*] "You are no Christian at all, unless you have received the Holy Ghost."

[*Physician:*] "How do you prove that you have received the Holy Ghost?"

[*Wesley:*] "By searching your heart, and showing you that you are a Pharisee."

Here he lifted up his cane and struck me. Mrs Philips intercepted and broke the blow. Felix Farley tripped up his heels, and the company rushed in between. My soul was immediately filled with the calm, recollected boldness of faith. There was a great outcry among the women. Several of them he struck, and hurt, and raged like one possessed, till the men forced him out and shut the door.

Soon after, it was broken open by a justice, and the bailiff, or head magistrate. The latter began expostulating with me upon the affront offered the doctor and said, "As it was a public injury, I ought to make him public satisfaction." I answered, "Mr Bailiff, I honour you for your office's sake. But was you yourself, or his Majesty King George, among my hearers, I should tell you both that you are by nature damned sinners. In the church, while preaching, I have no superior but God, and shall not ask man leave to show him his sins. As a ruler, it is your duty to be a terror to evil-doers, but a praise to them that do well." Upon my thus speaking, he became exceeding civil, assured me of his goodwill, and that he had come to prevent my being insulted, and none should touch an hair of my head.

While we were talking, the doctor made another attempt to break in and get at me, but the two justices and others with much trouble at last got him out. They went, and we continued our triumph in the name of the Lord our God. The shout of a king was among us.[158] We sang on unconcerned, though those sons of Belial, the players, had beset the house.[159] The ground of their quarrel with me is that the gospel has starved them. We prayed and sang with great tranquility till one in the morning. Then I lay down till three. Rose again, and was scarce got into the room, when they discovered a player just by me, who had stole in unobserved. They seized him, and Felix Farley wrested the sword from him. There

---

158. Cf. Num. 23:21.
159. Cf. 1 Sam. 2:12.

was no need of drawing it, for the point and blade were stripped an hand-breadth of the scabbard.

When the sword was brought in, the spirit of faith was kindled among us, at sight of the danger. Great was our rejoicing within, and the uproar of the players without, who strove to force their way after their companion. My female advisers were by no means for my venturing out, but deferring my journey. I preferred Mr Wells's advice of going with him, through the midst of our enemies. Called in on the poor creature they had secured. They talked of warrants, prosecutions, etc. On sight of me he cried, "Indeed, Mr Wesley, I did not intend to do you any harm." "That," I answered, "was best known to God, and his own heart," but my principle was to return good for evil. Wherefore I desired he might be released, assured him of my good wishes, and with Mr Wells walked peaceably to the water-side, no man forbidding me. Our friends stood on the shore, while we joined in hearty thanksgiving. "The fierceness of men shall turn to thy praise, and the fierceness of them shalt thou restrain" [Ps. 76:10].

Wednesday, November 19. Between five and six we were forced to return for want of water. Found Howell Harris and the flock still at Captain Philips's, and was strengthened to lay open the promise of sanctification, Ezek. 36[:24-30]. Took leave of my dear Howell and, with Mr Wells, waited upon the bailiff. Acknowledged his last night's civilities, and left him, as a trophy, the player's sword. In public prayer, Mr Wells returned thanks to God for our late deliverance.

At two I took my leave of the Society, and preached the pure gospel from the Woman of Canaan [Matt. 15:22-28]. A spirit of love constrained me to beseech them, with tears, to receive Christ Jesus. It ran through all. Some of the greatest opposers wept, especially a young lady, for whose entertainment the players had acted me, sang, and prayed, and humbled exceedingly. The word was as a fire that melteth the rocks. I saw why God had brought me back. Our parting was such as it ought to be.

About four, Mr Wells, etc., attended me to the vessel. I laid me down, and slept, and took my rest, "for it is thou, Lord, only, that makest me dwell in safety" [Ps. 4:8, BCP].

Thursday, November 20. By five the next morning, He who blest our going out, blest our coming to Bristol.

Found my brother at the Room, expounding Rom. 9. I confirmed his saying, and gave some account of my success in Wales. A great power accompanied the word, and I prayed in the Spirit. Joined with him in administering the Sacrament to a young woman I had baptized, but who had not kept her garments unspotted. Yet God healed her backslidings, and soon after she confidently resigned her spirit into the hands of Jesus.

Friday, November 21. My brother returned to London.

Sunday, November 23. I was very dead in delivering it, yet the word was mixed with faith in some that heard it, as they afterwards testified.

Thursday, November 27. At the Malt-house the spirit of love and supplication fell upon me. I was filled with the tenderest concern for the desolate Church of England, which I could not help expressing before the congregation in tears, and strong cries to God for her.

Sunday, November 30. Gave the Sacrament to our sister Taylor, dying in triumph. Here is another witness to the truth of the gospel. Commend me to a religion upon which I can trust my soul, while entering into eternity.

Expounded the lesson at Kingswood. It was 6th of Hebrews. I prayed Christ our Teacher to enlighten the people with me, and began my discourse with fear and trembling. The Spirit gave me utterance. I calmly warned them against apostasy, and spake with great tenderness and caution. But who can stand before envy, bigotry, and ~~predestination~~? The strong ones were offended. The poison of Calvin has drunk up their spirit of love. Anne Ayling and Anne Davis could not refrain from railing. John Cennick never offered to stop them. Alas! We have set the wolf to keep the sheep! God gave me great moderation toward him, who, for many months, has been undermining our doctrine and authority.

DECEMBER 1740

Monday, December 1. Passed two hours at Mrs Parsons's funeral, and looked with envy on the corpse in the coffin. Her soul, before it left the body, was sweetly and fully conscious of its reconciliation with God. The word has been a savour of life to her also.

While I was showing the universality of Christ's redemption, the flame was kindled all around, and the Holy Ghost bore witness with many consciences.

Tuesday, December 2. Had a conference in Kingswood with Mr Cennick and his friends, but could come to no agreement, though I offered entirely to drop the controversy, if he would.

I preached on the three-fold office of Christ,[160] but never with greater power. It constrained even the separatists to own that God was with us of a truth. Rode back in a glorious storm of thunder, lightning, and rain. My spirit rejoiced in hope of the glory of God.

He opened my mouth again at the Society, and I spoke in much grief and love of our desolate mother the Church of England. My heart yearns towards her when I think upon her ruins, and it pitieth me to see her in the dust.

Thursday, December 4. Administered the Sacrament to Mr Page, against hope believing in hope.[161] After receiving, he had power to believe his sins forgiven.

Friday, December 5. Was much refreshed in Spirit among some of my friends, the Quakers, by a writer of theirs, who strongly insists on the perfect death unto sin, and life unto righteousness, which every Christian experiences.[162] Death must precede life, and condemnation justification. This he as clearly teaches as any of our first Reformers.

Saturday, December 6. Wrote my brother a full account of the predestination party, their practices and designs, particularly "to have a church within themselves, and to give themselves the Sacrament in bread and water."

Sunday, December 21. Took my leave of the colliers in the words of the great Apostle (without comparing myself to him), "And now, brethren, I commend you to God, and to the word of his grace" [Acts 20:32]. The loving spirit was mightily among us, and more still at our Love-feast, for all the brethren of Kingswood and Bristol.

Monday, December 22. I showed, with demonstration of the Spirit, the (ordinary) necessity of our being bruised and broken *before*

---

160. Perhaps using Luke 4:18. Cf. August 28, 1743, entry.
161. Cf. Rom. 4:18.
162. One popular Quaker work that stresses this theme is John Crook, *Truth's Principles* (1662, original; reprint: London: T. Sowle, 1700), see pp. 16–18.

the Comforter would abide in us for ever. He who saith, "My work is before me," set to his seal.

Wednesday, December 24. At five set out for London, which I reached, with Thomas Maxfield, the next day by five in the afternoon. At six God renewed my strength to preach the glad tidings to a crowded audience at the Foundery. Great was our joy in the Lord, and in each other.

Friday, December 26. Rose at five, without feeling my journey, and expounded Isa. 40:9, "O Zion, that bringeth good tidings, get thee up into the high mountain," etc. He spake comfortably to his people by mouth, though I am nothing.

Talked with one who has entirely stopped the work of God in her own soul by judging of it in others.

A spirit of contrition fell upon me the moment I entered the Society-room. We made supplication for all men, especially the household of faith, and that small part of it at Bristol.

Saturday, December 27. From eleven to one met five or six hundred, to praise God with the voice of joy and thanksgiving. He had done great things for us already, but we shall see greater things than these.

Dined at a Dissenter's, armed cap-a-pie[163] with her faith of adherence, brim full of the five points, and going on to the perfection of Rom. 7.

At Mr Craven's a man abruptly accosted me, "Are you ready to receive my message?" "Yes," I answered, "if you speak not of yourself." "I speak to you from God." "Where are your credentials? What proof show you of your divine commission?" "Nay, nay," said he, "if you cannot receive my saying, I have nothing to do with you. I have delivered my own soul." With these he flung away and left his prophecy imperfect.

Sunday, December 28. In the evening the scoffers were very outrageous. God filled my mouth with threatenings and promises. I defied and invited them by turns, till he got himself the victory, and I freely published the glad tidings, "To us a son is born, to us a child is given" [Isa. 9:6].

---

163. *OED:* "head to toe."

I earnestly warned the bands not to fancy they had new hearts before they had seen the deceitfulness of the old; not to think they would ever be above the necessity of praying; not to yield for one moment to the spirit of judging.

Mrs Aspernel told me strange things, and I fear true, concerning some new creatures of their own making, particularly Anne Morris, Sarah Middleton, B. H., and George Angel, who have been caught in gross lies.

I appointed those who think they have new hearts to come and talk with me. Mrs Cannon came and stood to it that she neither could nor would pray for anything, that her very flesh was holy, and pure, and sinless as Christ's body.[164]

Among my visitants this morning I had a very ingenious person, who generously proffered to teach me the grand arcanum for the value of five shillings. Having no need of money, I declined his proffer, but gave him sixpence and told him, as he had the art of transmutation, it was the same as if I had given him half a guinea. We had more serious talk before parting: how to change an heart of stone into an heart of flesh.[165]

Tuesday, December 30. Exhorted the Society at Deptford with convincing power. A woman fell down under it.

Wednesday, December 31. Found the Spirit of prayer among the bands in London, and strongly exhorted them to humility.

APRIL 1741[1]

Friday, April [3].[2] Set out for Bristol, to which God brought me safe by Saturday evening. Expounded at the Malt-house Revelation 2:24, and God was with my mouth.

---

164. This and the preceding paragraph do not appear in Jackson.

165. Cf. Ezek. 11:19, 2 Cor. 3:3.

1. The period of January 1–March 31, 1741, is skipped in the MS Journal. From John Wesley's *Journal* it appears that Charles was briefly drawn toward the doctrine of "stillness" being taught by the English Moravians, and stopped preaching in London (see particularly the entries for January 18–February 12, *Works* 19:178–81). Lady Huntingdon (Selina Hastings, 1707–1791), who had recently initiated contact with the Wesley brothers, played an important role in helping Charles recover emphasis on holy living; cf. her letter to John Wesley (October 24, 1741) in *Works* 26:67–68.

2. MS is off by one in the numbering of all days in April, including creating an April 31. Hence, all the numbers have been adjusted one day backward.

Sunday, April [5]. Spake words of comfort to many mourners from Isaiah 30:18, "And therefore will the Lord wait, that he may be gracious unto you," etc.; and again God greatly to be feared[3] was in the midst of our congregation, and revived many drooping hearts.

Monday, April [6]. Prayed by one supposed at the point of death. He rejoiced to meet the king of terrors[4] and appeared so sweetly resigned, so ready for the Bridegroom, that I longed to change places with him.

Visited three murderers under sentence of death who were ready to say, "Blessed is he that cometh in the name of the Lord" [Ps. 118:26].

Thursday, April [9]. Got some hours for visiting our numerous sick, most of whom I found in a good way. Only one backslider, brother Hawks, was in the depth of despair.

Preached at Kendleshire[5] and gathered up the wreck. In riding back my horse threw me, but I know who caught me in his arms.

Friday, April [10]. Found a dying sinner rejoicing in God her Saviour. At sight of me she cried out, "O how loving is God to me, but he is loving to every man. He loves every soul, as well as he loves mine." Many like words she uttered in triumphant faith, and witnessed in death the universal love of Christ Jesus.

Saturday, April [11]. Today He called forth another of his dying witnesses, the young woman whom, at my last visit, I left in utter despair. This morning she broke out into, "I see, I see it now, that Jesus Christ died for me, and for all the world." From that time she testified with much assurance that Christ gave his life a ransom for all.[6] Some of her words to me were: "Death stares me in the face, but I fear him not. He cannot hurt me,

And death may shake his dart in vain!"[7]

Your report is true. God is love, pure love, love to every man. The Spirit, which is in me, tells me that Jesus Christ died for me and the whole world.

---

3. Cf. Neh. 1:5.
4. Cf. Job 18:14.
5. Charles spells "Kendalshire."
6. Cf. Mark 10:45.
7. "Written in the Beginning of a Recovery from Sickness," st. 7, ln 4, *HSP* (1739), 81 (*Poetical Works*, 1:76).

The next I saw was our brother S.,[8]

> with joyful eyes and looks divine,
> smiling and pleased in death.[9]

He likewise had in himself the witness of God's all-redeeming love, and could stake his soul upon the truth of it. Who will show me a predestinarian that dares die for the truth of reprobation?

Sunday, April [12]. At Kingswood while I was repeating B. H.'s dying testimony,[10] the Spirit came down as a mighty, rushing wind. Just then the predestinarians came in from hearing Cennick. In battles of shaking did he fight with them.[11] We were all in a flame of love.

Gave the Sacrament to the bands of Kingswood, not of Bristol, in obedience (as I told them) to the Church of England, which requires a weekly Sacrament at every cathedral. But as they had it not there and on this particular Sunday were refused it at Temple church (I myself, with many of them having been repelled), I therefore administered it to them in our school. And had we wanted an house, would justify doing it in the midst of the wood. I strongly urged the duty of their receiving it, as often as they could be admitted at the churches.

Had prayed God to show me some token if this was his will concerning me, and indeed my prayer was answered, for such a Sacrament was I never present at before. We received the sure pledges of our Saviour's dying love, and were, most of us, filled with all peace and joy in believing.

Preached a fourth time at Bristol. Read the bands my journal of which has lately passed in London. It occasioned a grief which, mixed with pity, violated not their joy. I gave them all the treatise on predestination.[12]

---

8. Likely the brother Stanley in the August 5, 1741, entry below.
9. Cf. Isaac Watts, "The Welcome Messenger," st. 1, *Horae lyricae* (London: Humfreys, 1709), 47:

> Lord, when we see a saint of thine
> Lie gasping out his breath,
> With longing eyes, and looks divine,
> Smiling and pleas'd in death.

10. Apparently one of the two women quoted on April 10–11.
11. Cf. Isa. 30:32.
12. *Serious Considerations on Absolute Predestination* (Bristol: Farley, 1741), which John Wesley

Monday, April [13]. While I was in great love warning the bands, the Spirit of power came down, the fountain was set open, my mouth and heart enlarged, and I spoke such words as I cannot repeat. Many sunk under the love of Christ crucified, and were constrained to break out, "Christ died for all." Some confessed with tears of joy, they were going to leave us, but could now die for the truth of the doctrine.

Tuesday, April [14]. Was enlarged in prayer for the malefactors, who are to die tomorrow.

Thursday, April [16]. One of our old men in the Wood[13] complained to me that the Separatists had got from him the treatise against predestination and burned it. In like manner they *answer* all they can lay hands on. But they do nothing unless they could burn one more book, the Bible.

At Kendleshire God gave me words to maintain his cause. I showed the end of Messiah[14] being cut off, namely, to finish the transgression and to make an end of sin, and to bring in everlasting righteousness [Dan. 9:24]. One soul, as I afterwards heard, was added to the witnesses of Jesus.

Friday, April [17]. For the sake of many poor soldiers present I enlarged on the faithful saying, "that Jesus Christ came into the world to save sinners" [1 Tim. 1:15].

Saturday, April [18]. Called to one that was a dying. It was Hannah Richardson, etc. (see printed account of her death[15]).

Sunday, April [19]. Returning from Baptist Mills, I heard that our sister Richardson finished her course. My soul was filled with strong consolation and struggled, as it were, to go out after her—"as heavenward endeavouring."[16] Jesu! My time is in thy hand.[17] Only let me follow her as she has followed thee![18]

---

had extracted from Robert Barclay's *Apology for the True Christian Divinity* (1678) and published in March 1741.

13. Likely a reference to the larger forested area around the school at Kingswood (originally, King's Wood).

14. Charles spells "Messias."

15. Charles is referring to the account he prepared for publication: *A Short Account of the Death of Hannah Richardson* (London: Strahan, 1741).

16. Cf. Phil. 3:14.

17. Cf. Ps. 31:10, BCP.

18. Cf. 1 Cor. 11:1.

The voice of joy and thanksgiving was in the congregation, while I spake of her death. Our sister Purnel has proved a true prophet that many of the Society would follow her, but God would first finish his work and cut it short in righteousness.

Monday, April [20]. The hand of the Lord was upon me at Downend,[19] while I enforced his universal call, "Look unto me and be ye saved, *all* the ends of the earth" [Isa. 45:22]. Many felt the earthquake, which preceded the coming of the Son of Man.[20] We prayed and sang alternately for two hours and the Lord, we trust, enlarged and established our hearts.

Tuesday, April [21]. Hastened to the joyful funeral of our sister Richardson. The room was crowded within and without. My subject was, "I know that my Redeemer liveth," etc. [Job 19:25]. Spoke searchingly to the hearsay-believers and then largely of her, whose faith they must safely follow. Great was my glorying and rejoicing over her. She being dead, yet spoke[21] in works of faith and love, which ought to be had in remembrance. Surely her spirit was present with us, and we were in a measure partakers of her joy, a joy unspeakable and full of glory.[22]

The whole Society followed her to her grave through all the city. Satan raged exceedingly in his children who threw dirt and stones at us, but the bridle was in their mouths. After the burial we joined in the following hymn.

> Come, let us who in Christ believe
> With saints and angels join.
> Glory and praise and blessing give,
> And thanks to grace divine.
>
> Our Friend in sure and certain hope
> Hath laid her body down.
> She knew that Christ will raise her up,
> And give the *heavenly*[23] crown.

---

19. Charles spells "Downing."
20. Cf. Rev. 16:18.
21. Cf. Heb. 11:4.
22. Cf. 1 Pet. 1:8.
23. In the margin Wesley writes "starry" as an alternative to "heavenly."

To all, who his appearing love,
    He opens paradise,
And we shall join the hosts above
    And we shall grasp the prize.

Then let us wait to see the day,
    To hear the welcome word,
To answer—Lo! We come away,
    We die to meet our Lord![24]

Wednesday, April [22]. Sharply improved three or four inflexible pharisees, then prayed the Lord to give me words of consolation, and immediately I was filled with power, which broke out as a mighty torrent. All our hearts caught fire as in a moment and such tears and strong crying followed as quite drowned my voice. I sat still while the prayer of the humble pierced the clouds and entered into the ears of the Lord of Sabaoth. All present received an answer of peace and from his love in their hearts, testified that Christ died for all.

The Spirit of Jesus is the Spirit of prophecy.[25] One prophecied in words that pierced my soul. At last I lifted up the book and cried, "The spirits of the prophets are subject to the prophets. Bow down to the written word." Immediately there was a profound silence, while I read Elijah's contention with the priests of Baal. The God that answereth by fire, received my appeal and at those words, "Then the fire of the Lord fell and consumed the burnt sacrifice" [1 Kings 18:38], a prisoner of hope broke loose and cried out, "Christ died for all." She was even filled with faith and the Holy Ghost. Not one soul was sent empty away. We were all amazed and glorified God the Saviour of all men, saying, "We never saw it on this fashion" [Mark 2:12].

News was brought me that the predestinarians had a design to get Kingswood School into their hands, and had made sure of the mistress, Hannah Barrow, a bold confident pharisee, a liar, backbiter, swearer, drunkard, and if she is not a whore, it is because others have more grace than herself. I rode over to Kingswood and the next morning—

---

24. "After the Funeral," *HSP* (1742), 131 (*Poetical Works*, 2:191). There are a series of variants in this later published version. 1:4 = And thanks to love divine. 2:2–4 = Hath laid his body down / He knew that Christ will raise him up, / And give the starry crown. 4:2 = To hear the welcome word.
25. Cf. Rev. 19:10.

Thursday, April [23]. After preaching, paid her above her wages and quickly dismissed her.[26]

In the evening gathered up a stray sheep at Bristol and carried her to the word, which she had long forsaken. Strongly exhorted the people to put on the whole armour of God [Eph. 6:11-17]. God doubly confirms the word, when it is denied.

Friday, April [24]. At the intercession had great faith in prayer, that all things shall happen for the furtherance of the gospel. The predestinarian was struck as with the pangs of death, and earnestly desired our prayers.

Spent the afternoon in confirming the weak. In the evening I left God to choose me a subject and opening the book where it was written, "And now, I beseech thee, let the power of my Lord be great, according as thou hast spoken," etc. [Num. 14:17], that famous history of the spies who brought up an evil report of the promised land.

I said, "let us go up at once and possess it, for we are well able to overcome it" [Num. 13:30]. God inclined their hearts to listen unto me, rather than the men that went up with us, who say, "We are not able to go up against the people, for they are stronger than we" [Num. 13:31]. We can never conquer *all* sin; we must sin sometimes.

Rode to Kingswood where many were come from far to spend the night in watching and prayer.[27] Had much of the divine presence, but remained myself like Gideon's fleece till at midnight a cry, "behold, the Bridegroom cometh!" [Matt. 25:6]. The flame was kindled and the Lord our God was among us, as in the holy place of Sinai.

Saturday, April [25]. The word at night was refreshing to our souls. Our thanksgiving notes multiply more and more, being convinced of judgment or that dreadful perfection, the living without sin. One wrote thus, "There was not a word came out of the mouth last night but I could apply it to my own soul, and witness it the doctrine of Christ. I know that Christ is a whole Saviour. I know the blood of Christ has washed away all my sins. I am sure the Lord will make me perfect in love, before I go hence, and am no more seen.

---

26. The preceding three paragraphs are omitted by Jackson.
27. I.e., they were holding a watch-night service.

O for a thousand tongues to sing
My dear Redeemer's praise!" etc.[28]

Sunday, April [26]. Proceeded in Numbers 14, and warned the hearers, lest a promise being made them of entering into rest, any of them should come short of it through unbelief.

God every day adds fresh seals to my ministry, as many testify in the notes of thanksgiving.

Thursday, April [30]. Went on in Numbers 14. Many eyes were opened to see that land of promises, which God hath sworn to give unto all who believe.

We find a continued increase of faith and strength. It is good for us to be assaulted by Satan and his children. They watch *for* our halting, which makes us watch *against* it.

MAY 1741

Friday, May 1. Visited a sister, dying in the Lord, and then two others, one mourning after, the other rejoicing in God her Saviour.

Found our sister Hooper sick of love. Her body too, sunk under it.

While I finished my discourse on Numbers 14, God fulfilled his promise, "Lo, I am with you always" [Matt. 28:20].

Was now informed that another of our sisters, E. Smith, is gone home in triumph. She witnessed a good confession of the universal Saviour, and gave up her spirit with those words, "I go to my heavenly Father."

Sunday, May 3. At Kingswood, as soon as I had named my text, "It is finished!" [John 19:30], the love of Christ crucified so constrained me that I burst into tears, and felt strong sympathy with him in his sufferings. In like manner the whole congregation looked upon Him, whom they had pierced, and mourned.[29]

Joined the Society in thanksgiving for our departed sister. We found where she was by the sweet power and solemn awe with which the divine presence filled us.

---

28. "For the Anniversary of One's Conversion," st. 7, *HSP* (1740), 121 (*Poetical Works*, 1:300).
29. Cf. Zech. 12:10.

Monday, May 4. Passed an hour in weeping with some that wept,[30] then rejoiced over our sister Hooper. The more the outward man decayeth, the inner is renewed.[31] For one whole night she had wrestled with the powers of darkness. This is that evil day, that fiery trial! But having done all, she stood unshaken! From henceforth she was kept in perfect peace, and that wicked one touched her not.

In conference B. Walker told me that last night ~~that~~ God had opened her eyes under the word, and the love of Christ, the Saviour of all men, quite overpowered her soul.

Saw my dear friend again in great bodily weakness, but strong in the Lord, and in the power of his might.[32] "The Spirit," said she, "bears witness every moment with my spirit, that I am a child of God." I spoke with her physician, who said he had little hope of her recovery. "Only," added he, "she has no dread upon her spirits, which is generally the worst symptom. Most people die for fear of dying, but I never met with such people as yours. They are, none of them, afraid of death, but calm, and patient, and resigned to the last." He had said to her, "Madam, be not cast down." She answered, "Sir, I shall never be cast down."

At Downend explained good old Simeon's confession, "Lord, now lettest thou," etc. [Luke 2:29]. Our sister Hooper was present in spirit. I hastened back, and asked, "How are you now?" Her answer was, "Full, full of love."

Met the bands in Kingswood. One, who in fear of God and mistrust of himself had heard Mr Whitefield, assured me he had preached barefaced reprobation. The people fled before the reprobating lion. But again and again, as he observed them depart, the preacher of sad tidings called them back with general offers of salvation. Vain and empty offers indeed! What availed his telling them that for *ought he knew*, they might be *all* elect. He did not believe them all elect; he could not. Therefore, he only mocked them with an empty word of invitation; and if God sent him to preach the gospel to *every creature*, God, according to his scheme, sent him to *deceive* the greatest part of mankind.

Tuesday, May 5. Had much of the spirit of supplication among our colliers. Could not but look on it as a good omen that while I

30. Cf. Rom. 12:15.
31. Cf. 2 Cor. 4:16.
32. Cf. Eph. 6:10.

was praying for the increase of our spiritual children, a wild collier brought me four of his children and threw the youngest on the table before me crying, "You have got the mother, take the bairns too."

Wednesday, May 6. Found our sister Hooper just at the haven. She expressed, while able to speak, her fullness of confidence and love, her desire to be with Christ, her grief at their preaching the other gospel.[33] Some of her words were, "Does Mr Cennick still preach his wretched doctrine?" O what has he to answer for turning his poor sister out of the way. But my Lord will pity, and not suffer to die in that delusion.

At my next visit I saw her in her latest conflict. The angel of death was coming and but a few moments between her and blessed eternity. We poured out our souls to God for her, her children, ourselves, the church and ministers, and all mankind. I had some perception of her joy. My soul was tenderly affected for her sufferings, yet the joy swallowed up the sorrow. How much more then did *her* consolations abound! The servants of Christ suffer nothing. I asked her whether she was not in great pain. "Yes," she answered, "but in greater joy. I would not be without either." "But do you not prefer life, or death?" She replied, "All is alike to me, let Christ choose. I have no will of my own."

This is that holiness, or absolute resignation, or Christian perfection!

Two days ago I asked her if she expected to recover. She answered, God had in the beginning of her sickness given her notice of her departure. And I now remember she told me some months ago that Mrs Parnel on her deathbed had said, "You shall shortly follow me."

A few moments before her last, I found such a complication of grief, joy, love, envy, as quite overpowered me. I fell upon the bed and in that instant her spirit ascended to God. I felt our souls were knit together by the violent struggle of mine to follow her.

When I saw the breathless temple of the Holy Ghost,[34] my heart was still, and a calm resignation took place. We knelt down and gave God thanks from the ground of our heart. Then had recourse to the book of comfort and found it written, "He was a burning and

---

33. Cf. Gal. 1:8-9.
34. Cf. 1 Cor. 6:19.

a shining light, and ye were willing for a season to rejoice in his light" [John 5:35]. The next word was for us, "Let us labour therefore to enter into that rest" [Heb. 4:11]. Even so, come, Lord Jesus,[35] and give us an inheritance among all them that are sanctified!

After her death they found a memorandum in her handwriting: "On such a day Mr W— came to town; the next day I received a fresh witness. Nov. 2, early in the morning such a manifestation of God's love as is not to be expressed."

One night, I remember, she told me she knew, while coming to us, we should have that extraordinary power among the bands; that in the way God had given her a sight of the new Jerusalem. This she did not mention to others, nor indeed many manifestations of Christ, being exceeding jealous lest she should take any glory to herself. O that all who tell what God hath done for their souls would tell it with like humble reverence!

Met the bands, a solemn assembly. Cautioned the unstable and comforted the feeble-minded. My mentioning our sister's release occasioned much thanksgiving.

Thursday, May 7. Visited Hannah Cennick full of love to her Saviour, crying out "~~Victory~~, Liberty, liberty! This is the glorious liberty of God's children![36] O who can name the name of Jesus and not depart from iniquity? God loves me. God loves every man. Jesus Christ the Saviour of the whole world."

I could not but observe, and bless God for, this answer to our dying sister's prayer.

At the Room I opened the book on "And I, if I be lifted up from the earth, will draw all men unto me" [John 12:32]. Was I to search after the strongest Scriptures for universal redemption, I could not choose so well as Providence chooses for me. God at this time made bare his arm.[37] I knew not how to give over, but continued my discourse till nine. Many witnesses stood forth and testified God's love to all.

Friday, May 8. We solemnized the funeral of our sister Hooper and rejoiced over her with singing, particularly that hymn which concludes:

---

35. Cf. Rev. 22:20.
36. Cf. Rom. 8:21.
37. Cf. Isa. 52:10.

> Thus may we all our parting breath
> Into the Saviour's hands resign!
> O sister! let *me* die thy death,
> And let thy latter end be mine![38]

My text was, "Lord, now lettest thou thy servant depart in peace" (Luke 2:29). A great multitude attended her to her grave. There we sang another hymn of triumph and I found myself pressed in spirit to speak to those who contradicted and blasphemed. While I reasoned on death and judgment to come, many humbled. One woman cried out in horrible agony. We returned to the Room and continued our solemn rejoicing, desiring all to be dissolved and to be with Christ.[39]

Sunday, May 10. Gave the Sacrament to the colliers. Preached on Elijah's small, still voice [1 Kings 19:12]. Went out into the highways and concluded the happy day with a feast in Kingswood.

Monday, May 11. At Downend explained, "I will heal thy backslidings. I will love thee freely" [Hosea 14:4]. He who gave the promise applied it. I was quite melted down by it. Several wept much and loved much, because they had much forgiven.

Thursday, May 14. Visited our sister Lillington whom her Saviour had brought to a bed of sickness before she knew he was *her* Saviour. She told me two nights ago she saw herself, as it were, dropping into hell, when suddenly a ray of light was darted into her soul and filled her with all peace and joy in believing. All fear of hell, death, and sin fled away in that same moment.

Saw two more of our sick sisters, then two of the brethren in Kingswood, who were all rejoicing in hope of a speedy dissolution. Preached at Kendleshire and visited one of the bands there, who walked through the valley of the shadow of death and feared no evil.[40] Prayed by a seventh in Bristol, who laughed at the king of terrors.[41] If God be not with us, who hath begotten us these?

---

38. Cf. "A Funeral Hymn. (Used first for Mrs Elizabeth Hooper)," st. 7, *HSP* (1742), 124–25 (*Poetical Works*, 2:184). The published form reads differently in lines 3 and 4: "O Jesu! Let me die her death / And let her latter end be mine!"
39. Cf. Phil. 1:23.
40. Cf. Ps. 23:4.
41. Cf. Job 18:14.

Friday, May 15. Saw our sister Lillington again; still without fear, desiring nothing but to be with Christ. "I never felt," said she, "such love before. I love every soul. I am all love and so is God. He is loving unto every man. He would have all men to be saved."

Saturday, May 16. Visited another of our sisters, who was triumphing over death. I asked her, "Do you know Christ died for you?" "Yes," she answered joyfully, "for me, and for the whole world. He has begun and he will finish his work in my soul." "But will he save you," I said, "from *all* sin?" She replied, "I know he will. Then shall no sin remain in me."

Sent for to another, who had lastly heard a preacher of reprobation. The tempter would not lose the advantage and immediately suggested, "You are one of those for whom Christ did not die." This threw her into a fever. I found her dying in despair. Preached the true gospel (gospel to every creature), prayed, and left her a prisoner of hope.

Whitsunday, May 17. The fire was kindled, while we were singing:

> Bear we witness unto thee
> Thou thy light to all dost give
> That the World through it may see
> Their Saviour and believe.[42]

One cried out, "It is the truth!" Several found the same constraint of the all-loving Spirit. We blessed the God and Saviour of all men, who never leaves himself without witness where his true gospel is preached.

Monday, May 18. A poor soldier confessed to me that God had opened his eyes to see his universal love. I was repeating that verse

> Arise, O God, arise,
> Thy glorious cause maintain,
> Hold forth the bloody sacrifice
> For every sinner slain.[43]

By all I can discern, he did in that moment receive the atonement.

---

42. "Gloria Patri, IV," st. 2, *Hymns on God's Everlasting Love*, 2nd series (London: Strahan, [1742]), 55 (*Poetical Works*, 3:99).

43. Hymn 17, st. 12, *Hymns on God's Everlasting Love* (Bristol: Farley, 1741), 36 (*Poetical Works*, 3:37).

Settled the bands in Kingswood. Toward the end an awful sense of God fell upon us and we trembled, seeing Him that is invisible.

Tuesday, May 19. I am more and more confirmed in the truth by its miserable opposers. Talked lately with Mr [William] Hooper and urged him with this dilemma: "For what did God make this reprobate? To be damned, or to be saved?" He durst not say God made even Judas to be damned, and would not say God made him to be saved. I desired to know for what third end he could make him, but all the answer I could get was: "It is not a fair question."

Next I asked whether he that believeth not shall not be damned because he believeth not? "Yes," he answered, and I replied, "Because he believeth not what?" Here he hesitated and I was forced to help him out with the Apostle's answer, "that they all might be damned who believed not the truth" [2 Thess. 2:12]. "What truth?" I asked again, "but the truth of the gospel of *their* salvation. If it is not the gospel of *their* salvation, and yet they are bound to believe it, then they are bound to believe a lie, under pain of damnation. And the Apostle should have said that they all might be damned, who believed not *a lie*." This drove him to assert that no man was damned for *actual* unbelief but only for what he called *original*, that is, for not believing before he was born. "But where," said I, "is the justice of this?" He answered, not over hastily, "I confess there is a mystery in reprobation." Or, to put it in Bèze's words, which I then read him, "We believe, though it is incomprehensible that [it] is just to damn such as do not deserve it."[44]

Farther I asked him, "Why does God command all men everywhere to repent? Why does he call and offer his grace to reprobates? Why does his Spirit strive with every child of man for *some* time, though not always?" I could get no answer, and so read him one of his friend Calvin's: "God speaketh to them that they may be the deafer, he gives light to them that they may be the blinder, he

---

44. This appears to be Charles's summary of Théodore de Bèze, *Briefe Declaration of the Chiefe Poyntes of Christian Religion* (London: D. Moptid, 1575), chapter 3 (on predestination): "We conclude therefore, that this fall of Adam . . . happened not without the will of God, whom it pleases by a miraculous and incomprehensible means that the thing which he does not allow (forasmuch as it is sin) should not happen without his will. . . . For the final end of God's counsel is neither the salvation of the elect, nor the damnation of the reprobate, but the setting forth of his own glory—in saving the one by his mercy, and condemning the other by his just judgment" (pp. 19–20, rendered in modern English). But note that Bèze does not say (and would never agree) that either Adam or fallen humanity do not deserve their condemnation.

offers instruction to them that they may be the more ignorant, and uses the remedy that they may *not* be healed." *Calvin's Institutes*, 3. c. 24.[45]

Never did I meet with a more pitiful advocate of a more pitiful cause. And yet I believe he could say as much for reprobation as another. I told him *his* predestination had got a millstone about its neck and would infallibly be drowned, if he did not part it from reprobation.

At Kingswood I preached on those much revisited words, "I pray not for the world, but for them which thou hast given me" [John 17:9], that is, his apostles. He does not take in believers of future ages till v. 20. Then in v. 21, he prays for the unbelieving world that, to use Mr Baxter's words on the place, "by *their* concord, the *world* may be won to Christianity" (*Paraphrase on New Testament*[46]). See again on v. 23, "That this luster of their excellency and concord may convince the world that thou hast sent me." So far is our Lord from not praying for the world *at all*. Yet in this very chapter he prays once for his first disciples, once for believers in after-ages, and *twice* for the *world* that believeth in wickedness, that the world may *believe*, that the world may *know*.

He who prays for all men himself and commands us to pray for all men, was with us, and showed us with the demonstration of his Spirit that he is not willing any should perish but that all should come to the knowledge of the truth and be saved.

Wednesday, May 20. Was called to a dying woman, who confessed she had often railed on me in her health but was now constrained to send for me and ask my pardon, or she could not die in peace. We prayed our Lord to speak peace and pardon to her soul. Several such instances have had of scoffers, when their feet came to stumble on the dark mountains.[47]

Friday, May 22. Preached a funeral sermon over sister Lillington and attended her to her grave, where we rejoiced in hope of quickly following her. Gave an exhortation to repentance though Satan greatly withstood me, thereby teaching me never to let go unwarned the poor sinners that come on such occasions.

45. This is a slight paraphrase of Calvin, *Institutes*, Bk. III, Ch. 24, ¶13.
46. Richard Baxter, *A Paraphrase on the New Testament; with notes, doctrinal and practical* (London: B. & T. Simmons, 1685).
47. Cf. Jer. 13:16.

Passed the night with my brother at Kingswood in watching unto prayer. I would this primitive custom were revived among all our brethren. The word of God encourages us to be in watchings often. Returned by two to Bristol and at five found strength to expound in my room.

Sunday, May 24. Preached on Jacob wrestling for the blessing [Gen. 32:24-31].[48] Many then I believe took hold on his strength and will not let him go till He bless them and tell them his name.

Heard my brother at the Mills and attended him to the Society. ~~The~~ We had the cloud on our assembly.[49] A woman was constrained to testify, "God this moment assures me that my pardon is sealed in heaven." The prince of this world was displeased. One of his subjects threw a stone into the room, which had no permission to hurt. We accepted it as a challenge to stay and continued an hour longer, singing and praising God.

Monday, May 25. Visited one who had been grievously tormented with the spirit of reprobation but now rejoiced on a bed of sickness, free from all her fear, and trouble, and *sense* of pain. "I am confident," she said, "that Jesus Christ will finish his work in me. That wicked one toucheth me not. He can no more make me doubt of God's universal love. Jesus is the stronger ~~and he is a dear Saviour~~! He is the Saviour of all mankind. It is a glorious gospel you preach. I stake my soul upon the truth of it."

While I was passing by the Bowling Green, a woman cried out, "The curse of God light upon you" with such uncommon bitterness that I could not but turn and stop to bless her. When I asked her why she cursed me, she answered, "For preaching against Mr —." I had indeed a suspicion from her dialect that she was one of the self-elect, but stayed heaping coals of his upon her head,[50] till at last she said, "God bless you all."

Thursday, May 28. In the evening I expounded Ezekiel 18. Some were grieved, and I myself also, at the necessity laid upon me to convince gainsayers and not to employ both hands in building. Yet

48. If Charles had a MS for this sermon, it has not survived. But one of his most famous poems, "Wrestling Jacob," is based on this passage. Cf. *HSP* (1742), 115–18 (*Poetical Works*, 2:173–76).

49. Cf. Exod. 40:34.

50. Cf. Prov. 25:22; Rom. 12:20.

our Lord owned me here also and the hammer of his word broke the rock[51] of absolute predestination into pieces. One, who had been long entangled with it, now testified that he had delivered his soul out of the snare of the fowler.[52]

Saturday, May 30. Passed an hour with a spiritual Quaker and rejoiced to find we were both of the same religion.

Sunday, May 31. Throughout this day I found my strength increase with my labour. Many at the Mills were affected deeply with our Lord's description (Matthew 24) of his coming to judgment.

Read in the Society my account of Hannah Richardson's death.[53] She, being dead, yet spoke so powerfully to our hearts that my voice was lost in sorrowful sighing of such as be in captivity. To several God showed himself the God of consolation also, particularly to two young Welshmen whom his providence sent hither from Carmarthen. They had heard most dreadful stories of us— Arminians, freewillers, perfectionists, Papists—which all vanished like smoke when they came to hear with their own ears. God applied to their hearts the word of his power. I carried them to my lodgings and stocked them with books, and sent them away, recommended to the grace of God which bringeth salvation unto all men.

JUNE 1741

Thursday, June 4. Met with one who said she was in the full liberty of the gospel and much displeased that I did not acknowledge her, "but that the spiritual man is discerned of none, though I discern you. You are justified but you have not my gifts." Upon my coming down, she was very abusive, called me child of the devil, etc., and denounced judgments against our whole Society for not receiving her.

In the evening Society, God wrought wonderfully. I have seldom known such a night. We rejoiced till near midnight with joy unspeakable.

---

51. Cf. Jer. 23:29.
52. Cf. Ps. 91:3.
53. *A Short Account of the Death of Hannah Richardson.*

Friday, June 5. The morning word was as a sharp, two-edged sword, a discerner of the thoughts and intents of the heart.[54] Mary Stratten, the poor self-deceiver I spoke with yesterday, could not bear it, but cried out, "You are a child of the devil, and the Society are all accursed." I let her speak on, that she might *show* herself, then warned the highminded least they also should fall into the condemnation of the devil. See the false assurance of unbelief and tremble! One in the gall of bitterness, the bond of iniquity, persuades herself that she is in the glorious liberty of the sons of God![55]

Visited one who had violently maintained the impossibility of knowing our sins forgiven in this life. But Christ hath taught her better on her deathbed. She was overjoyed to see me. I prayed over her in faith, and left her calmly waiting for the salvation of God.

Prayed by another of the bands, who has recovered in sickness the confidence she had long last.

Walked out of town to a third, who lay a-dying, and could not rest till she had seen me. She had been a great opposer of this way, which now she confesses to be the only way of salvation.

Sent for to rejoice with our brother G— in an high fever. The witness testified, "I come quickly!" [Rev. 22:20]. Therefore, consolation did much more abound.

Saturday, June 6. William Hooper informed me that last night he was delivered under the word from the snare of predestination.

Monday, June 8. A woman spoke to me of her husband. He was under strong convictions while he attended the word, but the first time he heard the *other gospel*[56] [he] came home *elect*, and in proof of it, *beat his wife.* His seriousness was at an end. His work was done, God doth not behold iniquity in Jacob,[57] therefore his iniquity and cruelty towards her abounds. He uses her worse than a Turk (his predestinarian brother), and tells her if he killed her he could not be damned.

Today I heard of another in the same delusion, Mrs Grevil's man, who lately favored me with a letter exhorting me to bow down at the foot of sovereign grace. His mistress has now sent him

54. Cf. Heb. 4:12.
55. Cf. Rom. 8:21.
56. Cf. Gal. 1:8-9.
57. Cf. Num. 23:21.

to Bridewell[58] and dragged her maid out of doors by the hair of the head, although naked, elect, and big with child.

Visited the woman whom I had left waiting for the redemption she had long denied.[59] She cried out at sight of me, "O blessed be God that ever I heard you! You have been the saving of my soul." I taught her to speak more exactly. Her faith wrought powerfully by love. Her mouth was full of prayers and blessings. She continued for two days praising God and then he took her to himself.

Wednesday, June 10. I warned one of the bands who, by his Ahab-like humility,[60] had deceived many. Prayed our Lord, if he approved my plainness of speech, to give us an answer of peace.

Immediately the Spirit of supplication burst forth. We wrestled with God for a blessing on ourselves, on all who wait for full redemption, on those who blaspheme the glorious liberty of his children. The Spirit made intercession with groans unutterable.[61] Many called upon God out of the deep. Others rejoiced with joy unspeakable and full assurance that we had the petitions we asked.

Saturday, June 13. Some days since I was sent for to one whom I had put out of our Society for disorderly walking. He earnestly desired to see me. I found him senseless and at the point of death, as was supposed. Surprised today at learning he was still alive and in his senses. He was overjoyed to see me and I to find the Lord had again been merciful unto him.

Tuesday, June 16. Seeking a sick man near Hanham, whose name I had forgot, I called at some of the huts for direction. At last a child informed me of one who lay a-dying. It was not the man whom I meant, but whom God meant, and sent me to bring him good news at the eleventh hour.

The woman asked me how Thomas Reed did, the very man I wanted to find and was now directed to. He was one that had drawn back, but gladly received me now. No dying man is grieved to hear Christ died for all!

---

58. A labor prison in Bristol.
59. I.e., the woman visited on June 5.
60. The story of Ahab's false humility is found in 1 Kings 21.
61. Cf. Rom. 8:26.

Spoke with one of the bands, most barbarously used by her husband, because she will not forsake God and his people. "An 100 times," she said, "he has carried a knife to bed with him to cut my throat." Her soul is always in her hand. She sleeps in the shadow of death and fears no evil,[62] knowing he can have no power over her except it be given him from above.[63] She ventures her life upon the word, "How knowest thou, O woman, but thou mayst save thy husband?" [1 Cor. 7:16].

Preached in the Wood on the dreadful word, "Sell all!" [Luke 18:22]. Never with more assistance. How has the devil baffled those teachers who, for fear of setting men upon works, forbear urging this *first universal* duty! If enforcing Christ's words is to preach works, I hope I shall preach works as long as I live.

Wednesday, June 17. Gave the Sacrament to our sister Brimble, dying in such strong agony as I have not seen before, no not in Hannah Richardson. She had no fear of hell, yet was so deeply convinced of original sin, as made all who heard her tremble. She could not let go her confidence that God would finish his work in her, though there were so few hours between her and eternity.

Met in Kingswood to humble our souls with fasting and deprecate the national judgments. In the evening God gave me words to stir up some who were settled upon their lees. How long have we called him, "Lord, Lord," and not done the things which he bade us, not denied ourselves and taken up our daily cross?[64]

Thursday, June 18. Visited our brother Haskins's father at Sison,[65] whom God had showed that he is a sinner, but not yet that he is the chief of sinners.[66] Left him desirous to know even as he is known.[67] Soon after he entered upon his last agony. By his vehement prayers to the Saviour of sinners and by the faith which God gave his son, I trust God made a short work in his soul, and received it without spot to himself.

Friday, June 19. Expounded the Fall of Jericho [Josh. 6] and felt the truth of every word I spoke. Howell Harris was present and

---

62. Cf. Ps. 23:4.
63. Cf. John 19:11.
64. Cf. Matt. 7:22; Mark 8:34.
65. Charles likely means Siston, Gloucestershire, seven miles east of Bristol.
66. Cf. 1 Tim. 1:15.
67. Cf. 1 Cor. 13:12.

afterwards confessed to me that he felt the power by which I spake, restraining him from denying the truth and telling him with strong desires of its accomplishments.

At the watch-night preached again on the same subject with double power. It was a glorious night indeed. We followed the ark and the shout of a King was in the midst of us.[68]

Monday, June 22. Visited one of the Society on her deathbed. God sent me to her that she might preach to me. She conjured me not to depart from the work; said, "The ministers will endure a great fight of afflictions, but go on to preach Christ the Saviour of all men, whose blood cleanseth from all sin. Christ died for all, none can resist this truth. I have not yet attained, but know He will fill up what is lacking in my faith."

Wednesday, June 24. I asked her if she had a new heart. She answered, "No, but I shall receive it with the Sacrament." After administering, I repeated the question and she bore witness to the truth, "Everyone that is perfect shall be as his Master" [Luke 6:40]. God, she said, had then taken away the evil heart and she had no sin remaining in her. I told her that time and temptation would show.

Thursday, June 25. Found her still the same, declaring she had felt no motion of evil or selfwill since the occasion of stumbling, as she thinks, was taken away.

Friday, June 26. Suky Harding informed me that Howell Harris, coming from the Room that night to his master's, had stopped their railings, saying he would hear nothing against his brothers Wesley, for they were true ministers of Christ and children of God. He confessed before a large company of our enemies he had found such power under the word that his soul was lifted to the third heaven.[69] He longed to be free from sin which he hated. He lay open to the light. "And if," said he, "the Scriptures say Christ died for all, I will say so too." By many such [words] he utterly confounded them. But who can touch pitch and not be defiled? The very next day he came and threatened to declare against me as a deceiver.

---

68. Cf. Num. 23:21.
69. Cf. 2 Cor. 12:2.

Sunday, June 28. A day much to be remembered. Preached in Bristol on repentance; at Kendleshire on temptation, with more life. My strength increased with my work so that in the afternoon I was filled with power and again at Baptist Mills.

Last night Howell Harris told me he would come to our Society. I bade him come in God's name. We were singing

> Thee triumphantly we praise,
> Vie with all thy hosts above,
> Shout thine universal grace,
> Thine everlasting love,[70]

when William Hooper, by my order, brought him. I prayed according to God, gave out an hymn which we might all join in. The hand of the Lord was upon me. I asked Howell whether he had a mind to speak and sat by for half an hour, while he gave an account of his conversion by *irresistible grace*, mixing with his experience the impossibility of falling, God's unchangeableness, etc. I could not but observe the ungenerousness of my friend, and after hearing him long and patiently was moved to rise up and ask in the name of Jesus, "Ye that are spiritual, doth the Spirit which is in you suffer me still to keep silence, and let my brother go on? Can I do it, without bringing the blood of these souls upon me?" A woman first cried (Mrs Rawlins, I think), "The wounds of Jesus answer, 'No!'" Then many others repeated, "No, no, no," and a whole cloud of witnesses arose, declaring, "Christ died for all!" [2 Cor. 5:15].

I asked again, "Would you have my brother Harris proceed, or would you not? If you would hear him, I will be silent all night." Again they forbade me in strong words upon which I gave out,

> Break forth into joy
> Your Comforter sing,[71] etc.

They did break forth as the voice of many waters or mighty thunderings. O what a burst of joy was there in the midst of us! The God and Saviour of all men was provoked to jealousy and magnified his universal love.

---

70. "Gloria Patri, IV," st. 4, *Hymns on God's Everlasting Love*, 2nd series (London: Strahan, [1742]), 56 (*Poetical Works*, 3:100).

71. "On the lii chapter of Isaiah, Part II," st. 6, *HSP* (1742), 113 (*Poetical Works*, 2:170).

Howell Harris would have entered into dispute but was stopped. "Then," said he, "you thrust me out." "No," said I, "we do not. You are welcome to stay as long as you please. We acknowledge you a child of God." Yet again he began, "If you do not believe irresistible grace," and I cut off the sentence of reprobation which I foresaw coming with:

> Praise God from whom ~~all~~ pure blessings flow,
> Whose bowels yearn on *all* below,
> Who would not have one sinner lost,
> Praise Father, Son, and Holy Ghost.[72]

Here Mr Labbè pulled him away and carried him from us. We betook ourselves to prayer in which the Spirit wonderfully helped our infirmities.[73] Great was the company both of mourners and rejoicers. We perceived God had taken the matter into his own hand, and was arose to maintain his own cause. My mouth and all their hearts were opened. I spake as I never spake before and all agreed in one testimony. John Doleman and Francis Vigor,[74] a young Quaker, received forgiveness of sins, and all that knew Christ, an increase of faith and love.

I acknowledged the grace given to our dear brother Harris and excused his estrangement from me through the wickedness of his counsellors. Spake I know not what words of exhortation and instruction.

The Spirit of their Father spake in many. And this I have found since, that just when I began to stop Howell, several felt in themselves that the time was come, and if I had deferred it, would themselves have rebuked the madness of the prophet.

Monday, June 29. Called on a sister in Bath and exhorted a few to "save themselves from this untoward generation" [Acts 2:40]. At their desire I opened the Scripture and warned them from the first words, "Depart, I pray you, from the tents of these wicked men, and touch nothing of theirs, least ye be consumed in all their sins" (Num. 16:26).

---

72. "Gloria Patri, V," *Hymns on God's Everlasting Love*, 2nd series (London: Strahan, [1742]), 56 (*Poetical Works*, 3:100).

73. Cf. Rom. 8:26.

74. This would be the son of Francis (d. 1733) and Elizabeth Vigor, who were married at the Society of Friends meeting house in Bristol in April 1722.

JULY 1741

Saturday, July 4. While the letters were reading,[75] we had a glimpse of the felicity of God's chosen, and rejoiced in the gladness of his people, and gave thanks with his inheritance.

Visited a dying woman, who fell upon me with revilings for not coming sooner to give her the Sacrament. She went on so violently that I feared her last breath would go in curses. I hoped she was not in her senses, but the attendants assured me that was her language continually. She had no trouble about her soul. When I told her she would be lost if she died unchanged, she answered, "Ye will go to hell before me." I could not account for it till they told me she was a constant hearer of the predestinarians. We joined in prayer for her, and God gave us a faint spark of hope.

Tuesday, July 7. Visited her a second time and perceived the strong man was bound![76] If so, he may be cast out. This is the Lord's doing!

Prayed by another who had been exceeding mad against Christ and his people. But the fierce persecutor is now struck to the ground and asks, "Lord, what wouldst thou have me to do?" I doubt not but the scales will fall from his eyes before they are closed in death.[77]

Received an earnest invitation to Cardiff where some are fallen asleep and some turned back in[to] Egypt.

Friday, July 10. Spent most of the afternoon in reading Gell on the Pentateuch.[78] Never man (uninspired) spake as this man speaks! I wonder where the devil hid him so long. But the good Providence, which has put him into our hands, will now, I trust, set him on a candlestick, that he may shine to all that are in the house.

Saturday, July 11. Preached at Bristol, then among the colliers, a third time at Bath, a fourth at Saltford,[79] and yet again in the Wood.

75. This wording indicates the Wesleys' habit of reading to the societies and bands letters from correspondents pertaining to growth in faith and the gospel.
76. Cf. Mark 3:27.
77. Cf. Acts 9:18.
78. Robert Gell (1595–1665), *An Essay towards the Amendment of the English Translation of the Bible; . . . The first part on the Pentateuch* (London: R. Norton, 1659). Note that Gell has a sermon on Christian Perfection in the appendix.
79. Charles spells "Sawford," a variant common in his day.

Let God have the glory. Preaching five times a day, when he calls me to it, no more wearies the flesh than preaching once.

Satan took it ill to be attacked in his headquarters, that Sodom of our land, Bath. While I was explaining the trembling jailer's question [Acts 16:30], he raged horribly in his children. They went out and came back again and mocked and at best roared, as if each man's name was Legion.[80] My power increased with the opposition. The sincere were melted into tears and strong desires of salvation.

Sunday, July 12. Preached from Titus 2:11, etc. The power and seal of God is never wanting while I declare the *two great truths* of the everlasting gospel: universal redemption and Christian perfection.

At Kingswood I received Jane Sheep into the fold by baptism, which she felt in that moment to be the redemption of sins.

Monday, July 13. Set out with our brother Hooper and by three reached Cardiff. At six I met and laboured to stir up the Society, and the Lord was with my mouth.

Tuesday, July 14. Warned them against apostasy from 1 Corinthians 10. Preached in the afternoon to the prisoners, "how shall I give thee up, O Ephraim!" [Hosea 11:8]. Above twenty were felons. The word melted them down. Many tears were shed at the singing that "Outcasts of men, to you I call," etc.[81] At night for near three hours I described the grace of God, which bringeth salvation to all men [Titus 2:11].

Wednesday, July 15. Encouraged them to expect salvation from indwelling sin by that blessed promise, "Who art thou, O great mountain? Before Zerubbabel thou shalt become a plain" [Zech. 4:7].

Rode to Wenvoe and asked brother [John] Hodges, if he had forbid letting me preach. He told me his church, while he had one, should be always open to me. It was full at so short a warning. I read prayers and preached from Isaiah 52: "Awake, awake, put on thy strength, O Zion," etc. [Isa. 52:1].

Rode on five miles farther with Mr [Nathaniel] Wells, Hodges, and others, to Fonmon Castle. Mr Jones,[82] who had sent for me,

---

80. Cf. Mark 5:9; Luke 8:30.
81. "Christ the Friend of Sinners," st. 5, *HSP* (1739), 102 (*Poetical Works*, 1:92).
82. Robert Jones (1706–1742) quickly become a supporter of Methodism. His untimely death led Charles to publish *An Elegy on the Death of Robert Jones* (Bristol: Felix Farley, 1742) (*Poetical Works*, 3:107–28).

received me very courteously. He civilly apologized for his first questions which he asked me as a magistrate—whether I was a Papist, whether a member of the established Church of England, etc. Was fully satisfied with my answers, and found we were contemporaries at the same college.

After dinner he sent by Porthkerry, where, at his desire, the minister lent me his pulpit. After Mr [John] Richards had made him a promise of it, he sent again, desiring him to act without bias or constraint, by either granting or refusing the church as his conscience directed.[83]

I read prayers and preached, "God so loved the world" [John 3:16]. God was amongst us and a mighty tempest was stirred up round about him. He shook many souls out of their carnal security. Never hath he given me more convincing words. The poor simple souls fell down at the feet of Jesus. Their shepherd, also, was deeply affected, and hid his face, and wept; especially while I was praying for him. After sermon he begged my pardon for believing the strange reports concerning me. God had spoke the contrary to his heart, and the hearts of his people, for when we were gone out of the church it was still filled with the cries of the wounded.

I yielded to Mr Jones's importunity and agreed to delay my return to Bristol, that I might preach here once more and pass a night at the castle. Mr Richards pressed me first to come to his house.

Hastened back to Cardiff and in great bodily weakness showed unawakened sinners their state in dead Lazarus [John 11]. The word was quick and powerful.

Thursday, July 16. Discoursed on Lazarus raised [John 11]. Dined at Llanishen and preached to the Society and a few others, chiefly predestinarians. Without touching the dispute, I simply declared the scriptural marks of election; whereby some I believe were cut off from their vain confidence. The sincere ones clave to me. Who can resist the power of love! A loving messenger of a loving God might drive reprobation out of Wales without once naming it.

In the evening, at Cardiff, Mr Wells and Hodges shamed me by patiently sitting by to hear *me* preach. My subject was Wrestling Jacob [Gen. 32:24-31]. Some whole sinners were offended at the

---

83. Rev. John Richards held the living at Porthkerry (1728–1757) as a gift of Robert Jones.

sick and wounded, who cried out for a physician, but such offences must needs come.

Friday, July 17. Expounded the Woman healed of her bloody issue.[84] The power of the Lord was present. We took leave of each other with many tears, and I earnestly exhorted them to continue in the grace of God.

Dropped most of my company on the road that I might meet Mr Jones at Mr Richards's. He came with Mrs [Mary] Jones and was met by a minister, whom, with some others, he had invited to his house, with a view of reconciling them to me. None but Mr Carne[85] accepted his invitation. His address was not so smooth as their's who dwell in king's palaces, but I said little till I could speak as one having authority.[86] With difficulty Mr Jones restrained him from breaking out.

He flew out on sight of the multitude in the churchyard and a motion made for my preaching there. It was then proposed to take down one of the windows, that those without might hear, but on Mr Carne's again threatening to go away, we went into the church, as many as could, and the rest stood without.

Mr Carne stood up all the prayers and sermon time. The first lesson was a remarkable word to me:

> Then said I, Ah, Lord God, behold I cannot speak, for I am a child. But the Lord said unto me, Say not, I am a child. For thou shalt go to all that I shall send thee, and whatsoever I command thee thou shalt speak. Be not afraid of their faces, for I am with thee to deliver thee, saith the Lord. Then the Lord put forth his hand, and touched my mouth, and the Lord said, Behold, I have put my words in thy mouth. . . . Thou, therefore, gird up thy loins, and arise, and speak unto them all that I command thee: be not dismayed at their faces, lest I confound thee before them. For, behold, I have made thee this day a defenced city and an iron pillar, and brazen walls. . . . And they shall fight against thee, but they shall not prevail against thee. For I am with thee, saith the Lord, to deliver thee (Jer. 1[:6-19]).

The second lesson was John 5. The psalms also spake nothing but encouragement. I expected that to be now fulfilled: "Show some

---

84. See the note on this sermon for the November 5, 1739, entry above.
85. Likely Rev. Charles Carne (b. c. 1708), rector of St Athan and Llanmaes.
86. Cf. Mark 1:22.

token for good upon thy servant that they who hate me may see it, and be ashamed, because thou, Lord God, hast holpen and comforted me" [Ps. 86:17, AV alt.].

I never read prayers with more inward feeling. Like strength was given me to explain the Good Samaritan [Luke 10:29-37] for two hours. Out of the abundance of my heart my mouth spake. Great was the company of mourners, whose tears God put into his bottle,[87] and they shall reap in joy.[88]

I could not help smiling at Mr Carne, who had come, as he said, on purpose to judge me, and his judgment was, "Sir, you have got very good lungs, but you will make the people melancholy. I saw them crying throughout the church." Then he turned on Mr Jones, told him he would make himself ridiculous all over the country by encouraging such a fellow. I was afraid of despising him, and therefore passed on and left them together. Mr Jones almost overcame his evil with good, but could not prevail upon him to come under the same roof with me.

However, the poor people were glad to accept of his invitation to hear me again at the castle. We eat our bread with gladness and singleness of heart, and at seven I preached to some hundreds in the courtyard. My three brethren, Richards, Wells, and Hodges stood in the midst of them, knelt on the ground in prayer, and cried after the Son of David. He breathed into our souls strong desires. O that he may confirm, increase, and satisfy them!

The voice of praise and thanksgiving was heard in this dwelling place.[89] Before, at, and after supper we sang and blessed God with joyful lips. Those in the parlor and kitchen were continually honouring by offering him praise. I thought it looked like the house of faithful Abraham. We called our brethren of Kingswood to be present with us in Spirit, and continued rejoicing with them till morning.

Saturday, July 18. Took sweet counsel with Mr Jones alone. The seed is sown in his heart and shall bring forth fruit unto perfection.[90] His wife, a simple innocent creature, joined us. I commended them to the grace of God in earnest prayer and then, with my Cardiff friends, went on my way rejoicing.

---

87. Cf. Ps. 56:8.
88. Cf. Ps. 126:5.
89. Cf. Ps. 42:4-5.
90. Cf. Luke 8:14.

Consented that some should ask Mr Colerick[91] for the use of his pulpit. He civilly answered that he would readily grant it, but the bishop had forbade him. Doth our law judge any man before it hear him and know what he doth?[92]

At two set out for the Passage.[93] The boat was just ready for us. By nine found my brother at the Room, the Lord having blest both my going out and my coming in.

Thursday, July 23. Sent for by a predestinarian (that *was* till death approached). Her miserable comforters she would none of now, but said, "'Blessed be [he] that cometh in the name of the Lord" [Matt. 21:9] and "Saviour of all men" [1 Tim. 4:10].

Visited one of our own flock, a joyful prisoner of hope. The Lord, when he came, found her watching for that great salvation.

Reproved an invincible Pharisee at Mr Farley's, whose whole discourse is of herself. She told us (as she does all the world) how often she goes to prayers and Sacrament, how many sermons she hears, what good she does, etc. She breathes out threatenings and woes against our Society for not acknowledging her gifts. "God loves no one upon earth as well as her." Never have I seen a professor more full of pride, and self, and the devil. Yet she pretends to the full assurance of faith.

Saturday, July 25. Met at ten to pray for a blessing on my brother's sermon, which he is preaching at this hour before the university.[94]

Sunday, July 26. Our hope was much confirmed by those words, which I enforced at Kingwood, "Stand still, and see the salvation of the Lord" [2 Chron. 20:17], or as it is afterwards expressed, "Speak unto the children of Israel, that they go forward" [Exod. 14:15].

Discoursed in the afternoon on the same subject from Isaiah 64:5, "Thou meetest . . . those that remember thee on the ways," etc. Hence,

---

91. Rev. Thomas Colerick (d. 1761), vicar of St John's Church, Cardiff. Charles spells "Coldrach."

92. Cf. John 7:51.

93. This is the ferry across the mouth of the River Severn to Wales. It appears that Charles normally crossed at "New Passage," departing east of Pilning, Gloucestershire, and landing near Black Rock, just north of Sudbrook, Monmouthshire (cf. the entries for October 31, 1743, and October 21, 1748, below). The alternative was "Old Passage," three miles farther north, running from Aust to Beachley.

94. Cf. John Wesley, Sermon 150, "Hypocrisy in Oxford," *Works* 4:392–407.

I magnified the love of Christian ordinances, exhorting those who wait for salvation to be as clay in the hand of the potter[95] by stirring themselves up to lay hold on the Lord. God gave me much freedom to explain that most active, vigorous, restless thing: true stillness.

Preached a fourth time at the Mills and a fifth time in the Room on "The One Thing Needful" [Luke 10:42].

Monday, July 27. The neighbourhood of the [Horse]fair fills our Room with strangers. Again God has put his words in my mouth and set me to root out, and to pull down, and to destroy, and to throw down—to build also and to plant,[96] if it be his blessed will concerning me.

Tuesday, July 28. God be praised, there is some ground for that complaint of a predestinarian that the plague of perfection reigns at Bristol, and many of the Welsh catch it. O that all mankind were infected with this plague, if it is a plague to be healed of every plague.

One serious youth I spake with today who did run well. But from the time that he was persuaded to believe there was no falling after justification, he did begin to fall, as he now confesses, into carelessness, self-indulgence, and at last into known sin.

Friday, July 31. Still by patience and comfort of God's Holy Word many daily lay hold on eternal life. He gave us this night strong consolation. O that in the strength thereof we might travel to his holy mountain!

AUGUST 1741

Sunday, August 2. In my way to Kingswood met Mr Wynn of Painswick, who informed me that when I was last there, a word I directed to another on a sick bed was applied to him, and he in that moment received remission of sins. He had heard of nothing farther and yet wanted something more. He knew not what, till God sent him hither. Now he rejoices in hope of redemption from all iniquity.

I got unawares with my chaise among the coalpits. We were going to alight when the horse started and overturned us. I leaped

95. Cf. Rom. 9:21, etc.
96. Cf. Jer. 1:10.

over both horse and chaise, but our sister Gaseath was thrown out upon her head and the chaise turned topsy turvy over her. She lay beneath the wheels untouched by either. The horse lay quiet upon his back. We all rose unhurt. "Thou, Lord, shalt save both man and beast" [Ps. 36:6, BCP]. How excellent is thy mercy!

Preached a funeral sermon over sister Rachel Peacock, who died in the Lord most triumphantly. She had continual joy in the Lord, which made her cry out, "Though I groan, I feel no pain at all. Christ so rejoices and fills my heart." Her mouth also was filled with laughter and her tongue with joy. She sang hymns incessantly. "Christ," said she, "is in my heart, and one minute with the Lord is worth a million of ages. O how brave it is to banquet with the Lamb!"

She was always praising God for giving her such patience. All her desires were unto the Lord and she continued calling upon him, in all the confidence of love, till he received her into his immediate presence.

At the sight of her coffin my soul was moved within me and struggled as a bird to break its cage. Some relief I found in tears, but still was so overpowered that, unless God had abated the vehemence of my desires, I could have had no utterance. The whole congregation partook with me in the blessedness of mourning.

Monday, August 3. Visited our sister Reed on a bed of sickness. All her doubts and fears are vanished at the approach of death, and she rejoices in confident hope that the Lord will sanctify her wholly, before he takes her hence.

Wednesday, August 5. Saw our brother Stanley in the same, if not an higher state, dying with eternal life abiding in him.

Thursday, August 6. Tonight God shook many souls by the word of his power. My subject was the Pool of Bethesda [John 5:1-15].

Coming to pray by a poor Welsh woman, she began with me, "Blessed be God that ever I heard you! Jesus, *my* Jesus, has visited me on a bed of sickness. He is in my heart. He is my strength. None shall pluck me out of his hand. I cannot leave him and he will not leave me." It was the Spirit of her Father spoke in her: "O, do not let me ask for death, if thou wouldst have me live. I know thou canst keep me from ever sinning more. If thou wouldst have me live, let me walk humbly with thee all my days."

I sat and heard her sing the new song till even my hard heart was melted. She glorified the Saviour of the world, who would have all men to be saved. "I know it, I feel it," said she, "He would not have one sinner lost. Believe, and he will give you all what he hath given me."

Sunday, August 9. Gave her the Sacrament, which she had never received before, but was taught to desire it by the Spirit that was in her, even as soon as she had received him. I asked what difference she found *after* communicating. She answered that she saw God and was full of him before, but that in the act of receiving she had the brightness of his presence and was filled as it were with all the fullness of God.

Friday, August 14. Went after a stray sheep, who was turned out of the way by the predestinarians, but the good Shepherd had found her himself and brought her to me rejoicing. For some days she had been under the full influence of that narrow opinion and could not bear any of her brethren and sisters. Then she cried unto the Lord to show her the truth, and he answered her by his own mouth. The true light broke in upon her, and in his light she saw that God is love. She is now humbled in the dust before him for having robbed him of his most darling attribute.

Our Kingswood School was crowded with those that came from all parts to the watch-night. I enforced our Lord's words "Have faith in God" [Mark 11:22] and indeed we had. The Spirit of faith was poured out. Many were there who could not keep it in, but out of the abundance of their heart their mouths spake. I triumphed till the morning with the voice of joy and thanksgiving among such as keep holiday.

Monday, August 17. Visited one who was forsaking the fellowship, when God arrested her in her flight by sickness, convinced, condemned, and justified her again. It is good for her to have been in trouble, since thereby He has plucked her as a brand out of the fire.

Saturday, August 22. While I was declaring at Saltford, "he shall save his people from their sins" [Matt. 1:21], the enemy stirred up his servants to great fierceness of opposition. But we defied them in the name of the Lord, who first restrained and then stilled the madness of the people.

Monday, August 24. Took ~~boat~~ horse with Felix Farley for Wales. In the passage I read on, while some gentlemen mocked. At last the chief of them asked, "What are you reading? Let us have a little with you." I read on the words that followed, "And behold I come quickly, and my reward is with me to give every man according as his work shall be" [Rev. 22:12]. This struck a damp upon them and silenced them in a moment, so that we reached the land without farther molestation.

The assizes brought many strangers to the Society in Cardiff, before whom I declared, "Other foundation can no man lay than that is laid, which is Jesus Christ" [1 Cor. 3:11]. Some, I doubt not, were enabled to receive the strange things I brought to their ears.

Tuesday, August 25. I found at five this morning, by the return of the strangers, that the word had not fallen to the ground.

Found our dear friend and brother at Wenvoe,[97] nothing terrified by his adversaries. Their threats, instead of shaking, have more deeply rooted him in the truth.

They have had the same effect upon Mr Jones. The poor prodigals, who are not yet come to themselves, say of him that he is beside himself, but he is content that they, fools, should count his life madness. Only when any of them come in his way, he speaks such words of truth and soberness as they cannot resist.

For three hours we sang, rejoiced, and gave thanks, then rode to Porthkerry where I read prayers and discoursed near two hours on the Pool of Bethesda [John 5:1-15]. The whole congregation were in tears.

Returned to the castle and met some hundreds of the poor neighbours in our chapel, the dining room. Exhorted them to build up one another from Malachi [3:16], "Then they that feared the Lord spake often one to another"; and at ten we departed. We kept on rejoicing till one in the morning.

Wednesday, August 26. Prayed by a dying woman, who waits for redemption from *all* iniquity *here*; otherwise, she knows she cannot see God. About noon applied at John Deer's Society, "But ye are washed, but ye are sanctified, etc." [1 Cor. 6:11]. Never have I spoke more closely to those who rest in the first gift. Some who seemed to be pillars began to find themselves shaken reeds.

Preached again in Wenvoe church and at night in Cardiff.

---

97. I.e., John Hodges.

Thursday, August 27. Great power was among us, while I spake on the walls of Jericho falling down [Josh. 6]; but much greater at the prison, where I recommended to two condemned malefactors the example of the penitent thief [Luke 23:40-43]. Both were melted into tears. The congregation sympathized, and joined in fervent prayer that our Lord would remember them, now he is come into his kingdom.

Went to a revel at Lanvans,[98] and dissuaded them from their *innocent* diversions in St Peter's words, "For the time past of our life may suffice us to have wrought the will of the gentiles, when we walked in lasciviousness, lusts, excess of wine, revellings, banqueting, and abominable idolatries" [1 Pet. 4:3]. An old dancer of three score fell down under the stroke of the hammer. She could never be convinced before that there was any harm in those innocent pleasures. O that all her fellows might likewise confess "she that liveth in pleasures is dead while she liveth" [1 Tim. 5:6].

Prayed by a poor persecutor, who had found mercy at the last hour. Then expounded Ezekiel's vision of dry bones [Ezek. 37:4]. A poor drunkard spoke the whole time, but without interrupting me or the congregation, for the hand of the Lord was over us.

Friday, August 28. Preached again at Porthkerry church. Many cried after Jesus with the Woman of Canaan [Matt. 15:22-28]. It was a time of great refreshing. Returned in the coach with Mr and Mrs Jones and a little girl of eight years old,[99] who has not outlived the simple life, or that breath of God which is the first enmity to the seed of the subtle serpent.

At six expounded Isaiah 53 in the courtyard and was greatly assisted to purge out the leaven of Calvin. Spent the evening in conference with those who desired to be of the Society, which was now begun in the name of Jesus Christ the Saviour of all men. Sang and prayed with them till ten, with the family till midnight.

Saturday, August 29. Preached our Lord's seven last cries on the cross and spoke to the men under sentence of death. God showed

---

98. Charles has surely misspelled the Welsh name for this locale, and it is unclear which of several similar names might be intended.
99. Their daughter Mary, born in 1733.

my thoughts were not as his thoughts,[100] for the most hardened, whom I had least hopes of, appeared truly justified. He told Mr Wells and me, he was quite easy, had no fear of death, no ill will to his prosecutors. "But had you never any fear of it?" I asked. "Yes," he replied, "till I heard you preach. Then it went away, and I have felt no trouble ever since."

Who knoweth the power of divine love? O gather this outcast of men, and show forth in him that thine arm is not shortened at all.[101]

Took horse with Mr Wynn and Mr Farley. Reached the Passage by seven, the English shore by nine, and Bristol before midnight.

Monday, August 31. Met with a sincere woman who did verily believe my brother to be a Papist, because when she asked him, he did not deny it. I asked her, "Are you a Turk? . . . Yes; for ye do not answer 'no'." Showed her from hence the folly of her conclusion. Would a Jesuit scruple to lie? However, I assured her now my brother was a true Protestant, and, if it would be any farther satisfaction to her, should tell her so himself.

Met with Kingswood bands and rejoiced in their steadfastness, none having turned either to the righthand or the left, either to stillness or predestination.

SEPTEMBER 1741

Wednesday, September 2. Sent for to Miss Gr.,[102] who has had no rest in her flesh since she left us (Papists) to follow Calvin. She often longed to return and would sometimes come by stealth to hear the word. The first time her mother heard of it she turned her out of doors, and has ever since treated her with true predestinarian meanness. All her relations joined in the same spirit, so that at last by their oppression they have fairly drove her distracted.

Now they sent for me in all haste. Never did I see a more pitiable spectacle. She was altogether untractable to them, but did just whatever I desired her. I led her to her chamber and returned to Mr Hooper's, but at midnight we were waked by her shrieks, and I sent for again. She lay in a manner inexpressible. Such outcries and

---

100. Cf. Ezek. 16:62.
101. See Isa. 50:2, 59:1.
102. Perhaps Mary Gregory; cf. John Wesley, *Journal* (September 24, 1742), *Works* 19:198–99.

distortions I have never heard or seen. Every breath they thought would be her last. She prayed to the Virgin Mary, Queen of heaven, in words which I am sure the devil taught her, for she had never seen a mass book. How justly does God suffer the stumbling block for those who have been continually suggesting to her the lies which they now believe!

I rebuked the lying spirit and prayed the One Mediator[103] in his time to bring her out of the furnace. This her relations afterwards represented as "unbewitching her."

In her ravings she would often say she was the lawful wife of Mr John Wesley. This also they believed. I laboured for an hour and an half to comfort them, who I knew would still return me evil for good, and then retired to rest.

Thursday, September 3. Preached a second time at the prison on the Lost Sheep [Luke 15:4-7], for the sake of a poor woman under condemnation, and the next day (*September 4*) on Christ crucified.[104] His dying words came with power to many hearts, being applied by his own Spirit.

Saturday, September 5. Heard that Justice Cr— and forty more, both the great vulgar and the small, had seized upon Mr Cennick's house and threatened to take ours on Tuesday next. They forget whose bridle is in their jaws.

Sunday, September 6. Preached morning and afternoon at Kingswood on our Lord's last cries, which sunk into the souls of many. At Baptist Mills administered that antidote of spiritual pride, 1 Cor. 10.

Astonished by a letter from my brother relating his conference with the apostle of the Moravians.[105]

If thou art he! but O! how false![106] Who would believe it of Count Zinzendorf, that he should utterly deny all Christian holiness! I never could, but for a saying of his which I heard with my own

---

103. Cf. 1 Tim. 2:5.
104. This sermon portraying Christ on the cross became a standard for Charles. As the next sentence suggests, it typically climaxed in Christ's dying words to sinners. But these were not the final words in the gospel accounts; they were the appeal of Lamentations 1:12, "Is it nothing to you, all you who pass by?" (which tradition had long associated with the crucifixion). Cf. Charles's descriptions of the sermon in the following entries below: November 28, 1746; September 1, 1747; February 24, 1748; September 8, 1748; and October 24, 1756.
105. See John Wesley's *Journal* (3 September 1741), *Works* 19:211–24.
106. See note for the April 5, 1740, entry.

ears. Speaking of St James's Epistle he said, if it was thrown out of the canon, "*ego non restituerem!*"[107]

Monday, September 7. Would have preached at Newgate [prison] to the poor penitent thief, but Satan hindered. Thou fool! 'Tis now too late, the prey is plucked out of the teeth. Jesus hath found his lost sheep and brought her home rejoicing. She was a sinner, but she is justified!

I went after another, a backslider, who had returned to folly and all outward wickedness. Now in her adversity she considered. God, who lifteth up them that are fallen, returned to her in sickness, and she bears the rod, and him that appointeth it.[108]

Tuesday, September 8. Being commended by the church to the grace of God, I took horse at four with William Hooper for the Passage. Preached Christ crucified[109] at Caldicot to an house full of simple souls, though wet through with the hard rain. But I live by the gospel. [That] which would *kill* another, shall not *hurt* a minister. By six God brought us safe to Cardiff, where we rejoiced with the little flock in the sure word of life and grace through Christ Jesus.

Wednesday, September 9. Preached to the two condemned malefactors and found them in the passage from death to life eternal.

Rode to Wenvoe to Fonmon and rejoiced with that household of faith. Went to fetch our little Society from Aberthaw and returned singing to the castle. Explained the Apostle's answer to the jailer: "Believe on the Lord Jesus Christ and thou shalt be saved" [Acts 16:31]. God gave me words to awaken some who were lulled fast asleep by the opiate of final perseverance.

Thursday, September 10. Read prayers at Porthkerry and applied our Lord's word, Matthew 11:5, "The blind receive their sight," etc.

Preached again from Acts 3, to the self-righteous predestinarians chiefly. Some of them afterwards complained to me that I should say, if they fell from grace after justification, they had better never have been justified at all. *Herra illae lachrymae!*[110] I cannot allow them Christ's righteousness for a cloak to their sins.

---

107. "I would not restore [it]."
108. Cf. Mic. 6:9.
109. On the sermon preached, see note for the September 3, 1741, entry.
110. Cf. Terence, *The Lady of Andros*, 126: "*hinc illae lacrumae*" ("that's the source of those tears").

Friday, September 11. Besought my guilty brethren at Cardiff, especially those who are to be executed tomorrow, to be reconciled unto God. Set out directly for Llantrisant, eight Welsh miles from Cardiff, and pointed them to the Son of Man lifted up, "that whosoever believeth on him might not perish, but have everlasting life" [John 3:16]. Hasted back, shifted my wet clothes, and attended Mr Wells and [Philip] Thomas to the prison. I asked one of the malefactors, "Are you afraid to die?" "No," he answered, "I should rejoice to die this moment?" Both behaved as believing penitents. We had strong consolation in prayer, the amen, and answer of God in our hearts.

Saturday, September 12. Had only time at the Society to offer up a prayer for the prisoners. At five went to them, the sheriff being resolved to hurry them away at six, some hours before the usual time. He would hardly let them stay to receive the Sacrament. Then he ordered them out, not allowing time to strike off their fetters.

They were very calm and composed, nothing afraid of death, or its consequences. One of them assured me, if it was now left to his choice, he would rather die than live. I asked the reason and he answered, "Was I to be any longer in this world, I might sin again." He also acknowledged that his punishment was just, not on account of the theft for which he was condemned, as to which he persisted in his innocence to the last, but for another offence of the same sort, which the justice of *man* had never taken hold of him.

Mr Wells rode by the side of the cart; Mr Thomas and I with the criminals in it. The sheriff's hurry often endangered our being overturned, but could not hinder our singing, till we came to the place of execution. I spoke a few minutes to the people from Galatians 3:13, "Christ hath redeemed us from [the curse of the law]," etc. Still I could not observe the least sign of fear or trouble on either of the dying men. They confessed their steadfast faith in Christ crucified, and are now, I make no doubt, with Him in paradise.

Preached at night to a numerous congregation of gentry and others. God gives me favour in their sight. O that I could make them displeased with themselves!

Sunday, September 13. Preached at Cardiff and then at Wenvoe, the third time at Porthkerry, and the last at Fonmon. The remainder of the night passed admonishing one another in psalms, and hymns, and spiritual songs.[111]

Monday, September 14. Sang on till two. Then I rode to a revel at Dinas Powys.[112] It was one of the greatest in the country, but is now dwindled down to nothing. I preached Jesus, the Saviour of his people from their sins [Matt. 1:21]. We rejoiced in hope of his great salvation.

Tuesday, September 15. At another famous revel in Whitchurch, which lasts a week and is honoured with the presence of the gentry and clergy, far and near, put myself in their way and called, "Awake thou that sleepest, and arise from the dead, and Christ shall give thee light" [Eph. 5:14]. I trust there was a great awakening among the dead souls. So again at Cardiff, while I showed the state of modern Christians in the church of Laodicea [Rev. 3:14-22].

Wednesday, September 16. Exhorted the Society in private. One accursed thing is discovered and removed, their abominably wicked custom of selling on Sundays.

Kept a watch-night at Fonmon and expounded the ten virgins [Matt. 25:1-13]. Continued singing and rejoicing till two in the morning. O that all the world were partakers with us!

Friday, September 18. Rose at six and took leave of our dear sister, who cheerfully parted with Mr Jones, to visit our beloved colliers.

Saturday, September 19. After exhorting and praying with the Society at Cardiff, set out with Mr Jones and Williams for Bristol. Thither the Lord brought us by seven in the evening, after a delightful journey.

Sunday, September 20. Most of the Society were at St James's Sacrament.

I carried Mr Jones to Kingswood where the Lord was mightily present in his own ordinance. At Baptist Mills I expounded the Bloody Issue.[113] Great disturbance was made behind me, till I turned upon the disturbers, and by the law first, and then the gospel, entirely silenced them.

---

111. Cf. Eph. 5:19.
112. Charles spells it "Dennis-Powis."
113. See the note on this sermon for the November 5, 1739, entry.

It was a glorious time at the Society, when God called forth his witnesses. Our guest was filled with consolation and acknowledged that God was with us of a truth.

Introduced him to the leaders of the colliers, with whom he had sweet fellowship. Met the bands and strongly urged them to press toward the mark. Read them a letter full of threatenings to take our house by violence. Immediately the power came down and we laughed all our enemies to scorn. Faith saw the mountain full of horsemen and chariots of fire.[114] Our brother from Wales was compelled to bear his testimony and declare before all what God had done for his soul. "At that time, when the power of the Holy Ghost so overshadowed him," (he assured them) "all bodily sufferings would have been as nothing. Neither would they feel them, if made partakers of the Holy Ghost in the *same measure*."

He warned us to prepare for the storm, which would surely fall upon us, if the work of God went on. His artless words were greatly blessed to us all, and our hearts were bowed and warmed by the Spirit of love, as the heart of one man.

Tuesday, September 22. He would have carried me to some great friends of his in the city, and particularly to a counselor, about the threatened seizure. I feared nothing but helping myself and trusting to an arm of flesh.[115] Our safety is to sit still. However, at his importunity I went with him a little way, but stopped and turned him back, and at last agreed to accompany him to Justice Cr—, the most forward of our adversaries.

He received us cautiously. I said I came to wait upon him, in respect to his office, having heard his name mentioned among some who were offended at the good we did to the poor colliers; that I should be sorry to give any just cause of complaint and willing to know from himself, if such had been given; that many vile reports were spread, as if he should countenance the violence of those who had seized Mr Cennick's house and now threatened to take away the collier's school.

I caught up an expression he dropped, that it would make a good workhouse, and said, "It is a workhouse already."

[*Justice:*] "Aye, but what work is done there?"

---

114. Cf. 2 Kings 6:17.
115. Cf. 2 Chron. 32:8.

[*Wesley:*] "We work the works of God, which man cannot hinder."

[*Justice:*] "But you occasion the increase of our poor."

[*Wesley:*] "Sir, you are misinformed. The reverse of that is true. None of our Society is chargeable to you. Even those who were so before they heard us, or who spent all their wages at the alehouse, now never go there at all, but keep their money to maintain their families, and have to give to those that want. Notorious swearers have now only the praise of God in their mouths. The good done among them is indisputable. Our worst enemies cannot deny it. None who hears us continues either to swear or drink."

[*Justice:*] "If I thought so," he hastily replied (*in eodem luto haesitans*[116]), "I would come and hear you myself."

I desired he would, said the grace of God was as sufficient for him as for our colliers, and who knew but he might be converted among us!

I gave him to know Mr Jones was in the commission, who then asked him on what pretence they had seized Mr Cennick's house. He utterly denied his having had any hand in it (his own servant, by the way, was one of the foremost in pulling up the hedge, etc.). Said he should not at all concern himself, "for if what you do, you do for gain, you have your reward. If for the sake of God, he will recompense you. I am of Gamaliel's mind: 'If this council or work be of men, it will come to nought.'" "'But if it be of God,'" I proceeded, "'ye cannot overthrow it, lest haply ye be found to fight against God.' Follow therefore Gamaliel's advice: 'take heed to yourselves, refrain from these men, and let them alone.'"[117]

He seemed determined so to do, and thus, through the blessing of God, we parted friends.

In our way home admired that hand which directs all our paths. Rejoiced at Bristol to hear that God had laid hold on poor William, Mr Jones's man, who is under strong convictions of sin, and continually in tears. In the evening we found under the word that there is none like unto the God of Jeshurun.[118] It was a time of sweet refreshment. Just when I had concluded, my brother came in from London, as if sent on purpose to be comforted together with

---

116. "Stuck in the same mud hole," Terence, *Phormio*, 780, though the original text reads "*in eodem luto hesitas.*"

117. Cf. Acts 5:34-39.

118. Cf. Deut. 32:26.

us. He exhorted and prayed with the congregation for another half-hour. Then we went to our Friend Vigor's, and for an hour or two longer our souls were satisfied as with marrow and fatness,[119] while our mouth praised God with joyful lips.

---

119. Cf. Ps. 63:5.

LaVergne, TN USA
07 April 2010
178462LV00003B/93/P